STALIN

Also by Walter Laqueur

COMMUNISM AND NATIONALISM IN THE MIDDLE EAST, *1956*

THE SOVIET UNION AND THE MIDDLE EAST, *1959*

YOUNG GERMANY, *1962*

RUSSIA AND GERMANY, *1966*

THE ROAD TO WAR, *1967*

EUROPE SINCE HITLER, *1970*

A HISTORY OF ZIONISM, *1972*

WEIMAR, *1975*

GUERRILLA, *1976*

TERRORISM, *1977*

THE MISSING YEARS, *1980*

THE TERRIBLE SECRET, *1981*

THE FATE OF THE REVOLUTION, Revised and Updated, *1987*

THE LONG ROAD TO FREEDOM, *1989*

STALIN

THE GLASNOST REVELATIONS

Walter Laqueur

UNWIN

HYMAN

LONDON SYDNEY WELLINGTON

First published by Charles Scribner's Sons, Macmillan
Publishing Company, New York, 1990

First published in Great Britain by the Trade Division
of Unwin Hyman Limited in 1990

UNWIN HYMAN LIMITED
15–17 Broadwick Street
London W1V 1FP

British Library Cataloguing in Publication Data

Laqueur, Walter, 1921–
    Stalin: the glasnost revelations.
    1. Soviet Union. Stalin, I. (Iosif) 1879–1953
    I. Title
    947.0842092

ISBN 0-04-440769-6

SI MONUMENTUM REQUIRIS, CIRCUMSPICE.
If you would see the man's monument, look around.

—Inscription in St. Paul's
Cathedral, London, written
by Sir Christopher Wren's son

Contents

Acknowledgments

My work on de-Stalinization and the debates on Stalinism have been supported by the Lynde and Harry Bradley Foundation and by Mr. Conrad Black, to whom I would like to express my gratitude. Professor John Erickson kindly agreed to read the chapter about Stalin as warlord to save me from committing mistakes in a field on which he knows much more than I shall ever know. Lastly my thanks go to my colleagues, assistants, and interns at both the Center for Strategic and International Studies in Washington and the Wiener Library and Institute of Contemporary History in London and, of course, above all to Naomi.

STALIN

Introduction

Stalin was in many respects a most unlikely leader of a great nation. Physically unattractive, devoid of warmth and spontaneous enthusiasm, not a good speaker and not a great thinker, Stalin failed to project any charisma at all, nor did he give the impression of being a great villain. Nevertheless, he left his mark on Soviet and world history like no other figure in this century.

The Stalin riddle—and the question "How could it have happened?"—will continue to preoccupy generations of biographers, historians, psychologists, and philosophers, as well as novelists and playwrights. Of course, to a large extent it is not just the mystery of the psychological profile and character of one man but of a whole period in the history of a nation.

Today we know considerably more about Stalin and Stalinism than even a few years ago as a result of the revelations and debates that are taking place under *glasnost*. This book is an attempt to review the new body of knowledge even though a great many questions are still shrouded in darkness and many will remain unsolved forever. *

In the 1930s, Karl Kraus wrote in the opening sentence of a long essay that as far as Hitler is concerned, "I cannot think of anything." He

---

* The present study is based predominantly on the revelations about Stalin and the debates on Stalinism in the Soviet media that began in 1987 and ended, as far as access to new documentation is concerned, in the summer of 1989. While the discussions on the origins and consequences of Stalinism will no doubt continue, there is but little hope that access to the truly important files concerning Stalin in the Soviet archives will be granted in the near future. Thus, V. V. Tsaplin, head of the Soviet main state archives, has made it known that the materials concerning "repression" have not yet been declassified and that reference to them in the press is not permitted (*Voprosy Istorii KPSS*, 1, 1990, p. 57). The same seems to be true with regard to other crucial aspects of the Stalinist era.

1

probably meant that Hitler was a repulsive subject, that it had been widely discussed, and that it was difficult to think of anything new to say. But it was still a very important topic, for Hitler's thoughts and actions affected the life of Kraus and of virtually everyone else in Europe and beyond in the most profound way. Broadly speaking, the same is true with regard to Stalin, whose name, in the words of Vasili Grossman, "has been inscribed for all eternity in Russian history."[1]

When Stalin died on March 5, 1953, time stood still. Perhaps not as many tears were shed as some contemporary Soviet accounts would have it, but the majority of Soviet people was stunned. They had been told for many years that they owed everything to the wise and strong boss (*khoziain*), who was omniscient and never mistaken and who had led the country to victory in the war. They had also been told that but for his leadership they would be lost, easy prey to the capitalist wolves.

Yet as soon as Stalin was laid to rest, there was a dramatic decline in the intensity of adulation of the leader. His name was but infrequently mentioned in the media; if previously no book, article, or speech was complete without one or more quotations from Stalin, that was no longer so. The publication of his works was stopped with the thirteenth volume; he no longer appeared in movies and paintings. Although no deliberate attempt was made to deride him, the giant shadow that he had cast for so long began to shrink and fade. A mere three months after his death, a *Pravda* editorial (June 10, 1953) used the term "cult of the individual"; at the meeting of the Central Committee a month later, George Malenkov raised the question of the Stalin cult and the distortion of Leninist norms under his rule. Within a few months it appeared that Stalin had not been as important as many had believed. The fear that the flock would be lost without the good shepherd rapidly waned.

Three years after his death, at the Twentieth Party Congress, some of Stalin's crimes were revealed for the first time by Nikita Khrushchev, who was about to emerge as the strongest figure in the collective leadership. This was followed by more revelations at the Twenty-second Party Congress in 1961. For many faithful party members, this came as a great shock. True, the text of the famous speech was not published for several decades. True again, its scope had been restricted in the first place: It mainly rehabilitated Stalinists who had perished in the terror. A real debate over Stalin and Stalinism could not take place in the prevailing political conditions; even the terms used, such as the "cult of the individual" or "repressions," were grossly misleading considering the enormity of Stalin's crimes. But even the limited de-Stalinization of 1956–64 caused considerable heartache to some and triggered off resistance for reasons that are easy to imagine.

With Khrushchev's fall, re-Stalinization was the order of the day, even though the cult never again became as pervasive as it had been during the lifetime of the great leader.

More of the truth about Stalinism and its consequences was revealed and became the subject of a national debate only after Mikhail Gorbachev had come to power. Paradoxically, at the very time when some in the West were playing down the general importance of Stalin, the extent of his crimes, and his attendant responsibility, there was an outburst of anger in the Soviet Union, all the more violent for having been suppressed for so long. However, not everyone in the Soviet Union became an anti-Stalinist; the late dictator still had advocates who deeply resented the revelations and claimed that many of the alleged crimes had not been committed in the first place, were perpetrated by others, or, in any case, that it was wrong to look at the events of the 1930s from the vantage point of the late 1980s.

Much has been written about Stalin's life and also about his political heritage. Most of this literature emanated from the West, and it presented a variety of viewpoints. Some admired Stalin, others loathed him, still others tried hard to take an objective, detached view. The studies of Stalinism diverged, perhaps most widely in their conclusions. They were written before the revelations of glasnost shed new light on almost every aspect of Soviet life.

How important are these revelations, and to what extent do they necessitate the need for a radical reconsideration of half a century of Soviet history? Conflicting answers to this question can be given with equal justification, always depending on one's vantage point. It can be argued that, all things considered, few sensations have emerged, and not many crucial new facts have been disclosed, whether because Soviet society was not leakproof even in the 1930s and 1940s, despite all the precautionary measures, or because even under glasnost many decisive historical sources were not accessible or had been destroyed. Some, in fact, may not have existed in the first place.[2]

Thus, even under glasnost, it could not be established with any certainty whether Stalin had been involved in the murder of Sergei Kirov or the death of Ordzhonikidze. Similarly, it could not be said with any certainty how many victims had died in the collectivization of agriculture, as the result of the purges, or in the war against Germany. Even the way decisions were made at the very top largely remained a secret.

Seen from another perspective, the evidence that came to light was of immense importance because much of the information about the Soviet Union that had reached the outside world in the 1930s and 1940s was no more than rumor and hearsay. Much of it later proved to be correct, but some was half true or distorted or entirely wrong. For corroboration (or refutation), one had to wait for glasnost.

But there was yet another aspect, probably of even greater importance. Until 1986, the assessments of and the discussions about Stalin and Stalinism had been almost exclusively the domain of non-Russians looking at the Soviet Union from the outside. Such a vantage point has much to recommend it, but it also involves obvious drawbacks. In fact, an entire dimension was frequently missing from the writings of foreign observers, namely, that of immediacy and the intimate experience of living under a certain political system that enabled one to know in one's bones certain imponderabilities that are essential to an understanding of Stalin's Russia.

All this is not to say (as some Soviet writers have argued) that outside observers could not possibly understand what it was like to live during Stalin's time. Not everything written in the Soviet Union about Stalin and Stalinism under glasnost exuded great wisdom. Some was plainly wrong, and some writers repeated ideas and arguments that had been voiced decades earlier in the West; even the Nazi literature on the Soviet Union found some latter-day emulators. But it is also true that many Soviet writings on the subject have an empathy, and hence an authority, that might come to outsiders only as the result of a major effort of both intellect and imagination. For these reasons, the accounts and interpretations of Stalin and Stalinism published in the Soviet Union in recent years are of crucial importance not just because of new facts but also because of interpretations that came from the inside.

Stalin's personality and policies will be discussed for many years to come, and it is fruitless even to dream of a definitive assessment of them that is universally agreed upon. History is written and rewritten until a certain period ceases to command interest, which is unlikely to be the case for a long time in the case of Stalin and Stalinism.

I did not feel compelled to deal with every aspect of Stalin's rule in equal detail; the reader will find much more about purges and terror than about the Five-Year Plans. I felt that within a limited framework I had to concentrate on that which is specific and unique to the Stalinist period. Most societies have gone through a process of industrialization, but the Soviet purges, the show trials, and the "cult" were unique. The writer will therefore be excused for devoting more space to the specifics of Stalinism than to the economic history of the Soviet Union, just as a student of the Third Reich might favor devoting more time and space to the role of propaganda and terror than to the construction of superhighways, the *Reichsautobahnen*, under Hitler.

Most of the book deals with events that took place half a century or more ago, but the issues involved have remained amazingly topical. According to one of the official slogans in Moscow in the 1960s and 1970s, Lenin, though dead for a long time, was more alive than any other contemporary. The same is true with regard to Stalin, for so deep was the impact of Stalinism that, to this day, it has remained the central issue in Soviet society. Real lasting change is possible only if Stalinism is eradicated—that is, the climate of fear and the lack of initiative in the economy and in social life—and this has proved to be much more difficult than many thought.

Under glasnost there have been promising new beginnings in various directions, startling in many ways in view of the lack of freedom, Stalin's main legacy, that prevailed for so long. Can it be said that the changes are irreversible, the break with the past final? I very much hope so, but only time will tell. The decline and fall of Stalinism seems to me certain, but I also believe that it will be a long journey to the very end. Stalin's ghost has not yet been exorcised; it will haunt his native country for years to come.

1. Josef Stalin, 1879–1953

The essential facts about Stalin's youth and early career are relatively few, and they have been known to his biographers for a long time. While Stalin was alive, he was not interested in permitting more than a minimum amount of detail in the public realm; when he died and a freer investigation became possible, it was too late to uncover any major new details. Perhaps there was nothing to discover.

Stalin was born Josef Dzhugashvili on December 20, 1879, in Gori, a little town in the Caucasus not far from Tiflis. His father was a hard-drinking shoemaker who died when his son was eleven years of age. Josef ("Soso") was brought up by his mother, a washerwoman. He went to the local church school, and because he was a good pupil, he won a scholarship to the Tiflis Theological Seminary. At the age of eighteen he joined a clandestine local Social Democratic party. This led to his expulsion from the seminary in 1899. One year later, following a police search of his room, he went underground. A year later, his first articles appeared in the illegal press, and he became a member of the local party executive. His party nickname was "Koba," but he also used several other aliases.

Between 1901 and 1917, he lived the life of a professional revolutionary, mainly in Baku, the main industrial center in the Caucasus, but also, for a shorter period, in Petersburg, the capital. There were four or five arrests. On one occasion, he was exiled to Siberia, but escaped. Gradually he became known to the central leadership; in a letter to Maksim Gorky, Lenin referred to Stalin as that "splendid Georgian." A few years later, however, Lenin had forgotten Stalin's name. Stalin participated at party congresses in Finland (1905), Stockholm (1906), and London (1907). When the Prague Conference was convened in 1912,

Stalin was under arrest; in his absence, he was co-opted as a member of the Central Committee.

Stalin had the reputation of a hardworking, reliable, and able party worker. Unlike many other revolutionary leaders, he was neither an outstanding orator nor a theoretician. His only major publication to appear before the revolution of 1917, "Marxism and the National Question," was written at the level of a superior seminar paper. Essentially a doer, he excelled in conspirative organizational work that included the smuggling and distribution of party literature. He also helped organize the "expropriation" of banks, that is to say, armed holdups. For this reason, in 1917, the Mensheviks revealed that he had been excluded from the Tiflis party organization; Stalin claimed that he had never been excluded but did not deny the substance of the charge against him. He was a hard-liner who, in the various splits that occurred in Russian social democracy, always opted for the most radical wing, that is, the Bolsheviks. He had great self-discipline, and if he nursed political ambitions, he knew well to hide them. He was a dynamic, fearless, indefatigable party workhorse, at least until his last, longest internment in 1913.

During the next four years of exile in Turukhansk, Siberia, he became curiously lethargic. He did not attempt to escape, and although other Bolshevik exiles used their years in Siberia to study, read, and write, Stalin's only passion seems to have been hunting and fishing. There were rumors that he had been enlisted as an agent by the Okhrana, the tsarist secret police, but this has never been proved. He left Siberia only after the February Revolution and the fall of the tsarist regime.

Stalin had no close friends; he was sullen, rude, and had other (unspecified) character traits that made many party comrades shun his company. In 1903, he married a girl, Ekaterina (Keke) Svanidze, from a neighboring Georgian village, who died four years later. There was one child from this marriage, Yasha, who was taken prisoner of war in 1941 and died in a German camp. Stalin is said to have fathered another child in his Siberian exile;[1] if so, he showed no interest in his offspring at the time or in later years. But then, Stalin was never a family man; his mother went on to live for many years after the Revolution, yet Stalin saw her only once. Perhaps he felt embarrassed by the presence of the illiterate washerwoman; perhaps he did not care one way or another.

The man who arrived in Petrograd in 1917 and who had adopted the name Stalin a number of years earlier (between 1910 and 1912) was thirty-eight years of age—not a youngster by the standard of those days but a mature revolutionary. (Lenin, his elder by nine years, was known as *Starik*, the "old man.")

Stalin was small in stature but of powerful physique; he had a pock-marked face, and his famous mustache seems to have been in place since the year 1900. He had a quick intelligence and a phenomenal memory but little education and few interests outside Russian working-class politics. His command of the Russian language was perfect, but he spoke with a strong Georgian accent. As a member of the "Russian bureau" of the Bolsheviks, he was a high-ranking official; yet, in 1917, he was probably the least-known leader of comparable rank both inside the party and, *a fortiori*, outside it.

He played no leading role in the year of the two revolutions. In accounts at the time of the Revolution, he is seldom, if ever, mentioned, except as a member of the Executive Committee of the party. One such report characterized him as creating the impression of a "gray blur, looming up now and then dimly and not leaving any trace" (N. N. Sukhanov). In later years, after most of his erstwhile comrades had died or had been executed, Stalin rewrote Soviet history to include his participation, together with Lenin, in planning and carrying out the Revolution. Nothing could be further from the truth; his role in 1917 was exceedingly modest. True, he was not a gray blur or a mediocrity or the "creature of the party bureaucracy" claimed by Trotsky in later years. His career was not made as a people's tribune; his influence was based on patient organizational work carried out in small meetings in back rooms, far from street crowds and large assemblies. Yet his work was recognized, and when the first list of fifteen ministers ("people's commissars") was published after the uprising, Stalin's name was among them—the people's commissar for nationalities.

There are interesting divergences between the Stalin legend and the real facts, even prior to 1917. He came from modest beginnings in a border area of the Russian Empire, which had to be played down because it was not befitting the image of the great leader, just as the terrorist incidents had to be suppressed. These aspects of his background were not compatible with the image of a wise statesman, the father of his people. He thought of himself as a Russian, and he was to be described as such. But how significant is it, in the final analysis, that Stalin, at the age of twenty-three in Batum, or a few years later in Baku, was not yet a leader of world stature and renown, but instead played second fiddle to Shaumyan and others, and that the stage of his activities was a little sideshow? He had not yet arrived at the center of the Russian political scene, and for this reason, if for no other, after 1930, the rewriting of history about his early years is not of great importance.

All this begins to change with the October Revolution, when the biography of Josef Stalin gradually turns into the history of the Soviet Union. During the civil war he played a role of some importance, above all in the defense of Tsaritsyn; later, Stalingrad; later yet, Volgograd. He was also sent on special missions to other parts of the front. In the year 1919, he was appointed a member of the Politburo, the highest executive body of the party. Three years later, Stalin became secretary-general of the party. The office of the secretariat, founded in 1919, had been of no great consequence before, but Stalin made it into the seat of real power. When, shortly before his death, Lenin tried to remove Stalin, it was too late; Lenin's famous "Testament" was ignored by the party. Trotsky, the leader next in stature to Lenin, was a brilliant speaker and writer but an incompetent tactician. Trotsky maneuvered himself into a position that effectively debarred him from the struggle for the succession. From 1923, the country was ruled by a triumvirate consisting of Stalin, G. E. Zinoviev, and L. B. Kamenev.

In 1925, Stalin made a turn to the right, got rid of his two companions, and established a coalition with such moderate leaders as Bukharin, Rykov, and Tomsky, which lasted until 1928, when the collectivization of agriculture and the forced industrialization of the Five-Year Plans came about. By that time, Stalin had established his own apparatus within the party, and those who were not his faithful followers were systematically replaced. By 1930, his rule was absolute, and within another few years, the Stalinist system had been established— euphemistically labeled "cult of the individual," rule by propaganda and terror.

The purges and mass trials at first seemed rational inasmuch as the main victims were former enemies and rivals, or at least potential foes. But gradually they became quite unpredictable, and they began to affect Stalin's blind, unquestioning followers.

During the 1930s, Stalin the boss (*khoziain*) became a great statesman, a great ideologist—for the time being, merely continuing Lenin's work, whose most faithful pupil he was—and a great economist. With the

German invasion in June 1941, Stalin also became a supreme military leader. No leader in modern history, with the possible exception of Adolf Hitler, had concentrated so much power in his hands. But Hitler led his country to defeat, whereas the Soviet Union emerged triumphant from the war. Thus, in 1945, Stalin was at the height of his power; his prestige was equally great at home and abroad. Under his leadership, the Soviet Union had emerged as the strongest power in Europe by far and as a world power equal to the United States.

That Stalin's last years were, in most respects, anticlimactic appears most clearly only after his death in 1953. Those who had hoped for more freedom and greater prosperity inside the Soviet Union were disappointed; the propaganda and terror machine relentlessly continued its work, the arrests and the executions continued, and the Soviet Union remained an empire of fear. Stalin's intellectual preoccupations and ambitions became even more splenetic; he even wrote pseudoscientific essays on linguistics. The economic rebuilding of the ravaged country was initiated and made some progress, but less so than in many other countries. Soviet power was consolidated in the Eastern European countries, which had been occupied in the last phase of the war. But it was imposed in such a way as to plant the seeds of opposition and conflict—first with Yugoslavia, later with other Communist countries.

When Stalin died in 1953, he was mourned by many of his subjects; whether there was a genuine feeling of bereavement or whether they were fearful about the future, we do not know. Stalin had systematically inculcated the belief that only he was farsighted enough to lead the country, that without him the Soviet people would be lost, an easy prey to the country's many enemies.

However, a good number of Stalin's subjects genuinely admired him and sincerely thought his form of rule the most adequate for their country. Why they should have thought so, why they should have genuinely missed him, is one of the central questions this study wishes to address.

That Stalin made no provisions for his succession led to a struggle for power that was to last for years. The party and state apparatus were cumbersome and increasingly incapable of coping with the economic problems facing the country. Foreign policy had no clear aim or strategy, being geared neither to engage in wars of conquest nor to make peace. Yet so deeply ingrained was the Stalinist legacy that, even after 1956, when certain excesses of the "cult of personality" were announced, the

Stalinist imprint on the mentality of leaders and followers alike resulted in institutions that had hardly changed. A man who had such an enormous impact on his people in his time, and for many years after, the man who put his imprint on a whole period in history, was obviously a great leader. He was not necessarily a positive hero, but he was great inasmuch as his deeds affected the lives of many millions. Much of it depended, of course, on the size of the historical stage; had he been born and ruled in Persia or Afghanistan, Stalin would have been remembered only as a marginal figure in world history.

What made his rise possible? What did he have that other Communist leaders of his generation lacked? Stalin was in no way designed to be an idol of the masses: He was neither a demonic, hypnotic figure like Hitler or Mussolini, who could impart emotions to millions, nor a "Pied Piper," seductive in leadership. Unlike Lenin, he could not impose his authority naturally on his peers. He was no intellectual; Trotsky, Bukharin, and many others were superior to him in this respect. He certainly did not attain leadership because of his outstanding moral qualities; on the contrary, there was in him a strong streak of both criminality and madness that became more pronounced with age.

Stalin, the great villain, would have been a more suitable subject for an ancient historian such as Plutarch (who would, no doubt, have juxtaposed him to Hitler), rather than for contemporary academic Western biographers, who are ill prepared both for the scale of his crimes and motives that seem to belong to another time and civilization. Stalin and Hitler certainly had this much in common: Both were greatly underrated until they seized power. What a recent biographer wrote of Hitler is also true with regard to Stalin:

> The author Kurt Tucholski voiced the opinion of many when he wrote: "The man [Hitler] does not really exist—he is only the noise he makes." When, after 1933, the man turned out to be an exceedingly energetic, inventive, and efficient operator, the psychological reaction was great.[2]

In Stalin's case, it was not even a question of noise, for unlike Hitler, he was not known as a spellbinder and demagogue; nor had Stalin made any significant contribution to Marxism in a movement characterized by a heavy emphasis on ideology.

The answer to this seeming riddle is twofold. Stalin was a man of enormous self-confidence and had a single-minded sense of purpose. If he was not an intellectual and if he indeed despised intellectuals, he was not affected by the hesitation and self-doubt of an intellectual. However, these qualities were of crucial importance as the Bolshevik party emerged from the underground and became the ruling state party. If once the leader had to be an agitator, above all, mobilizing the masses, now he had to be a technician of power. Stalin mastered that art better than his contemporaries; he was a first-rate tactician, intriguer, and plotter, playing enemies and potential enemies one against the other. It has been mentioned that he had common sense and a quick intelligence. Trotsky was much more clever and had read many more books, but, unlike Stalin, he failed to understand certain simple truths—for example, the fact that once the world revolution had not come, building socialism in Russia was the only possible alternative. That the final outcome would not be socialism, as the old Bolsheviks and virtually everyone else had envisaged, was yet another question.

The old Bolsheviks were no saints, and their revolutionary convictions induced them to increasingly use violence. But Stalin was infinitely more ruthless; he was, in fact, devoid of any scruples, a quality of decisive importance in his rise and in his successful stay in power. A man of great brutality, he would seldom boast of his ruthlessness. On the contrary, he was a master of sanctimoniousness, hypocrisy, and mendacity—unlike Hitler, who made virtually no secret of his murderous intentions. Hitler, as a Soviet author has pointed out, never pretended to be a friend of Jews, Slavs, and other such "inferior" people.[3] Among many other things, Stalin thought it important to also be known as the greatest humanist of his time, perhaps of all time.

And yet, everything considered, these qualifications alone are not sufficient to explain his phenomenal rise to power and the fact that he remained in power for three decades and continued to influence Soviet politics long after his death. It became increasingly obvious that his leadership corresponded with certain traditions dating further back, some connected with the origins and practices of Bolshevism and others with the autocratic tradition in Russian history. The connection between Stalinism and Leninism has been endlessly discussed and vehemently denied by Leninists. There is no denying that there is a world of difference between Lenin's and Stalin's style and between many of Lenin's and Stalin's views. But it is also true that there was a strong dictatorial, antidemocratic element in Lenin from the very beginning. Bolshevism came to power as the result of a coup against the majority of Petrograd and Moscow, and once engaged in this course of action, there were no guarantees that the dictatorship of the supreme party committee might not turn into the dictatorship of a single individual.

Farsighted leaders of the Left, like Rosa Luxemburg, had predicted this only weeks after the Bolsheviks had come to power. Only a very naive man—and Lenin was not naive—could have believed that the dictatorship of the proletariat, that is to say, of the Politburo, would more or less automatically give way to a higher form of democracy. Which may explain the relative ease with which Stalin established his ascendancy over the party. But it does not explain the popularity of Stalinism during its heyday.

Stalin and his system were apparently genuinely popular; he was an excellent father figure for tens of millions of his subjects, strict but fair and wise. It does not explain, however, why many of his subjects continued to believe, at least to some extent, in Stalin and Stalinism even after his death, when the crimes and failures of the system had already become common knowledge. This can be explained only against the background of the lack of a democratic tradition in Russia, a country ruled for centuries by autocrats, unfettered by constitutional restraints. True, some of the rulers had been more autocratic than others, but the people by and large had accepted them not just dutifully as a necessary evil but with genuine respect and even love (as if they were sent by God), not to be resisted, however foolishly or cruelly they behaved.

Even with all these psychological and historical explanations, however, it is also true that Stalin needed luck. He could have been felled by an assassin's bullet or by disease; he was lucky not only because he was blessed with an iron constitution but also because he had to deal with the long-suffering Russian people and because, among his antagonists in the party, there was no one who had the courage and the ability to oppose him effectively. Even if Trotsky had been a better politician, he would still have been debarred as a Jew, and Bukharin lacked ambition. While it is true that thousands could have ruled Russia, there were no effective plotters in the 1930s. Many were overawed by Stalin or felt bound by ties of loyalty to the party, a loyalty utterly strange to him. It is fascinating to speculate what Soviet history would have been like under another leader, but history deals principally with events that did take place, not with those that might have taken place. Initially there existed many alternatives to

Stalin, but it was part of his "greatness" to make it appear that there were none, and it is, of course, true that each of his actions led to another, thus narrowing the freedom of choice. To give but one obvious example: Once he had ordered the execution of the supreme commanders of the Red Army, the stature of the Soviet Union as a military power (and as a potential ally) greatly diminished. This contributed to a breakdown in the negotiations between Moscow and the Western powers in the summer of 1939 and ultimately led to the pact with Nazi Germany.

Leading sociologists have established various types of leadership: the charismatic, the rational-legal, and the traditional. Stalin did not fit into any pattern, not even the traditional. Ivan Grozny (Ivan the Terrible) perhaps resembled Stalin the most closely, though he had lived more than three centuries before; Stalin seems to have been fascinated by Grozny, but he criticized him for not being *grozny* enough. Other historians and philosophers have drawn parallels between Stalin and certain Roman (Nero, Commodus) or Byzantine emperors, while some invoked Oriental despotism. None of these parallels is of much help in explaining the Stalin phenomenon.

The fascinating story of the Stalinist cult has not yet been written. It began in 1929, on the occasion of his fiftieth birthday, and by the time of the Seventeenth Party Congress in January 1934 (of which a post-Stalin official history was to say that it was "the scene of the most excessive praise of his services"), it had reached a first climax. The short official biography published in1940 called him the great strategist of the socialist revolution, an omniscient genius. Everyone, it said, knew the irresistible, crushing strength of the Stalinist logic, the crystal clarity of his mind, his steely will, his devotion to the party, his burning belief in the people, and his love of the people: "Everyone knows his modesty, his simpleness, his delicacy toward people, and his lack of mercy vis-à-vis the enemies of the people."[4]

But these were the restrained words of the party theoreticians. In many thousands of editorials, speeches, pictures, poems, plays, songs, and movies, there was far more extravagant praise. He was compared to a mountain eagle (with thousands of eaglets) and a falcon, to the sun, the moon, and the stars; he was not only the undisputed leader of the Soviet Union, but of all progressive mankind, the greatest man who had ever lived. Little children were writing poems such as "Stalin! Thou art dearer to us than anything in the world," and a delegate to a party conference (the writer A. Avdeenko) solemnly declared that the first word of his child, as yet unborn, would be "Stalin." In his biography, Barbusse had this to say: "In his country, if the cobbles in the street could talk, they would say: Stalin." His sixtieth and seventieth birthdays were further occasions for organized mass enthusiasm, essays written by Politburo members, verse by leading poets, statues and pictures by leading artists, and songs by the foremost composers. Astronomers, surgeons, specialists in Romance philology, everyone stressed how much they had learned from and been inspired by Stalin and his works.

Stalin, the poets claimed, had the attributes of the king-god of earlier civilizations. He made the sun rise and shine; he had created the moon and the stars; he made mankind breathe; he had fructified the earth; he made the spring bloom and the musical chords vibrate. But these were mere repetitions; the apex of the cult had been reached earlier on, and, in substance, there was nothing more to add. Some of the stories and poems were written by people in fear of their lives (such as Bulgakov, Mandelstam, and Pasternak), but much of the enthusiasm was no doubt genuine. On a few occasions, Stalin himself was mildly critical of the excessive praise heaped on him as unbecoming to the Bolshevik tradition. But far more often, he helped to organize the adulation and took a hand in rewriting official histories, as well as editorials, novels, and movies, to give more prominence to his own role.

Foreigners added to the cult. Perhaps the most widely read biography at the time was the one written by Henri Barbusse, the author of the most famous antiwar novel of the century and later a member of the French Communist party. In seventeen years, under Stalin's leadership, the Soviet Union had become the most civilized country on earth in every respect. His story was a chain of successes in the face of unheard-of difficulties. He was a man of iron and steel and of enormous common sense; he had the wisdom and the caution of a lion. He was a man of the widest knowledge, of passionate purity, of unshakable resolution, the Lenin of his age. He had written a great number of important books. In some ways, he was even greater than Lenin, who had been a mere agitator, because Stalin was, above all, the statesman. His "terrible patience" was one of his outstanding features.

He was one of the most modest of men, taking care of everything, having only one secretary—unlike Lloyd George, who had thirty-two. He wrote his speeches himself and answered all his mail. He laughed like a child and loved children. He was kind, cordial, delicate, and gay. He never tried to shine, but always preferred to stay in the background. His simplicity and his uncomplicated nature made it sometimes difficult to understand him.

He was motivated not by personal vanity but by his conviction and faith. Stalin believed in the masses as the masses believed in him. He was the most important of all contemporaries. The other Soviet leaders believed in him and needed him. Under Stalin's guidance, scientists were endeavoring to raise the dead and save the living with the blood of the dead. In his way, Stalin towered, with all his greatness, over Europe and Asia, over yesterday and today at the same time. The biography ended with an apotheosis on Red Square:

> Here is the paternal brother who is watching everyone. Although you do not know him, he knows you and is thinking of you. Whoever you may be, you have need of this benefactor. Whoever you may be, the finest part of your destiny is in the hands of that other man, who also watches over you and who works for you—the man with a scholar's mind, a workman's face, and the dress of a simple soldier.[5]

The Barbusse biography was written by a Communist, an extreme manifestation of the adulation of Stalin. But there were other works almost equally laudatory, if more restrained in tone. J. T. Murphy was a former Communist, but this did not prevent him from writing of Stalin as the "great human powerhouse," as a statesman whose gigantic achievements and assured prospects were greater than those of any contemporary:

> He can confidently face his people with frontiers secure and an era of economic and social expansion ahead such as the world has never known. The full power of the country's vast productive machinery and resources will be turned to healing the wounds of war and enriching the social well being of every man, woman and child in the Union. Thus the new world, born on November 7th, 1917, will grow from strength to strength, and all men will testify that in its creation and development Joseph Stalin has earned his title of "The Great."[6]

Isaac Deutscher, a former Trotskyite and an independent Marxist author, was not uncritical of certain aspects of Stalin's rule. But he, too, was overawed in his overall assessment of the man:

Many Allied visitors who called at the Kremlin during the war were astonished to see on how many issues, great and small, military, political and diplomatic, Stalin personally took the final decision. He was in fact, his own commander-in-chief, his own minister of defense, his own quartermaster, his own minister of supply, his own foreign minister, and even his own chef de protocol. . . . Thus he went on, day after day, throughout four years of hostilities—a prodigy of patience, tenacity and vigilance, almost omnipresent, almost omniscient.[7]

Years later, Deutscher was to argue that the "omnipresence" and the "omniscience" were not to be understood literally, that the terms had been written tongue in cheek, but there is no certainty that the writer's memory did not fail him. Russian nationalists and neo-Stalinists would adduce in later years such writings as evidence for their argument that, far from being a specific Russian (or Soviet) affair, the Stalinist cult was a global phenomenon, "from Madrid to Shanghai."[8] For a quarter of a century, many Western intellectuals attributed all victories and achievements to Stalin and the idea of the cult as it gripped the masses and was transformed into a very powerful material force. This is an interesting theory, but it suffered from a fatal flaw. For Stalinism, after all, had not triumphed in Spain or in France, or anywhere else at the time. And if some Western intellectuals had been carried away in their enthusiasm, the reason had been a fear of Hitler rather than a love of Stalin. Others had sharply attacked Stalin, and their numbers had grown with the purges and the German-Soviet pact. With equal or greater justification, the 1930s could have been called "the age of fascism"; there were Fascist parties, big and small, in virtually every European country. In Italy and Germany, they came to power; in Britain and France, they remained sects of marginal importance.

Stalin died on March 5, 1953, and within a few days the Stalin cult was frozen. It did not come to an abrupt end. Stalingrad and all the other cities, villages, and streets retained their names, and for the time being no open criticism was uttered concerning the late leader. His name was but seldom mentioned in the press and on the radio; the last terror campaign (against the "medical poisoners") was discontinued; the surviving victims were released from prison; and gradually a general amnesty was promulgated.

2. War Against the Peasants: The Bukharin Alternative

In a testament written in the form of a letter to a party conference, Lenin singled out six leaders, on whom, as he saw it, rested the future of the party and the Revolution. About Bukharin, Lenin said he was not only the most valuable and greatest theoretician of the party but also its favorite son. Nevertheless, Bukharin's theoretical views could only with grave doubt be regarded as wholly Marxist. There was something scholastic about him; he had never learned and might never master the essence of dialectics. It was certainly a candid statement, but it was no more critical than Lenin's assessments of the other top leaders.

Lenin was in some ways a farsighted leader, a fact of which Soviet citizens are constantly reminded to this day. Yet the thought never crossed his mind that of the six mentioned in his "Testament," five would be killed by the sixth. True, he had some misgivings about the sixth man, who he said had concentrated immeasurable power in his hands. Lenin was not sure whether this sixth man would use such power "always with sufficient caution"—a prediction that has entered history as one of the grossest understatements ever made. Ten days later, in a postscript, Lenin suggested that Stalin be deposed from the post of secretary general. But the party leadership took no notice; it was decided not to make the contents of the letter known.

Like many others, the "favorite of the party" was shot in 1938 as an enemy of the people; his place of execution and burial, if indeed he was buried, are not known. After Stalin's death, the more absurd charges against Bukharin were dropped. It was unofficially conceded that he had not been a foreign spy or assassin. But there was no legal rehabilitation, and he remained by and large a "nonperson" until 1988, fifty years after his death. Only then did a group of legal experts acting on behalf of the

U.S.S.R. Supreme Court, after having given careful study to "hundreds of volumes and thousands upon thousands of documents concerning his case," reach the conclusion that he had been innocent of the charges against him.[1] Then, in rapid succession, a number of favorable articles were published in the Soviet media, and eventually even his party membership was reinstated.

Respect was paid to many of Stalin's victims, albeit sometimes grudgingly, but only Bukharin became the object of a political cult. Frequently it was stated that if the party had only followed the course of action proposed in the 1920s by Bukharin, a very different and much better society would have emerged. Many sacrifices would not have been necessary, and a socialism with a human face—rather than a horrible grimace—would have emerged. In brief, this opinion gained ground: Bukharinism was seen as a historical alternative to Stalinism, and even fifty years after his death, Bukharin's views were thought to be relevant.

Nikolai Ivanovich Bukharin, born in 1888, was among the youngest of the first cohort of Bolshevik leaders; like most of them, he hailed from a middle-class family. Those who knew him in his early years, such as his Moscow classmate Ilya Erenburg, have described him as a bookworm with insatiable intellectual interests even as a boy. He was small of stature, enthusiastic, emotional, with an open, friendly face, and had no personal enemy in the world. He joined the revolutionary movement as a high school student. At twenty he organized strikes, made speeches on behalf of the party, and became a member of the Executive Committee of the Moscow Committee of the Bolshevik party. One year later, he was arrested for the first time, which was followed by administrative exile to northern Russia, from which he escaped in 1911.

The next six years he spent abroad: in Austria, where he studied economics at Vienna University, in Switzerland, Sweden, and ultimately in the United States. He fell under the spell of Lenin, who valued him as a Marxist economist but felt uneasy about his political instability and thought him "too soft." Occasional disagreements with Lenin were probably inevitable because the leader of the party brooked no contradiction, irrespective of whether it concerned some recondite philosophical question or a tactical maneuver. Bukharin, on the other hand, was an intellectual who, with all his loyalty to the party, was sometimes unwilling to give up independent, critical thought. As a result, he would find himself on occasion to the left of Lenin; at other times, his views would be with the right wing of the party. His political judgment was not always reliable, perhaps because of a certain lack of realism and a surfeit of dogmatism, a quality that he shared with Trotsky. For instance, the negative stand he took against the armistice with the Germans in February 1918 was a mistake he subsequently admitted.

Bukharin played no central role in either the planning of the Revolution or the civil war. Virtually alone among the Bolshevik leaders, he accepted no position in either the Soviet government or the supreme party hierarchy. He was a member of the Central Committee, later of the Politburo, editor in chief of *Pravda* (later of *Izvestiia*), but he had no power base, no ministry, no appointment except the intangible one as a major ideologist. His *ABC of Communism* remained the basic doctrinal text of the party for mass audiences for many years. His *Economics of the Transformation Period* fared less well; it was a manifesto of the period of "war communism." Only one section was finished when the bankruptcy of war communism had become all too obvious and when the radically different New Economic Policy (NEP) was about to be ushered in.[2]

At the time of Lenin's death, Bukharin was a highly esteemed member of the party leadership, but not one of the contenders for the role of leader; among the members of the top echelon, he was certainly the least ambitious. Yet even if he had craved power, there might have been no room in the top leadership for a man of so many contradictions. He would utter bloodthirsty pronouncements concerning the fate of the enemies of the Bolshevik party. Essentially, however, he was a mild man; on various occasions, he tried to save people who had been condemned to death. He was one of the staunchest supporters of Proletkult (the literary group advocating strict cultural regimentation), yet advocated at the same time a more liberal attitude toward the old, Russian, non-Communist intelligentsia. Many other examples could be included.

When Lenin died, Trotsky had been outmaneuvered in the struggle for the succession, largely owing to his own ineptitude. Effective power was in the hands of a troika consisting of Stalin, Kamenev, and Zinoviev. Within less than two years, Kamenev and Zinoviev found themselves in opposition to the new general secretary. Although there were political differences between them, they are not sufficient to explain the split; the real reason was that Stalin no longer needed them. He had built up his own power base with people such as Molotov who were to serve him faithfully to the end of his days. However, he was not yet strong enough to serve as the sole dictator, nor was the party ready for political rule of this style. A coalition between Stalin and Bukharin came into being that lasted for almost three years. Stalin left the ideological pronouncements to Bukharin, who was also in charge of the Communist International (Comintern). In the meantime, Stalin dealt with practical issues and further strengthened the bureaucratic apparatus. It would have been an unequal partnership except that Bukharin had the support of several powerful figures in the Soviet hierarchy, such as Aleksei Rykov, successor to Lenin as chairman of the Council of People's Commissar (i.e., prime minister), as well as Tomsky, head of the trade unions, and others, whose fate we shall return to later.

During 1926 and 1927, there seems to have been by and large a degree of unanimity between Stalin and Bukharin. True, Bukharin went a bit further in his enthusiasm for the NEP than the general secretary; at one stage, Bukharin coined the slogan "Enrich yourself" for the prosperous peasants, which he was later to regret. Stalin, on the other hand, became increasingly preoccupied with the idea that "there would be no bread" without decisive changes in the Soviet village. He began to envisage the abolition of private property and the collectivization of agriculture.[3]

The showdown in 1928 between Stalin and what later became known as the "right-wing deviationists" ended with a decisive victory for the general secretary. Not only was the policy advocated by Bukharin and his supporters defeated; they lost their key positions in the party and in government. Within a couple of years, they had to engage in abject admissions that they had been wrong and "the party" had been right. In the meantime, the collectivization of agriculture was carried out in break-neck speed, and the first Five-Year Plan, aimed at the expansion of Soviet industry, began. The country was undergoing a second economic, social, and political revolution.

There is no denying that the political differences between Stalin and the "right-wing deviationists" were real and far more important than those that had caused the split between him and Zinoviev and Kamenev a few years earlier. The issue at stake was the end of the NEP; 1929 entered Soviet history as the year of the (great) turning point, the transition to a socialist economy. However, in principle, Bukharin was by no means opposed to the collectivization of agriculture; he recognized the importance of the expansion of heavy industry and fully realized that it was impossible to effect it in a country in which agriculture was backward and agricultural supplies uncertain. Stalin, on the other hand, was by character a cautious man, always calculating the cost of his actions. He did not really have a clear, detailed concept, and he advanced in a series of fitful stop-and-go movements. The differences between Stalin and the "deviationists," in short, were not so much rooted in questions of principle; rather, they concerned the speed of development in agriculture and industry. They had more to do with the kind of party and society Stalin envisaged; there was room only for blind obedience, not for collective leadership. It was for this reason, more than for any other, that Bukharin and his allies had to be removed, broken, and ultimately destroyed.

Bukharin continued to be active along the margins of the party leadership after his downfall. He was still a member of the Central Committee; he published articles and made speeches to academic audiences and at Soviet writers' conferences. He admitted some of his mistakes at the party plenum in November 1929; one year later, he took his self-criticism even further and stated that he regarded Stalin's policy as a full success, praising Stalin as an "energetic, iron figure" who "entirely deserved the right to lead the party in the future." Only a few years earlier, Bukharin had compared Stalin with Genghis Khan. At the Seventeenth Party Congress, Bukharin declared that Stalin had been wholly correct in destroying the "right-wing deviationists." Every party member had a duty to rally around Stalin, the embodiment of the mind and will of the party, its theoretical and practical leader.

Such declarations were in line with the other speeches at the "congress of the victors"; many took adulation much further. A new political style had emerged. For a little while it seemed as if Bukharin might be restored to a modest position in the higher echelons of power. To the extent that Stalin liked anyone among the old guard, he probably preferred Bukharin to most others. But such feelings made not the slightest difference with regard to Bukharin's ultimate fate. Once Stalin had made up his mind to exterminate the Bolshevik old guard, Bukharin's fate was sealed.

The agony lasted for almost three years. Bukharin was implicated as a fellow conspirator by the accused in the Zinoviev-Kamenev trial of August 1936. An investigation against him was launched but was discontinued one month later for "want of legal evidence." However, soon after, the accusations were renewed, and Bukharin was arrested on February 27, 1937, brought to trial a year later, and executed on March 15, 1938—two days after having been sentenced to death. In his evidence,

Bukharin incriminated himself (like all defendants in all trials), although he denied many of the more specific, grotesque accusations, such as having been a foreign spy and having plotted to kill Lenin, Stalin, Gorky, and others.

A few days before his arrest, Bukharin had dictated a letter "to the future generation of party leaders" and asked his young wife to memorize it by heart. The letter said that in the face of death, confronting a diabolical machine applying medieval methods, he wanted to state for a last time that he had been an honest revolutionary ever since joining the party at the age of sixteen. He had never wanted to destroy the achievements of the Revolution or to reintroduce capitalism. He had never been a traitor and would have given his life for Lenin. If he had committed mistakes, he hoped that posterity would not judge him more harshly than Lenin had done. And he ended with the request that a new generation of honest leaders read his letter at a plenary meeting of the Central Committee and restore him to party membership.

Following the release of Anna Larina (Bukharina) after many years in the gulag, the letter was submitted to the party authorities in 1961. But it took another twenty-seven years for it to be published and for Bukharin's party membership to be restored.[4]

What made Bukharin capitulate in such an abject way after his political defeat in 1929? Even if he believed that his policy had been mistaken—which is by no means clear—the self-flagellation and the Byzantine eulogies to Stalin are difficult to understand, even with the benefit of hindsight. He was a loyal party man and seemed to have put loyalty above truth. He feared political isolation. He was afraid for his young wife and his newborn child. He had always been a little soft, as Lenin recognized many years earlier, but then, many men who were even tougher behaved exactly as he did. The question of motives will preoccupy us later on in the general context of the trials and the purges.

In the light of Stalin's rise to dictatorship, we still know too little about Bukharin's true opinions after his political defeat. For a long time our knowledge rested mainly on the "Letter of the Old Bolshevik" and conversations in Paris with Lydia Dan, the wife of the Menshevik leader. Together with some officials of the Marx-Engels Institute in Moscow, Bukharin had been sent to Paris in early 1936 to negotiate the purchase of portions of Marx's archives held by the exiled German Social Democrats. They, in turn, asked Boris Nikolaevsky, a Russian socialist and outstanding Marxologist, to act as their negotiator. He was a scrupulous historian and, incidentally, also Rykov's brother-in-law; Nikolaevsky's integrity as a source has seldom, if ever, been questioned. At the same time, there is much reason to assume that Bukharin was by no means Nikolaevsky's only source; the "Letter" also referred to events after Bukharin's departure from Paris.[5] Furthermore, certain precautions were taken to obfuscate the origins of the letter. According to Nikolaevsky, Bukharin said: "We are all obliged to lie; it is impossible to manage otherwise." In the beginning, Bukharin and other critics had believed that the terror inside the party was an exaggerated aftermath of Kirov's murder but that this would pass and that an internal party reconciliation would take place:

> All that was necessary (it was believed) was for Stalin's morbid mistrust to pass. To this end it was maintained that the loyalty of the party to its present leadership must be stressed as often and as emphatically as possible; that the thing to do was to burn incense before Stalin and extol his person on all occasions. . . . He has a weakness for such adulation, and his revengefulness can be appeased only by huge doses of flattery laid on with a trowel; there is nothing else to be done about it. Moreover, it was added, we must learn to forgive these trifles because of the big things Stalin has done for the party in guiding it through the critical years of the first Five-Year Plan, and at the same time we must speak even louder and with increasing emphasis of the tremendous changes now taking place, of the new "happy days" into which we were now entering, of the new party policy, the basis of which was to cultivate in the masses feeling of human dignity, respect for human personality, and the development of "proletarian humanism." Alas, how naive were all these hopes of ours! Looking back now, we find it hard to understand how we could have failed to note the symptoms that indicated that the trend was in quite the opposite direction: not toward reconciliation inside the party but toward intensification of the terror inside the party to its logical conclusion, to the stage of physical extermination of all those whose party past might make them opponents of Stalin or aspirants to his power.[6]

In conversation with Lydia Dan and others, Bukharin noted that people in the West had no idea what kind of person Stalin was—not just a malicious man but a devil. Bukharin also noted that his own fate was sealed and that Stalin waited only for an opportunity to have him killed.

Yet, at the same time, he refused to entertain the idea of defecting; he could not live as an émigré. And there was his faith that the stream (of history) was still going forward, that the (Soviet) people were becoming stronger, and that the building of a new society was taking place.

This account, the source of much of our knowledge, has been violently disputed by Bukharin's widow in her memoirs published under glasnost.[7] She went as far as accusing the Paris Mensheviks of collaborating, knowingly or unknowingly, in the preparation of Stalin's case against Bukharin, although she conceded that such a "provocation" was by no means essential from Stalin's point of view. Larina, according to her evidence, was present at all meetings with Nikolaevsky after her arrival in Paris in March 1936, and though there had been some talks before that date, she thought it utterly inconceivable that Bukharin would confide in a political enemy. On the contrary, Bukharin told Nikolaevsky of the few occasions when discussions were held on the politics of the stormy growth of industry in the Soviet Union and the building of giant new enterprises. Although the collectivization of agriculture had been a difficult period, it was now a thing of the past, and there were no longer differences of opinion among the leadership. Bukharin (according to Larina) concluded by telling Nikolaevsky that if he were now to visit the Soviet Union, he would no longer recognize the country.

Which of the two versions is the correct one? If Bukharin's real views were expressed in his talks with Nikolaevsky, it is not easy to understand why he returned to Moscow—and to certain death. Perhaps his loyalty to the party prevailed over all other considerations; perhaps there was in Bukharin's mental makeup a streak of the *stradalets*, the great sufferer, the early Christian martyr. This has been noted by many observers, including his widow, who wrote about a recurring nightmare during the first year after his murder: "I saw, as on Golgotha, a crucified person; not Christ but rather a worn-out, paler Bukharin. . . . A black raven was pecking at the martyr's bloodied, lifeless body." More recent Soviet writers have referred to Bukharin as a great martyr and to his stay in Paris as his Golgotha.[8]

But there was an essential difference: The early Christian martyrs did not renege on their faith, and they were tortured by their enemies rather than by fellow Christians. The purpose of the Moscow trials was precisely to show groups of people obediently repeating the lies invented for them by their tormentors.

According to Larina, Bukharin was a man of great intelligence but equally profound naïveté. She claims that up until the first Moscow trial, which took place after his return from Paris, he did not believe in any impending danger. Even after the trial he tended to blame Zinoviev and Kamenev rather than Stalin. Even after Bukharin had become the target of open attacks in Moscow, he tried to reach Stalin by phone and through letters, assuming that the attacks had been launched without the knowledge of the dictator.[9] Could it be that after years of close collaboration Bukharin had no inkling regarding the true character of "Koba"? In defense of this thesis, it could be argued that Radek and others, less naive than Bukharin, behaved exactly as he did.

On the other side of the ledger, there is the fact that Stalin's campaign against the old guard had started many years earlier. In some cases (such as Ryutin's), Stalin had asked for the death sentence, despite Lenin's appeal: "Let there be no blood among you." What could have induced Bukharin to appeal to the chief hangman after so many of the old Bolsheviks had already been executed? How does one explain that (as Volkogonov, Stalin's Soviet biographer, notes) the *Sotsialisticheski Vestnik*, the exiled Menshevik organ, had correctly predicted six years earlier that although the supporters of the NEP had only been demoted, it was merely a question of time until they would become "enemies of the people."[10] The Mensheviks quite obviously had no firsthand knowledge with regard to Stalin's personality, why did they see the future so much more clearly than the leading theoretician of the Communist party?

In some respects, questions of this kind resemble the mysteries of the "final solution." True, the Soviet executions, in contrast to the German ones, were not kept secret; at least there was no secret with regard to the fate of the leading Bolsheviks. But there was initially the same belief that "such things cannot happen in a civilized country," and, *a fortiori*, not between comrades belonging to the same political party. Larina invokes the "instinct of self-preservation" that induced Bukharin not to accept the bitter truth about the confessions of the Zinoviev-Kamenev trial (namely, that they were faked), and this has a parallel in the belief among some European Jews in 1942 that what had occurred elsewhere (in Russia or Poland, for example) would not happen in Denmark, Holland, or France.

The instinct of self-preservation should have induced Bukharin to stay in Paris in 1936 rather than return; the problem with Bukharin, as with so many others, was that their optimism regarding the future of the regime prevailed over their instinct of self-preservation. They used their considerable intelligence to find all kinds of reasons why the terror would soon cease and not affect them. As a French observer remarked about his coreligionists:

> The Jews were divided into two categories—the pessimists and the optimists. The former tried to reach the United States or Switzerland, or to hide as best they could. The other, cherishing fanciful hopes, became the principal candidates for the journey to Auschwitz and Treblinka.[11]

Bukharin was a man of wide intellectual interest and a high order of intelligence, yet he wrote letters to Stalin, to Voroshilov, and to Ordzhonikidze to clear up the "horrible misunderstandings" well after it should have been clear that there were no misunderstandings at all. Tomsky, who was not an intellectual and had only a passing knowledge of Marxist works, shot himself the moment the first accusations against him appeared in print. When Rykov saw Bukharin for the last time before their arrest on February 23, 1937, he said: "Tomsky was the most far-sighted among us. . . ."[12] There are various explanations for the behavior of Bukharin and those who acted like him. Usually there was a mixture of motives involved, and those threatened would be torn between pessimism and optimism; on some days, they would tend toward a rational explanation, which also happened to be a worst-case interpretation of the situation. On other days, they would see things in an optimistic light. There is no doubt that there was a great deal of naïveté still prevailing. When Ilya Erenburg, one of the survivors, referred to this in his autobiography years later, another survivor (Evgeni Gnedin) noted that these references to the naive posture of an otherwise wholly sober people would encounter an attitude of total disbelief among a later generation. Here again, there is a striking similarity to the Holocaust period: There is a period in which information about mass murder had been received but was rejected. In both instances, people were disorientated because they had to cope with a situation that was essentially new, for which there was no precedent and for which there existed no compass to guide their actions. Ideological bias acted as a further impediment: The more faithful and loyal the believer in communism and the Bolshevik party, the more difficult it was for him or her to confront the reality of Stalinism.

The horrible dilemma facing Bukharin in 1936–37 was shared by many others. In one respect, in historical perspective, his case was unique. Only with regard to Bukharin has it been claimed that his views constituted a real alternative to Stalin's policies. [13] Had he been a better politician, more clever, more forceful and ambitious, is it not conceivable that the history of the Soviet Union might have taken a different turn? This has been argued in some circles in the West since the 1960s and increasingly also in the Soviet Union under Gorbachev.

What was the essence of the Bukharin alternative? The question has been discussed for a long time, and it usually refers to the economic policies followed by the Communist party after 1927: the precipitate liquidation of the NEP, collectivization of agriculture in record time, and the enormous targets imposed on Soviet industry. However, the issues at stake were by no means entirely economic in character. The issue of power in the party and the country, of a new style of leadership, was in the long run even more important. The decision to collectivize agriculture and to destroy the kulaks (the richer peasants—rich by Russian standards) as a class was made mainly for political and ideological reasons rather than because it was assumed that it would bring about abundant food supplies or help finance the expansion of industry.

The NEP had been a great success inasmuch as it got the Soviet economy going again: Industrial output grew more than fivefold between 1921 and 1926; the output of electricity, always a reliable indicator, grew sevenfold; the grain harvest doubled in size. However, grain marketing was still a little smaller than before World War I. The peasants (about 80 percent of the population) were eating better, and their standard of living improved faster than that of urban workers. This was a matter of concern to many party leaders; the urban proletariat was their political mainstay; its interests were closest to the heart of the party. Furthermore, party leaders had always expected that substantial grain exports would pay for the import of capital goods needed for industrialization. The left wing, Trotsky, and his followers had pressed in the early 1920s for higher growth rates—a demand resisted at the time by Stalin and Bukharin. The "left-wing opposition" had argued that because needed investments could not come from colonial profits (as in the case of nineteenth-century Britain), there would have to be "primitive accumulation"; the well-to-do peasants would have to be squeezed. However, even Trotsky merely envisaged forced loans from the kulaks. He did not suggest killing the goose that lay the golden eggs.

Bukharin ("Bukharshik" to his friends), on the contrary, thought that the NEP would last not just a few years but a generation or perhaps even longer. Stalin had originally shared Bukharin's view, but by early 1928 he persuaded himself that the NEP no longer worked. Growth rates declined, and, above all, the peasants were holding back the wheat rather than selling it at the (low) prices that had been fixed by the state. This kind of crisis could have been foreseen (and, indeed, was foreseen) by several Bolshevik leaders. It could most probably have been solved by applying some pressure to the peasantry while at the same time increasing the supply of consumer goods to the village. However, Stalin opted for a radical solution, for a big stick without any carrot. He decided to collectivize agriculture within the shortest possible time so as to put an end, once and for all, to the danger of the "peasants' blackmailing" and to simultaneously press forward with industrialization at breakneck speed. According to the first Five-Year Plan promulgated in 1929, coal and oil production were to double, and the output of steel and pig iron was to grow threefold. Stalin and his supporters deliberately exaggerated the extent of the immediate crisis; their basic argument was that "'exceptional measures" had to be applied and that the victory of socialism could be secured only as the result of the destruction of private agriculture, which, as they saw it, was constantly reproducing capitalism.

Finally, Stalin argued that for foreign policy reasons the Soviet Union simply had no time to engage in gradual industrialization at a measured rate. Unless it established a heavy industrial base for defense industry within ten to fifteen years, it would relapse into backwardness and be defeated, as it so often had earlier in Russian history. Although this argument was articulated only after collectivization had already been carried out, there is reason to believe that such concerns did play a certain role earlier on. Because less than fifteen years were to pass between the first Five-Year Plan and the Nazi invasion, it became in retrospect the strongest argument of those justifying Stalin's "wild rates of growth."

The dispute with Bukharin was not about long-term perspectives. Bukharin was by no means averse to speeding up industrial production, and he voted, albeit with some reluctance, for the application of extraordinary measures in January 1928. But he and his colleagues regarded the policy as an emergency measure, which should not become a norm. He suggested that the NEP policy should be continued, by and large, in agriculture, that temporary crises could be averted by importing grain from abroad, and that the policy need not impede the expansion of industry on a broad front. In the final analysis, Bukharin lacked an overall concept of Russia's economic future as much as Stalin; perhaps Bukharin needed it less because he did not advocate immediate, radical changes. He remembered Lenin's admonitions that the agricultural problem should be solved with great caution and without exerting too much pressure on the peasants. On the other hand, he was the prisoner of his own dogmatic concepts: If he agreed that there was an immediate danger of war and that there was a political threat to the Communist leadership on the part of the rural and urban bourgeoisie, how could he justify a *peredishka*, "a breathing space," even of a year or two?

Invoking dangers that were partly imaginary, partly exaggerated, Bukharin reached the conclusion that the party leadership had little room to maneuver. This, in turn, deprived him of his strongest arguments in the debate with Stalin. He could have insisted on a much longer transition period with regard to collectivization. He should have protested against the deportation (and consequent death) of millions of kulaks and others, whose only fault had been that they had been enterprising and hardworking. He could have advocated more careful and rational preparation of the first Five-Year Plan, which would have resulted in higher-quality products and more balanced targets without necessarily impairing overall output. But he lacked the courage of his convictions—or perhaps it was because "making haste slowly" had never been part of the Bolshevik vocabulary.

Within a fairly short time, the mistakes and shortcomings of the new course would become all too obvious. About agriculture, there is virtual unanimity: Collectivization, as carried out by Stalin, was a disaster. It resulted not only in the destruction of the kulaks as a class but in the near-destruction of Soviet agriculture, which, to this day, has not recovered from the consequences. But for radical reform, it is likely to remain the weakest link in the Soviet economy. True, by 1935, bread rationing was abolished, but the production and consumption of virtually all other agricultural products remained lower on a per capita basis than before 1929—and before 1914. This, despite the investment of hundreds of billions of dollars over many decades, infinitely higher sums than spent in any other country. Between 1971 and 1986, 680 billion rubles was invested in Soviet agriculture; over the years, the value of fixed investment tripled, and the result was that output just barely kept pace with the growth of population and that, in case of a bad harvest, the country still had to import grain.

The traditional Russian village was destroyed. The *kolkhoz* and *sovkhoz* that replaced the village were depressing and inefficient places. The peasants who remained derived an essential part of their income from produce grown on tiny private plots, which the regime had left them as a concession. The supply to the cities of vegetables, fruit, and even meat continued to depend, even sixty years later, on these tiny plots outside the "socialist" sector. One of the results of collectivization was the great famine of 1932–33 in the Ukraine, once among the richest agricultural regions, which exacted a toll of millions of lives.

But even after the immediate crisis had been overcome, life in the Soviet village remained miserable, worst of all in the non-black earth region of central and northern Russia. If, according to one Soviet novelist, the advancing German troops in 1941 were welcomed as liberators by White Russian peasants, the reason was, above all, the suffering from collectivization. But the main danger to the regime was not peasant resistance; it was peasant apathy. The backbone of the peasantry was effectively broken by the persecution of 1929–33, but so was all initiative.

For decades after, the leadership continued to tinker more or less permanently with the agricultural system: Lysenko was given a long (and destructive) try, and so were many other schemes, especially under Khrushchev. The Soviet Union had more tractors and combine harvesters than the United States and Europe combined, but it continued to depend on grain imports from abroad. Having been taught that everything in old, rural Russia had been backward, poor, and obscurantist, a new generation of Russians began to idolize the old Russian village. The slogan of the idiocy of rural life was replaced by references to the idiocy of big-city life.

Seen in historical perspective, the only defense that can be made for the 1929–32 revolution from above is that, with all its tragic consequences, it was a historical necessity: The Soviet Union had to engage in rapid industrialization to strengthen the Communist regime, to increase the standard of living of the country as a whole, and to create a massive heavy-industry basis to enable the country to defend itself in an impending war. Hence, the need for coercion; the resources for industrialization could only be squeezed out of agriculture. Moreover, what alternative had the authorities once the peasants had decided in 1928–29 to withdraw from the market?

But there was no permanent "withdrawal" of the peasantry, only temporary difficulties caused by two consecutive bad harvests and an ill-advised price policy. There were various ways and means of coping with the grain crisis, but politically they were not acceptable to the majority of the party leadership, which would have interpreted it as a surrender to the nonsocialized sector. To this day, the debate continues whether "squeezing" agriculture contributed to industrial expansion, whether it made no difference at all, or whether it actually had a negative impact. Having destroyed the traditional village and established collective farms, the authorities had to equip them with tractors and other machinery. In the words of one historian:

> Agriculture was a net recipient of real resources in the first Five-Year Plan from 1929–32. Far from there being a net flow of resources out of agriculture into the industrial sector, there was a reverse flow of some consequence when measured in 1928 prices.[14]

It could be argued that the peasants who escaped to the cities and who were deported to Siberia and other distant parts provided a reservoir of cheap labor for some of the giant projects of industrial construction. In the end, the debate boils down to whether Stalin and the majority in the party leadership, regarding the market as the main enemy of socialist planning, were psychologically and politically in a position to accept any solution other than the "military-feudal exploitation of the peasantry" (Bukharin's words of early 1928). And this was clearly not the case.

Since Stalin's death, beginning with Khrushchev's famous "secret speech," no secret has been made of the miserable quality of life in the Soviet countryside. True, the historians and the economists would still argue that Stalin's collectivization was, everything considered, a progressive measure. True, mistakes had been committed and innocent people had suffered, but then there was no making omelets without breaking eggs. A few historians and economists expressed more critical views, but they were reprimanded because of their lack of ideological vigilance.[15] However, once the reader turned from the abstract debates to concrete descriptions of conditions in the Soviet village from the late 1920s onward in the books of Fyodor Abramov, Sergei Zalygin, and the whole group of writers that became later known as the *derevenshchiki* ("the village writers"), a dark, depressing picture emerged. In 1987, it was conceded that every third kolkhoz was operating at a loss; it probably had been the case all along.

Beyond agriculture, what were the general long-term consequences of the second revolution of 1929? Soviet authors of the glasnost period tend to put most of the blame for the subsequent failure of the Soviet economy on wrong decisions that were taken in 1928, which shaped Communist strategy for decades to come, and they did this for two reasons: The style of the command economy, headed by a parasitic and paralyzing bureaucracy, became deeply ingrained. It killed all initiative in the national economy, which eventually ground to a halt. But more fateful yet were the political-psychological consequences, the dehumanization of the party apparatus as related by Bukharin to Nikolaevsky:

> Deep changes took place in the psychological outlook of those who participated in this [collectivization] campaign. Instead of going mad they became professional bureaucrats for whom terror was henceforth a normal method of administration and obedience to any order from above a high virtue.

To what extent is Stalin personally to blame for the results of the "great turning point"? Without Stalin's initiative following his visit to Siberia in early 1928 and his subsequent turnabout, the great campaign would never have started, and the war against the peasantry would not have been pursued as its economic and political consequences became gradually obvious. But it is also true that this policy was quite popular not only in the top echelons of the party but also further down in the hierarchy. It was based on the fear that the hold of Soviet power would not be secure until agriculture was no longer in private hands. The traditional attitude toward the peasantry was one of suspicion. The peasantry was regarded as a class that did not understand its own interests and that, childlike, needed constant guidance and, if necessary, punishment.

Nor was the idea that industrialization had to proceed at a more rapid pace a brainchild of Stalin's; such demands had been voiced in previous years by Trotsky, Zinoviev, Kamenev, and above all, by Preobrazhensky, many of whose arguments Stalin made his own after 1928. There was a great deal of "revolutionary impatience" in the ranks of the party, especially among the younger generation, that needed an outlet. The world revolution, predicted by Lenin and Trotsky, had not materialized; instead, a new effort was needed inside the Soviet Union to develop more rapidly than ever before the economy and, above all, heavy industry. There is no denying that the regime succeeded to a considerable extent in channeling the enthusiasm of the younger generation to building up mammoth projects such as Magnitogorsk and Kuznetsk, Dneproges, Zaporozhe, and Stalingrad. There was widespread feeling that young Communists could (and would) "storm heavens." The mood proved infectious: The Soviet example of seemingly lifting oneself up by one's own bootstraps found increasing interest and support in the West at the very time when the capitalist world faced a severe recession. The "socialist sixth of the world" was transforming itself, and the Russian example, as many enthusiastic visitors predicted, would serve as an inspiration for everyone else. A few outside experts followed the victory reports with a skeptical eye, but their comments were largely ignored.

The story of Soviet industry, unlike the annals of agriculture after 1929, is not one of unmitigated disaster. The steel and machine-tool industries made impressive quantitative progress; the targets of other industries for the end of the first Five-Year Plan (1933) were reached only in the 1950s. According to official figures, very high growth rates in industrial production (20 percent during each of the first three years of the plan) were followed by a sharp decline during the last year of the plan. There was a further advance in 1934–36, to be followed by new stagnation in 1937–38. This uneven progress had many causes, above all the single-minded concentration on a few strategically important industries. The transport infrastructure, for example, was neglected, and this had an indirect impact on the growth of heavy industry.

How successful was Soviet industrialization in a comparative historical perspective? The figures published at the time that remained official until the era of glasnost were vastly exaggerated. Furthermore, they offer no clue to quality; that a million tons of steel was produced does not indicate whether it was of sufficient quality to be used for the intended purpose— or for any purpose. According to figures published under glasnost, the Soviet GNP (gross national product) grew between 1929 and 1941 not fivefold (as official statisticians claimed) but only by a factor of 1.5. This is still impressive growth, but not more than the economic development of, say, Hitler's Germany between 1933 and 1939; during the very years that Soviet industrial production grew by 20 percent or more, so did German industry.

It can be argued that German industrial capacity had existed before but was not exploited, whereas Soviet factories had to be built from scratch. Furthermore, it could be maintained that the German economic upswing largely depended on preparations for war, but this was true, too, in the case of the Soviet Union. Perhaps it is more useful to compare the performance during the 1930s with Russian industrial growth before the Revolution. Between 1880 and 1914, a longish period, including good years as well as periods of stagnation and decline, the annual growth rate was 5–6 percent annually, higher than in any other country. Average annual industrial growth was 5.7 percent, more than in any other industrial country, including the United States. Again, it could be said in explanation that Russia was industrially less developed at the time than the United States, Germany, or Britain. And it is, of course, well known that backward economies tend to grow faster than developed ones—the so-called advantages of backwardness. But the same is true with regard to the starting point in the late 1920s: Russia was still an underdeveloped country at the time of the first Five-Year Plan, and its progress was likely to be faster than elsewhere. All of which is to say that although Soviet industrial growth was impressive, it was by no means unprecedented either in Russian history or in comparison with other countries.

Given the benefit of hindsight, how real was the Bukharin alternative? Virtually no one claims any longer that Stalin's approach was the only possible one; the very fact that Bukharin's ideas were so widely discussed fifty years after his death point to the conviction that alternatives must have existed. But the meaning of "alternative" is by no means unambiguous.

Some Soviet authors still believe that collectivization was basically unavoidable simply because the country could not procrastinate for domestic and foreign political reasons. Violence had to be employed, for the kulaks would not have cooperated unless subjected to pressure.[16] However, the excesses committed by Stalin and his underlings were unnecessary and counterproductive. It was not, in other words, necessary to kill millions of people or starve large sections of the country to establish a new system of management that, to say the least, was not very effective. Stalin and a majority of the party had a clear aim only in the negative sense. They wanted to destroy the capitalist system in the countryside, but they had no overall concept of what should replace it. Hence, there were many changes in Soviet agriculture during the subsequent decades.

Such criticism is perfectly legitimate, but it does not provide an answer to the question: What other system should have been adopted once it had been agreed that there was no time to be lost, that the land should be taken away from the peasants who cultivated it, and that unless this was done the country would face recurrent crises?

Stalin and most members of the party leadership deeply distrusted the peasantry and were firmly convinced that its instincts were, and would always remain, "petty bourgeois." They believed that the peasants would never voluntarily part with their land, and they were probably right. But because peasants at the time still constituted some 80 percent of the population, the party faced not only external enemies but an internal foe, and the party leadership felt as if it were in a besieged fortress.[17] Stalin, after all, did not spoil for a fight; he referred in later years to the struggle against the peasantry as bitter civil war. Had he seen another, less wasteful way to achieve his aim, he might have well adopted it—a "solution without a crisis," to use Bukharin's term. But Stalin believed that the NEP no longer worked in agriculture, that agricultural cooperatives (based on foreign patterns) would probably not function in the Soviet Union, and that, in any case, there was no time for patient persuasion, for teaching the peasant by trial and error.

Both his political and economic assumptions were wrong: The "commanding heights" were in the hands of the Communist party, and there was no threat to Communist power, even if some peasants fared markedly better than others. Furthermore, the Stalinist model did not bring about, as he had assumed, a radical improvement in the economic situation. If one believed that the land had to be taken away at once, there was no solution radically different from Stalin's. Thus, not a few contemporary Soviet authors tend to believe that although the way Stalin's revolution from above was carried out was a scandal and caused great harm, he was right in assuming that it was a dire necessity. If he was too harsh, Bukharin, on the contrary, was too soft, and, in this situation, it was probably less dangerous to err on the side of harshness. At best, some of these critics propagate a mixture of Stalinist and Bukharinist ideas, whereby the Stalinist approach would have been carried out somewhat more humanely and over a somewhat longer period. It is not certain whether this was feasible and, if feasible, whether the results would have been essentially different.

There were basic alternatives, but only if one dissociated oneself from Stalin's political assumptions, which, to repeat once again, were also those of the majority of the party leadership.[18] And last, it was not only a question of ideological purity; it was also one of the new, despotic style of leadership that had developed in the party and that was not compatible with concessions and gradualism.

A case for the Bukharin alternative was made by some Western historians in the 1970s and, following glasnost, also by Soviet writers. Their argument runs, very briefly, as follows: Lenin, toward the end of his life, reached the conclusion that the seizure of power by the Bolsheviks in 1917 had been premature because social conditions had not been ripe for it. But they could and should not have missed the opportunity. The consequences of the premature seizure of power could only be undone if a harmonious society was created, if peace existed between town and countryside, if the peasants were converted to socialism by persuasion. This was the tenor of Lenin's last articles, with an emphasis on the NEP and cooperation. Bukharin's doctrine was based on Lenin's last thoughts: The peasants were to "grow into socialism," and although industrialization would have to be stepped up, due regard was to be given to the needs of the peasants, which is to say, light industry was to cater to the needs of the peasantry.

We shall never know whether Lenin thought in 1922 that the NEP would last five years. It is doubtful that he was fully aware what the political consequences of the "premature seizure of power" were bound to be. It is unlikely that he was converted late in life to what the Mensheviks and Kautsky had preached all along. His political suggestions certainly do not point to such awareness; there is no evidence that he advocated a more democratic regime, let alone renewed cooperation with other left-wing parties. There was no readiness to retreat from the idea and practice of dictatorship, and Bukharin fully shared his views. True, he denounced the growth of the bureaucracy, the danger of which he had not been aware before. But such criticism was shared by every faction in the party, from Trotsky and Preobrazhensky to Stalin. Denouncing the bureaucracy was by no means tantamount to promoting democracy inside the party, let alone inside the country. If Bukharin had misgivings about the political trials of the late 1920s, which were in some respects the forerunner of the Moscow trials, he did not make them public. In brief, neither Lenin nor Bukharin had a clear idea of how to proceed toward a more harmonious society without undoing the Communist Revolution in a largely backward country. We are not even sure how important these concerns figured in their political agenda. And finally, it is doubtful whether there was a way to "undo the consequences" short of, at the very least, sharing powers with other left-wing parties—that is, collaborating with Mensheviks and Social Revolutionaries. But this was altogether unthinkable, for they had been the political enemies of the Bolsheviks from the very beginning.

The October Revolution had been carried out against these other parties as much as against the "bourgeois" factions. Given the specific character of the Bolshevik party, such a course of action must have appeared as utter foolishness, if not political suicide. Sharing power was never a serious alternative: This door had been closed when the Bolsheviks took power. The most that could be hoped was that at least a measure of inner-party democracy could be preserved, thus refuting Rosa Luxemburg's famous prediction that the dictatorship of the Central Committee would inevitably lead to the dictatorship of a handful of leaders and, ultimately, to the rule of one dictator.

There had been factions and differences of opinion inside the Bolshevik party, but after the October Revolution, the pressures to create a monolithic party increased all the time. Although doing so was much in line with Stalin's mentality, Bukharin, too, contributed to its development. V. P. Danilov, the leading Soviet historian of collectivization, has observed that although some writers have argued that a real alternative no longer existed after Stalin had become secretary-general of the party, there still was a chance to remove Stalin or to reduce his power:

> Such a possibility continued to exist up to the end of 1927, when Bukharin and his supporters retreated facing the Stalinist pressure and voted for the exclusion of Trotsky, Zinoviev, Kamenev, and a number of other leaders of the "new opposition." This was a tragic mistake that cost the party dearly—and Bukharin personally. It was the end of the balance of power that had existed in the top leadership since Lenin's death. This made it possible for the Stalinist faction to gain complete power, to destroy decisively inner-party democracy, and to establish Stalinist autocracy based on the bureaucratic-command system of management. From this moment on, the Bukharin alternative, and Bukharin himself, were doomed. . . ."[19]

Even if Bukharin and his supporters were doomed after 1927, was there a need for abject surrender? Instead of engaging in wholesale self-incrimination ("the right-wing deviation was the gravest danger to the party and the Communist International" said Bukharin), they could have gone under fighting or at least withdrawn from active politics and refrained from commenting on political developments instead of singing Stalin's praise. As far as their ultimate fate is concerned, it would not have made any difference. Instead, they behaved, at least in public, in a way without precedent in any other country or party. They were not people without courage, but they had grown up with a belief that there was no truth except in the ranks of the party, and they feared isolation.

Perhaps it was not just a question of pressure and loyalty; perhaps they might have lost their self-confidence and gradually came to believe that Stalin's course had been right, that subsequent events had justified his course of action rather than their line of 1928. The attitude of the supreme German military command toward Hitler comes to mind: They had counseled prudence and, on many occasions, pointed to the grave risks involved in Hitler's blueprint for reckless military aggression. However, after Hitler succeeded time and again, from the invasion of Austria and Czechoslovakia to the victory over France and in the Balkans, the marshals and generals, although perhaps not yet entirely convinced of his genius and not wholly free of apprehensions, were reluctant to engage in criticism. It is difficult to reason with success. True, Hitler's military victories were more clear-cut than Stalin's domestic achievements. But with all their misgivings, the leaders of the right wing had to admit to themselves that the industrial capacity of the country had greatly increased. There was an atmosphere of enthusiasm, and the voices of those who were not enthusiastic would seldom reach them. Under these conditions, they may well have thought that Stalin had, after all, been right, and because there was no going back to the state of affairs before collectivization, what was the point of playing Cassandra?

That the fate of Bukharin was deeply tragic should not blind the historian to his great responsibility. After 1929, Bukharin could no longer command any respect as a political leader. His moral backbone had been broken. In December 1934, after Kirov's murder, Bukharin wrote an article in *Izvestiia*, the newspaper he edited, that stated that any opposition and deviation inevitably led to a break with the party, a break with Soviet legality, and to counterrevolution. For such was the logic of the class struggle: "This lesson is confirmed once again in all its frightful depth by the Fascist degeneration of the dregs of the former Zinoviev antiparty group," Bukharin continued, stating that following the years after Lenin's death, during the great reconstruction era that had transformed the country, the party had been led by Stalin. The former leaders who no longer found themselves at the helm had suffered bankruptcy at a major historical turning point: "The Stalinist leadership has not been selected accidentally. It is history; it is the party. . . ."

It is important to recall the date: December 1934. The great terror was just beginning. Bukharin was not writing under the threat of immediate execution and the murder of his family. Whatever the reason, he was a willing collaborator with the Stalinist regime. If he could write about the "Fascist degeneration" of his former comrades, he had lost all self-respect, his moral and political bankruptcy was complete, though not for the reason he indicated.[20]

However, it is not at all certain whether a Bukharin alternative existed even before 1928. For intolerance toward opposition was not the monopoly of any faction inside the Bolshevik party; Kamenev and Zinoviev had behaved in a similar way when they collaborated with Stalin in 1925. It is more than doubtful whether Trotsky would have maintained Bolshevik unity if it had been up to him to make the decision.

Tolerance vis-à-vis dissenting opinions had never been a characteristic feature of the Bolshevik party. They would not have murdered their opponents, but they would certainly have removed them from all positions of influence. The general attitude among the rank and file was even more emphatically in favor of a style that Stalin represented better than the other old Bolsheviks. It was a system based on "command from above," on the presence of a single ruler rather than committees, on propaganda and terror rather than on consultation and persuasion, and on hardness rather than harmony.

It has often been asked why the Bolshevik party developed in this particular way, and various explanations have been offered: the patriarchal structure of the old Russian village, the general lack of a democratic tradition in prerevolutionary Russia, the low level of political culture among the party leadership, and so on. These questions ought to be discussed in the general framework of the origins of Stalinism rather than the specific context of the Bukharin alternative. Given the character of the party, a "Bukharin alternative" stood little chance of support if it had been interpreted as a true policy alternative and not as some minor changes in the timetable and the execution of the "great leap forward."

Mention has been made that Khrushchev wanted to rehabilitate Bukharin following the Twentieth Party Congress. Various versions have been given as to why the attempt failed at the time. According to one source, leading foreign Communists opposed it, which is most unlikely, for the Soviet leaders were never greatly influenced by what Thorez or Togliatti would think or say, and the latter, in any case, would certainly have favored rehabilitation. The opposition by Stalinists like Suslov was undoubtedly the decisive factor. After Khrushchev's fall, the attacks against Bukharin were renewed[21] even though the specific accusations concerning espionage on behalf of foreign powers were dropped. Thus, rehabilitation came only under glasnost, and though opposition persisted in some quarters, a veritable Bukharin cult developed. The continued opposition to Bukharin was strongest among the right-wing nationalist and neo-Stalinist circles. That the ultraorthodox should resent it was not surprising, but the unease among the Russia-firsters was more difficult to explain. They claimed that Bukharin had not been close to Lenin, that his ideological contribution had been modest, and that, as a true internationalist, he had no sympathy for traditional Russian nationalist culture: He had criticized the poet Esenin after his suicide in 1929. In their view, Bukharin's opposition to Stalinist collectivization (which they in part shared) was less important in an overall assessment than his cosmopolitanism, that is, the "national nihilism" that he shared with the entire old guard of the Bolshevik party.[22] That Bukharin also advocated a more consistent anti-Nazi policy than Stalin did not endear him to the extreme right, either.[23]

The new Bukharin cult manifested itself in the emergence of Bukharin youth clubs studying his heritage, in conferences devoted to his memory (in Wuppertal, Budapest, Oxford, and Beijing), and in exhibitions as well as in many publications.[24] The first glasnost biography to be written was authored by a Hungarian (Miklos Kun). It was followed by countless articles and memoirs—above all, those of his widow—and by novels as well as plays in which Bukharin made an appearance. Some of Bukharin's articles appeared in Soviet periodicals during 1988, and a further selection was published as a book, Etiudy (Studies), in 1989.[25]

As far as the party leadership is concerned, the Bukharin alternative of 1928 did not become the new orthodoxy. The announcement of his rehabilitation and reinstatement in the party made it clear that Bukharin's political views were by no means all approved in retrospect. As Lukyanov, a member of the Gorbachev Politburo, put it, the collectivization of agriculture as much as the industrialization had been an absolute necessity for the building of socialism and the victory over fascism. If so, Stalin had been basically right; the NEP could not have been continued because there was no time to lose. Since there was no way to persuade the peasants to cooperate, they had to be forcibly driven into the collectives. Thus, the debate is narrowed down to a question of how much pressure should have been applied and whether the same results could not have been achieved with fewer victims and less general dislocation.

The renewed interest in Bukharin is rooted in part in his attractive personality and tragic fate. Bukharin's "communism with a human face" also provides inspiration to latter-day Marxists who believe that although Lenin's ideas were essentially correct, they were distorted by Stalin but that this was not inevitable.

It goes without saying that under Bukharin's leadership a political system different from Stalinism would have emerged and that the country would have been spared the horrors of the great purge. However, he did not seek a leading position, and it is doubtful that he would have prevailed in the struggle for power, had he tried. His style was too much against the true Bolshevik grain, given the mentality of the 1920s.[26] Nor is it certain that Bukharin's economic proposals would have led to results radically different from Stalin's. His ideas of an alliance between the working class and the peasantry, his apprehension about the growing role of the bureaucracy and the state monopolies, had much to recommend them. He counseled greater caution and moderation. But it is doubtful whether such positions amount to an overall stragegy. Bukharin's weakness was not that he had failed to master dialectics or that he radically changed his stand from time to time but that he could not, and would not, go beyond Leninist doctrine in tackling the economic problems of the Soviet Union. Given that his party had come to power in a backward country and also given his close attachment to Bolshevik ideology, truly alternative strategies of agricultural and industrial development were closed to him.

3. Trotsky:
"Demon of the Revolution"

Lev Davidovich Trotsky has entered Soviet history as Stalin's greatest antagonist, yet in actual fact the paths of the two men seldom crossed. Trotsky had maneuvered himself out of the race for leadership well before the decisive phase in Stalin's rise to power. For decades Soviet citizens were educated in the belief that Trotsky was the incarnation of evil, and after Stalin's death, too, the political rehabilitation of Trotsky remained unthinkable. Even under glasnost, his personality and role in history remained a major bone of contention.

Born in southern Russia in 1879—a few weeks before Stalin—the son of a Jewish landowner, he joined the revolutionary movement while in high school.[1] He was first arrested at the age of nineteen and exiled to Siberia. He devoted his time in exile to the study of Marx; he then escaped and joined Lenin in London as an editor of *Iskra*. Between 1902 and 1907, at times he supported the Bolsheviks; at others, the Mensheviks. During World War I, he drew closer to the former but did not join them until his return to Russia in 1917.

In the Revolution of 1905, he had played a major role and served as the last president of the St. Petersburg Soviet of Workers Deputies. He owed his rise to fame mainly to his outstanding gift as an orator; he was also a prolific writer. In the preparation of the Revolution of 1917, he also showed considerable organizational skill. His place next to Lenin was never seriously disputed at the time. And when Lenin had to go into hiding, Trotsky became the leader of the party in practice, if not in name. Even Stalin later wrote that all work of practical organization and preparation for the seizure of power was done under the "immediate leadership of the president of the Petrograd Soviet, Comrade Trotsky."

Trotsky served for a short time as the first foreign commissar of the

Soviet Union; later, for a much longer period (until January 1925), as commissar and president of the Supreme War Council. In between, he also was commissar for transport. In all these appointments, he proved himself a hard taskmaster, dynamic and efficient. Although he committed many mistakes, considering his utter lack of experience and the enormity of the tasks facing the young state, the Soviet Union probably owes its survival during the early period of its existence more to Trotsky than to anyone else except Lenin.

His decline in power and political standing began with the end of the civil war, and soon after Lenin's death he was almost totally isolated. The reasons were largely personal; quarrelsome and a man of uncommon arrogance, Trotsky found it difficult to work with others. He had neither the patience nor the political instinct to build up a power base; instead, he involved himself in constant ideological and political controversies with the other leaders, more befitting a prerevolutionary littérateur than a postrevolutionary statesman.

In 1927, Trotsky was expelled from the party and, two years later, deported from the Soviet Union. He lived first in Turkey, later in France and Norway, and ultimately in Mexico, where he was assassinated on August 20, 1940, at Stalin's behest. He wrote a great deal in exile, but his political activities (such as the establishment of the Fourth International) were ineffectual. His erstwhile supporters in the Soviet Union dissociated themselves from him early on; the more prominent among them perished in the purges. His followers in other countries formed small sects that constituted no danger to the local Communist parties, let alone the Soviet Union.

Lenin, who had frequently been engaged in ideological and political quarrels with Trotsky, thought highly of him and argued that there had been no better Bolshevik since Trotsky joined the party. In his "Testament" published under glasnost, Lenin wrote that Trotsky was perhaps the most capable man in the party leadership but that he displayed excessive self-assurance and excessive preoccupation with the purely administrative side of the work. Trotsky's ideological innovations, such as the "permanent revolution" (originally developed by Parvus), caused endless debate among the Bolsheviks but was of little practical consequence. The same is true, *mutatis mutandis*, with regard to the dispute in the 1920s about Stalin's doctrine of "socialism in one country." Once it appeared that the Russian Revolution would not be followed by similar revolutions elsewhere, Trotsky was as eager as Stalin to develop Russia's agriculture and industry and to build up socialist structures inside the Soviet Union. However, not for the first time, he had maneuvered himself into an unpopular position largely because of his ideological rigidity, his lack of pragmatic instinct, and his inability to understand what was and what was not possible in a given situation. On various occasions, he was more right than Stalin, for instance, in his opposition to the liquidation of the kulaks as a class and his recognizing the danger of Nazism. He misjudged the phenomenon of Stalin (a "mediocrity, created by the party machine") and overrated the importance of the Soviet bureaucracy during the Stalinist period. Because to the end of his life he refused to modify his orthodox Marxist approach, he wasted an inordinate amount of time in debates over whether a new "Thermidor" had taken place, whether the Soviet Union was state capitalist or a degenerate workers' state, and whether the dictatorship of the bureaucracy was still essentially socialist in character because the means of production were still nationalized.

Under Stalin, Trotsky personified for most Soviet citizens all that was evil, criminal, and treacherous; he was the enemy par excellence. All of Lenin's negative comments about Trotsky were dredged up; all positive ones, suppressed. According to the party line, throughout the Stalinist period Trotsky had been a criminal and a traitor right from the beginning. He had tried all in his power to subvert Lenin and the Revolution. He was the greatest enemy of the working class and the Communist party; to be a "Trotskyite" was much worse than being a "Fascist." With the latter, one could do business; with the former, even a temporary arrangement was impossible. Individual Fascists could be redeemed; Trotskyites— never.

After Stalin's death, during the first thaw, the more outrageous falsifications were toned down. It was conceded, to begin with, that Trotsky, albeit usually mistaken, had served in key positions before, during, and after the Revolution and that despite his "Bonapartist" inclinations, he had done some good for the cause of Bolshevism as a mass orator and organizer. However, by and large, the deliberate falsification of Trotsky's role persisted in textbooks; the general trend was to describe Trotsky as a minor figure who had not been an agent of foreign powers (as previously maintained) but a negative influence on the party who had greatly contributed to its disorientation. Whatever good he had done was outweighed by his mistakes and misdeeds.[2]

This, in its broadest outline, was the party line on Trotsky until 1987, and there was little inclination among the party leadership to undertake a fundamental revision. In his speech on the seventieth anniversary of the October Revolution, Gorbachev implied that in his struggle with Stalin, Trotsky had been wrong.[3] Although the overwhelming majority of those accused in the Moscow trials were rehabilitated—including virtually all "Trotskyites" (real and alleged)—Trotsky was excluded, and not for purely technical reasons; he, too, had been sentenced to death—in absentia. The only change in attitude at first was the restoration of Trotsky's figure in photographs from which he had been excised for almost sixty years. As one of the spokesmen of the establishment liberals argued, the rehabilitation of Trotsky would take a long time and come at the very end of glasnost. For the belief in his guilt was so deeply rooted among the public that there was tremendous resistance to facing the true facts.

A first dent in the traditional Trotsky image was made by a few individual historians and essayists. Pavel Volobuyev, a corresponding member of the Academy of Sciences, wrote that although Trotsky had never really been a true Bolshevik, he still was a revolutionary who had played a leading role in the party.[4] Yuri Afanasiev, director of the Institute of Historical Archives, went considerably further and demanded both the legal rehabilitation of Trotsky and the publication of his books.[5] Subsequently, during 1988 and 1989, articles about Trotsky began to appear that expressed a variety of points of view; Trotsky's grandson Esteban visited Moscow, as did his most recent biographer, Pierre Broué. It was announced in early 1989 that some of Trotsky's works would be published in the not too distant future. On November 15, 1988, the Memorial association arranged an evening devoted to the memory of Trotsky and an appeal for his rehabilitation. The 400 tickets were sold out well in advance, even though there had been no publicity at all.[6] The meeting was presided over by the historian V. Lysenko; among the main speakers were the historians Bulgakov and Yuri Heller and the economist Dzarasov. Among others who were present were Igor Piatnitsky, Nadezhda Yoffe, Tatyana Smilga, Galina Antonov Ovseenko, and the children and grandchildren of the Bolshevik old guard.

The great-grandchildren of Trotsky, as well as the son of Victor Serge

(Vladimir Kibalchich), and various American left-wingers asked the Kremlin to revoke the bans on Trotsky; they argued that everyone should be in a position to make up his (or her) mind about Trotsky. But this could be done only if his writings were accessible to the public.[7]

Such applications were by no means universally welcomed; articles appeared in the Soviet media under the title "They Try to Embellish Little Judas,"[8] and in the literary magazines of the extreme Right, hardly a month passed without a denunciation of Trotsky.

Outside the extremist circles, Trotsky fared somewhat better under glasnost. The general assessment was more positive than during the Stalinist era. Soviet writers concluded that Trotsky had been a talented political leader, much closer to Lenin than Stalin, and that, with all his faults, Trotsky and Trotskyism had remained a trend within the working-class movement. Trotskyism was muddleheaded and should have been attacked on the political-ideological level.[9] They even went as far as to admit that in his criticism of Stalin, Trotsky had been right more than once. However, the overall thrust of the writings was still negative. According to Vasetsky, as a military leader Trotsky was unimpressive. The Red Army repelled the imperialist intervention and prevailed in the civil war not because of him but despite his presence.

Vasetsky also claimed that Trotsky did not play any active role either in planning the Revolution or in its execution. If so, how does one explain that even Stalin wrote in November 1918, when the events were still fresh in his mind, that Trotsky had played a central role?[10] Did Stalin suffer from hallucinations, or did he perhaps want to ingratiate himself with Trotsky? But if Trotsky was not a central figure, there was no need for Stalin to cultivate him. Soviet readers are bound to remain confused in the face of such curious contradictions. They are also told that the concept of war communism, the militarization of work and public life, and the bureaucratization of the country were all essentially flawed and were all Trotsky's brainchildren.

This is part of the truth; the other part was not divulged, even under glasnost. If Trotsky was not an accomplished strategist, the other major military figures of the civil war, including Tukhachevsky, also committed major errors. With all his extremism and rigidity, Trotsky could be more liberal than most of his comrades. If eventually almost a thousand tsarist generals served in the Red Army, it was mainly owing to him, not to the Stalins and Voroshilovs, who were up in arms against the employment of these experts of the old order. (In a similar way, Trotsky took a more liberal line in literature and cultural life in general, in contrast to the protagonists of pure working-class culture. He became a merciless critic of the new Soviet bureaucracy that developed in the 1920s (in his book *The New Course*) and the most ardent fighter for inner-party democracy, even something akin to a (socialist) multiparty system. As the historian of Trotsky's ideas summarized:

> The real concern running through *The New Course* is the preservation of the revolutionary spirit. At a time when the social revolution in the Soviet Union, not to mention the revolution in the West, had hardly begun, it seemed to him that already the party was turning into a conservative institutionalized force, more concerned with protecting the little that had been achieved than pursuing the much that remained to be fulfilled. New blood, new ideas, criticism, discussion, mass enthusiasm—all these, he believed, would not only democratize the party, but preserve its revolutionary character, its original sources of inspiration, its very obsession with the real goals of socialism. . . .[11]

It is true that Trotsky became the great champion of democracy and against bureaucracy only when in opposition, but it does not entirely invalidate his campaign. His ideas were very popular among the young Communists at the time, and it was, in fact, his principal aim to mobilize youth against the party apparatus.[12]

If, for many decades, the good Stalin had been juxtaposed to the archvillain Trotsky, under glasnost both became problematical characters, but with Trotsky still more negative and destructive in an overall perspective. The old myths were replaced by new ones. It was now believed that Stalin had inherited (and assimilated) most of his ideas from Trotsky and that he was so afraid of Trotsky that he engaged in the bloody purges of the 1930s only after having been provoked to do so by Trotsky. Such speculation could be found in a pronounced way not only among the extreme nationalists and the neo-Stalinists but also quite frequently among those to the center of the political spectrum, and they therefore deserve closer scrutiny.

According to the new mythology that made its appearance under glasnost, much of the blame for the terror, the show trials, and the purges has to go to Trotsky because he called for the physical elimination of Stalin. Thus, Volkogonov: Trotsky's book *The Revolution Betrayed*, which was handed to Stalin in early 1937, was one of the last straws that broke the camel's back.[13] An earlier version of this farfetched theory can be found in Roy Medvedev's *Let History Judge*, published in the Soviet Union in 1988.

> At the very beginning of the thirties, Trotsky's articles did not call for the overthrow of Stalin. On the contrary, he wrote that under existing conditions the overthrow of the Stalinist bureaucratic apparat would inevitably lead to the triumph of counterrevolution. Thus he recommended that his supporters limit themselves to ideological propaganda. But in the mid-thirties, that is, when mass repression began, Trotsky and some of his closest advisers apparently came to the conclusion that it was necessary to destroy Stalin as a tyrant. It was then that Stalin directed the NKVD to arrange Trotsky's assassination.[14]

What should one make of assertions of this kind? To begin with, the chronology does not fit. The first copies of *The Revolution Betrayed* appeared in May 1937, and even if the NKVD had worked day and night translating the book, they could not possibly have handed it to Stalin in 1936 at the time of the first trials. Indeed, in an earlier publication, Volkogonov had written that Stalin had received the translated manuscript only in late 1937.[15]

We do not know what made him change the chronology; but whatever the reason, Trotsky's book could not possibly have driven Stalin to his "desperate decision."

But there is yet another difficulty with this version; hard as he may try, the reader will find it impossible to locate in *The Revolution Betrayed* any statement, or even hint, to the effect that the tyrant Stalin should be killed, either because Trotsky lacked the courage of his convictions or, more likely, because, as an orthodox Marxist, he, unlike Stalin, did not believe in individual terror. Trotsky never called for Stalin's physical elimination, nor did he engage in any activities to this end.

Vasetsky, not an admirer of Trotsky, stressed this important point, quoting Trotsky to the effect that "through murder one cannot change the correlation of social forces and stop the objective course of development. The removal of Stalin, the individual, would mean today nothing else but his replacement by one of the Kaganovitches. . . ."[16]

To a certain extent, Stalin's (and Trotsky's) Western biographers bear some responsibility for the fantasies about Trotsky's role as an instigator of the trials. Thus, Deutscher argued that it is possible that if the leaders of the opposition had lived to witness the terrible defeats of the Red Army in 1941–42, to see Hitler at the gates of Moscow, they might have attempted to overthrow Stalin.[17] And Stalin was determined not to allow that to happen. Forty years later, in Volkogonov's simplified version, Stalin, anticipating the war, envisaged that Hitler would appoint Trotsky as his viceroy in Moscow. The idea of Hitler's appointing a Jewish Communist does not lack a certain originality, but even if Stalin was a madman, he was still not a fool, and such a "fear" could not possibly have struck him even in his wildest delirium.[18]

Generally speaking, Soviet authors tend grossly to overrate Trotsky's international ties, his impact on public opinion, and his general political importance in the 1930s. Their judgment may be based on lack of information: having been cut off from Western sources for so long and largely denied access to crucial evidence in Soviet secret archives even under glasnost, they are not in a good position to make realistic assessments. Thus, Volkogonov points to the ties that Trotsky maintained with his followers in the Soviet Union by means of the Lithuanian-German correspondent Sobolevicius. He does not mention and probably does not know that said Sobolevicius (better known in later years as Jack Soble) was an NKVD agent. Elsewhere Volkogonov maintains that Trotsky's writings appeared in dozens of countries and that Stalin's image, as far as world public opinion was concerned, was shaped not by Feuchtwanger and Barbusse but, above all, by the works of Trotsky.[19] This again is a wild exaggeration; the writings of foreign Communists and fellow travelers reached an infinitely larger circle of readers than did Trotsky's books.

Biographers of Stalin, Trotsky, and other political leaders are frequently tempted to engage in descriptions and explanations beyond what the evidence will bear out. Doing so is sometimes inevitable in view of the lack of evidence, and a good case can be made for informed guesses, as long as they are not presented as fact and certitude. Thus, there is no harm if Volkogonov describes how Stalin entered his office around noon on August 21, 1940, the day the news about Trotsky's murder was received, said "Good morning" to Poskrebyshev, and sat down to smoke a pipe. It is equally possible that he came to work earlier or later or not at all, that Poskrebyshev was away that day, or that Stalin was in bad humor and entered his room without saying a word. It is even possible that he had temporarily run out of tobacco.[20] Stalin might have said in a small circle that it had been a mistake to let Trotsky go in 1929 in the first place, even though there is no evidence to this effect.

But even now, after all the revelations, we cannot possibly know what Stalin thought when he read Trotsky's books or articles or when he received reports about Trotsky's activities in exile, for there is no evidence. Perhaps Stalin thought Trotsky was a political figure of far greater stature than those surrounding him in the Kremlin (as Volkogonov claims); perhaps Stalin was so preoccupied with what Trotsky might do or think about his policy that it became a compulsion, an overriding motive force in his life. Yet it is equally possible that Stalin did not lose any sleep over Trotsky. Stalin had told Emil Ludwig, who interviewed him in 1931, that Trotsky was virtually forgotten in the Soviet Union. Had this been mere pretense, or had Stalin changed his views, reaching the conclusion Trotsky, even in exile, lacking any political bases, was the most dangerous enemy he was facing? True, Stalin gave instructions to kill Trotsky, but the same is true with regard to quite a few other émigrés, which is no proof that he was mortally afraid of them.

Volkogonov describes Trotsky as the "great master of intrigue,"[21] yet, in actual fact, Trotsky seldom engaged in intrigues and was not good at it; he was a rank amateur compared with Stalin. Had he been a more astute plotter, Stalin would not have been able to oust him with such contemptuous ease. True, Stalin's political logic was not that of a normal human being, and there is no accounting for all his thoughts and fears in the late 1930s. But the idea that he had millions of people killed because he genuinely thought that they were part of a giant Trotskyite conspiracy is as farfetched as the notion that they had been hirelings of the Japanese or the Romanian secret service. If Stalin really believed that Trotsky was a deadly threat, there would have been a change in his behavior once Trotsky had been killed. But that did not transpire; Stalin's behavior in 1950 was essentially the same as it had been in the 1930s.

Inevitably, there were differences in the appraisal of Trotsky among Soviet authors writing under glasnost. Thus, Roy Medvedev has disagreed with Volkogonov's "demon of the revolution" concept, a term, in his view, that is far more applicable to Stalin.[22] Grigori Pomerants has noted that after 1917 there were only tactical political differences between Lenin and Trotsky and that, seen in historical perspective, Trotsky was much closer to Lenin than to Stalin.[23]

But these were the heretical thoughts of outsiders; mainline historians remained negative: "Trotsky always loved himself in the revolution more than the revolution as such." "Under the banner of the struggle against Stalin, Trotsky merely wanted to replace Stalinism by Trotskyism, which was equally hostile to Leninism."[24] According to the same line of thought, Trotskyism was never a true alternative to Stalinism partly because it was impractical (the concept of the world revolution) and partly because it was too similar in inspiration (the militarization and bureaucratization of public life, the use of various kinds of repression, etc.).

The ability to make friends and influence people was not among Trotsky's many talents. And yet one cannot be but struck by the unpleasant inclination of Soviet authors—not necessarily anti-Semites or neo-Stalinists—to draw negative inferences from everything Trotsky did or wrote. Two examples should suffice: On March 25, 1935, Trotsky noted in his diary that but for the fact that Lenin and he were in Petersburg at the time, there would have been no revolution. It may not be a modest remark, but it was essentially correct.

Or another entry in his diary: Trotsky had read the autobiography of the priest Avakuum, the seventeenth-century leader of the Old Believers, who underwent many persecutions and was eventually burned at the stake. Trotsky notes:

> Reflecting on the blows that had fallen to our lot, I reminded Natasha [his wife] the other day of the life of the Archpriest Avakuum. They were stumbling on together in Siberia, the rebellious priest and his faithful spouse, their feet sunk in the snow, and the poor exhausted woman kept falling in the snowdrifts. Avakuum relates: "And I came up, and she began to reproach me, saying: 'How long, Archpriest, is this suffering to be?' And I said: 'Markovna, unto our very death.' And she, with a sigh, answered: 'So be it, Petrovich, let us be getting on our way.' "

The entry was made by a man whose son and most members of his family had already been killed by the NKVD, who was driven from country to country, unable to find permanent exile. Seen in this light—and also in view of his subsequent fate—the story of Avakuum seems by no means inappropriate. Yet all the Soviet historians can offer are some snide remarks that Trotsky was boasting, implying that his own willpower and persistence were even greater than those of the unfortunate cleric.[25]

There is some truth in the ideological critique of Trotsky. He did not inspire Stalin, but he failed to recognize Stalinism for what it really was.

He believed that even under Stalin the Soviet Union had basically remained a socialist workers' state, more progressive than any other. Trotsky's arrogance, egocentrism, and his many political misjudgments are not in serious question. If he favored inner-party democracy, even a (limited) multiparty system after 1927, he had not practiced such beliefs while in power. If Kamenev, Bukharin, Zinoviev, and many others made common cause with Stalin in 1923, it was mainly because they were afraid of Trotsky and his ambitions. If by historical accident he had found himself in power in the Soviet Union, his regime would have been dictatorial and harsh in the Jacobin-Leninist tradition.

But there was one fundamental difference between him and Stalin: Trotsky was an authoritarian personality but did not have the mentality of an Oriental despot; nor was he a paranoid mass murderer. Equating Trotskyism with Stalinism is therefore unjust and unhistorical, and the attempts to explain Stalin's terror campaign with reference to Trotsky's "provocations" belong to the realm of fantasy. Some Soviet historians blame Trotsky for having called for the overthrow of the Stalinist regime in 1937 and after. They would have called him a coward had he kept silent. But how could he have done so in the face of such constant vilification emanating from Moscow? Poor Trotsky, whatever he had done, Soviet historians would have found fault with him; even his suicide would not have produced a sympathetic reaction.

When Trotsky was killed in Mexico in August 1940, *Pravda* reported, with a delay of three days, that the "international spy" had been killed by one of his close supporters. After that, for decades, there was no elaboration. Only under glasnost was the issue reopened. Although the official Soviet version was believed by no one in the West or East, a formula of the kind used by *Pravda* was quite proper at the time; governments did not in those days boast of acts of terror abroad as they would in the age of Khomeini and Khaddafi.

Thus, no publicity was given to the killing in 1937 of Ignaz Reiss, an intelligence defector, or of Erwin Wolf and Rudolf Klement, two militant Trotskyites in Spain and Paris, respectively; there were other mysterious deaths, such as those of Leon Sedov (Trotsky's son) and Walter Krivitsky (another intelligence defector), that might have been murder, but the assassins (if there had been such) had succeeded so well in obliterating their traces that there was no proof.[26]

A considerable amount of information emerged from the trial of Jacson-Mornard Mercader even though the murderer kept his real motive and the background of his mission secret. Mercader left a letter in which he claimed that he had been originally a devoted follower of Trotsky's, "ready to shed his last drop of blood for him." But once in Mexico, he had realized that the beloved leader was merely a criminal counterrevolutionary in the service of (unnamed) capitalist governments.[27] Then, and only then, did he decide to liberate the world from this monster.

The true identity of Mercader (and some of his motives and the general context of the affair) became known in 1948 with the defection from the Soviet Union of Enrique Castro, one of the leaders of the Spanish Communist party, who received the information from Caridad, Mercader's mother.

In fact, Ramón Mercader, like some other Soviet agents such as Mark Zborowsky and the Soblens, had been infiltrated by the NKVD into Trotsky's entourage. It appeared from various sources that he had been enlisted in Paris by an NKVD colonel named Eitingon (aka Kotov, Leontev, and Rabinovich), who had handed him a forged passport and several thousand dollars. Mercader, sentenced to a twenty-year prison term, was released in 1960, whereupon he went to Moscow. He lived in the Soviet capital, not very happily, it would appear, was seen in Czechoslovakia, and then moved to Havana, where he died in 1978. He had been made a Hero of the Soviet Union by Stalin. Eitingon also was awarded the Order of Lenin and, more important, a promise that, unlike many other NKVD predecessors, he would not be executed. After Stalin's death, he was apparently arrested, but he was released after a few years and worked in a Soviet publishing house. He died in the Soviet capital in 1981.

The story of how Stalin planned the murder of his old rival was, of course, of considerable interest to Soviet citizens, who also wanted to know more about the personality of the assassin. They were to be disappointed, for the archives of the NKVD remain closed; the revelations published under glasnost were essentially those that had been published in the West decades earlier, including some that were almost certainly erroneous—such as the story that Mercader's mother had been Eitingon's mistress. A few of Mercader's acquaintances published their recollections, among them a fellow Spaniard and a Soviet specialist on Latin

America. But it appeared that none had known Mercader very well; nor was it certain that Mercader, a mere cog in a giant wheel, had known everything about the origins of the master plan.

Juan Kobo, a fellow Spaniard, angered by suggestions in the Soviet media that Mercader was a mere hireling, argued that he was both hangman and victim.[28] Why a victim? He was firmly convinced that the Trotskyites had cooperated in Spain with the anarchists, whom Mercader, as a lieutenant and a commissar in the Spanish Republican army, regarded as dangerous enemies. To "liquidate" Trotsky was therefore tantamount to killing an ally of fascism, an enemy of Spain, and not just of the Soviet Union. Kobo compares his deed with that of a Soviet partisan who killed a high-ranking Nazi official during the war: "One must not judge Mercader's behavior in 1940 by present-day standards, for the situation at that time was much more complicated."

The comparison is wholly unconvincing because, all other considerations apart, Mercader must have been aware of the fact that the Spanish civil war was over by 1939. If no attempt was made to kill Franco, why murder Trotsky? The author reveals incidentally that the operation aiming at the liquidation of Trotsky had been launched three years earlier, that a great many people were involved, but that the Spaniards among them, including Mercader, were not originally meant to play a central role.

While glasnost produced the demand for the (legal) rehabilitation of Trotsky, it also gave rise to bitter denunciations of the founder of the Red Army.[29] Under Stalin, it had been the habit to blame Trotsky for all sorts of crimes but not for official Soviet policies after 1923. Only the Russian émigrés of the 1920s and 1930s argued that Stalin was a hidden Trotskyite or that there was no difference between the two leaders. But these views did not gain much currency, were not widely discussed, and would have been considered sacrilege in the Soviet Union.

There is an irony of history in the fact that the leader (Trotsky) who had said that "Stalinism is the syphilis of the working-class movement" became, in later years, in the eyes of not a few Russians, Stalin's guru. In part, it was the fault of the Trotskyite radical phraseology—the charges against Stalin of having become a Menshevik, reformist, and opportunist, of having betrayed Lenin, even, at a certain stage, of having stolen ("confiscated") some of Trotsky's ideas. But with all this, it is also true that Trotsky, like Bukharin, did not favor a violent end to the NEP, but instead, a gradual transition to socialism.

No one in the 1930s, during the war, and in the postwar period would have considered Trotsky responsible for collectivization, mainly, no doubt, because it was considered a great success. This began to change only in the 1960s, when Trotsky was increasingly attacked inside Russia not for his opposition to Stalin, not for acts of sabotage, but, on the contrary, for having been the source of inspiration to Stalin. This new school of thought had its inspiration in the ranks of the right-wing patriotic-religious dissidents, small in number and influence. But it soon spread to the establishment Right, to journals such as *Nash Sovremennik*, *Molodaia Gvardia*, and *Moskva*, and it could even be found, albeit far more rarely, among the writings of some liberal authors in the 1970s.[30] There was a basic difference inasmuch as the "liberals" made Trotsky responsible for the civil-war terror of the 1920s but did not accept the Trotsky-as-Stalin's-guru concept.

The charges against Trotsky were specifically that he had tried to militarize Soviet civilian life (e.g., the organization of labor unions along military lines) and that he had inspired Stalin to implement the ruinous collectivization of agriculture.[31] He had provoked Stalin into the blood-bath of the 1930s by engaging in all kind of provocations and had systematically tried to ruin traditional Russian culture. While one right-wing writer held Trotsky responsible for the destruction of Moscow's churches at a time when he was in exile in France,[32] another blamed him for the invasion of Afghanistan, and a third for the persecution of Russian writers such as Esenin and Bulgakov.[33] The evidence produced, if any, did not lack ingenuity; thus, one literary critic discovered in an Esenin poem an obscure negative reference to "a man from Weimar." The poet Stanislav Kunyaev concluded that because Trotsky lived at one time in Weimar,[34] he must have been the villain referred to. The collectivization of agriculture took place well after Trotsky had been exiled from the Soviet Union. But this has not dissuaded Soviet authors from making him responsible for the catastrophe rather than Stalin. Thus, Vasili Belov, one of the most popular Soviet writers, wrote in a novel published in 1989: "The trip last year to Siberia has persuaded him [Stalin] that Trotsky was absolutely right with regard to the peasantry; these bags of shit are not even suitable as cannon fodder on the barricades."[35] Trotsky did not have a high opinion of the revolutionary potential of the peasantry, but he had never talked about them in offensive terms, as did Gorky, for example.

Leading Soviet newspapers published bitter political attacks against Trotsky; others made him responsible for the growing popularity in the Soviet Union of such undesirable writers as Mandelstam and Pasternak.[36] They did not mention that he thought highly of Esenin, who, in later years, became the hero of the Right. As V. Khatiushin wrote in the literary monthly *Moskva*:

> Trotsky dreamed of turning the country into a feudal-military state so as to carry out by this means the world revolution. . . . This is to say that he dreamed of giving legal sanction to the Masonic idea of establishing its rule worldwide. The main obstacle on Trotsky's road was Stalin, who, in all probability, realized the adventurist character of this Masonic-Zionist conspiracy against mankind.[37]

What were the reasons underlying these attacks? As long as Trotsky had been in a position of influence, that is to say, until roughly 1923, he was, of course, as much to blame for all the shortcomings, defeats, and crimes of the ruling group to which he belonged as the other leaders. The harshness of his approach has been noted; the same charges could be leveled against Lenin or the other Communist leaders, and, *a fortiori*, against Dzerzhinsky, the head of the Cheka. But Lenin and Dzerzhinsky were sacrosanct—they could not be blamed—at least not prior to 1990, whereas Trotsky was an obvious and easy target. This changed to a certain extent under glasnost; the Bolshevik old guard—many of them Jews— could be singled out for attack. They included Sverdlov, who was made responsible for the killing of the tsar's family and the pogrom of the Cossacks. It even affected some *déraciné* Russians, like Bukharin and Lunacharsky, who had helped with the "destruction of traditional Russian culture."

To a certain extent, Trotsky was a mere stand-in, as long as those really culpable (including, above all, Lenin) could not be named by the right-wingers. But it would be wrong to underrate the real hatred for Trotsky among sections of the Russian Right and the neo-Stalinists. He was the personification of all evil, and he was doubly vulnerable as a Communist and a Jew; his "original name," Leiba Bronstein, was always stressed with loving care by his enemies, a practice that had once been the monopoly of the Nazis.[38] No one would have dreamed of referring to Lenin as Ulyanov, to Gorky as Peshkov, or to Kirov as Kostrikov. The prediction of a Russian Jew ("the Trotskys make the Revolution, the Bronsteins will have to pay the price for it") came true more strikingly than anyone had imagined.

Little did it matter that Trotsky had, in fact, been opposed to collectivization. He had written that without modern machinery it was just as impossible to turn private small holdings into a viable collective farm as it was to merge small boats into an ocean liner. He predicted the impending catastrophe, the slaughter of cattle, the destruction of Russian agriculture, and even after much of the damage had already been done, he called for the Kremlin, on many occasions from his exile, to desist from its savage enterprise.[39] All this was ignored by Trotsky's critics. Although Stalin and his henchmen, who had been the designers and executors of collectivization, were at least in part forgiven, Trotsky, who had opposed it, was not.

Trotsky was frequently mistaken in his judgment, but there is no evidence that, once expelled from the leadership, he had any influence whatsoever either on the ideology of Stalinism or on practical politics. On the contrary, that Trotsky was suggesting a certain course of action was probably enough to induce Stalin to reject it.[40]

Under Stalin scapegoats were essential, and Trotsky was an ideal choice. For decades he had been Satan, and to preserve continuity, under glasnost he still remains a villain of sorts, albeit for different reasons. As the patriarch in Lessing's *Nathan* said upon listening to all kinds of evidence proving that Nathan was innocent: "Never mind, the Jew is for burning." True, the comparison between Trotsky and Lessing's Nathan, a good man as well as a wise one, is not wholly satisfactory. But whatever Trotsky's many sins of commission and omission, one's sense of fairness rebels against making him the main villain in the company of saints headed by Lenin.

4. The Great Terror: How It Came About

The "purges" of the 1930s, the killing of millions of people, including virtually the whole old guard of the Bolshevik party, is an event unique in world history. More people may have perished during the collectivization and in the famine of 1933 than in the purges, and Hitler engaged in more systematic murder, as did Pol Pot, who, more recently, has exterminated a greater percentage of his own people. There have been wars of extermination and destructive civil wars throughout history in which Catholics have been pitted against Protestants, Muslims against infidels, and various sectarians against each other around the world. What distinguished the events in the Soviet Union was such distinct features as the fantastic allegations and self-incriminations of the show trials and the ironic absence of apparent motives, which in other lands and periods had fueled mass murder.

The *terreur* in the French Revolution had been directed against the people of the old regime and, later, against all moderates. Hitler sought to destroy as many Jews and other "racial enemies" as possible; in Stalin's case, however, the arrests and executions were far more arbitrary and accidental. There were no conspiracies against the regime other than imaginary ones; there was not even a potential opposition against Stalin. Many, probably most, of the victims were his supporters. There was virtually no resistance against the terror machine, no Vendée, no plot like the one hatched by senior German officers against Hitler in 1943–44. The absurd allegations were frequently believed and often fervently supported, sometime even outside the Soviet Union—all of which has made the purges extremely difficult to understand.

Many theories in respect to the purges have been voiced over the years, some more plausible than others, and it was only natural that under glasnost—in the light of many new revelations and official admissions—this darkest chapter in Soviet history came to be reexamined. There was resistance against the "unhealthy preoccupation with the past." But the quest for truth proved stronger, not surprisingly, because so many families throughout this vast country had been affected and because the great terror so deeply influenced the subsequent course of Soviet history.

The main stages of the great terror will be briefly recapitulated before we turn to the new light that has been shed on the tragic and seemingly inexplicable events of the late 1930s.

Neither the arrests nor the show trials of the 1930s were altogether unprecedented. Prison camps and *polit-isolators* had existed even in the 1920s, although the overall number of political prisoners was then much smaller. Executions were as yet rare. Only with the four show trials of sundry "wreckers and saboteurs" that took place in the late 1920s and early 1930s was a new era inaugurated. Although limited in scope, these trials are of relevance because the charges against the accused were largely false and the techniques employed to extract confessions were also novel. For those stage-managing and conducting the trials, these were limbering-up exercises for the big events that were to follow in 1936–38.[1]

The period of the great terror proper was ushered in by the murder of Sergei Kirov, the Leningrad party boss and, after Stalin, one of the central figures in the land. Although many circumstances point to Stalin's involvement in Kirov's assassination, no irrefutable evidence has been discovered so far and perhaps never will.[2] Following the Kirov murder there were mass arrests among members of the former Zinoviev-Kamenev opposition. This group was brought to a (secret) trial in January 1935 and was sentenced to five to ten years in prison. But there were also arrests among the Leningrad NKVD and fairly large numbers of other people from all ranks of society. ("The usual suspects" were rounded up.) As in the trials that were to follow, Vyshinsky and Ulrich were presiding judge and chief prosecutor, respectively.

The next stage began with the second Zinoviev-Kamenev trial in August 1936. This time the proceedings were public; it was claimed that the defendants had deceived the authorities in their first trial. They bore not only moral responsibility for Kirov's murder (as claimed the year before) but had actually killed him and also tried to murder Stalin, Lenin, and many others. They had been agents of foreign intelligence services, European as well as Japanese;[3] they had sabotaged agriculture, industrial plants, and railway lines. The same charges, with but minor variations, figured in the subsequent trials: the Piatakov-Radek trial of February 1937, the case against the Red Army leadership in June 1937, and the trial of Bukharin, Rykov, and others.

In the show trials, all the accused confessed, some more readily than others. Most were sentenced to death, but even the few who received lesser sentences were killed. "Ten years without the right of correspondence" was synonymous with almost immediate execution. In the meantime, Yagoda, the people's commissar of the interior, who had been instrumental in engineering the early stages of the "purges," was removed from his job (September 1936) and eventually sentenced to death in the Bukharin trial. His successor, Nikolai Ezhov, lasted for little more than a year and was then replaced by Lavrenti Beria. Beria headed the security services until shortly after Stalin's death, when he, too, was executed for, among other things, having been a British spy since 1918.

But the trials were only the tip of the iceberg. Whereas the various Moscow court proceedings concerned no more than about 50 people, the number of victims was in the millions. The whole Bolshevik old guard was decimated, and the same is true with regard to the Red Army officer corps and NKVD leadership, down to the local level, altogether some 20,000 people. Many foreign Communist leaders were among the victims; Stalin had more German and Polish Communist leaders killed than Hitler.

The arrests and executions affected people in Moscow and Leningrad as much as in the outlying districts; it affected peasants and workers as well as managers, writers, and scientists. Frequently, the families of the "enemies of the people" were also arrested and executed. It would be easier to count the categories of people who were seldom "repressed," to use post-Stalinist jargon: There were few movie directors and actors among those liquidated, few painters, composers, and musicians. As in the Third Reich, entertainers enjoyed by and large an immunity of sorts.

Most of the bloodletting took place in the years 1936–38, but the terror by no means ceased during the years that followed. Some of those who had been tried in earlier years were executed in 1939–41. True, some military leaders who had escaped the firing squads in 1937 were actually released from the labor camps in 1940, but others were arrested in 1940–41.

During the war, the institutionalized terror took, by necessity, different forms. Among those affected were officers and soldiers who were accused of not having obeyed orders as well as members of nationalities deemed suspect, such as the Crimean Tartars, the Volga Germans, the Kalmyk, various Caucasian nationalities, and others. When the war ended, it was the turn of officers and soldiers who had been taken prisoner by the Germans. Between 1945 and Stalin's death, there were two major, and a great number of smaller, "purges." Above all the Leningrad case should be mentioned in which a member of the Politburo (N. Voznesensky) and many other local leaders were arrested and shot. The other concerned the drive against the "Cosmopolitans," which resulted in the killing of most Yiddish-language writers. When Stalin died, yet another terror wave was under way, the "doctors' plot," but it was stopped the day after the dictator suffered his fatal stroke.

Our list does not even contain all of the more important categories; no mention, for instance, has been made of the destruction of Soviet genetics and the killing of leading geneticists, such as N. Vavilov. After Stalin's death, the survivors were gradually released from the camps. Their legal rehabilitation took much longer. Although the army commanders were among the first, the leading political victims of the purge were rehabilitated only in 1988, and a few, for a variety of reasons, were not rehabilitated at all. There were all kinds of variations: Some were rehabilitated under Khruschev but "dehabilitated" under Brezhnev, to be rehabilitated again under Gorbachev.

Stalinist terror differed in essential aspects from the terrorist practice of fascism. Mussolini's followers certainly used violent means prior to the March on Rome. But once *Il Duce* was in power, only a handful of people in twenty years were executed for political reasons, and the number of those exiled was in the hundreds.

Nazi terrorism was predominantly directed against Jews, foreigners, and active oppositionists. There were concentration camps inside Germany from an early date, and millions perished in the death camps during the war, but the machinery was programmed to destroy certain groups of people; it did not operate indiscriminately.

There were no purges under the Italian Fascist leadership; in Germany, there was one, the so-called Night of the Long Knives, on June 30, 1934. Many arrests and executions took place in Germany in the latter part of the war, but they were directed against true opponents of the regime. All this is not to say that Hitler and Mussolini were less cruel than Stalin. It simply means that they assumed, correctly, that the majority of the population was loyal and that the mere threat of terror was sufficient to intimidate potential enemies. If Hitler needed forced labor, there were plenty of foreign workers to be exploited, and Italy never experienced an acute labor shortage.

How much was known about the extent of terror during Stalin's lifetime? The fate of the accused in the show trials was, of course, no secret, and it was also made known that certain prominent officials had been sentenced or shot. But in the great majority of cases of victims who were not well known, there was no publicity. In some instances in which foreigners were affected (such as Katyn), there were even official denials. Ordzhonikidze, a member of the Politburo, was either killed or committed suicide; according to official version, however, he died of natural causes.

At the time, no one could say with any assurance whether tens of thousands of people had been killed or 10 million, and estimates varied between those extremes. Yet, considering that the Soviet Union from about 1936 was a country almost hermetically sealed (far more so than Nazi Germany), an astonishing amount of information became known, even before the first thaw.

What were the sources, how was the information transmitted to the outside world, and how was it received there? Defectors, especially from the Soviet security services, were the most important early sources. Although even relatively high placed NKVD agents had only a limited purview—especially those stationed outside Russia—and although the number of defections was not great, it is astonishing, in historical perspective, how much became known as the result of their revelations and how many of their accounts were confirmed forty or fifty years later.[4]

The second important source was men and women who had been arrested but were released and reintegrated into Soviet society or, if they were German nationals, deported to Nazi Germany. Some Russian victims of collectivization and the purges became collaborators under the German occupation. Although former inmates of the gulag had, by necessity, only a limited purview, their accounts, taken together, constituted a valuable and wide-ranging source of information. With the first thaw, more witnesses returned; some of them made their way to the

West, which, together with the revelations published in Moscow after Stalin's death, created the basis for the first major accounts of the terror, the executions, and gulag.[5]

Soon after Stalin's death, a major amnesty was declared that almost exclusively covered ordinary criminals. True, there were also a few releases of political prisoners, such as the physicians whose trial had been prepared during the last months of Stalin's life. As far as they were concerned, there was no case against them.

The release of most survivors came only in 1954–55, and the rehabilitation of those dead and alive began only after Khrushchev's famous secret speech at the Twentieth Party Congress. Rehabilitation took different forms. In some cases, it was done publicly; more often, it was kept secret even from the closest relations of those concerned. There were first- and second-rate, sometimes even third- and fourth-rate, rehabilitations. Some victims were reinstated into the party, but this was by no means always the case. Some were rehabilitated fully and without any reservations; some were not. Sometimes the procedure was carried out by the Central Committee; more often it was carried out on the local level. Khrushchev encountered strong resistance from old Stalinists. That close collaborators of the late dictator, such as Molotov, Andreev, and Pospelov, were key figures in committees charged with de-Stalinization did not inspire confidence and pointed to the limits that had been set.

Rehabilitation was strictly selective; from among the better-known political figures who had appeared in the Moscow show trials, only a very few, such as Krestinsky, Ikramov, and Hodzaev, were rehabilitated. Those who had been liquidated without the benefit of a trial, and particularly the senior army commanders, stood a much better chance. In his secret speech, Khrushchev singled out his own friends and contemporaries, those who had been members of Stalin's Politburo and Central Committee throughout the 1930s (Chubar, Eikhe, Postyshev, Kosior, Rudzutak) and who fell victim toward the end of the great purge. He seems also to have tried to rehabilitate Bukharin but gave up when he encountered resistance. Bukharin's widow and son, from 1961 to 1976, applied to the party leadership, but their requests were turned down on all occasions.

The first wave of de-Stalinization came to an end in 1959, but the issue was unexpectedly raised again by Khrushchev at the Twenty-second Party

Congress (October 1961). It was part of his campaign against the Stalinist old guard (the "antiparty group") that increasingly opposed his political initiatives. Thus, in speeches at the congress, Malenkov was blamed for complicity in the crimes that had been committed in White Russia; Kaganovich, for the part he had played in the Ukraine; Voroshilov, for his role in the murder of the "flower of the Red Army"; and Molotov, for his duplicity all along. There were relatively few specific rehabilitations after the Twenty-second Party Congress except that it was now generally admitted that the terror had commenced well before 1937.

After the fall of Khrushchev, another revaluation of Soviet history took place. Although the "cult of the individual" was not reinstated, Stalin's actions were viewed in a far more positive light. No more victims were rehabilitated; on the contrary, some who had been rehabilitated earlier again became nonpersons or remained "enemies." The only further revelations that took place were made in samizdat.

The practice continued to prevail under Andropov, Chernenko, and even during the first two years of Gorbachev. Then, in early 1987, the second wave of unofficial rehabilitations began with the showing of various television documentaries on Lenin and his comrades-in-arms, with plays such as those by Mikhail Shatrov (*Brestski Mir*) and the reprinting of Lenin's famous "Testament" of 1922. It was followed by Gorbachev's speech on the seventieth anniversary of the October Revolution. It had been widely assumed that there would be a wholesale rehabilitation of all Stalin's victims on this occasion. Instead, there were merely general references to Stalin's misdeeds and his achievements. But Gorbachev also demanded that there should be no "white spaces" in Soviet history, which opened the door to many further publications and eventually to the legal rehabilitation of Stalin's victims who had not benefited from the first thaw.

Initially, in 1985–86, Gorbachev opposed the reopening of "divisive debates." Later, he stated that the causes of the situation in the U.S.S.R. went back far into the past. In a talk with leading intellectuals in July 1987, he said, "We never will be able to forgive or justify what happened in 1937–1938."

The first group to be rehabilitated in July 1987 by the Supreme Soviet was composed of some fifteen economists, many of them agricultural experts (the Working Peasants party) who had been accused of sabotage in the late 1920s and disappeared following a secret trial. Their rehabilitation was less than sensational. Because they had not been party members, their case was not controversial. They had been de facto half-rehabilitated even under Brezhnev, when some of the books of Chayanov, their "leader," had been published. It was also implied in 1987–88 that the other two show trials that had taken place at about the same time had to be reexamined: Professor Ramzin's Prompartia (Industrial party) and the Union Buro of Mensheviks. But this created complications with regard to the man who had conducted the trials: Krylenko, the predecessor of the notorious Vyshinsky. He was an old Bolshevik who was himself "repressed" in 1938 following a trial that lasted only a few minutes. He had helped to establish the murderous system that in the end swallowed him. It comes as no surprise, then, that he became a "contradictory, deeply tragic figure" as far as the media were concerned; it is of little wonder that his daughter should continue to defend him as a man who had done his revolutionary duty against enemies who had allegedly prepared a military invasion of the Soviet Union.[6]

This was followed by the legal rehabilitation in 1988 of the defendants in the Bukharin-Rykov trial, exactly fifty years earlier. There was one notable exception, Genrich Yagoda, who had been responsible, as chief of the NKVD, for much of the killing in the early phase of the terror. His case remained in abeyance.

Finally, on June 13, 1988, the sentences of the accused in the first (Zinoviev-Kamenev) and the second Moscow trial (Piatakov-Radek) were quashed. The Supreme Court, however, did not examine, in the words of one commentator, the "party image" of the criminals of 1936–37. In fact, official comment in the media made it clear that they had committed political mistakes during various stages of their careers and that the same was true of Bukharin. But it was stated clearly that before the law, before the state and the people, they were not guilty.[7]

Of the major party figures, this left only Trotsky. For many years, he had been described as the devil incarnate, the worst enemy of socialism and the Soviet people. But because Trotsky had never been officially charged with any crime (merely assassinated during his Mexico exile), no legal rehabilitation was called for. Instead, a variety of articles on Trotsky appeared in the media, some bitterly hostile, others more lenient in their appraisal, pointing to the merits (as well as to the demerits) of a man who, at one time, had been second only to Lenin in the hierarchy, had been the founder of the Red Army, and had been first foreign minister.

Generally speaking, the main importance of the new revelations was that facts previously circulated only in samizdat now became common knowledge. Frequently, the essential facts about the repression had been known for a long time, but the documents and detailed accounts published in 1987–88 had a far greater impact than the mere statement that a certain individual had vanished. Mikhail Koltsov had been a very popular journalist in the 1930s of impeccable Stalinist credentials who had been arrested in 1938 and shot soon after. His story, written by his brother Boris Efimov, a prominent cartoonist, had first been published in the 1960s. A more detailed account, which appeared in a popular weekly in 1988, reached a much larger audience and made a shattering impression. The same is true, to provide a few other examples, with regard to Isaac Babel and Osip Mandelstam, to Alexander Kosarev, the head of the Komsomol (the Communist Youth League), and to Fyodor Raskolnikov, one of the early heroes of the Revolution who had defected in Spain in 1938.

Babel and Mandelstam had ceased to be "enemies of the people" in the 1950s. Some of their work had been published under Khrushchev and even under Brezhnev, in limited editions. They had reappeared in the official histories of literature, albeit as marginal figures on the sidelines. The same was true, *mutatis mutandis*, with regard to Kosarev and Raskolnikov. But the full text of Raskolnikov's "open letter" to Stalin had never been published, nor had the fact registered that it was not just Kosarev who had been "repressed" but the whole leadership of the Komsomol throughout the Soviet Union.

The intensity of the debate on Stalinist terror was one new aspect of the second thaw, but there were others. In 1956, following Khrushchev's speech, the party line had simply changed; there was no public debate. In 1987, however, there were open controversies: Although many strongly supported the revelations about the mass murders under Stalin, others, to the contrary, expressed the belief that although there had been regrettable excesses, these negative features of Stalinism should be seen in a broader historical perspective, approached in a "detached way and not be exaggerated." Given the tremendous domestic and external pressures of the period, they argued, it had been unavoidable that some innocent people should have suffered. Furthermore, it was argued, the purges of 1937–38 affected a relatively small segment of the population, mainly old Communists; many more people had perished under collectivization. Some considered 1937–38 just punishment meted out to Communists who had previously engaged in the repression of non-Communists. Although this was certainly true with regard to the organs of state security and some members of the Politburo, it was not, of course, correct with regard to the great majority of the victims.

There were other new aspects to the second thaw. Under Khrushchev, all the blame had been placed on Stalin and some of his closest collaborators. But the fact that Molotov had been a close collaborator had not prevented his subsequent reinstatement by the party. Beria and some of his leading henchmen had been shot in 1953, and some of the most active "investigators" had been sentenced in secret trials. Thus, the impression had been created that the murder of millions of people had been carried out by Stalin and Beria more or less single-handedly, which was, of course, absurd. Tens of thousands of people must have been involved in a crime of such magnitude.

During the second thaw, new names were revealed, and further documentary evidence was disclosed. Yet, even then, there was considerable reluctance to reopen old wounds. Most of the hangmen, informers, and extortionists were no longer among the living. Furthermore, research into the crimes of the 1930s and 1940s was made very difficult because most of the incriminating source material had been well hidden in the archives of the Ministries of Justice and Defense or destroyed;[8] the archives of the organs of state security were not accessible in any case. True, a select few were permitted to use some of the material in the Ministry of Justice; what they reported was both shattering and of great historical interest. But it was not remotely sufficient to engage in a systematic, exhaustive research of that tragic period. Very often the researchers had to rely on the recollections of survivors or their families; "oral history" flourished in the Soviet Union as never before.

On December 5, 1988, *Vlast Solovetskaia* (Solovetsk Power), a documentary film, was first shown in Moscow. The film examined the first Soviet labor camp, which was located in a big sixteenth-century monastery on the largest of a group of islands in the White Sea. Far away from populated centers, it had served as a prison throughout its history. It had also served as a refuge for seventeenth-century religious schismatics. In 1923, it became a camp for both political prisoners and common criminals. It ceased to function in 1939, when the surviving inmates were transferred to other camps farther east.

The existence of the camp was not unknown in the West. In the late 1920s, one or more inmates had succeeded in escaping over the ice to Finland; one of them wrote a book that was translated into several languages.[9] Furthermore, not a few inmates were released after three or four years, and their stories, too, percolated to the outside world. Solovki was the most intellectual of all the Soviet camps; a great many famous historians, philosophers, and scientists were confined there, and Pimen, the patriarch of all Russia, had died there. The most prominent living survivor at the time of the showing of the film was the academician Dmitri Likhachev, who had been arrested as a young historian in Leningrad. The makers of the film initially believed that no other inmates were alive, but as they prepared their movie, they found others, all in their eighties: Adamova-Sluisberg, who had been accused of attempting to assassinate Kaganovich (whom she had never seen in her life); Alexander Prokhorov, a well-known engineer of the early 1930s; Samuel Epstein, then a young journalist and lawyer; and Andrei Roshin, who had known the camp both as deputy commander and subsequently as an inmate. Another important source of information was the unexpected discovery of a huge file of letters written by the inmates but never dispatched by the camp authorities.

The story of Solovki covers a period that, even today, is known as the "humanist era" of Soviet power. The NKVD commanders were so proud of their record (and so angry about the adverse publicity abroad) that they decided to have a film produced about conditions in the camp. With Maksim Gorky as the star, the film's purpose was to show how errant sons and daughters were reeducated by work. A copy of this old film was found and added authenticity to the new movie. However, the makers of the Solovki documentary soon realized that the socialist humanism so frequently invoked did not extend to Solovki. New arrivals were told by the guards that the only power on the island was the local one; hence, the title of the documentary.

The percentage of survivors was higher than in the camps of the Stalin era. But it was also true that, in the words of the producer (Dr. Goldovskaia), 300 inmates were killed in a single night in 1929, almost as many as the *total* number of those incarcerated in the monastery during four centuries.[10] Still, compared with the camps of later years, Solovki was almost a luxury resort. It had a theater ("Paris of the North"), a newspaper, and visits from close relatives were occasionally permitted. The number of political prisoners counted in the tens of thousands rather than millions. According to official reports, there were 800,000 inmates in the labor camps all over the Soviet Union in 1934, but this figure may have included criminals.[11] There were few Communists among the inmates; instead, the inmates were mainly people deemed to be "class enemies," that is to say, of "bourgeois" origin, rather liberally interpreted.

The systematic persecution of Communist oppositionists began with the Fifteenth Party Congress in 1927 and was directed against the Trotskyites; eventually it encompassed everyone else. During the early years, the oppositionists were generally exiled; if they recanted, they were usually permitted to return to European Russia.

Mention has been made of the rehabilitation in 1987 of the agricultural experts, which was not unrelated to the new agrarian policy advocated by Gorbachev and his colleagues. In the 1920s, Chayanov had suggested rural cooperatives rather than wholesale collectivization, which made him very popular under perestroika; his academic books (he also wrote children's stories) were reissued. Virtually every issue of the leading Soviet agricultural magazine contained an article about aspects of his work and views under the general heading "Readings from (or on) Chayanov."

Equally striking was the rehabilitation of Nikolai Kondratiev. His was a household name in the West; even first-year economics students and laymen had heard of "Kondratiev cycles" and his "long waves," although not everyone would accept his theory. But until 1988 the Soviet encyclopedic dictionary listed only a Kondratiev who was a textile-industry innovator, another who was a ballet dancer, and a third who was an athlete; the economist was still a nonperson except in highly specialized publications, in which he occasionally figured as a counterrevolutionary wrecker who had propagated ideas that were both wrong and harmful. Even in the library of the Soviet Academy of Sciences, three of his main works had been lost.[12]

Following his legal rehabilitation, Kondratiev was proudly reinstated as part of the heritage of Soviet economic thought. Incidentally, it was discovered that while he was an inmate of the Suzdal *polit-isolator* ("prison for political prisoners") between 1930 and 1934, he had written two books on macroeconomic modeling (only one had survived but was never published) that showed, according to the Soviet discoverers, that he had been ten to fifteen years ahead of his U.S. colleagues in this field. Publicity was given to the others, among them V. Novozhilov, who were accused at the same trial.[13]

If Chayanov's and his colleagues' views on agriculture were right, this created serious ideological problems not only with regard to party decisions taken in 1928–31 but also with such classics of Soviet literature as Sholokhov's *Virgin Soil Upturned*, which had given a strongly embellished account of the collectivization at the grass roots. In 1937, Sholokhov's well-wishers discovered just in time that the writer was in acute danger of being arrested and possibly shot; he dashed to Moscow from his Cossack village, stayed there anonymously, and allegedly appeared at a Politburo meeting at which, owing to Stalin's personal intervention, he was given a clean bill of health.[14]

The case of the "Ryutin platform" has been known in broad outline outside the Soviet Union ever since the arrest of Martimian Ryutin in 1932. However, only in 1988 under glasnost were many details revealed. It was the one and only time that a conspiracy to remove Stalin did, in fact, exist—even though it never progressed beyond the stage of vague talk. It was also the first time that those accused were sentenced under paragraph 58 (10), that is, anti-Soviet agitation and propaganda. It was the first time that Stalin demanded the death sentence for fellow party members.

By origin, Ryutin was an old working-class Bolshevik who had played a role of some importance in the civil war. At the time of his arrest, he served as party secretary of a leading Moscow district (Krasnaia Presnia). He had reached the conclusion that Stalin's economic and social policy was disastrous and, if unchecked, would lead the country to ruin. Ryutin compared Stalin with Azev, the famous tsarist police agent in the Russian revolutionary movement in the first decade of the century, noting that no enemy had ever caused as much damage as Stalin and his clique. A climate of terror and fear was prevailing in the country, and Ryutin called on all true, courageous Leninists to join the new Union of Marxists-Leninists and depose Stalin.[15]

Because there were often police agents among the oppositionists, the Ryutin initiative soon became known to Stalin. The case went first to the party control commission, which referred the case to the Politburo, where Stalin demanded Ryutin's head. But he was overruled by the majority.[16]

Stalin never forgot his defeat and, in later years, reminded his followers that he had been right to demand that most severe punishment. When deposing Yagoda in 1936 for showing a lack of initiative, he sent a cable to the other members of the Politburo that said "the OGPU [secret police] is four years behind. . . ." As Robert Conquest has noted, it was almost four years to the day of the September 1932 meeting of the Politburo that had blocked him.

Ryutin and his colleagues were ousted from the party and given prison sentences. Most of them were shot in 1937–38; a few marginal figures survived in the camps. One was forgiven and reinstated by Stalin: Sergei Kavtaradze, who became a deputy foreign minister.[17]

The Ryutin case raises a question that will have to be discussed again in our account: Why was there so little resistance to Stalin? As Lev Razgon and others observed after Ryutin's rehabilitation, the Soviet Union would have been spared a great deal of misfortune if there had been more courageous people, such as Ryutin, who would have gotten rid of Stalin in the early 1930s. More surprisingly, perhaps, Ryutin's courage and sober assessment were singled out for praise in 1988 by *Krasnaia zvezda*, the army organ. That Ryutin had been an early Red Army commander and that he had served at one time as deputy editor of the newspaper no doubt helped in this context.

Kirov's Murder

The case of Sergei Mironovich Kirov is probably the most intriguing in a period filled with mysteries. The possibility that Stalin might have planned the murder of one of his most faithful lieutenants seems to have occurred to many even before the first show trials were staged. Perhaps Kirov was too popular for Stalin's liking; in any case, his murder offered a unique opportunity to carry out a widespread purge, leading to the wholescale massacre of the old party leadership, as well as many others. But for the killing of one of the party's central leaders, allegedly carried out by Trotskyite terrorists and other enemies of Soviet society, it would have been difficult to persuade the party and the public that measures of extraordinary severity were needed to crush an enemy lurking everywhere and willing to strike at any moment at all targets.

Khrushchev said in his secret speech in February 1956 that "to this day the circumstances surrounding Kirov's murder hide many things that are inexplicable and mysterious and demand the most careful examination." Five years later, at the Twenty-second Party Congress, he again referred to this issue:

> Great efforts are still needed to find out who was really to blame for his death. The more deeply we study the materials connected with Kirov's death, the more questions arise. . . . A thorough inquiry is now being made into the circumstances of this complicated case.

What became of the inquiry? For three decades there was total silence. In a roundtable discussion in 1988, a historian working at the Academy of Sciences announced, "It is said that more than one Commission had delved into this murky affair." But the materials it had investigated and the reports issued were never produced.[18] In 1987, Anatoly Rybakov published *The Children of the Arbat*, his famous roman à clef, in which it was strongly suggested that Stalin had been instrumental in engineering Kirov's murder. But the author stopped short of producing proof or going into details; in any case, indicting Stalin was not in the province of a novelist.

Naturally Volkogonov, Stalin's Soviet biographer, tried to find out as much as he could about this very event. But he did not succeed. The relevant source material did not apparently exist any longer or was inconclusive:

> In the archives to which the author received access, there are no materials that permit one with a great degree of certainty to comment on the Kirov affair—except that the murder was *not* committed at the behest of Trotsky, Zinoviev, or Kamenev.

Volkogonov rejected the versions published outside the Soviet Union as "tendentious," but he also noted that "knowing Stalin as we know him today, his exceptional cruelty, his intrigues and perfidy, it is quite possible that this was done by him."[19]

However, no conclusive documentary evidence has been discovered so far. The Soviet security authorities have been reluctant, to say the least, to give access even to their own, most trusted people. It could well be that some written evidence was destroyed or that such evidence never existed. But if there had been no evidence, the work of the various Soviet committees of investigation would have been much shorter and less complicated. They could have concluded that in view of the disappearance of all the key witnesses and the absence of relevant documentary material, it was impossible to examine the case any further and that in the circumstances Stalin ought to be given the benefit of the doubt. They could have concluded that all the available evidence pointed to the involvement of one man and one man only (Nikolaev), just as the Reichstag, contrary to all appearances, had been set on fire by one individual, van der Lubbe, without the assistance of anyone else.[20] But the case was left hanging in midair; hence, the possibility that one day further light will be shed on the Kirov murder.

According to yet another version, a central role in the whole affair was played by a semiliterate woman named Maria Volkova, who worked for the NKVD in Leningrad. She claimed that there was a major counterrevolutionary plot named the Green Lamp in which some 700 people were involved and that they had been behind the Kirov murder. Stalin was told about this informer and demanded to see her during his stay in Leningrad. He soon realized, however, that her story belonged wholly to the realm of fantasy. Volkova died in an asylum in the 1960s, but some of the people who had known her were still alive when a new investigation began during glasnost. Because there is no reason to believe that Stalin gave any credence to the Volkova evidence, this strange story in no way helps to explain either the circumstances of the Kirov murder or the terror campaign thereafter.[21]

The First Show Trial

The murder of Kirov led to the trial against the Trotskyite-Zinovievite Center in August 1936. The preparations began a year before; Kamenev and Zinoviev, the main defendants, had, in fact, been arrested almost immediately after the assassination of Kirov in Leningrad. They were given lengthy prison terms in a first trial. When they were tried for the second time, they were made to confess that they had withheld from the court the full extent of their guilt. Unprejudiced observers found this impossible to accept, yet far more unlikely accusations were to follow. Ivan Smirnov, another defendant in the trial, had actually been in prison since 1932. An incorrigible old oppositionist who had not recanted, he quite obviously was physically incapable of planning and executing Kirov's murder from a prison cell far from Moscow. But such incongruities did not bother the investigators who prepared the trials.[22] Those who might have dared to question the accusations fell ill or died during this time, including Maksim Gorky, Krupskaia (Lenin's widow), Ordzhonikidze, Kuibyshev, members of the Politburo, and a few others.

On August 15, 1936, the Soviet press announced that Zinoviev and Kamenev had been handed over to the court. Immediately a stream of anger and indignation broke out. From Minsk and Brest Litovsk to the Far East, there were calls for capital punishment for the vile traitors. The trial had not yet started, nor had the accused been found guilty. But the popular outcry seemed quite appropriate because the verdict was clear even before the trial started. It was a mere formality; if previously the hands of the NKVD (formerly GPU) had been tied by various administrative regulations, on the very day of Kirov's murder a special decree was passed removing the restrictions. From then on, the organs of state security had a free hand in bringing "terrorists" to trial and interrogating them. There was to be no appeal for clemency, and executions were to be immediate.

Abroad, the first show trial came as a bombshell, as did the fantastic confessions of the defendants, to even a greater extent. How to explain that the old Leninist guard had committed such dastardly deeds? Even more mysterious: How to explain that they readily admitted all their crimes? Not a few foreign observers, including some Russian experts, reached the conclusion that there was only one logical explanation: They had indeed been guilty as charged, and they had no alternative but to confess under the weight of the evidence. Thus, Sir Bernard Pares, the leading British expert who had followed Russian affairs closely since the turn of the century, stated:

> Nearly all of them admitted having done so [conspiring against Stalin], and at this point it is not necessary that we should doubt them, in whatever way their evidence was originally obtained. The bulky verbatim reports were in any case impressive. . . . Some of these men . . . were at their intellectual best in their last words at the trial. Zinoviev, who had escaped by the skin

of his teeth in former trials, was now firmly brought to book and died still
fawning, like the coward he had always been (August 24, 1936).[23]

The book that contained these pearls of wisdom was reprinted fourteen
times in seventeen years; those who find Soviet comment on the trials
under Stalin difficult to understand and more difficult to stomach are
well advised not to lose sight of such contemporary Western commentators as Bernard Pares.

As a Soviet commentator was to write many years later: Poor deluded
Westerners, "they could not understand what was going on."[24] It was
easy for Pares tu write with disdain about Zinoviev, a sick man who had
not shown much physical courage at the best of times. But hardened
revolutionaries who had spent many years in tsarist prisons and in the
civil war, professional soldiers unlikely to be cowards, behaved the same
way. There is every reason to believe that experts like Pares, having been
exposed to a week or two in the cellars of the Lubyanka, would have
admitted at the very least to the poisoning of the royal family in Buck-
ingham Palace. In actual fact, the accused—including such intellectuals
as Kamenev and Radek, who were to appear in the second show trial—
put up, as it was to emerge in later years, considerable resistance. Kamenev's resistance was broken after a meeting with Stalin and other
members of the Politburo in which both he and Radek were promised
that either their lives, or the lives of their closest relatives, would be
spared.

At about the same time, Stalin gave free rein to the application of
physical and mental torture: When it produced no immediate results, he
threatened the NKVD for their inefficiency. On July 29, 1936, Stalin
gave another order to apply whatever methods deemed necessary to extract confessions from those accused of espionage, Trotskyism, or other
charges.

The total mendacity of the first, as of the other Moscow trials, was
obvious from the very beginning, but it took the Soviet authorities more
than fifty years to admit that much. True, under Khrushchev in 1960–
61, the accusations of treason and of the murder of Kirov were withdrawn. But there was no public announcement, and the defendants of
1936–38 were not posthumously admitted to the party. As far as the
history books were concerned, they remained "enemies of the party" who
had done considerable harm to the cause of communism in 1917 and

thereafter. Only in February 1988 did the Presidium of the Supreme Soviet decide at long last that "impermissible methods" had been applied against all the accused in the first Moscow trial. Their full rehabilitation came in July 1988.

However, even then, as legal experts pointed out, rehabilitation was less than full and unconditional. For the formula used implied that the crime (treason, terrorism, etc.) had indeed taken place but that the accused had not participated in it, whereas in actual fact there had been no crime in the first place. The definition used was tantamount to legal-criminal rehabilitation, but it did not necessarily preclude civil-administrative (or political) responsibility on the part of the defendants. It meant that the act had been committed, and though it was not criminal, it remained to be analyzed to discover its real character.[25]

These admissions did not come easily to the Soviet authorities. For too long, the victims had been at the very top of the list of enemies; generations of Soviet citizens had been educated in the belief that Zinoviev, Kamenev, and Bukharin had been at least as bad as Hitler. Now it had to be explained that Zinoviev had been Lenin's closest associate in exile and that Kamenev had served after the Revolution in various key positions. True, with all his undoubted gifts, especially as an orator, there had always been a streak of hysteria and exaggeration in Zinoviev. Therefore, it was not surprising that even after the full rehabilitation, some Soviet historians published articles on Zinoviev with a heavy emphasis on his political errors. It was conceded that he had faithfully served Lenin for many years. But on the other side of the ledger were his vacillations on the eve of the armed uprising in November 1917, the hyperbole in his bloodthirsty speeches, his style of work as a Leningrad party boss, and his unwillingness to publish Lenin's "Testament."[26]

The attitude toward Kamenev was a little warmer, though not very much so. He had fewer enemies than Zinoviev; his interests, after having been forced out of politics, had been mainly cultural; he had edited Herzen and written a biography of the Russian nineteenth-century radical writer Nikolai Chernyshevsky. His tragic fate was regretted, but unlike Bukharin's, his writings were not republished. In brief, he remained a person of historical interest only.

It should be mentioned in passing that in this case, as in others, Stalin gave instructions to kill not just the "enemies of the people" but to exterminate all their relations near and far. (In Leningrad, after Kirov's murder, all persons who bore the name of the assassin Nikolaev—a fairly common one in Russia—were exiled from the city.) In the case of Kamenev, the whole family—brothers, children, sisters-in-law, and grandchildren—were arrested; some were immediately shot, while others died in exile. The last to be arrested was his grandson, Vitali, in 1951, shortly after his nineteenth birthday. The only ones to survive were Kamenev's daughter-in-law, the actor and movie star G. S. Kravchenko, and his youngest son, Vitali, who had been six at the time of his father's arrest. He was detained for the first time when he was ten, spent his childhood and adolescence in various camps, but was released after the Twentieth Party Congress and became a lecturer in philosophy at the Novosibirsk technical college.[27]

The rehabilitation of the defendants in the second Moscow trial took place at the very same time. Only a few months before their arrest, Piatakov and Radek had joined the chorus of those asking for the execution of Zinoviev, Kamenev, and the others accused in the first trial—a pattern that was to repeat itself from then on.

Karl Radek, who was born in Lvov in 1885, had been one of the old-guard Bolsheviks, perhaps the most gifted journalist of his generation. He had joined the revolutionary movement at the age of fourteen and ever since had been a faithful Leninist, serving his party in Russia and abroad. His daughter Sonya Radek had been arrested when she was eighteen but miraculously survived a lifetime in the camp. When she was interviewed in 1988 about her father's attitude toward Stalin, she replied: "What a question! He hated and despised him. . . ."[28] What about her father's book *Portraits and Pamphlets*, which was circulated in tens of thousands of copies and in which he had described Stalin as the greatest, wisest, and most benign of all rulers and had described the Soviet Union as a factory for the mass production of heroes? Sonya Radek said that it was bitter and painful to read these pages now; a most gifted and clever publicist had used his talent to sing Stalin's praise.

Radek's pro-Stalinist essays have been singled out by latter-day historians,[29] unfairly, I believe, because virtually everyone else, from Bukharin to Piatakov, behaved in the same way, asking for the death penalty for Zinoviev and Kamenev. In the January 1, 1934, issue of *Pravda*, Radek had written about Stalin as Lenin's best pupil, the model of the Leninist party, personifying the entire historical experience of the party, and as farsighted as Lenin. The article helped to open a new era in the adulation of the leader by former oppositionists.

The second Moscow trial was, in some respects, better prepared than the first; the investigators and the judges had learned from experience. There were still some mishaps: the meeting between one of the accused and Trotsky's son in a Copenhagen hotel that had been demolished many years earlier and Piatakov's flight to Oslo to meet Trotsky, which could not have taken place because there had been no such flights at the time, as the Norwegian government pointed out. But such minor points can be easily glossed over in a totalitarian regime.

The accused of 1937 (the "parallel Trotskyite anti-Soviet center") were rehabilitated fifty-one years after their trial and execution. Two, Radek and Sokolnikov, had been given a ten-year sentence but were killed in the camp in 1939.[30] In 1988, it was conceded that all the defendants had certain merits with regard to the cause of the revolution and socialist reconstruction. Piatakov, after all, had been one of the few mentioned in Lenin's testament. At the time of his arrest, he had been deputy minister of heavy industry; but for his independent line in the 1920s, he would have been minister. Sokolnikov had been the first people's commissar of finance, the architect of the currency reform of 1922–24, and later a deputy minister of foreign affairs. Muralov had been an inspector general of the Red Army. A giant of a man, he was the only one of this group who had been formally rehabilitated under Khrushchev,[31] probably in view of his military background. It clearly made no sense to keep him a nonperson at the time that all other military commanders had been rehabilitated.

Following the rehabilitation in 1988, the party historians were at a loss as to how to treat those who had been "restored to our history."[32] Unlike Bukharin and the others accused in the 1938 show trial, they did not become cult figures; with some exceptions, their writings were not reissued. There were occasional references to their record and achievements, but on the whole, there was the impression that this was out of a feeling of duty rather than genuine enthusiasm.[33] Most of the close relations of those accused had been arrested, but more of the descendants of the second and third trial survived than had been assumed. The most prominent of the survivors was Galina Serebryakova, who was best known as an author of children's books and who had been married first to Serebryakov and later to Sokolnikov; she had returned to Moscow under Khrushchev. Like some other prominent figures, such as Mrs. Karp-Molotov, her faith in the party was unbroken; she remained a conservative figure opposed to the anti-Stalinist thaw.

Those who were the accused in the third right-wing Trotskyite trial of 1938 fared best of all, which of course had to do with the specific political situation in 1988. Some of the minor figures, such as the Central Asians, Ikramov, and Hodzaev, and at least one major figure (Krestinsky) had been cleared already under the first thaw; the rest were reinstated under Gorbachev. The composition of the 1938 trial was curious; among the accused were leading members of the right-wing opposition of the late 1920s who had recanted long before and were readmitted to the party. There were diplomats who had nothing to do with Bukharin and Rykov, party leaders from the periphery, and also some nonpolitical figures, physicians who were charged with having killed some, and had intended to poison other leading figures in the Soviet state and in society.

Bukharin's politics have been discussed in some detail earlier. Khrushchev had tried to rehabilitate him in 1956 but encountered stiff opposition in the Presidium. Certain allegations, such as the charges of treason and terrorism, were tacitly dropped, but in the textbooks Bukharin still appeared negatively. New efforts on the part of his wife and son in the 1970s to have him reinstated were in vain. Nor was there unanimity when, at long last, rehabilitation was accomplished. Neo-Stalinists claimed that Bukharin had never been close to Lenin and had committed many political mistakes. The far Right continued to attack him because of his disdainful attitude toward the pre-1917 Russian patriotic tradition. [34] This he had in common with Lenin, but Lenin could not be attacked. Bukharin, like Trotsky and other old Bolsheviks, had to serve as a scapegoat.

However, despite such opposition, a veritable Bukharin cult developed. His writings were republished, and a full-scale biography was written by an American scholar. [35] "Bukharin clubs" were founded, and conferences were held to honor him on the occasion of his one hundredth birthday. Pride of place was given to the memoirs of Larina, Bukharin's widow. [36] There were many other accounts and references to him; the "favorite of the party" (as stated by Lenin) was again becoming a favorite. True, not all the new revelations did him great credit. Volkogonov published the text of a letter Bukharin had sent, shortly before his arrest, to Voroshilov. Written in an abject tone, he justified the killing of the "dogs" but asked for justice for himself. The author of this letter had been driven half crazy by the attacks against him, and he was not a good student of human character in the first place. How could he have failed to understand with what kind of moral imbeciles Stalin had surrounded himself? Voroshilov returned the letter and demanded not to be bothered with such offensive supplications in the future.[37]

Bukharin's appearance before the Central Committee was less than dignified. He must have known that he was doomed; self-respect as well as a sober assessment of his situation should have induced him to take a more courageous stand, that is, to go under with all flags flying. If he was concerned with his standing as far as future generations of Communists were concerned—and the last letter dictated to his wife points in that direction—he should have behaved as an accuser rather than a pitiable defendant. Trotsky was not remotely as nice a man as Bukharin, but it is unlikely that he would have capitulated in such an abject manner.

Mention has been made of the fact that there was much greater enthusiasm under glasnost for the accused in the third Moscow trial than for those who had appeared in the first and second. The main reason for this has also been adduced: Their ideas were much more aligned with the orientation of the party in the late 1980s.[38] However, the rehabilitation of the victims of the great terror was by no means unanimous, and even during the heyday of glasnost a campaign was launched by neo-Stalinists to prove that the opposition had been "parasitical" all along, forever trying to sabotage the party line.[39]

5. A Murky Affair: The Destruction of the Red Army Command

As the result of the glasnost revelations, much new light has been shed on one of the most mysterious chapters in recent Soviet history—the decapitation of the Red Army high command and officer corps. Preparations for the trial against the Red Army's top commanders were initiated many months before the event, and traces of the plot lead to Paris, Berlin, and Prague. The NKVD was given the assignment of collecting evidence against the marshals and generals both at home and abroad. That forged documents came from Berlin alleging that Marshal Tukhachevsky, commander in chief of the Red Army, was involved with German military circles was first mentioned in 1938–39. It appeared in *I Was Stalin's Agent*, a book by Walter Krivitsky, a high-ranking defector from Stalin's secret service. It was confirmed soon after the war in the Schellenberg memoirs and a book by Wilhelm Höttl, both of whom were leading members of German foreign intelligence. More recently, additional information has come to light from Czech and White Russian sources. Even the names of the forgers and the go-betweens are no longer secret.

Walter Krivitsky writes that Skoblin, a White Russian general residing in Paris, was the man at the center of the NKVD conspiracy against Tukhachevsky and the other generals. Stalin, he says, knew that the "evidence" provided was disinformation of the rawest kind and that General Miller (Skoblin's boss, chairman of the émigré officers association) had to be liquidated because he was the only man who could expose the intrigue to the whole world. Although this specific assertion seems unlikely, the general information about the plot seems correct and has since been confirmed by various other sources.[1]

The question arises whether material incriminating the Red Army was actually planted in Paris by the NKVD on Stalin's order or whether this occurred quite independently, by way of some private initiative. The Russian émigré organizations did, after all, engage in political warfare against the U.S.S.R. and disseminated all kinds of disinformation. Were the stories about an anti-Stalin military plot the work of an enterprising journalist? For a long time, some Western authors have believed in the existence of a military conspiracy.[2]

After all, it was a period of constant ferment and trouble in Moscow. During the purge, with leaders disappearing regularly or being unmasked as "enemies of the people," almost anything seemed possible. Among those who, even in later years, were convinced that there had been a conspiracy were such public figures as Winston Churchill—although, after Khrushchev's speech at the Twentieth Party Congress in 1956, the issue should have been regarded as closed.

The alleged existence of a plot among Soviet marshals and generals was mentioned more than once in the émigré press before 1937, particularly in right-wing journals. A story proclaiming this ran in several installments in the Prague *Znamia Rossii* during the first months of 1936, and, in Paris, *Vozroshdenie* announced that Marshal Tukhachevsky had been a German agent ever since he had been a German prisoner of war in World War I.[3]

Who were the authors of the articles? And who inspired them? One of the instigators was General Count Ignatiev, the last tsarist military attaché in Paris, who was soon to return to the Soviet Union, where, under Stalin, he became something of a celebrity. Another informant was Kotypin-Liubsky, whom a French investigating magistrate described as an agent of the Soviet secret service, a contemptible character, *une cynique crapule*, who openly sold any information he could lay his hands on. The magistrate described him in almost poetic terms: "*La provocation est sa volupté physique.*"

This creature had wormed his way into the confidence of Vladimir Burtsev, once the grand inquisitor and chief detective of the Russian revolutionary movements: He had unmasked countless tsarist agents, including the notorious Azev and the Bolshevik Malinovsky. But Burtsev had become old and gullible, and he fell victim to the confidence trickster.[4] Last, there was N. N. Alekseev, author of the article in *Vozroshdenie*. He was another NKVD agent—a *stukach* ("informant and provocateur") in the words of Roman Gul, who published a vehement reply in the same journal on February 16, 1936.[5] As Walter Krivitsky boasted, the resident agent of the NKVD could publish in the right-wing *Vozrosh-denie* whatever material he wanted.

Yet another relevant article, "The Soviet Union on the Road to Bona-partism," appeared in the semiofficial German military journal *Deutsche Wehr*, but only after the event. Its author had no doubt that Tukhachev-sky had indeed plotted against Stalin but was betrayed at the very last moment. His article, which attracted much attention and was widely translated and disseminated, was signed by one "A. Agricola"—none other than Russian-born Alexander Gustavovich Bauermeister, who, dur-ing World War I, was the most effective German spy master on the Eastern Front.

Agricola said that every true Soviet expert knew that the conspiracy had not been just a matter of espionage; it aspired to be a truly enormous military coup. The commanders of the most important military districts were involved in the plot. Tukhachevsky had made his first preparations in 1935, and zero hour was fixed for June 1937. Only because of General Skoblin's betrayal had the coup been averted.

Agricola's article greatly puzzled Western observers. If the allegations were true, why did the Germans reveal what should have been a closely guarded secret? Was the rivalry between the army and the Gestapo? Did the Germans want to dissociate themselves from Skoblin? But there is a simpler explanation. Skoblin's involvement in the whole affair had been mentioned before—for instance, by Walter Krivitsky in articles published in the émigré press before his famous book appeared. Agricola had ob-viously read the articles.

The campaign against Tukhachevsky was prepared and orchestrated by the NKVD, and it is impossible that it could have been done without the knowledge of Stalin. Volkogonov has not been able to shed new light on this specific aspect of the affair. In an interview, he complained that after the Twentieth Party Congress many files had been removed from the archives of the Soviet Ministry of Defense and from army archives. As for the NKVD archives, Volkogonov clearly had no access to them.[6] After Volkogonov's book had been published, someone high up in the Soviet hierarchy decided that the veil of secrecy should be lifted, at least in part; as a result, it was revealed that General Skoblin, far from being a Nazi agent, had actually been a Soviet spy since 1930, when he had been recruited, together with his wife. The revelations contained many inter-esting details about "Mr. and Mrs. Farmer" (the code names given to the

Skoblins by the NKVD), including verbatim reports sent from Paris. On one issue, alas, the veil was not lifted, and it happened to be the most important one—Skoblin's involvement in the preparation of the case against the Red Army command.[7]

The second source of disinformation was Heydrich and his SS (secret service). Throughout 1936, President Beneš and other Czech leaders had been approached by various informants who told them that Soviet generals were conspiring against Stalin. These sources included both Russians and White Russian émigrés, German double agents (Dr. Wittig, for example), German diplomats such as Count Trautmannsdorf, Nazi leaders like Hermann Goering, and the head of the Gestapo, Heinrich Müller. The handing over of forged documents implicated Tukhachevsky; they had been prepared by the Gestapo, with the help of White Russian émigrés.

The plan was apparently Skoblin's, or to be precise, because Skoblin was not an "ideas man," it must have been inspired by people behind Skoblin. He had met Heydrich in Berlin. We do not know the date of the Heydrich-Skoblin meeting or the exact date of the transmission of the incriminating material, but it probably took place sometime in February 1937. Beneš hesitated for several weeks, but then, between April 26 and May 4, 1937, he had four meetings with the Soviet ambassador in Prague, together with Krofta, the foreign minister, and handed over the evidence.[8]

Beneš was no doubt convinced that his decision was the only proper one and that the Soviet leaders would be extremely grateful to him. But he was no Soviet expert and in no position to judge whether the material that had been handed to him was at all credible. He might, however, have asked himself why the Germans, who were in no way amicably disposed toward Czechoslovakia, should have chosen him as a conduit.

Even if Beneš had been utterly convinced of the authenticity of the forgeries—even if he had been able to think of a satisfactory explanation as to why the Nazis were using him as their chosen instrument—it could still be argued that he should not have acted as middleman. For the very survival of Czechoslovakia rested on the existence of the Paris-Prague-Moscow axis, and anything likely to weaken Czechoslovakia's partners was bound to weaken the Czech prospects of survival. This was precisely the result of the purges of 1937. But for at least another year Beneš continued to believe that he had done a great service to his country and its allies.

Marshal Tukhachevsky and Generals Yakir, Kork, Uborevich, and the other Red Army commanders were arrested on various dates during May 1937. In June, they were brought to a secret trial—although the term "trial" is inappropriate, because the accused were given no opportunity to defend themselves. The accusations were irrelevant. Tukhachevsky and most of the others were charged with having plotted with the Germans. But this was not much publicized, for Stalin himself was beginning at that time to explore whether there was common ground for a pact with Hitler. Within two years of the trial, a pact was signed. It was probably for this reason that no public use was made of the "evidence" received from Paris, Berlin, and Prague, because this could have caused political complications.

In later years, some authors have argued that Stalin did not need elaborate "evidence" from abroad, received in a roundabout, complicated way. Would it not have been sufficient had he claimed that Tukhachevsky and Co. had conspired to kill him, together with Voroshilov and other members of the Politburo? Was it not too risky to involve forgeries from foreign sources that could one day be exposed?

True enough, but Stalin was never a straightforward operator, and complicated intrigues seldom deterred him. Why, in the end, he should have made little, if any, use of the Skoblin-Heydrich-Beneš material remains yet another mystery. But it was standard procedure, as we know now from the revelations that have occurred under glasnost, that Soviet security organs had instructions to collect evidence against virtually everyone in Stalin's entourage. This did not mean that everyone was purged and shot, however.

After Khrushchev's "secret speech," it became the practice to accuse Stalin of murdering the "flower of the Red Army." At the same time, mitigating circumstances were adduced: Stalin had fallen victim to the forgeries of the Nazi secret service. Some argued that Stalin was a great believer in written evidence. But there were thousands of documents that Stalin ignored; for example, those telling him of an impending German attack in June 1941. Above all, it has been known for a long time that the first arrests (of General Putna and Primakov) took place almost a year before the Nazi forgeries reached the Kremlin. Furthermore, Tukhachevsky had already been incriminated during the second Moscow show trial of former leading Bolsheviks (G. L. Piatakov, K. B. Radek, et al.), which took place in early 1937.

In brief, the "gullible Stalin" version seems most unlikely.[9] Even the editors of the official Soviet history of "the great fatherlandic war" could not make up their mind in this respect. The East German edition (1962) claims that Stalin fell victim to a diabolical provocation by the Fascist secret service. In the original Russian, this passage is missing.[10]

The doubts have been reinforced by General Pavlenko, a leading military historian and former editor of *Military-Historical Archives*. He stated in an interview that Stalin began to undermine Tukhachevsky's position as early as 1930 and that the organs of state security began preparations for the trial of Soviet generals nine months before the German forgeries reached Moscow. Pavlenko had it on the authority of Major General Golushkevich (who was present at the 1937 trial) that the Heydrich documents were never once brought up in the course of the proceedings. General Pavlenko believed that Stalin's ill will toward Tukhachevsky, who was too gifted and had become too popular for Stalin's taste, was nourished by various denunciations made by Klim Voroshilov, the people's commissar of defense and an old rival of Tukhachevsky's. Stalin knew what the sensationalist foreign press was writing about Tukhachevsky, whom they had chosen for the role of a "red Bonaparte." But, Pavlenko continues,

> Stalin was not so naive as to swallow this very ordinary bait, of the sort that can be found in all elementary textbooks on intelligence. . . . Stalin would have carried out his sinister design (he managed to kill more senior officers of the Red Army than Hitler) even without the notorious forgery. After all, although there were no more such forgeries after the Tukhachevsky affair, the repressions continued with renewed vigor.

Pavlenko quotes an entry from the diary of the chief of the German general staff, Franz Halder. It is dated May 5, 1941: "The Russian officer corps makes a very bad impression, much worse than in 1933. They need twenty years to recover their previous level according to the impressions of Krebs [military attaché in Moscow in 1941]."

What induced Stalin to have certain commanders killed and to spare others, we do not know. The prospects for survival of the more gifted and independent minded were the dimmest. However, that a great many mediocrities and toadies were also executed does not really clarify the situation. Some of the answers will perhaps come to light; others may remain shrouded in mystery forever because the secret files have been destroyed or because there were never any documents in the first place.[11]

Was Stalin not afraid that he might dangerously weaken the Soviet armed forces as the result of killing most of the commanders? Here again, it is unlikely that we shall find answers in the archives. Obviously the issue did not figure very high on Stalin's scale of priorities. He must have thought the outbreak of war quite likely at the time; otherwise, he would have ceased to invest so heavily in the defense industry. He probably thought that marshals, generals, and admirals were expendable, "mere cogs in a wheel," to use his famous phrase. After all, he never thought very highly of the military profession; if he could be the *generalissimus* and Marshal Voroshilov could be people's commissar of defense, others could command armies and divisions without much preparation.

Did he really believe that military leaders who had never conspired against him and were personally devoted to him constituted a potential danger? We shall have to return to this question in another context.

The purge played a greater havoc on the military command than on any other segment of society. According to a survey by General Todorsky undertaken in the Khrushchev era, the great majority of senior officers were arrested, and most of them were killed; virtually all military district commanders and army commanders were shot. According to a report by Voroshilov in 1938, some 40,000 officers were affected; according to Volkogonov, writing in 1988, it was 43,000. Volkogonov notes in passing that although during World War II some thousand Soviet generals were killed, more perished in peacetime under Stalin. According to Todorsky, 3 out of 5 marshals, 15 out of 16 army commanders, 60 out of 67 corps commanders, and 136 out of 199 divisional commanders were murdered.[12]

Even slightly higher figures with regard to the military victims of the purges were given by Colonel Korenblat in 1989, who lays a great deal of the blame on Voroshilov.[13] A writer in the semiofficial *Voenny Vestnik*, on the other hand, argues that the losses were smaller than quoted by other recent authors. Although 37,000 officers were discharged for political reasons between 1937 and 1939, based on figures contained in a report by Yefim Shchadenko, deputy people's commissar for defense, delivered on May 5, 1940, more than 10,000 were reinstated prior to 1940. According to Colonel Borodin, only 10 percent of regiment commanders, 26 percent of division commanders, and 27 percent of corps commanders (compared with 90 percent given by Todorov and 93 percent quoted by Korenblat) are said to have perished. The lower figure mentioned by Borodin could perhaps be explained with reference to the framework of time: Todorsky and others refer to the Red Army command staff as of 1937, whereas Borodin takes January 1, 1941, as his starting point. Between these two dates, of course, many new appointments and promotions had been made. Kornilov, too, concludes that the top commanders were hardest hit and that the damage was truly irreparable.[14]

Their fate figured prominently in Khrushchev's secret speech, in which he reported such details as Yakir shouting "Long live Stalin" as he faced the firing squad. In the 1950s all those who had been murdered in the 1930s were rehabilitated. A few survivors were released from the camps; several had already been freed in 1940–41, such as Gorbatov, Rokossovksy, and Meretskov, who rose to fame during the war. Commemorative articles and books were devoted to these national heroes. Among those rehabilitated were also the senior commanders of the period of the civil war who had left the army in the 1920s as well as senior officers arrested between 1938 and 1941, of whom there were not a few. Thus, the second thaw added little but some personal memoirs, such as interviews with Tukhachevsky's younger sister, Elizaveta (the rest of the family had perished in the camps), and with the daughters of Gamarnik, Smushkevich, Feldman, and Uborevich. Male members of the families were almost all killed; one exception was Piotr Yakir, another Anton Antonov-Ovseenko.

But the revelations of the 1950s and 1960s did not delve into the deeper issues involved; they remained too hot to handle. Although many commanders contemptuously denied the absurd charges against them, others confessed and turned against their comrades. Among them was General Primakov, commander of the Red Cossacks in the civil war, the recipient of three Orders of the Red Banner. He named no less than seventy senior officers who he said had been members of the "military-fascist conspiracy." In his final speech, Primakov said, "Neither in the history of our country nor in the history of other revolutions had there ever been such a plot, as far as its extent, means, and ends are concerned. Who was united under Trotsky's Fascist banner? All the counterrevolutionary elements rallied under that banner. What means did this conspiracy use? High treason, the defeat of their own country, sabotage, espionage and terror."[15] How does one explain Primakov's behavior? Perhaps it was that he had been in prison for a year, whereas the other accused generals had been arrested just two weeks earlier.

There had also been denunciations against the most senior officers on the part of the brigade generals and the colonels.[16] Worse yet, the names of Marshal Blyukher and of Generals Dybenko, Belov, and Alksnis appear on the death sentences of their own comrades handed down in June 1937 by the military tribunals. How could they have given their hand to this bloody farce? And if they had lacked civic courage, was it right to rehabilitate victims and executioners alike just because Blyukher, Dybenko, Belov, and Alksnis were arrested and shot a year later? This caused heated debates, and though it could always be claimed that they had acted under tremendous pressure, a bitter aftertaste remained.

The Old Bolsheviks

The defendants in the Moscow show trials represented only the tip of the iceberg. The "purge" affected millions of others who disappeared without any publicity whatsoever. They were taken from their homes, their place of work, from a meeting, or in the middle of a lecture. Most of them were posthumously rehabilitated during the first thaw. Precisely because there had been little publicity in the first place, it was easier for the authorities to rehabilitate them. Among them were members of the Politburo, such as Rudzutak, who was arrested in his dacha in the middle of a conversation with a group of painters; there were such old Bolsheviks as Vladimir Nevsky, who had joined the party in 1897 and had served as people's commissar for communication and later as head of the Communist Academy. As his daughter wrote in later years, Nevsky had been arrested eleven times under the tsar, but only the twelfth arrest under Stalin proved to be fatal. Another such case was Andrei Bubnov, formerly people's commissar of education and former head of the political directorate of the Red Army. His daughter Elena, an art historian, got off relatively lightly; although accused of planning a terrorist act against Stalin, she received a seven-and-a-half-year prison sentence and, after her release from prison, lifelong exile in a remote location.[17]

Alexander Shliapnikov had been people's commissar in the very first Soviet government and, subsequently, one of the first oppositionists. He had been out of politics for a long time but was arrested in 1935 and shot in 1937. Most of his family survived the camps, and after their release they fought to clear his name. He was rehabilitated in 1963, but the decision was not made public until 1988. As far as the public at large was concerned, Shliapnikov continued to be an enemy of the people.[18]

The fate of two old-guard Bolsheviks, Antonov-Ovseenko and Fyodor Raskolnikov, was particularly interesting. Both played a role of importance in the military uprising of 1917. The former was responsible for the seizure of the Winter Palace (and the arrest of the provisional government), and Raskolnikov, a naval officer, headed the mutinous Kronstadt sailors in 1917. Both were delegated to represent their country abroad, Antonov-Ovseenko in Czechoslovakia and Poland, Raskolnikov in Afghanistan, Estonia, Denmark, Bulgaria, and, finally, in Spain during the civil war. Both were recalled to Moscow in 1937, but whereas Antonov-Ovseenko dutifully returned and was almost immediately executed, Raskolnikov refused to obey and published a public letter to Stalin in which he accused the tyrant of mass murder and betrayal of the cause of communism. Both were rehabilitated in the wake of the first thaw, but Raskolnikov was again "dehabilitated" in 1969, following Khrushchev's fall and as a result of the strong resentment of such neo-Stalinist historians as Trapetsnikov.[19]

Under glasnost both leaders again came into their own. When Antonov-Ovseenko's son returned to Moscow after many years in camps, he devoted his life to the writing of biographies—of his father, of Stalin, and of Beria. Some of his writings appeared abroad and, after 1987, also in the Soviet Union. Even more attention was given to the memory of Raskolnikov; his widow, a professor at Strasbourg University, revisited Moscow, and his daughter studied for a while in a Soviet university. The "open letter to Stalin" had been circulated in the Soviet Union in samizdat for years; in 1987, it was featured in the Soviet media, much to the chagrin of the neo-Stalinists, who continued to consider him a traitor.[20]

Last, the case of Mikhail Koltsov, one of the most famous Soviet journalists of the 1930s and an ardent Stalinist. Returning from the front of the Spanish civil war, he was given an audience by Stalin. Soon after, he disappeared, to be rehabilitated twenty years later under Khrushchev. Interesting details came to light under glasnost: Koltsov's brother Boris

Efimov, perhaps the leading Soviet cartoonist of the day, was seen by Ulrich, the chief prosecutor, who revealed that Koltsov had been sentenced to ten years in a remote camp without the right to write or receive letters. The meeting took place many months after Koltsov's execution, but Efimov did not know what "deprivation of the right of correspondence" meant. He continued to hope, as did so many others. Major A. T. Rybin, who served in Stalin's personal guard unit, related in 1988 that when Stalin first received an oral denunciation of Koltsov, he refused to believe it. But, soon after, when he was handed the same information in writing, he issued orders for Koltsov's arrest. Several sources relate that Stalin was a glutton for written information and tended to believe such evidence more than the spoken word.[21] It seems highly dubious, however, because in those days virtually everyone was denounced by someone else but not everyone was executed. If there was some method to this madness, there was also much that was accidental.

Almost all military leaders who had perished in the great purge were rehabilitated, but hardly anyone from among the secret police officials. The massacres took place under three people's commissars of the interior—Yagoda, Ezhov, and Beria. All three were executed, albeit Beria after a long and regrettable delay. Yagoda had been people's commissar since 1929, and although torture and extortion were introduced under his leadership, he was instrumental only in the preparation of the first Moscow trial. Stalin distrusted him, and perhaps rightly so, for although he fulfilled his orders, he seems to have acted without enthusiasm. Soon after the Zinoviev-Kamenev trial, he was dismissed and, the year after, arrested. He figured among the accused in the Bukharin trial and was the only one accused in the 1938 trial not to be rehabilitated in 1988.

Yagoda's case presented the authorities with a serious dilemma, because he was obviously responsible for the murder of many innocent people. But he was not guilty of the specific crimes for which he was charged at the time. The correct course of action would have been to clear him of the trumped-up charges of 1938 while at the same time charging him with the crimes of which he really had been guilty. But the Politburo of 1988 did not believe in posthumous trials, and it is easy to see why: It would have been tantamount to opening a Pandora's box. Why charge Yagoda and not the man who had given him the instructions?[22]

Yagoda was succeeded by Nikolai Ezhov, under whose leadership and active participation (he took part in the interrogation of prisoners) the purge reached its climax. He had previously been a member of Stalin's secretariat; a man small by stature and of no outstanding gifts except his devotion to his master. Like his successor, Beria, he seems to have been quite apolitical, even though his contemporaries praised him in the most extravagant terms as a true Bolshevik, a man of iron, of great intelligence, enormous vigilance, and so forth, for everyone was afraid of him. Everyone, that is, but Stalin, who seems to have despised him; according to Volkogonov, Ezhov was an alcoholic, and Stalin took a dim view of people who had no self-discipline. The explanation might be correct, but there is no certainty. Ezhov's drunkenness did not interfere with the execution of his duties. It is more likely that once most of the dirty work had been done, Stalin wanted a new face to head the security apparatus. On December 7, 1938, Ezhov was deposed and became people's commissar of water transport; he was arrested early in the new year. (For Yagoda, the stepping-stone to the cellars of the Lubyanka had been the ministry of communications.) Even under glasnost, neither the exact charges against Ezhov nor the date and place of his execution became known. According to rumor, he became clinically mad under interrogation, but even Stalin's official biographer failed to turn up any documentary evidence. Ezhov, as well as his family, disappeared, and those who possessed the relevant files refused to let anyone see them.

With Yagoda and Ezhov, a whole generation of highly placed Chekists disappeared. It happened not infrequently that those confined in the main prisons and camps sooner or later would welcome their investigators as cellmates.

All this caused considerable distress to the KGB in later years. All other institutions had their histories rewritten and heroes reinstalled; only the security services had no one to look back to with admiration, except for the founder, Dzerzhinski, who had died in the mid-twenties. Attempts were made to find at least some blameless minor figures who could serve as models. Thus, the reputations of some old Chekists, such as Peters, Latsis, Boky, Trilisser, Messing, Deribas and Kedrov, were refurbished. All had been old Bolsheviks, all had served under Dzerzhinski, and, with few exceptions, they had left the security services in the 1920s, taking jobs in the economic section or in the party. The exceptions were Deribas and Boky.[23] But Deribas had served as head of the NKVD in the Far East, far from the center of action, and Boky, too, was not prominently involved in the terror of the 1930s. In addition, a few local police chiefs outside Moscow were rehabilitated. But, by and large, the whole period from the early 1930s onward remained blotted out from memory. Worse yet, as the result of the evidence of the survivors who returned from the camps, the names of chief "investigators," such as Ushakov, Rodos, and Shvartsman, became known.

Some of them were arrested, brought to secret trial, and shot after 1956; others survived. Their defense, broadly speaking, was very similar to that used by war criminals who were brought to trial in Germany after 1945: They had merely obeyed orders; so great was Stalin's prestige, so unlimited his power, that resistance was unthinkable. Such a defense, in turn, triggered passionate discussions as to whether the torturers and executioners of 1936–39 should be brought to trial. If there had been no amnesty for crimes against humanity committed by the Nazis, why have an amnesty in the Soviet Union?[24]

Purges Far from Moscow

It was frequently thought that the purges were, in the main, limited to Moscow and Leningrad and, more specifically, to leading party and state officials residing there. But the revelations under glasnost demonstrated that the terror had raged in all the Soviet republics and had affected every segment of the population. Under the first thaw, many rehabilitations in various parts of the country had taken place, but a general picture had only emerged under glasnost.

A few examples will have to suffice: Virtually the entire leadership of the Central Asian republics was purged, but many members of the intelligentsia were also killed, as were simple people, who, for one reason or another, had been selected as victims. The victims included old Bolsheviks like Isaac Zelensky, a party member since 1906 who had been active in Tashkent since 1924. He was picked as a codefendant in the Bukharin trial; according to Vyshinsky, he had been a tsarist spy, only one of many charges against him. Elsewhere, as in Kazakhstan, Kirghizia, and the Caucasus, leading cadres and intellectuals were executed because of alleged right-wing nationalist separatism. A typical case was that of Akmal Ikramov, first party secretary in Uzbekistan, also a codefendant in the Bukharin trial. His son survived the camps and wrote a detailed and moving account of the "case of my father."[25] In the Ukraine, the Komsomol was decapitated several times over. In some of the smaller Caucasian autonomous republics, the majority of the local intelligentsia was arrested and killed.

The charge leveled was very often espionage on behalf of a foreign power in accordance with the geographic location: Thus, residents of Odessa would be accused of being Romanian agents; those in White Russia had allegedly cooperated with the Poles; in the Far East, a link with the Japanese was frequently found; and those in Central Asia and the Caucasus were said to work for the British.

That the suspect had once talked for five minutes to a visiting delegation from the United States, Turkey, or Germany was sufficient cause to accuse him of being an agent of one of those countries. And if the person had not talked, he would of course, be even more suspect. The initiative for a purge would come from Moscow; a member of the Politburo, such as Zhdanov, Kaganovich, Malenkov, or Molotov, or a secretary of the Central Committee would visit the city and complain that the local cadres were not showing sufficient vigilance, whereupon arrests and executions would begin. There seems to have been an unwritten law that everywhere in the Soviet Union a certain percentage of the population were bound to be enemies of the people.[26] The rest was left to local security organs headed by men such as Jafar Bagirov in Baku, Beria's trusted aide who was executed in July 1956.[27]

Individual cases quite apart, there were mass executions of people who had not been charged with any crime. In the Rainai Forest in Latvia, the graves of political prisoners were discovered; near Kiev, in the Bykovnya Forest, there was a mass grave of 6,329 Soviet soldiers and partisans; in November 1988, it was suddenly made known that Soviets—not Fascist occupants—had killed them.[28] There were many other such cases, the most widely publicized of which was Kuropaty near Minsk: The lowest estimate gave a figure of 30,000 victims; the highest, 300,000. White Russia had been heavily hit by the collectivization campaign in 1933, when many villagers had been arrested and deported; the second wave of arrests, in 1937–38, left whole villages depopulated.

In May 1988, two local schoolboys discovered a number of skeletons in a recreation area just outside the capital of White Russia. Even earlier, a group of local archaeologists and historians, following reports by villagers in the vicinity, had been searching for mass graves. The first article on the subject appeared in early June 1988, and to quote a Soviet commentator, it came as a bombshell.[29] The diggings continued. At first the remains of twenty-three bodies were found, then fifteen in another site. Eventually it emerged that many thousands of corpses had been buried there in layers separated by ten inches of sand. At the end of the war, many corpses had been exhumed by Soviet soldiers, but they had not exhumed the bottom layer. Although various circumstances point to the fact that many victims hailed from White Russia, there was also evidence that thousands from the Baltic republics had also been buried in Kuropaty. According to Pozniak, our main source (and a deputy of the Supreme Soviet in 1989), the total figure could well have been in excess of 300,000. Some of the NKVD personnel involved at the time were still alive, and old people from neighboring villages also gave evidence. Altogether, more than 200 witnesses were interrogated, but written evidence of the burials could not be found: It had either been destroyed before or during the war or it was in the archives of the state security organs. A government investigation committee was appointed, but mass meetings that had been planned to honor the memory of the victims were banned.[30]

There was much reason to assume that Kuropaty was not a singular case; in Minsk, yet another mass grave was found. Excavations there proved to be difficult because a garage and other installations had been constructed over the site. In brief, Kuropaty was not an exception, and, as Vasil Bykov, the leading White Russian writer and member of the investigation committee, put it, there were powerful forces still actively trying to cover up the crimes of the Stalinist era: "They understand that if the people should begin to cross all the T's and dot all the I's this could serve as an example for the discovery of the other such crimes."[31] One of the most striking aspects of the whole affair was that the secret had been kept for so long, although the burial site was not in sparsely populated Siberia or Kazakhstan but in the suburbs of a city with a million inhabitants. Although thousands of people must have seen and heard what went on in the forest of Kuropaty, the secret had been kept for fifty years.

The authorities in Minsk apparently wanted to keep the secret forever. There were attempts to prevent the publication of articles; participants in meetings commemorating the victims were photographed by the local organs of state security and, in some instances, interrogated and even arrested. Pozniak, the man who had contributed more than any other to uncovering and publicizing the Kuropaty murders, was elected president of the Belorussian Popular Front (Adradzhenie). But the first full meeting of this organization had to take place in neighboring Lithuania because the authorities in Minsk would not have it. It was a bitter irony that a region that had suffered more than most during the great terror acquired the reputation of a Soviet Vendée, one of the most resistant to glasnost and to change.[32]

6. Purges Everywhere

As the result of the many publications during the glasnost period, certain clear patterns have emerged with regard to the character and extent of the purges. As far as physical survival was concerned, Soviet culture fared better than the Red Army under the terror; many more writers, painters, scientists, and composers survived than marshals and generals. True, the price of survival meant accepting the strictest regimentation, making creative work virtually impossible. However, many leading figures survived the Stalinist era and resumed work in a later, more relaxed period.

But some of the most outstanding writers, poets, and playwrights did not survive, and it took many years even to realize the extent of the disaster. Unlike the ministers and generals, the poets and playwrights were not brought to trial; they were arrested and disappeared. By 1950, even foreign experts on Soviet literature did not know what had happened to a leading writer like Isaac Babel, who had been translated into many languages, or to Osip Mandelstam, one of Russia's greatest poets. It was known that they were no longer published, and works of reference did not mention them. No one could say for certain whether they were in labor camps, had perhaps died during the war, or lived somewhere in exile. Frequently, even their closest relations did not know. Sometimes there were rumors, perhaps deliberately spread by the authorities, that they were still alive even though they had been shot more than ten years earlier. Mandelstam had once written an epigram deriding Stalin, and Budyonni, the famous civil war military leader, had not liked the stories of Babel. Boris Pilnyak was the author of a famous story in which the death of a military commander (Frunze) was imputed to the intrigues of a politician; this was read by many as a condemnation of Stalin. But the cases in which a political motive, however slight, could be established were an exception. Stalin had probably never heard of a single Bashkir or Udmurt writer, living far from the capital, yet virtually all of them were wiped out. The same was true with regard to the literature of the Altai people and the northern Caucasians, such as the Ossetine. Many Ukrainian, White Russian, Armenian, and Azerbaijani writers were murdered. After the purge elsewhere had come to a halt, all the leading Yiddish-language writers were still being arrested and killed.

When rehabilitation began in the late 1950s, a figure of 600–625 writers was mentioned.[1] Eduard Beltov, a journalist who began to investigate the fate of Soviet writers, initially thought the number exaggerated. But when he had concluded his investigations thirty years later, he realized that the true figure was in excess of a thousand.[2]

Those who had perished included writers and poets well known in the Soviet Union and the West, such as Serge Tretiakov, Artem Vesoli, Nikolai Zabolotsky, Tarasov-Rodionov, Bruno Yasenski, Ivan Kataev, and Pavel Vasilev. They also included critics, essayists, literary historians, playwrights, editors, producers, actors, as well as some of the most famous directors of theaters in the world, such as Meyerhold. Many had been party members, but there were an equally large number who had never been Communists. There were working-class writers who had belonged to the Proletkult group, but there were as many writers of peasant origins. Many members of the RAPP (Association of Proletarian Writers) faction (the orthodoxy of the 1920s) disappeared, but almost an equal number of the "liberal" Pereval group, the "Akmeists," and former members of the Kuznets group also disappeared.

There was no detectable pattern or motive in the selection of the victims; of the RAPP leadership, Averbach and Kirshon were executed as enemies of the people, while their colleagues Fadeev and Ermilov became the literary dictators of "high" (between 1935 and 1953) Stalinism. The Pereval group was virtually wiped out, but Andrei Platonov miraculously survived and attained great posthumous fame. Most of those arrested were executed soon after, but a few were released after a year or two in prison (such as Olga Berggolts) or, more often, after Stalin's death.

Boris Pasternak was never arrested, even though he had written Bukharin expressing his sympathy at a time when such behavior was tantamount to suicide. Koltsov, the most faithful Stalinist, personally well known to the leader, was accused of having served no less than three espionage services (German, French, and American) as well as having been a Trotskyite since 1923 and a terrorist since 1932. One of the main charges against Koltsov was that his brother, Professor Fridlender, dean of the Department of History at Moscow State University, had been shot as an enemy of the people. Soon it emerged that Fridlender was no relation of Koltsov's and that his real brother, Boris Efimov, was at liberty. But this did not make the slightest difference as far as Koltsov's fate was concerned.[3]

The trials invariably took twenty minutes or less; Koltsov withdrew all his confessions, claiming they had been extracted following protracted torture. On the same day Koltsov was shot (February 2, 1940), they also killed Meyerhold, who was in his sixties. He had been tortured for seven months; his left arm had been broken, the right one, his investigator said, was needed to sign the confession. Meyerhold had admitted that he had spied for both the British and the Japanese.[4] There was a curious twist to his case inasmuch as the interrogators made him confess that his spy master had been the special correspondent of *Izvestiia* in Paris, Ilya Erenburg. According to this and other evidence extracted, Erenburg was also the controller of Pasternak and other famous writers.

Babel was compelled to make a similar confession; the group of Trotskyites and terrorists to whom he belonged was again headed by Ilya Erenburg; other members included Shostakovich, André Malraux, Eisenstein, Leonid Leonov, and many other leading figures.[5]

Meyerhold and Babel were shot, but Erenburg—the great spy master—returned to Moscow and lived out his days without major inconvenience. And other leading cultural figures were similarly untouched despite their implication in the trials.

How to explain these grotesque incongruencies? In part, it was sheer ignorance. The interrogators often did not know with whom they were dealing. When the notorious Rodos, who had tortured Babel, was arrested after Stalin's death, he was asked by one of the judges, "Do you know what Babel's profession was?" Rodos replied: "I was told he was a writer. . . ." "Did you read a single line of his books?" "What for?" Rodos replied. But ignorance can explain the events of 1936–40 only in part. It stands to reason that the organizers of the purges were collecting incriminating material against every major and many minor figures so that, when necessary, they could be immediately arrested and charged.

The great purge did not ignore any cultural discipline, although painters, composers, actors, and singers happened to be of less interest to

Stalin and the organs of state security than writers and playwrights. Stalin read a great deal, but he seldom, if ever, went to a concert or an exhibition. He saw many movies, but few filmmakers were shot. Science, too, was beyond Stalin's immediate preoccupation, and one might assume that scientists would therefore escape lightly, but this was not so.

The party sciences (philosophy, history, economics) were under close scrutiny, and many leading figures of the 1920s fell victim to the great purge. But the natural sciences and even technology were not bypassed.

The most notorious case was that of genetics, a discipline that was banned altogether. Even after Stalin's death, it took a long time for this branch of science to be rehabilitated, because Khrushchev, like Stalin, had a great weakness for Lysenko, who promised to work miracles in agricultural yields. In November 1987, the centenary of the birth of Nikolai Vavilov was celebrated in the Soviet Union, as in the rest of the world. He had been the most outstanding Soviet biologist, the first president of the All-Union Academy of Agricultural Sciences, and also the most prominent victim of the antigenetics purge. He was arrested in late July 1940, accused of espionage as well as sabotage, and died (apparently of starvation) in a prison in Saratov in late 1942. He was buried in a common grave for criminals.[6]

At the time of the hundredth anniversary of Vavilov's birth, his NKVD interrogator, Alexander Khvat, was still alive. Journalists asked him whether he ever thought that Vavilov was guilty. He answered: "I didn't believe the spying charges, of course—there was no proof. As for sabotage—he was doing something in a strange direction in science. . . ."

Vavilov was rehabilitated soon after Stalin's death, but it took a much longer time for the whole scandalous history of the destruction of Soviet genetics to emerge. As one scientist noted in 1988, "It is no accident that the works on this subject by Mark Popovsky, Zh. Medvedev, and S. Reznik have been published abroad but not in the Soviet Union. . . . Abroad, the history of Soviet genetics and biology is better known than in our own country."[7]

That the historical circumstances of the rise and fall of Lysenko remained shrouded in mystery gave rise to all kinds of strange theories, even under glasnost. Thus, one spokesman of the extreme Right, Vadim Kozhinov, interpreted the rise of Lysenkoism as yet another manifestation of a worldwide Judaeo-Masonic plot. Was it not true that Lysenko had been a mere tool in the hands of such (Jewish) wire-pullers as philosophers Present and Deborin? That many of the repressed victims of the purge (Agol, Levit, and others) were also "rootless cosmopolitans" was considered a matter of no consequence.[8]

As in other fields, such novelists as V. Dudintsev (*White Coats*) and V. Amlinsky, with their romans à clef, were both quicker and more courageous in revealing the truth than the professionals. Too many vested interests impeded the revelation of the whole truth.

The Soviet system could function, if necessary, without poets and novelists, but given the growing danger of war, one should have assumed that every effort would be made to strengthen its defensive capacity. However, the chief designers and constructors of the armament industry were hit by the purge as strongly as other branches of science and technology, if not more so. Andrei Nikolaevich Tupolev was the leading Soviet aircraft designer of the day; his planes had established seventy-eight world records, he had received five Stalin Prizes, and he was a hero of Socialist Labor three times over. All this did not prevent his arrest in October 1937. He was threatened with the most dire of consequences for his wife (who was arrested in any case) and his children. As a result, he confessed after a mere five days that he had been a French spy since 1924. Subsequently, he withdrew most of the confession but was given a fifteen-year sentence, anyway.[9]

However, French spy or not, he still could not be spared, and because a great many other experts were also in prison, he received a laboratory to design a new bomber. He stayed there four years and was pardoned a few weeks after the Nazi invasion. For his full rehabilitation, he had to wait another fourteen years. Tupolev was lucky in comparison with Korolev, the leading Soviet missile designer, who had been arrested at about the same time and remained in a camp almost to the end of the war. Many leading figures of the Soviet aircraft industry were shot soon after their arrest. Those who survived were eventually reintegrated into the war effort and duly collected further state prizes and other awards.

In a few cases, Stalin and Beria were ready to compromise. When Lev Landau was arrested on April 28, 1938, he was not yet thirty years of age but already a physicist of world renown. He was charged with various counterrevolutionary actions, and his life hung in the balance. However, he had a powerful friend and protector, Pyotr Kapitsa, who in missives to Molotov and Beria explained that Landau was engaged in work of the greatest importance, that he was irreplaceable, and that he should be released under Kapitsa's personal guarantee. Landau was released within a year[10]—a show of considerable courage, because the authorities, with equal ease, could have given instructions to arrest Kapitsa and liquidate him.

The Communist International (Comintern)

The fate of the Comintern under the terror still remains to be studied in detail. Given the defeat of communism in many European countries, the preponderant role of the Soviet Union in the Comintern was, of course, inevitable. But the cynical manipulation of the organization as a (minor) instrument of Soviet foreign policy, the grave mistakes committed, and eventually the murder of so many leading foreign Communists were certainly not inevitable. It will be recalled that the Comintern adopted the Popular Front policy in 1935 after years of an ultraleft line during which, in total misjudgment of the world situation, social democracy had been attacked as the "left wing of fascism" and therefore the worst enemy of the working class.

Whether history would have taken a different turn but for the fratricidal struggle on the Left, as some Soviet historians claim under glasnost, is not certain.[11] That this struggle facilitated the rise of Nazism and heralded the advent of World War II is beyond doubt. There was no reason why the Communist appeal for a popular anti-Fascist front should have been given credence after so many years of relentless hostility. And when the German-Soviet rapprochement began, the anti-Fascist slogans were dropped.

Because many foreign Communists were stationed in the Soviet Union, they were bound to fall victim to the purge. They included some of the most prominent Comintern leaders, such as Piatnitsky, a contemporary of Lenin's, and Béla Kun, the leader of the Hungarian Communists in their bid for power in 1919. At the June 1937 meeting of the Central Committee, Piatnitsky had opposed the death penalty for Bukharin and the other defendants in the coming show trial. He had also spoken out about the violation of law by Ezhov and his underlings. A few days later, Piatnitsky was arrested and accused of spying for both tsarist Russia and foreign powers. According to evidence by Mikhail Mendeleev that became known in 1988, there was a most elaborate frame-up to prepare evidence against Piatnitsky:

> In May 1938 I was transferred from a special regime camp in Vorkuta to a Moscow prison. At the end of June or the beginning of July, after I had been interrogated by Sharok, I was taken to a different cell. Looking around in the dimness, I discerned an inhabitant and said "Hello" to him. As the man approached me, I extended my hand, but he said, "Don't be in a hurry to shake my hand. First hear me out and then see if you still want to.
>
> "I have been sentenced to death and am waiting. . . . Perhaps you will survive and tell people about everything. My name is Melnikov, Boris Nikolaevich, I was consul general in Harbin. I was asked to confirm that Piatnitsky was a spy working for Japan and other capitalist countries. Since I knew personally that Piatnitsky was an active member of the Communist International and since I deeply respected him for his honesty and high principles, I did my best to prove that what was said about him was a lie, slander, and that he was held in high esteem in the Comintern. But once, after prolonged beatings and torture, I broke down and agreed to give evidence against Piatnitsky. . . .
>
> "A few days later, they brought my suit (it had been pressed), my tie, and polished shoes to my cell and then took me to my interrogator. There they carefully looked me over and said: 'This will do.' The next day a barber was brought to my cell. He gave me a shave and cut my hair. After that I was again taken to the interrogator and sternly told, 'This is the last time that we'll warn you about the need to conduct yourself according to our instructions. You will be very sorry if you don't.'
>
> "Twenty or thirty minutes later I was led out to the courtyard and ordered to take my seat in a car between two men, one of whom was my interrogator. I was brought to the Kremlin, ushered into a room, seated near one of the doors, and told to wait.
>
> "In about 15 or 20 minutes I was taken into a spacious room. Looking around, I saw Stalin sitting at a large desk. Not far from him there were ten or twelve people. I recognized Molotov, Voroshilov, Kaganovich, and, at some distance, Nadezhda Krupskaya.
>
> "I heard Stalin speak. 'Comrade Krupskaya,' he said, 'refuses to believe that Piatnitsky was a spy. Comrade Ezhov will now report on the matter and will convince you by quoting facts.'

"Ezhov got up, took a sheet of paper out of his briefcase, and having looked around at the people sitting in the room, turned to me: 'Citizen Melnikov.' Then he started asking me questions which I knew. I answered in keeping with the instructions. Suddenly I heard Krupskaya's sharp and indignant voice. 'He lies! He is a Fascist; he is a scoundrel!' And then she cried: 'Viacheslav Mikhailovich, Kliment Yefremovich, Lazar Moiseevich, you know Piatnitsky well. He is the most honest person. Lenin was very fond of him and respected him!'

"Krupskaya was very agitated, searching the faces around her for sympathy. But there was only oppressive silence in the room. The silence was broken by Stalin: 'Comrade Krupskaya does not believe Melnikov's evidence. Well, we'll do some more checking.'

"I was taken out of the room and brought to Lubyanka."[12]

It is doubtful whether any foreign Communist party remained unaffected by the purges, except perhaps the Chinese; among those murdered were even Persian and Indian Communists. Worst hit were the Polish; some 5,000 Polish Communists lived in the Soviet Union at the time. In spring and summer of 1937, the majority was arrested and killed, including the entire leadership. The Polish Politburo had been based in Paris; its members were invited for a meeting and then arrested as they arrived in Moscow.[13] Dimitrov, the secretary general of the Comintern, closely collaborated with the NKVD in the liquidation of the Polish party; in 1938 it was officially dissolved. When the German attack came in September 1939, there was no Polish Communist party in existence. The Polish party and its leading members were rehabilitated in February 1956, but their fate remained a major bone of contention in relations between Moscow and Warsaw.

The German Communist party was not dissolved, but many of its members perished, including seven members of the pre-1933 Politburo. A juxtaposition of the fate of German Communists in Nazi Germany and Stalin's Russia is of some interest. Of the pre-1933 German Politburo members, 5 were killed by the Gestapo and 7 in the Soviet Union. Of the Central Committee, 17 were killed in Nazi Germany compared with 12 in Russia. Of the 100 Communist parliamentarians in 1932, 27 died under Hitler, 8 under Stalin.[14] The Soviet party leadership seems to have left the decision of whom to rehabilitate to the East German party, which announced in 1988 that there must be "no white spots in our history" and that, in any case, all those who were repressed had been rehabilitated long ago.[15]

But this is not true. Some of the nonpersons had reappeared in the specialized literature without mention of the circumstances, date, or place of their death. In some cases, families had been privately informed that there had been a regrettable miscarriage of justice. But there had been no public rehabilitation either in the case of the party leaders or of the hundreds of the rank-and-file members and the left-wing writers, journalists, painters, actors, and scientists who also disappeared in the Soviet Union. Great efforts have been made under glasnost to show that the leadership of the German Communist party in Moscow had tried very hard to get their arrested comrades released. They found a letter by Wilhelm Pieck sent in May 1939 to Manuilsky, another survivor, that contained a reference to earlier letters to Beria (April 1939) and Ezhov (April 1938). But it is feeble evidence, for Pieck must have known that by 1939 most of those arrested had been executed and that, in any case, the only relevant address for letters of this kind was that of Stalin himself. Millions of Russians wrote Stalin about the "mistakes" that had been committed. Pieck did not even dare to do this.[16]

Another group that fared very badly were the members of the Austrian Socialist party (the Schutzbund) who had escaped to the Soviet Union after their defeat in Vienna in 1934. Under glasnost, new light was also shed on the fate of a family of Swiss sympathizers who had settled in the Soviet Union. The name Fritz Platten is well known to all students of Lenin because this left-wing socialist leader had been his close supporter during his Swiss exile. He had been instrumental in organizing the famous "sealed train" in which Lenin, Zinoviev, and others had reached Petrograd on their way from Zurich in April 1917. Like so many others, Platten was arrested in March 1938, but for unknown reasons his trial was postponed time and again; his turn came only in October 1939. Perhaps alone among the millions of victims, he was charged with crimes that were not even political in character. He received a four-year prison sentence for "illegal possession of weapons." He died in a camp near Arkhangelsk in April 1942; according to a Soviet newspaper, the revolver in question had allegedly been given to him as a present by Lenin.[17]

Among those who perished were hundreds of Communists from Yugoslavia, Bulgaria, and Hungary, but also from smaller parties, such as the Finnish.[18] Sometimes they included the wives or the close relations of leaders apparently in good standing; Aino Kuusinen, the wife of the leader of the Finnish party, spent seventeen years in prison and camps. More than 100 Italian Communists died, as well as a large number of Spaniards who had escaped at the end of the civil war.

Many details have come to light under glasnost about individuals killed, circumstances of their arrest and execution, and the accusations against them. But many essential questions still remain shrouded in darkness. Why did Dimitrov survive, and why was Béla Kun murdered?[19] Perhaps it was a matter of accident; Stalin probably liked the Bulgarian more than the Hungarian Jew. Perhaps it was a little more inconvenient to liquidate the hero of the Reichstag trial rather than the leader of the abortive Hungarian Revolution? There was a traditional anti-Polish feeling in Russia, which may explain why the Polish party suffered so grievously and the Czech party much less so. In some cases, the victims had been members of various opposition groups, but equally often they were faithful Stalinists or quite nonpolitical. There is much reason to believe that once the purges began the opportunity was used by some foreign Communists in Moscow to settle old scores with rivals. Not a few of those who died were denounced by informers. But we may not know details about such intrigues in the foreseeable future, if only because they concern foreign Communist parties.

Terror and the Common People

So far mention has been made of the fate of well-known men and women: party leaders, generals, famous writers, and the like. In the annals of the great terror, their names figure first and foremost. Even under glasnost, most of the attention has been focused on their fate and that of their families. Hence the impression that most of the victims of the purge belonged to the elite and that the events of the late 1930s should be considered as a circulation of elites, that although the great and famous suffered, life for the common people went on, more or less, as usual.

This is true inasmuch as no individual and no group can possibly live in a permanent state of fear. Even in the period of the Holocaust there were concerts in the ghettos, and people celebrated holidays and other joyous occasions on the eve of their departure for the death camps. A Soviet author in a book that could be published only under glasnost (*The*

Faculty of Unnecessary Things) made reference to "singing and dancing in the streets," albeit in a surreal mood, not one of true joy and relaxation. Russia is a very great country; some communities were less severely affected by the purge for one reason or another. Many thousands benefited from the terror; to a certain extent, it eased the housing shortage in the cities. Others enjoyed the spectacle of individuals and groups whom they despised being decimated by the terror.

When Robert Conquest wrote that the ratio of nonparty to party arrests runs at between seven and nine to one, he was criticized by some U.S. scholars for exaggeration. But the academician A. Sakharov, not a man given to wild statements, put the ratio at ten to one. According to some preglasnost critics, it was wrong to claim that the majority of people in the Soviet Union and in Germany was terrorized in the 1930s.[20] There were two major differences between Germany and Russia at the time: The number of the inmates of the German concentration camps did not exceed 100,000 until the outbreak of the war. Furthermore, no one in Nazi Germany had reason to fear arrest unless he was an active anti-Fascist, a Jew, or belonged to some other undesirable group. The situation in the Soviet Union was different because even the most enthusiastic Stalinists could not feel secure. It may be literally true that the majority of people in the Soviet Union were in no immediate danger of being executed and, to this extent, could feel reasonably secure—including children, who were told in school that Stalin loved them and who did not understand what went on around them, and the very old, who, as a rule, were not seized. It is also true that much fewer women were arrested than men. Fewer peasants were arrested than city dwellers; the countryside had experienced the terror in earlier years.

The above categories constituted the majority of the population. But inasmuch as the politically and socially active sections of the population were concerned, the situation was quite different. One example should suffice: According to an official source, the purges of the late 1930s resulted in about 40,000 victims in the Donetsk region of the Ukraine.[21] The Donetsk region was predominantly working class in character; the categories particularly severely hit in the purges were hardly represented in Donetsk. Nevertheless, it transpires from these figures that about 5 percent, perhaps more, of the male population between the ages of eighteen and sixty disappeared.

The real extent of the horror has become known only in recent years from reports in the Soviet media, from the letters of the children of the victims, or, in some cases, from the survivors of camps. These accounts came from lone survivors of erstwhile big families, from family members who were shot, died of starvation, or froze to death because there was no one left to care for them. The fate of a Bukharin or a Kamenev was deeply tragic, but they had opted for radical politics, a calling notoriously associated with high risk. It is more difficult to make sense of the arrest and the murder of a poet or a philosopher or an engineer; their world was not that of affairs of state; they were just following their vocation as best they could. Why should they, their families, and friends have been singled out for destruction? And the issue becomes altogether unfathomable once we reach the "great unwashed masses"—semiliterate, poor peasants or unskilled workers. To give but one example: A young porter, Ivan Demura, twenty-four years of age, from Blagoveshshensk in Siberia, was arrested on April 4, 1938. Under interrogation, he admitted having been a member of the right-wing Trotskyite bloc that plotted to assist Japan in restoring the capitalist order in the Far East. They found in his possession an antiquated single-barreled shotgun. Under pressure, Demura gave the names of fellow conspirators—porters like him, some fishermen, a builder's mate, and a carpenter. The end of the protocol read: "There was no material evidence found." But poor Ivan Demura was nevertheless found guilty under paragraph 58 (1A), 58 (2), 58 (7), and 58 (11), which covered not only high treason but also anti-Soviet propaganda—as if a spy would reveal his true identity by also engaging in propaganda. Consequently, the "highest measure of social defense," execution, was called for. He was killed on May 16, 1938, the same day the sentence had been pronounced.[22]

Poor, semiliterate Ivan Demura had surely never heard of Trotskyism and right-wingers, let alone the alleged bloc between them. He probably had never seen a Japanese in his life, and he was a loyal citizen of his country. Who had picked him and millions of other unlikely plotters against Stalin? One may never know the answer to this question. Perhaps the NKVD had arrested an occasional driver or a tractor operator or a nightwatchman by mistake, and because they were always interested in extracting the names of fellow conspirators and because everyone undergoing the full "treatment" would provide lists of fellow conspirators from their own milieu, the security organs ended up with countless Ivan Demuras.

Schedules of arrests of "enemies of the people" were established for every district. After Stalin's death, authorities in the Kuzbas industrial region dealt with the cases of 11,000 local people who had been "repressed," but it then became too much work and was stopped. In 1988, the authorities announced that at least another 11,000 cases had to be dealt with.[23] The terror machine did not ignore small villages. In a hamlet of sixty families in White Russia, twenty-six men were "taken" as Trotskyite spies and Fascist agents in 1937–38—nearly one-half the families were affected. Of these, only one returned after his rehabilitation. "But from this man nothing could be found out. He kept to himself and did not talk. He died soon after his return. The others had been shot near Bobruisk."[24]

Many of those who were arrested did not suffer long. They were kept for a few weeks and interrogated for a few days. Their trial—in front of special courts of two or three "judges"—took only a few minutes, and then they were shot or sent to a camp. The suffering of their wives and children was lifelong. It is difficult for outsiders even to begin to imagine in what conditions these women and children survived: "We lived in an unfinished hut," wrote the daughter of an "enemy of the people." "The frost in Siberia reached 60 degrees below freezing point. There was no wood, no food for the cow. Everyone shunned us; even our relations were afraid of inviting trouble."[25] The father had received an eight-year sentence. In 1957, he was rehabilitated posthumously: "We heard about this only ten years later. . . ."

Under glasnost, an old file sometimes has fallen into the hands of an enterprising investigative journalist. There was the case of a member of a kolkhoz in Siberia, a woman of little education, who had allegedly said that while working in the fields the situation would be better if people were permitted to pray freely. It was not at all clear whether she had actually said it or whether some personal enemy had informed on her. Nor was it clear whether Matrena Chuchalina, the woman in question, was quite sane; her memory had suffered earlier in life when she had been struck by lightning. But the case dragged on for eight months and involved many trips by highly placed NKVD personnel and many official statements (in illiterate Russian), until she was finally given a six-year sentence in a labor camp, without confiscation of her property. All this happened in the middle of a most destructive war in which the survival of the country was in question and in which two of her sons were serving on the front lines. Perhaps her case was singled out because she lived to celebrate her ninetieth birthday in 1989; most others were less fortunate.[26]

It was widely believed in the West that the great terror and the pervasive fear ended sometime toward the end of 1938, when Ezhov was ousted. But this is only half true. The great meat grinder was no longer running at full capacity, mainly, no doubt, because it had run out of raw material. There were actually some releases in 1939–40, perhaps tens of thousands. But as the doors of the camps opened in one direction, they remained open to give entrance to new categories of prisoners: Russian soldiers who had fallen into Finnish hands during the winter war of 1939–40, for example. New victims included, above all, many thousands of citizens of the Baltic republics, which were annexed in 1940, as well as Poles from eastern Poland, which became part of the Soviet Union under the treaty with Germany.

Inside the Soviet Union, the arrests also continued. On February 23, 1939, Kosarev, former secretary-general of the Komsomol, was executed, as was A. Egorov, deputy minister for defense. Two days later, it was the turn of A. Ugarov, head of the Moscow region and city committee; A. Smorodin, first party secretary at Stalingrad; and B. Pozern, Leningrad public prosecutor, who knew too much about the Kirov trial. On the following day, three members of the Politburo were shot—Kosior, Chubar, and Postyshev—as well as Mirzoian, first secretary of the Kazakhstan Central Committee. Not one of them had ever belonged to any oppositionist faction. Their Stalinist zeal had been second to none, and they had been very active during the first phase of the purges.

Other members of the Central Committee shot in 1939 included I. Vareikis, first party secretary in the Far East; P. Alekseev of Leningrad; M. Kulkov of Rostov; and I. Deribas, chief of the NKVD in the Far East. Central Committee members shot in 1940 included yet another alternate member of the Politburo, Eikhe, as well as Bubnov, the former people's commissar of education, Y. Evdokimov and I. Zhukov, two more members of the Central Committee, not to mention Ezhov, the great killer himself. The arrests and executions continued well into 1941, right up until the outbreak of war—and beyond.[27]

Arrests continued of Red Army commanders and leading officials of the armament industry. In September 1939, World War II had broken out; how long would it take until the Soviet Union became involved in the battle for survival? But the executions continued, as is now revealed under glasnost, not only after September 1939 but even after Hitler's attack against the Soviet Union. Those arrested just before or after June 22, 1941, included the people's commissar for armaments, the deputy head of the general staff, three deputies of the people's commissar for defense, the commander in chief of antiair defense, and other senior officers and officials. Most of them were shot in October 1941. Revealing these facts, a distinguished commentator wrote:

> Let us recall the date, October 28, 1941. The Fascists are at the gates of Moscow, Leningrad is cut off; the Ukraine, Moldavia, White Russia, and the Baltic countries are occupied. And on this very day the salvos are fired in Kuibyshev and Saratov, barely muffled by truck engines. Military leaders, army commanders, and leading weapons designers, all totally innocent, are liquidated. Three of them are dying together with their wives—victims of their own people. Their own people?[28]

The terror continued throughout the war: Generals, captains, and privates were sentenced to death for not obeying orders or for a great many other reasons, only to be rehabilitated in later years. Many prisoners who had not been sentenced to death in the great purge were nevertheless killed during the first year of the war. We do not know for certain when the Katyn massacre took place, whether it was in 1940 or during the first months after the Nazi invasion. Various Soviet-Polish commissions investigated the issue in 1986–89, but there was no clear admission of guilt until 1990. In Kuibyshev, Alter and Erlich, two leading Polish Jewish socialists, were arrested in their hotel and murdered; again, there was no admission of guilt or rehabilitation.

As the war ended, there was a widespread feeling of hope. It was generally expected that the purges, the arbitrary arrests, and the executions would not recur. But these were vain hopes; hundreds of thousands of Soviet prisoners of war found themselves in the gulag after the war. There were also attacks in the media reminiscent of the 1930s, including the campaign against the biologists who refused to subscribe to Lysenkoism. Scientists were arrested, and many others lost their jobs. The same was true with regard to the cosmopolitans, that is to say, the Jews, who were so bitterly denounced. Again, literary critics, writers, moviemakers, and some scientists lost their jobs and income, but no one was actually brought to court, nor were there initially any executions.[29]

However, after a few years, the campaigns became more savage. First, in chronological order, was the "Leningrad affair" in July and August 1949, in the course of which virtually all leading Communists in Leningrad were arrested. Most were subsequently executed, including M. I. Rodionov, A. A. Kuznetsov, and P. S. Popkov. Altogether some 2,000 people were arrested and executed.[30] But the NKVD cast its nets wider: Not only was the present Leningrad leadership seized but also those who had served there at some time in the past, including M. Basov, first secretary in the Crimea; P. Smorodin, a Stalingrad party secretary; N. Solovyov, first secretary at Yaroslavl; and, above all, Nikolai Voznesensky, the youngest member of the Politburo, who was regarded by many as Stalin's crown prince. He had been a member of the Supreme Defense Committee during the war and, as such, was repsonsible for the economic war effort.

There was to be no show trial; the accused were charged with antiparty activities, various kinds of sabotage aimed at the nonfulfillment of the state plan, and preparing the Leningrad organization to challenge the Moscow Central Committee. Some were also accused with espionage on behalf of Britain; one of them had once been dispatched to England to study some engineering problem. Several of the defendants confessed after the application of the usual pressure. But Voznesensky declared that he had committed no crimes whatsoever, and Kuznetsov said he was and continued to be a true Bolshevik, whatever the sentence would be, and that historical justice would eventually prevail. Such justice did indeed prevail; the Leningrad accused were among the first to be rehabilitated by the Soviet Supreme Court in April 1954. There was a second rehabilitation wave under the auspices of a subcommittee of the Politburo in March 1988, when those who had been excluded from the party were reinstated.[31] But for all the major figures, such rehabilitation was posthumous because the court had pronounced death sentences—illegally, it should be noted, for capital punishment had been abolished in the Soviet Union at the end of the war.

As for the underlying reasons of the Leningrad affair, there are even now only speculations and question marks. It is known that Malenkov played a leading role in this affair, but he would not have dared to take a single step without Stalin's full support. Why did Stalin want to destroy the party organization of the country's second city? Why did he pick on the youngest member of his own Politburo who was totally devoted to him? Did he suspect Leningrad of showing too much independence?

Was he jealous of Voznesensky's growing reputation as an economist? Or did he have a grudge against him because he had protected his employees in the Gosplan in 1938? There are, as yet, no answers to these questions, and perhaps there might never be.

The preparation for the anti-Jewish campaign began in late 1947. Solomon Mikhoels, the leading Jewish actor of his generation, an unforgettable King Lear, was killed in a faked automobile accident in Minsk in January 1948. Why was he singled out? Why, if he was deemed suspect, was he not brought to secret trial? These and many other questions have remained unanswered. After the revelations under glasnost it seems certain that it was a case of murder, not accident. [32]

During the year 1949, virtually all authors writing in Yiddish were arrested. They included David Bergelson and Itzik Feffer, Peretz Markish, David Hofstein, Lev Kvitko, and others, as well as Lozovsky, a former deputy foreign minister, who was seventy. They were shot on August 12, 1952. The accusations against them were so ludicrous that even some of the military judges had their doubts. Nor was it clear why the writers were held in prison for three years before they were shot. It was equally strange that their secret trial should have lasted three months. They were rehabilitated under the first thaw, and their works were again published.

From the files that were discovered under glasnost, it appeared that five of the accused denied all guilt. The main witness of the prosecution was apparently Itzik Feffer, who implicated all the others in various anti-Soviet activities. But then Feffer also confessed that, under the nickname "Zorin," he had been a secret informer of the organs of state security since 1944, which was, of course, the last thing the "organs" wanted him to reveal. A. Cheptsov, one of the military judges, complained to Malenkov that the evidence was quite unconvincing but was told in no uncertain terms not to cause "legalistic difficulties."[33]

Finally, the doctors' plot broke in January 1953. Efim Smirnov, a distinguished Russian physician and minister of health after 1945, related many years later that he went to see Stalin during the winter of 1952–53 and that Stalin suddenly asked him which doctor had treated Zhdanov and Dimitrov. Smirnov mentioned the doctor's name, and Stalin said: "Strange, the same doctor and both of them died. . . ." Smirnov said that the doctor was in no way responsible, that there was nothing he could have done, but Stalin remained unconvinced.[34]

It seems that, about the same time, Stalin had a regular checkup by Professor Vinogradov, who found a marked deterioration in his health, stated it in his report, and suggested absolute rest.[35] Stalin was furious and ordered Vinogradov's arrest. (Vinogradov had been a witness for the prosecution in the Bukharin trial in 1938.) There were four other Russians among the victims, but the majority was Jewish—M. S. Vovsi, M. B. Kogan, A. Feldman, Y. Etinger, and others—the leading doctors in the country. They were accused of having killed Zhdanov and Sherbakov (a member of the Politburo in wartime) and of having tried to poison a group of Soviet military leaders. Some of them were also charged with having been British agents for a long time; others were said to have been Jewish bourgeois nationalists who, through the Joint (a Jewish welfare agency), had cooperated with U.S. intelligence. Vovsi, who had been the chief physician of the Red Army, was forced to confess that he had been a Nazi spy all along. It was also made known that the infamous plot would not have been revealed but for the vigilance of Lidia Timashuk, a junior doctor employed in the Kremlin hospital, who, in recognition of her great services, was given the Order of Lenin.

The political background of the arrests and the trial is not entirely clear to this day except that it followed a recurrent pattern. The case was prepared by Ryumin, who was in charge of "especially important affairs" in the state security office. At the time, Beria was still in overall control of the state security apparatus, but the head of the MGB was Ignatiev. It is possible that Ignatiev might have plotted with Ryumin against Beria or, more likely, Beria with Ryumin against Ignatiev. Be that as it may, nothing could have happened without Stalin's permission, who apparently thought that time had come for another major bloodletting. Molotov, Mikoyan, and even Voroshilov, as potential British spies, were in disfavor at the time. Khrushchev said in later years that had Stalin lived, he would have gotten rid of the whole Politburo. Seen in historical perspective, doing so might not have been an unmitigated disaster; it would have made the transition to freedom in the Soviet Union much easier.

Those arrested were submitted to intensive interrogation, that is to say, by the "conveyer" system and also by physical torture. Professor Etinger died under interrogation; others were permanently crippled and died soon after. Some admitted their guilt immediately.[36] When Vasilenko (who refused to admit any guilt) was confronted with Vovsi and Vinogradov (who had caved in), they told him to stop playing the fool, for "he must have remembered how they together plotted to kill their patients." Vasilenko later said that he thought that he was dealing with madmen. Vinogradov said in his defense that because of his impressions of the trials of 1937, he had decided to sign everything that was demanded to escape torture, such was the general fear. As for Vovsi (a relation of Mikhoels's), he told Rapoport many years later, after the amputation of a leg, that having become a cripple hurt him less than having become a moral cripple under arrest and interrogation. ("Then I ceased to be a man.")[37]

Meanwhile, the situation of the families of those arrested was not much better; they were treated like lepers—and worse. Rumors spread that all Jews were poisoners, that all drugs in the pharmacies had been contaminated.[38] Then, less than eight weeks after the original announcement, Stalin died. The case was dismissed; the surviving accused (the "killer doctors," the "scum of the earth") were freed, Ryumin was arrested and eventually shot, and Dr. Timashuk had to return her Order of Lenin. When glasnost came, only one of the accused, Y. Rapoport, who belonged to the second echelon of those arrested, was still alive. He kept his party membership and said in 1988 that he had always hoped that he would live to see the day when common sense would triumph. His daughter, who had been fourteen at the time, said that she had been more reluctant to forgive and forget.[39]

Before turning to the more general questions arising from the reign of terror, some other issues remain: the fate of Stalin's main assistants in preparing and carrying out the "purges," the role of a small number of people who helped make the details of the purges known before and under glasnost, and, finally, the estimates of victims of the terror.

Beria's personality will preoccupy us later. Suffice it to say that since his execution in 1953 he has figured in Soviet historiography as the greatest villain by far. If mitigating circumstances were found for Stalin, no one had anything good to say about Beria, and this, justifiably. Beria was a major criminal who was responsible for the death of countless people. He was devoid of character, a liar, who tried to anticipate every whim of Stalin and who was brutal to his inferiors. He may have been a sadist; he certainly took part in interrogations. He used his influential position to settle all kinds of personal accounts, especially concerning those who knew too much about his early political career. As a young man in Baku, Beria had been, in all probability, an active member of a nationalist, anti-Bolshevik group, the Mussavetists. He devoted much energy to destroying material evidence and all potential witnesses.[40] However, if it had not have been for Stalin, it is more than doubtful whether there would have been hecatombs of victims. Beria had not the slightest moral scruples about giving orders to kill thousands of people. But his motivation was that of the common gangster, not of a political mass murderer; he did not believe in killing people for political and social, that is to say, "objective," reasons.

He was liquidated by his Politburo colleagues not because he had been Stalin's chief hangman, certainly not because of his role in Baku in 1917–18, but because he was too powerful and because his colleagues were afraid of him.[41]

The most loathsome creature connected with the purges was not any of the thugs of the NKVD but a civilian, the chief prosecutor, Andrei Yanuarevich Vyshinsky. He was apparently a scion of a lower aristocratic family, perhaps partly of Polish origin. Like Beria, he had belonged to the wrong party in 1917—the Mensheviks. In fact, he had signed an order to find, arrest, and to bring to trial the German spy Lenin.[42]

Vyshinsky was apparently mortally afraid that his past would be dredged up one day, and for this reason, as well as for some others, he became a pliant tool in Stalin's hands. A man of some education, he was no mean demagogue, and a most accomplished liar and therefore eminently suited for his assignment.

It is interesting to compare his role with that of Roland Freisler, who played a cardinal role in the main trials of the Nazi regime during its last years. Both liked to call the defendants "pigs," "scum," "filth," "stinking," "reeking heap of human garbage," "accursed vermin," and so on. But there was one crucial difference: Freisler, a younger man, was a committed, fanatical Nazi; Vyshinsky, an utter cynic, believed in nothing except his own survival and career. Both had the good fortune to escape justice: Freisler was killed in a bombing raid a few months before the end of the war, and Vyshinsky died eighteen months before the Twentieth Party Congress. According to Volkogonov, the "boss" liked Vyshinsky—a diligent man without any moral scruples, mendacious, brutal, the ideal producer of the show trials.[43] He also liked V. Ulrich, who served as the head of the military collegium of the Supreme Court, the presiding judge in all the important trials. A native of Riga, Ulrich was a man of few words, rather dry, but he, too, could be relied upon always to do the right thing—a cynic, a pathological liar, an utter scoundrel, and, from Stalin's point of view, an ideal tool.[44]

That Vyshinsky ceased to be prosecutor general in1939 did not mark the end of his career. He became a professor and later rector at Moscow University, deputy prime minister, and eventually foreign minister after Molotov. His book *Theory of Court Evidence in Soviet Law* (1941), for which he received the Stalin Prize, greatly helped to shape the practice of Soviet justice. In this book, there was no presumption of innocence; instead, admission extracted by torture became the last word in jurisprudence.[45] But despite his standing as the first and foremost jurist in the country, Vyshinsky was mortally afraid as long as Stalin was alive.

> He knew too much; he had been personally involved in too much. After all, did not tens and indeed hundreds of the butchers follow their victims? It is easy to imagine Vyshinsky's terror when, while in the highly honored post of foreign minister, he was suddenly stripped of his deputy's seat on the Supreme Soviet. What lay behind this "joke" in 1950? A warning? A hint? Intrigues and machinations by someone or other? Who knows. . . . Stalin loved to frighten people, after which the slaves would lick his boots even more assiduously.[46]

This was the man about whom Harold Laski, the British socialist theorist, had written a few years earlier. After a long and amicable conversation, Vyshinsky did not observe much difference between the general character of a trial in Russia and in Britain. Vyshinsky, he concluded, was a man whose passion was legal reform.

> He was doing what an ideal minister of justice would do if we had such a person in Great Britain—forcing his colleagues to consider what is meant by actual experience of the law in action. He brought to the study of the law in operation an energy that we have not seen in this country since the days of Jeremy Bentham.[47]

When Vyshinsky died, his remains were buried at the Kremlin wall, as befitting the merits of a man of such distinction. At the time of this writing, they are still there, unlike the remains of his many victims. Perhaps it is the right thing not to make any change, for as one critic has said, removing them would not erase the Vyshinsky chapter from Soviet history.

7. Why They Confessed

How many people died as the result of the great terror? No certain answer has been given to this question even under glasnost. Gorbachev spoke on one occasion about "many thousands"; unofficial Soviet spokesmen have mentioned many millions, including the victims of collectivization. Volkogonov, Stalin's biographer, wrote that he had no reliable overall figures at his disposal and that there perhaps never would be any available.

Estimates varied greatly even on a local scale. While the official White Russian government committee concluded in 1988 that not less than 30,000 people were buried in Kuropaty near Minsk, others gave a figure ten times as large. From the many accounts published in the Soviet Union after 1985 it appeared that in many families at least one member or two had been arrested. This included the seemingly most powerful in the land, such as Molotov, Kalinin, and Poskrebyshev (their wives were arrested), or Kaganovich, who lost a brother without batting an eyelid. It affected not only intellectuals but industry and transport; in agriculture, most of the bloodletting had taken place before. According to a progress report sent by Ulrich to Beria in October 1938, 36,157 people had been sentenced by the supreme military court, of them 30,514 by firing squad, between October 1, 1936, and September 1938, that is, about 500 a day, including Sundays and holidays.[1] But this number referred only to VIPs. The great majority of people were dealt with by the so-called *osoboe soveshanie* ("special consultation"), that is, three judges, or even two, and sometimes none at all. According to the historian Polikarpov, appearing as a witness in a trial in Moscow in October 1988, there had been altogether 19.8 million cases of repression.

Sometimes the local figures were revealing. It was thus reported in

November 1988 that in Azerbaijan alone 50,000 cases of "repression" were as yet to be reexamined. The number of Azerbaijanis is less than 2 percent of the Soviet total. Considering that a considerable number of cases of "repression," perhaps half, were dealt with under the first thaw, one reaches a figure in excess of millions, projecting the Azerbaijani experience on the country as a whole, which is close to the calculations made by Robert Conquest in his "Great Terror" (6–9 million) or by Boris Nikolaevsky in the 1940s (5–8 million.) The numbers of victims in Georgia was higher than in Azerbaijan.

How many of these were party members, how many were killed immediately, how many sent to the gulag, and what percentage survived there? There have been heated discussions on these topics beginning in the 1930s right up to the dawn of the age of glasnost.[2]

Trotsky's *Biuleten Oppositsii* thought that 300,000 men and women had been arrested by May 1937; the Menshevik *Sotsialisticheski Vestnik* (July 1938) gave a far higher figure for the inmates of the gulag alone—7 million. Souvarine, Stalin's biographer, quoted Anton Ciliga, a well-known Yugoslav Communist, who had been an inmate of a camp; according to him, there were at least 5 million, possibly many more inmates.[3] Isaac Deutscher, writing ten years later, was more restrained: "He sent thousands to their death and tens and hundreds of thousands into prisons and concentration camps."[4]

A great deal of ingenuity has gone into more recent assessments, such as the analysis of demographic statistics and party membership and of newspapers distributed among camp inmates, evidence by defectors, information collected by dissidents in the Soviet Union, and so on.[5] But these calculations referred mainly to "involuntary laborers"; they left many questions open; above all, the total number of people affected by the terror.

Western estimates also differed widely, from "tens of thousands" (George Kennan) to 16–18 million victims. A Yugoslav (Dedijer) gave a figure of 3 million people who had been executed. Conquest mentioned that in 1943 a mass grave of thousands of political prisoners had been found near Vinnitsa. Critics argued that this might have been an exception; did every district have its Vinnitsa? Revelations after 1986 (from Minsk to the Altai) tended to show that Vinnitsa had not been an isolated case.

During the 1960s and 1970s there was a tendency in the West to regard the earlier estimates as greatly exaggerated—not only the revisionist historians but also the research section of the State Department, which, in 1960, reached the conclusion that the earlier estimates (of 10–12 million inmates of the camps) would have meant that one-fifth of all males had been imprisoned, a figure that was clearly much too high.[6]

As a result of the revelations under glasnost, the estimates rose. Even according to the estimates of so cautious a writer as Volkogonov, between 3.5 and 4 million people had been "repressed" between 1937 and 1939, out of which between 600,000 and 650,000 had been shot. According to an author writing in *Neva* (October 1988), the Leningrad periodical, at least 16 million were arrested under Stalin, of which some 8 to 10 million died in the camps. If one adds the numbers of peasants who perished as the result of collectivization, one reaches a figure of no less than 20 million. Roy Medvedev, writing in the semiofficial *Argumenty i Fakty*, reached an even higher figure, 40 million.[7] True, he included the victims of 1929–33 as well as those who had been deported during the Second World War and after. For the great terror his figure was 5 to 7 million, including almost 1 million party members: "Of those arrested in 1937/38, almost 1 million were sentenced to be shot, and the rest were sent to the camps. However, few of them lived long enough to be rehabilitated." These figures were higher than the highest Western estimates twenty and thirty years earlier.

A highly placed demographer, following some very complicated analysis of past censuses, reached the conclusion that 7.9 million people starved to death and died in prisons and camps between 1927 and 1958, that an additional 2 million left the Soviet Union during this period, but that this was not, however, the full blood toll of the Stalinist crimes.[8] Another author has stated that about 8 million people died as the result of the "destruction of the Kulaks as a class," and yet another Soviet writer, who served in the administration of the gulag from 1953, contends that the number of victims in the camps was 7 million.[9] But Yulian Semenov, the well-connected Soviet writer, had access to a secret memorandum to Stalin by Semyon Ignatiev, according to which there were about 12 million inmates in the camps in early 1953 (*Moskovski Komsomolets*, quoted in *Times*, London, February 26, 1988).[10]

Soviet ideologues of the far Right, such as Kozhinov and Perevertsev, have claimed that the population of the Soviet Union fell by 15 million during the civil war and that an additional 9.4 million perished as the result of collectivization and the famine of 1932–33. According to these spokesmen, there has been a deliberate attempt on the part of Communists and "liberals" to play down or ignore altogether the number of victims and to exaggerate the number during the terror of the late 1930s. But in actual fact the population losses for the civil war period were put at 20 million by a textbook published in the Soviet Union during the Stalinist period, and the Kozhinov figures of the collectivization period are not at great variance with those of leading experts in both West and East. The most specific figures on the population of the gulag were given in 1989 by a researcher named Viktor Zemskov.[11] According to the evidence discovered by him, or put at his disposal, there existed, in 1940, 53 major and 425 minor camps that were guarded by 107,000 special police. The population of the gulag according to this source had been about 190,000 in 1930, rose to 1.3 million in 1938, remained fairly constant (1.3 to 1.5 million) until 1943, when it declined to 731,000, and rose again to over 1 million in 1947. Again, according to the same source, about 1 million inmates of the Gulag died between 1930 and 1947. Of those kept in the camps only between 20 to 30 percent were political prisoners. However, these figures are almost certainly incomplete; many victims of the terror were executed immediately after the investigation against them had been concluded (and there are no statistics with regard to their number), others were kept in special prisons that were not part of the gulag archipelago.

The lowest numbers of victims published so far under glasnost were those revealed by the KGB. According to this source, 3,778,234 people were arrested between 1930 and 1953 under paragraph 58 (counterrevolutionary activities and crimes against the state) and 786,098 were shot. This figure is based on a perusal of the files in the KGB archives. It does not cover the victims of collectivization, victims who were killed by the security forces in peace and war without a trial, nor is it known how complete existing files are.[12] Yet another set of figures was given in an article by V. Zemskov and D. Nokhotovich. They are based on a report allegedly prepared for Khrushchev by the KGB and dated February 1, 1955. According to this source (covering the period from 1921 to 1954), the number of those arrested was 3,777,380; of those executed, 642,980. It will be noted that the number of those arrested is virtually identical with the one given in the TASS report, even though it covers a period shorter by nine years. Such discrepancies have not so far been explained.

Whether we opt for the lower figures or those in the higher range, they are, of course quite unique in times of peace. The number of victims during St. Bartholomew's Day was 3,000 in Paris and perhaps 10,000 elsewhere. Some 17,000 people perished under the terror during the French Revolution. Even in Nazi Germany, up to the outbreak of war, the number of those sentenced to death and killed in the camps was measured only in thousands; some 120–150 were "liquidated" in the "Night of the Long Knives" (June 30, 1934), and only a few dozen perished under Mussolini. What happened in the Soviet Union was without precedent in peacetime in modern history.

We owe the revelations under glasnost about the arrests, the interrogations, and the executions to a small number of indefatigable investigators. The authorities seldom volunteered information. Leading journalists such as Yuri Feofanov and Arkadi Vaksberg were given access to some files in the ministries, and their articles were of the greatest interest. Neither Roy Medvedev nor Anton Antonov-Ovseenko, who had written about this subject under Brezhnev and whose books were published in the West (but not, before 1988, in the Soviet Union), had been given access to archival material. Like Solzhenitsyn, they relied almost entirely on oral history, that is, the recollections of prominent and not so prominent survivors. Medvedev revealed that his one-man enterprise had the moral support of Andropov, who strongly advised him, however, not to publish abroad, advice that was disregarded by the author.[13]

A subcommittee of the Politburo that was appointed in October 1987 to study material and documents related to the repression during the Stalinist period should also be mentioned. Its first chairman was Mikhail Solomontsev, who was succeeded by Alexander Yakovlev. Among its members were three top figures of the KGB, the head of the Central Committee General Department, the director of the Marx-Engels-Lenin Institute and three other high-ranking officials. To this committee we owe the rehabilitation (except for Yagoda) of the accused in the three Moscow show trials. The committee seems not to have dealt with other individual cases, but it was probably owing to its initiative that all sentences passed by the *osoboe soveshanie* were declared null and void in January 1989.

The greatest single quantitative contribution to our knowledge was made, however, by a student in his twenties, Dmitri (Dima) Yurasov.

He was not a dissident, nor had anyone in his own family been affected by the terror. He became interested in the subject even before he served as a paratrooper in Afghanistan, a lonely researcher who had not even heard of Solzhenitsyn but wanted an answer to the questions that bothered him: Why had so many people mentioned in works of reference been "repressed," and what did it mean? At the age of sixteen (in 1981), he installed himself in the state archives as a "palaeographer, second rank." He was not supposed to study the files of those who had been killed, but he did so, anyway, thus collecting cards of 123,000 individuals; the whole register he had seen amounted to 16 million files.[14]

Yurasov first became known to the public when he appeared at a historical seminar in the central writers' building on April 30, 1987. When speaker after speaker had complained about the dearth of information, Yurasov got up and said quietly: "I have statistical material, incomplete, of course, but it gives a general idea." He quoted Meyerhold's last letter to Vyshinsky. ("My confessions are all wrong, I could not suffer the torture.") He mentioned the report according to which in Orel the wives and children of military leaders, such as Egorov, Kork, Uborevich, and Gamarnik, had been murdered. There was much more sensational information.

From this date on, Yurasov, a mere student, was in constant demand, even though he was still barred from official meetings and institutions. As far as the authorities were concerned, he had illegally acquired information from secret archives. They withdrew his reader's ticket to the archives. But no one even dreamed of suing him. For many others he became a hero almost overnight; volunteers from all over the Soviet Union offered their help in preparing a fuller register of victims than the authorities were either unwilling or unable to provide.

Yurasov's story is amazing for a variety of reasons, for it showed what an enormous contribution to the restoration of historical truth could be made by a single individual. A role similar to Yurasov's was played in the late 1950s and early 1960s by General Todorsky. Most of the figures quoted about the victims of the Red Army Command in 1937–39 are based on the work done in earlier years by Todorsky and circulated in samizdat.[15] Todorsky had been a corps commander (three-star general) when he was arrested in 1937 but was neither shot nor released from the camps in 1940–41 and emerged from the gulag in 1953. From that date to his death in 1965, he collected dates concerning the fate of the Red

Army Command. Under glasnost many more details have become accessible at least to a select few who had access to the archives.[16] The facts they uncovered are of great historical and human interest, but much of the pioneering work had been done by an amateur historian, the ex-general Todorsky.

The many revelations about the age of terror caused searching debates inside the Soviet Union over the deeper issues involved. These issues had been discussed in the West for years past, and for some of them there are no answers even now. Why had the purges been launched in the first place? Why were they relentlessly pursued for years and fitfully continued even after the war? Why had so many people believed for so long in the guilt of those arrested and executed? Why had many accepted the guilt for grotesque crimes they had never committed? Why had there been so many willing assistants ready to serve the terror machine even though they must have known that their own chances for survival were poor? And why had there been virtually no resistance?

True, some of the more farfetched ideas that had some currency at the time in the West could now safely be dismissed, for no evidence was found to support them. The defendants in the show trials had certainly not been drugged. Had they confessed to nonexistent crimes because of loyalty to the Communist party? Many were not even members of that party. True, some Bolsheviks kept their faith in the party throughout all their tribulations. Their belief was exceptionally deep; they were fanatics or very naive people who had persuaded themselves that Stalin was unaware of the reign of terror, that a group of criminals had usurped the NKVD, and so on. There was a similar syndrome in Nazi Germany, albeit not so widespread: "If the Führer only knew . . . ." The loyalty-to-the-end concept might have been part of the clue to the confessions in some cases, but only in the context of the general "treatment," including constant interrogations ("the conveyor system"), moral and sometimes physical torture, threats, and the systematic destruction of the person's dignity.

The loyalty-to-the-end concept was widely discussed in the Soviet Union following the publication of Arthur Koestler's *Darkness at Noon*.[17] Reviews noted that readers of the novel in 1988 would reject the "Koestler version" out of hand because it seemed too theatrical, too much opposed to common sense; it too much resembled the theater of the absurd. But the younger reader of 1988 tended to forget (or not to know) that once upon a time a different type of Communist had existed whose loyalty to the party had been boundless, who had been willing to undergo any sacrifice. Arthur London's account (*L'Aveu*) of his role in the Slanski trial of the early 1950s was very much in the Koestlerian spirit. Furthermore, one ought to recall that Koestler had never argued that his interpretation was true with regard to all the accused who had confessed; it referred only to some of the old-guard Bolsheviks.[18]

Furthermore, the "Koestler version" seems to have been concerned with only some of the minor figures among the accused. Shatskin, who was one of Bukharin's followers, complained that he had been asked to confess "in the interests of the party." Very few other such cases are known.[19]

However, even if some of the more outlandish interpretations could be discarded, many question marks remained. That Stalin was perfectly aware of what went on in his empire had been clear for a long time; he had not been the prisoner of a bureaucracy, not the dupe of the security service, as some had argued at the time and also for decades after.[20] It was a concept voiced by neo-Stalinists and, in a somewhat more sophisticated way, by some Western commentators. The same argument (Hitler as a weak ruler, half the time unaware of what was going on in his empire) had been adduced with regard to the final solution and other Nazi crimes.[21]

No one has ever argued that either Hitler or Stalin could possibly know everything that went on under their rule; it was a sheer physical impossibility. But Stalin still knew everything of importance; no member of the Central Committee, no minister or deputy minister, no party district secretary or person of similar standing, could be executed without his sanction having been obtained, through his secretary, Poskrebyshev.[22] In all probability, there was no grand design, no master plan, and it is quite likely that at the time of the first trial Stalin had no clear idea whether there would be a second or third trial, how far the purge would go, or how many victims it would devour. History seldom if ever works this way.

Among the seemingly rational theories that were discussed ever since the 1930s, some referred to plots and conspiracies that either existed or might have developed if Stalin had not acted decisively, harshly, and in time. Molotov seems to have believed this up to the end of his days. Joseph Davis, the U.S. ambassador, traveled around the United States during the Second World War proclaiming that in Russia alone of all countries there had been no fifth column because Stalin had it shot. In a more sophisticated way we find the same idea in the work of one of Stalin's best-known biographers, Isaac Deutscher. He believed that there was an actual conspiracy between the generals and the moderates in the Politburo. He also thought there was a plot *in statu nascendi*: There would be a war against Hitler, in the course of which there would be setbacks. In such a situation, the leaders of the opposition would try to overthrow him. [23]

But these pseudorational explanations do not lead anywhere. There is no evidence that Stalin was mortally afraid of Hitler in 1936–37; on the contrary, he seems to have underrated the Nazi danger. There was no plot on the part of the opposition; in fact, there was no opposition at all. On the other hand, there developed a fifth column in later years, such as the Vlassov army, precisely because of Stalin's harsh rule; that Hitler did not want to make use of Russian collaborators is yet another issue. If Stalin was suspicious of people with an independent mind and if he wanted to liquidate them, he faced an insoluble problem. For most people have potentially a mind of his (or her) own and constitute therefore a potential danger. The closer they are to the dictator, the greater the danger.

Did Stalin perhaps want to get rid of the old-guard Bolsheviks, thus preparing the way for a rapprochement with Hitler, or to promote a circulation of elites, with younger people personally devoted to him rising to the top? These are serious questions. With so many of Lenin's contemporaries still around, his position as undisputed leader may not have seemed secure. They had to disappear in order to make room for the kind of political system that Stalin envisaged. But this does not explain the murder of so many committed Stalinists and nonparty members, of the killing of the leadership of the Komsomol and the army and of Stalin's own family.

There is no evidence that considerations of foreign policy played a predominant role in the terror campaign. On the contrary, the accusations of foreign involvement were bandied about indiscriminately and frivolously; one day a defendant would be charged with being a Romanian agent; on the next, he would be accused of spying for Japan; on the third, he would be confronted with evidence that he acted on behalf of three countries at one and the same time. Everyone knew that these charges were not meant seriously: There existed orders to eliminate a certain person; the evidence was of no importance.

Or was the terror necessary because of the way Stalin was reading Russia's history and the psychology of mankind in general: Unless the Russians were kept in fear, they would neither work nor fight. These could well have been Stalin's innermost thoughts. But it is not enough to know that he underlined in a history book the lines Genghis Khan had allegedly said, that the death of the vanquished is needed for the calm of the victors, or that, in conversation with Eisenstein, Stalin criticized Ivan IV for not having killed enough Boyars.[24]

It is the privilege of novelists to discuss such ideas; Stalin never put his secret thoughts on paper, nor did he discuss them with those close to him. Even if he had done so, it is doubtful whether any credence could be given to the writings of this most devious man. Caligula was fond of saying, "Oderint dum metuant" ("Let them hate, as long as they fear"); it could have also been Stalin's motto. He was a strict authoritarian, believing that the country needed an iron hand and would be lost without him; he was the only one who really understood Russia's deeper needs. But Stalin wanted not only to be hated; also be loved, and the reign of terror was not a good instrument to instill feelings of love. It created not so much a climate of order as of uncertainty. That one could no longer assume that blind obedience to the leader would be awarded and disloyalty punished was not conducive to discipline or to the feeling that the country was making progress. On the contrary, such conflicting signals led to confusion and disorientation.

It was not surprising that some observers would look for the origins of the purges in Russian history in the authoritarian structure of Russian village life, in a mentality produced by centuries of servitude. Even Karamzin had invoked the "vile artifices of slavery," the blind and boundless devotion to the monarch's will, "even when in his violent fits of caprice, he trampled upon every law of justice." The parallel with Ivan the Terrible seemed obvious; he had also created an NKVD of sorts, the oprichnina, headed by Malyuta Skuratov, a precursor of Ezhov and Beria. True, Ivan IV was in some ways an even more complicated individual; from time to time he would withdraw and reproach himself as a "vile murderer of innocent people,"[25] whereas Stalin never suffered from guilt feelings and fits of sudden remorse.

It was, quite obviously, not just the question of the supreme leader but also of those who revered him. As one Soviet citizen commented many years after the event:

> The time has come for us to look at ourselves openly and honestly and try to understand what kind of people we are. Why did we permit Stalin to do with us whatever he wanted, to kill us, to send us to prison, to turn us into prison guards and informers?
>
> I believe that we share the responsibility equally for all the crimes committed bewteen the 1930s and 1950s. All this was done with our agreement, loudly and silently, with our hands and brains. There were no witnesses; all turned accomplices. How could it happen that a people almost voluntarily submitted itself to destruction. Where are the roots, in our history, our mentality, our genetic structure?[26]

These are harsh words, and in part perhaps unfair. Students of totalitarianism know how difficult resistance becomes once the system has been installed. But it is a legitimate question all the same.

For some, especially Russian nationalists, such interpretations of the terror are anathema. As they see it, there was nothing specifically Russian in the events of 1936–40; it was a global phenomenon, "from Madrid to Shanghai," as one of their spokesmen put it. They offered various arguments: Was it not true that Western intellectuals like Feuchtwanger, Barbusse, Shaw, the Webbs, Dreiser, Thomas Mann, and Einstein had approved of Stalin and Stalinism, even though, unlike Russian intellectuals, they were under no duress. Show trials took place in other Eastern European countries after the Second World War, and the defendants had confessed exactly on the pattern of the Moscow trials. But such theories lacked conviction. If some Western intellectuals had voiced support for Stalin even in the late 1930s, it was because they knew little about contemporary Russia. Their support stemmed primarily from the assumption that Nazism was the main enemy and that Stalin's help was essential. The show trials in Prague, Budapest, and Sofia proved that Soviet methods worked also in other countries. But the methods had still originated in Moscow.

The purges and the terror were explained by some against the background of the Russian revolution in 1917. The Revolution had carried the day in a country in which the objective conditions had not yet ripened. Before 1918, the party had consisted of a small elite, but as its membership grew in the 1920s and 1930s, the general cultural level declined.

These various interpretations probably all contained a grain of truth, but the Stalinist terror still remained a unique phenomenon. The various preconditions mentioned could at most explain the circumstances in which the terror had taken place but not why it had occurred in the Soviet Union and not elsewhere.

What if Stalin had been mentally ill? This is a possibility, widely discussed under glasnost, that finds many supporters. It was prominently mentioned by Volkogonov,[27] but the origins of the story went back to 1927, to the case of Vladimir Bekhterev, the leading Russian psychiatrist of his time, who died under mysterious circumstances in December 1927, a few days after he had seen Stalin and made a fatal diagnosis.[28] Others, such as Kaminsky, had allegedly said in the early 1930s, "Comrade Stalin was a very sick man." Kaminsky was both a doctor and people's commissar of health. He perished in the purges.[29] Khrushchev was not a psychiatrist by training but a man of considerable common sense; he had known Stalin well and repeatedly stressed after 1953 that it was not easy to work under a leader who was raving mad.

The idea that Stalin was a paranoiac, or at the very least had pronounced paranoid tendencies, had occurred to many, perhaps most Western biographers.[30] Even the Bekhterev anecdote had been published well before glasnost.[31] Stalin's suspiciousness was proverbial. It was also known that he had more than a touch of megalomania, that he was vindictive and probably also a bit of a sadist.

If there are differences of opinion, they concern not so much the presence of such mental traits but their relative importance. Thus, in contrast to Volkogonov, Medvedev argued that while Stalin was morbidly suspicious, he was not a true paranoiac; he acted with great self-control and was therefore responsible, inasmuch as he was fully aware of what he was doing. If there were McNaughton rules in the court of history, he would be found responsible for his actions. Others, such as Rancour Lafferiere, argued that even true paranoiacs can function as Stalin. Most Soviet psychiatrists were reluctant at first to comment on Stalin's mental health; some agreed that he was a paranoiac and that his disease became progressively worse toward the end of his life.

One psychiatrist who did comment argued that the whole issue was not of decisive importance. Pathological features can easily be found in the mental makeup of many famous personalities. But in Stalin's case they do not explain his exceptional cruelty. Psychiatry does not provide mitigating circumstances, and to prevent a recurrence of Stalinism, political factors, such as the readiness of the people to defend its freedom, are of much greater importance than medical diagnoses. [32]

Stalin's disease, if indeed he was sick in conformity with the textbooks, was a historical accident. But Russia and other countries have had mad rulers before, and it should not absolve us from looking for deeper reasons for the reign of terror. For Stalin's madness fails to explain how a mentally disturbed man found so many willing supporters and victims, how he managed to stay in power for decades enjoying immense popularity, how he succeeded to impart his paranoia to a great many others, creating something akin to a collective psychosis.

If Stalin was not ill in a clinical sense, the same questions still remain: What kind of people welcomed and supported him? What kind of party made him its leader and blindly followed him? Or was it perhaps that the position of the leader in a totalitarian regime was so immensely strong that it prevailed over all other factors?

The Fascist experience in Italy and Germany has shown the crucial role of the Duce and the Führer. Hitler and Mussolini created their parties in their image, and it is perfectly legitimate to talk about the Hitler and the Mussolini "movement," for theirs were not political parties in the traditional sense. However auspicious the conditions for the rise of parties of this kind, it is unlikely that but for the presence of these specific individuals they would have come to power, stayed in power, and have unleashed a Second World War with all its consequences. But Stalin's role in the Soviet Union was initially less decisive. When he concentrated power in his hands, Communist power was already firmly established. There is every reason to believe that even if Stalin had been shot or had died of a disease or had never existed, the party would have still remained in power in the 1920s and 1930s.

True, he played an enormous role in shaping the character of the party and of Soviet society; he was the unquestioned leader, an idol of many. His authority was enormous. If he said that the country was surrounded by enemies, that there were countless internal enemies, and that the class struggle would not decrease but intensify the more the country approached socialism, this had a very great impact on the mentality of a great many people. It helps to explain that the wild accusations against so many people, high and low, did not become a matter of ridicule but were believed, or at least half-believed, by many for a long time.

But it still leaves unexplained the basic issues that have been mentioned, such as, for instance, the question of why so many people signed confessions of crimes they had never committed. What new light has been shed by the revelations of glasnost?

It is likely that some of the defendants in the early trials (1936) were promised a prison term rather than the death sentence if they confessed. There is some recent factual evidence to this effect. A. I. Katsafa, who was head of the NKVD detachment in charge of Kamenev at the time of the 1935 trial, reported in 1956, when interrogated, that immediately before the trial A. F. Rutkovsky, the head of the NKVD secret political department, assured Kamenev that his life would be spared if he confirmed at the trial his admission of guilt. The whole world would be watching the trial, and Kamenev's cooperation was needed in the circumstances.[33] But this was in 1935; by 1937 such promises could no longer have been very impressive. True, some members of the families of Bukharin, Tomsky, and the generals survived, but many did not, and the survival chances seem to have been ruled by accident rather than by design.

It should be noted furthermore that most old Bolsheviks were not brought to show trials in the first place. Fifty or more were lined up for the first trial (Zinoviev-Kamenev), but only eighteen defendants eventually appeared in open court. Opposition leaders, such as Smilga, Preobrazhensky, and others, may not, for all we know, have been broken by the interrogators. According to a rumor frequently heard, there were several dress rehearsals for each show trial, so that the defendants did not know in the end when the true "public" performance was taking place. Roy Medvedev repeated this allegation in 1989 and even named the chief stage manager (L. M. Zakovsky).[34]

One case that sheds some light on the motives for confession is that of Ivan Smirnov. He was an old Bolshevik, a party member since 1899; he had taken a leading part in all the uprisings since 1905. During the civil war he was head of the Siberian Central Committee, and the victory over Kolchak was to a great degree his achievement.[35] An early Trotsykite, he was arrested, released in 1929, and made people's commissar of post and telegraph, but he was rearrested in 1933. In 1936 he was a codefendant in the Zinoviev-Kamenev trial and was shot.

In the interrogation he flatly denied that he had been a member of a terrorist group that intended to kill Stalin. Since Smirnov was in prison, he could, of course, not have been an active member of any terrorist center even if he had wanted, but apparently Stalin particularly wanted his confession. It was therefore decided to confront him with his wife, Alexandra Safonova. She also was an old revolutionary; her life story was one of arrests and escapes; as prisoner of the White armies in Siberia, she had undergone torture. Yet when she was told by Yezhov in person that evidence against her husband was needed by the party, she capitulated and agreed to collaborate.

Smirnov told his interrogator that he had met Trotsky's son in Berlin and exchanged letters with Trotsky. But terrorism had never been mentioned in the exchange as a method of political struggle. There had been no "instructions," no "center," and even less a terrorist conspiracy. But Safonova said, when the two were confronted: "Ivan Nikitovich, the talk about terrorism took place in my apartment; you yourself talked about killing Stalin." The confrontation took place one week before the opening of the trial, and Safonova repeated her accusation against her husband in open court. Smirnov, who had been holding out for so long, now admitted everything and was duly executed. He was betrayed by a person close and dear to him; as usual, the interrogators had looked for the chink in his armor.

Safonova survived, and after her release her turn came to explain her behavior. She said that 90 percent of her evidence had been lies. If so, what was the true 10 percent? She had been accused at the time of being the "finance minister" of the "terrorist center." In fact, she had once collected money for Ryazanov, an elderly comrade and the leading Marxologist of the day, who had been banished by Stalin to Saratov because of his reluctance to participate in the Stalinist cult and was destitute. Thus, an act of charity became a terrorist operation not just as far as the NKVD was concerned but in Safonova's own imagination. True, Mrachkovsky (a friend of Smirnov's) had once said in conversation that he had talked with Stalin and that the idea had crossed his mind, how easy it would be to liquidate him. Whereupon Ivan Smirnov had said: "But we cannot do this." On another occasion, when discussing the consequences of collectivization of agriculture, Smirnov had said that for such crimes even to kill a man would be insufficient punishment. And on another occasion Ivan Smirnov asked himself, according to Safonova: "Has Stalin become a real Fascist?" But he answered his own question: "No, his past in the party makes this impossible."

But why was the opposition so much opposed to terror? According to Safonova, its members were not cowards, nor did they lack conspirational experience. They opposed terror in principle. Furthermore, they thought Stalin's policy by and large correct; they only disliked his methods.

Why did she lie and betray her husband? According to Safonova, Kirov's murder was the key event. She felt somehow morally responsible for it, and Stalin and his henchmen played on this.[36]

At this point, her explanation becomes difficult to believe. Let us assume that the old oppositionists knew nothing about the truth behind the murder, that Nikolaev had either acted alone or had been manipulated by the NKVD. (We have it from many sources that rumors to this effect were widespread in the Soviet Union at the time.) But even then it is impossible to understand the psychology of the Safonovas and the Smirnovs. Guilt implies that they had in some way prepared the ground for the murder by incitement or by other attempts to destabilize the regime. But they had surrendered to Stalin well before 1934; they had nothing against him, and even less against Kirov. How could they have felt any guilt on account of Kirov's murder? During the first days after the murder, when information was as yet sparse, it is just possible that Safonova might have feared that "one of them" might, after all, have been involved. But the interrogation took place eighteen months after the murder.

Safonova explained that the opposition respected Stalin, but it did not love or idolize him. If so, why should a wife accuse her husband, both old revolutionaries, of fantastic crimes just because Stalin wanted her to? A noted Soviet author writing in 1988 has said that it might appear incomprehensible fifty years after the events but that in 1936 the psychology of the people involved was totally different. A great mental effort is certainly needed to try to understand the mentality of the defendants of 1936–38. But hard as one may try, the explanations given by Safonova and others still lack the ring of conviction. Even if we assume that a true Bolshevik had to be ready to give his life for the party, there was nothing in the party statutes that said he also had to incriminate himself of treason, espionage, and terrorism, the worst political crimes on the calendar. Such behavior makes sense only if we assume that the old-guard Bolsheviks were men and women of morbid guilt feelings, willing to accept the responsibility for all the imperfections of the world, spending sleepless nights because of crimes they had never committed. But they did not suffer from such hypersensitivity. Safonova's evidence was not 90 percent or 99 percent wrong, but totally mendacious, and she must have known it. There might have been one or two among the defendants suffering from a surfeit of misplaced guilt feeling, willing to act as martyrs for a cause that did not carry conviction. But this does not account for the behavior of all the others.

Why should Safonova have said less than the whole truth in 1958 when there was no more risk? Perhaps she wanted to rationalize her behavior twenty years earlier to find excuses for her betrayal. One cannot possibly comment with assurance about individual cases. Perhaps she had been more afraid than she wanted to admit. It was one thing to be tortured by the "class enemy" in 1918, another, more difficult, to stand up to her own people in 1936. In 1918 she must have felt that even if she was to die, she was dying for the right cause, that she had the moral support of her party. Life outside the party was difficult to envisage for this generation of Bolsheviks. In 1936 there was the feeling of total isolation that made resistance infinitely more difficult.

Whatever the means of extraction of confessions in the case of Zinoviev, Piatakov, and Bukharin, we have it on the authority of NKVD people in the field that "without beating (*mordoboi*) and torture there were no confessions."[37] Instead, those arrested would claim that they had been the victims of false and malicious denunciation. In other words, those who were interrogated in accordance with legal procedure did not collaborate; it was only as the result of beating and more beating that results were achieved. There were a great many forms of physical torture. It began with the conveyor system. The defendants were interrogated without interruption; they had to stand up and were not permitted to sleep. If this did not produce quick results, they were beaten, and bones were broken. They were not permitted to drink or were given very salty water or compelled to eat and drink excrement. They were kept in very hot or freezing rooms and knifed or burned on various parts of the body. There was an extensive *instrumentarium* of torture, and the interrogators learned from experience. A favorite gambit was to beat them on the mouth right at the start of the interrogation so that they lost a few teeth. [38] If this did not work, more elaborate and painful methods were used.

Mental torture played an equally important role. Those beaten up by young professional gangsters were men and women of consequence; only yesterday they had been ministers, generals, or directors of factories. Such unceremonious treatment came as an enormous shock. They were threatened with the murder of their relations; furthermore, they were told that if they did not confess, they would be shot without the benefit of a trial. No one would know about their fate; they would simply disappear. As in the case of the Gestapo, the image of the secret police became so frightening that the application of violence was unnecessary in many cases. Those arrested trembled even before the interrogation started. They came to believe that all resistance was completely useless. In many cases this approach seems to have worked; the defendants immediately volunteered whatever information was wanted.

More became known under glasnost about the Bukharin trial than about any other episode of the great terror, and the revelations shed some light on the questions that have preoccupied us. The key figures were mercilessly bullied, isolated, and subjected to all kinds of blackmail; many were tortured. There was no appeal to their loyalty to Stalin and the party. [39] Many resisted to the end, denying all along any guilt. Among them were, for instance Slepkov and Ryutin, who repeatedly tried to commit suicide. [40] These "hard-core cases" were never brought to trial but liquidated in the cellars of the Lubyanka. Stalin repeatedly intervened, demanding the use of harsher measures in the extraction of "confessions." Thus he wrote in a note to Yezhov, dated May 26, 1937, that Beloborodov, a former member of the Left opposition who had not been broken by the interrogators, should be made to feel that he was "in a prison, not a hotel." [41]

In the preparation of the Bukharin case, unlike the other show trials, the Central Committee was involved. A special commission headed by Mikoyan was appointed, and it practically sealed the fate of the accused well before the trial took place. The only question left open was whether Bukharin and the others should be immediately tried or whether their case should be transmitted to the NKVD for further "treatment," as Stalin proposed—not out of any humanitarian feelings but because many members of the commission had spoken in favor of a trial without application of the death penalty. (Among them were Khrushchev and Litvi-nov.) On the very day this decision was taken, February 27, 1937, Bukharin and Rykov were arrested.

The glasnost revelations also confirmed some suspicions that had been widespread for a long time; that the NKVD used undercover agents to break the accused. One such case was that of Vladimir Astrov, who had been used as a key witness against Bukharin and who survived to tell his story, or at least a good part of it, under glasnost. An old Bolshevik—he had joined the party before the October Revolution—he was a leading journalist and historian who belonged to Bukharin's circle in the 1920s. Arrested for the first time in 1933, he became a *seksot*, a secret collab-orator of the NKVD, which used him in confrontations with Bukharin in which he claimed that the right-wing opposition had advocated terrorism in general and Stalin's murder in particular.[42]

Writing in 1989 at the age of ninety, Astrov said that he regarded the Astrov of 1932 a different human being, for so much had changed since. He had regarded the investigators as representatives of the party and complied with their demands, culminating in the confrontation with Bukharin, whereupon, a unique case, he was released from prison.[43]

Astrov's advice to the young generation was not to retreat even under duress one step from the truth; otherwise, "who ever had said A would be compelled to say B" and, like him, "objectively" becomes a helper in the horrible raging of the repression.

Astrov's confession many years after the event is a valuable contribu-tion toward an understanding of the functioning of the terror machinery, even though the memory of the writer fifty years after the event was at times faulty; at other times, he let his behavior appear in a more favorable light than warranted.[44]

The question of why there was no more resistance among the Jewish communities in the Second World War has been discussed for a long time. The same question arises, a fortiori, with regard to the victims of the Stalinist terror. The Jewish victims were often children, the elderly, or sick people, whereas most of the Soviet victims were men in the prime of their life; tens of thousands were military people. Why did they col-lapse so easily, implicating not only themselves but falsely accusing so many others? What could they hope for? Logic and the sense of self-preservation should have guided their steps. It was only to be expected that under glasnost searching and painful questions would be asked: Why admire Marshal Blyukher, who had been a member of the court-martial that had condemned Yakir to death?[45] The answer given was that

> there is no denying that Blyukher signed a monstrous sentence. But if he had not signed it, he would immediately have been on the other side of the barrier. And he was frightened. Anyone who remembers the atmosphere of those years will understand him, though possibly not forgive him. A renowned hero of the civil war, a man who was legend, but he was frightened. . . . Like Tomsky, like Bukharin, like Yakir, he was conscious of being part of the system personified by Stalin. And that paralyzed his will, confused him, disorientated him. . . .[46]

A similar explanation was given by a former inmate of Stalinist prisons: He referred to the horrible mental devastation, the feeling of loneliness, of utter helplessness, of a world that had become wholly absurd.[47] All of which may be true, but it is also true that soldiers are paid not to be afraid. It does not explain why General Primakov ("a man of absolutely outstanding bravery," according to Zatonsky) confessed not only to the existence of a plot but gave the names of seventy others whom he had recruited or who knew of the plot—although there was no plot and he had recruited no one. Nor does it explain why Yona Yakir ("a man of rare bravery and rare honesty who seemed to understand everything"—Zatonsky) shouted "Long live Stalin" when facing the firing squad. There were, after all, people who did resist, who were not broken, or who were broken partly only and after a long time. According to a highly placed Soviet official, some seventy-four military prosecutors were "repressed" because they refused to cooperate, that is, to sanction illegal arrests.[48] Some of these officials might have been arrested for other reasons or because they were shielding friends. But at least some of them seem to have acted like decent people, quite irrespective of the consequences.

Bukharin's first wife, Nadezhda Mikhailovna Lukina, was one of the true heroes of the terror. She was arrested in November 1938, interrogated for thirteen months, and shot in March 1940.[49] Lukina was no military hero; she was a bedridden cripple who, before Bukharin's arrest, had returned in protest her party-membership card. She was abused and beaten; her medical corset, without which she could not move, was broken. But her resistance was stronger than that of most of the military heroes. Unlike them, she had morally opted out of the Stalinist universe; she must have known that she would soon die in any case.

Another of the unsung heroes of the terror was Osip Piatnitsky. One of the oldest Bolsheviks alive, he had been one of the key figures in the Communist International. A member of the Central Committee, he was the only one to speak out against the preparation of the Bukharin trial in 1937 at the Central Committee meeting on June 24, 1937.[50] What made this deeply civilian man approaching old age act courageously at a time when the military heroes voted for the immediate execution of Bukharin, Rykov, et al.? And how could they be surprised and shocked when, a mere three months later, a similar fate befell them?

The courage of the military commanders who confessed and informed—some, for all we know, did not—was the courage of men fighting together. Left to their individual resources, their type of courage was ineffectual. Some, at least, were willing to betray their relations and their friends not because of a feeling of greater loyalty but because they could not bear the torture any longer—which does not reflect very well on their generation and its adherence to truth and moral values. Stalinism, after all, was of relatively recent vintage; they had been educated in a different spirit and had other ideals.

What could be said in their defense? That they were ill prepared for such a situation. That many had been active in the tsarist underground was of little relevance. The life of a political convict in tsarist Russia, in contrast to conditions under Stalin, had been paradisiacal. No leading Bolshevik had ever been executed before 1917; many had escaped from their exile, during which they enjoyed a great deal of freedom. It was the tragedy of a generation that many did not know how to resist evil and how to die.

One of the facts that was of paramount importance with regard to pretrial preparation was the near total demoralization of the victims even before they were arrested. It remains to be investigated in detail what had caused this—fear, a feeling of isolation, the conviction that Stalin had been right all along? A few examples that became known should suffice to shed some light on a state of mind that is difficult to understand even with the benefit of hindsight.

On August 11, 1936, Ezhov reported to Stalin that he had summoned Piatakov and conveyed to him that the Central Committee had decided to appoint him, Piatakov, star witness in the forthcoming trial against the "parallel anti-Soviet Trotskyite center." Piatakov said in reply that he regarded this appointment as evidence of enormous confidence in him. He suggested that he himself should carry out the execution of those sentenced to be shot, including his former wife, and that this should be announced in the press.[51] Even Ezhov found the offer exaggerated and called it absurd; but Piatakov still insisted that his request should be committed to the Central Committee.

Piatakov, it should be remembered, was one of the leading old Bolsheviks; he had fought in the underground and in the civil war. Lenin had mentioned him in his "Testament" as one of the six most important and promising successors. Above all, Piatakov was not yet even under arrest when he made this suggestion; he was arrested only a month later, on September 12, while on a mission in the Urals.

Karl Radek published in *Izvestiia* of August 1936 an article in which he had called Trotsky "a bloody clown" and "Fascist *oberbandit*"; *Pravda* on the same day featured an article by Piatakov in which the author demanded to "destroy without mercy the despicable murderers and traitors," referring to the Zinoviev-Kamenev trial. But Radek was not under arrest at the time; he had been neither starved nor beaten to extract from him these lines; his arrest came only in mid-September.

In view of such utter loss of self-respect, it is remarkable that Piatakov held out for more than a month in prison until he signed the confession that had been drawn up by his interrogators; Radek refused to sign for two months and eighteen days, and Muralov, the most resilient of the lot, refused to cooperate for seven months and seventeen days. Most of the marshals and the generals, on the other hand, collapsed within a few days. But it could well be that they were subjected to merciless beatings and other torture from the first moment; until the circumstances of their "interrogation" are known in detail, it would be inappropriate to judge them harshly.[52]

It is one of the mysteries of the Stalin era that no serious attempt was ever made to kill the dictator. There were attempts against Hitler's life, but there is no known case of a conspiracy against Stalin. Which is all the more surprising in view of the terrorist tradition of long standing in Russia. Was it the effectiveness of the security organs that prevented an attempt on Stalin's life? It is unlikely, for they were not as efficient as their reputation would suggest; in any case, the attempt could have come from

within the NKVD. By late 1937, at the very latest, any rational assessment of the situation should have persuaded high-ranking army officers
or NKVD officials that they had little to lose: their chances of survival
were problematical, to say the least. Self-interest, if not patriotism, should
have induced some of them to depose Stalin. Did they believe that any
such attempt was doomed? But even in this case a single individual might
have acted; experience shows that against action by individuals even the
most accomplished secret service is powerless: There is no weak link in a
one-man conspiracy. Since it is unlikely that the whole population of the
Soviet Union was hypnotized and paralyzed by Stalin, that no such
attempt was made remains a fascinating conundrum that thus far remains
unsolved.

In some respects the study of the great terror has only just begun, now
that so many facts have been collated; many, unfortunately, are still
missing. At some future stage it will be possible to conclude with greater
assurance how important accident was in the selection of the victims.
Why, for instance, did Litvinov and Petrovsky survive and most other old
Bolsheviks perish? Nikolai Starostin, the most famous soccer player of his
generation, was about to be shot but received instead a ten-year sentence
because his daughter was a classmate and friend of Molotov's daughter.
From the new evidence available so far it would appear that the less
prominent the individual involved, the greater the scope of accident.
General Gorbatov says he survived because a member of the military
tribunal knew him well. But if Gorbatov had been an officer of higher
rank at the time or if his trial had taken place in 1937 or 1938 (he was
sentenced in May 1939), he would probably have been less lucky.

It still remains to be investigated why some victims volunteered false
information and readily informed on their comrades, while others could
not be broken. Of the less prominent victims, more could have saved
themselves if they had simply disappeared from their normal place of
residence. The Soviet Union is a vast country, and the resources of the
security organs were stretched; it took them a long time to catch up with
people who frequently changed their whereabouts. Not a few were, in
fact, saved because they adopted a peripatetic life-style during the critical
months.

It will be one of the most difficult assignments to establish who knew
what by what time. Everyone knew, of course, from radio and newspapers that many "enemies of the people" had been caught, tried, and

executed. But to what extent and for how long was the official propaganda believed by various segments of the population, among the party and the nonparty members, in the cities and the countryside? At what stage did the conviction gain ground that the purges would snowball and ultimately affect, directly or indirectly, a considerable portion of the population? There are no public opinion polls in totalitarian societies; it is dangerous to put on paper one's innermost thoughts and fears. Most of those involved are now dead, and even the reminiscences written after 1953 must be read with some caution.

Perhaps, in the end, there will exist more clarity as to Stalin's motives, even though chances are that they will remain open to divergent interpretations. Nevertheless, we may be one day in a better position to assess the terror in history and its impact on Soviet society and politics. For a long time there was a greater willingness to suppress the memories than to come to terms with them. Only under glasnost has a serious attempt been made to exorcise the ghost. But first the disease that had affected Soviet society has to be diagnosed—a painful process, unpalatable to some even now fifty years after the great terror.

8. Stalin at Home

Information about Stalin's private life was kept to the very minimum and was in inverse ratio to the enormous publicity given his public activities. Little was known about the way he lived, his family, and his personal habits. Soviet citizens knew, of course, that he worked and lived in the Kremlin; some knew that he had a dacha in Kuntsevo and another, more distant, in Zubalovo. Soviet citizens also knew that his wife had died suddenly in the early 1930s. There was a famous picture showing Stalin carrying his little daughter, Svetlana. It was, of course, known how he dressed and that he smoked a pipe. Broadly speaking, however, this was the extent of public knowledge about Stalin. It was as if he had no private life or that, more likely, some impenetrable curtain had been drawn around him as a shield from profane curiosity.

The only biographies of Stalin published in the Soviet Union were short tracts that contained no frivolous details about his private life. The few foreigners who wrote about Stalin had no access to his personal sphere, either, even though at least one of them, Barbusse, was received at his dacha. Rumors abounded, of course, but in actual fact there was not much to report about his private life. He was not a colorful figure like the extrovert Mussolini. His work day was so long that there was virtually no time for other pursuits. Nor did he have any major interests or hobbies outside politics. He seldom traveled; during the last twenty years of his life, he never once visited an agricultural settlement. From time to time, Stalin would spend a few weeks in Yalta, Sochi, Tshaltubo, or some other resort in the south. He had a fairly sizable library and enjoyed reading. His work hours were irregular, with a preference for working at night. But he also entertained his cronies from the Politburo until the last years of his life, when, with increasing frequency, he complained about his state of health. Women were seldom among his guests; Jakob Berman, the veteran Polish Communist, related how he had to dance with Molotov while Stalin operated the gramophone. Khrushchev reported similar experiences about performing the Ukrainian gopak. After Stalin's death, the curtain covering the private sphere was lifted to a certain extent by those who had been in contact with him. Physicians, guards, writers, and artists reported their impressions, but political leaders, on the whole, remained silent.[1] It took thirty-five years after Stalin's death and the glasnost era for more detailed accounts to emerge. They emanated from those who had been given some access to the archives; others collected oral evidence.

Of these sources, Major Aleksei Trofimovich Rybin had perhaps been the one closest physically to Stalin. He had been a member of the NKVD detachment in charge of Stalin's personal security.[2] Provoked by Rybakov's novel *The Children of the Arbat,* Rybin more or less systematically collected evidence from other members of Stalin's household, mainly NKVD personnel. The general picture that emerged was certainly more flattering than the image of Stalin presented by Rybakov. It was not true that Stalin had been afraid to mix with people, as Rybakov had argued, or that he had a morbid fear of terrorists. His car slowly traversed the streets of Moscow (in particular, the Arbat) whenever he traveled from his dacha to the Kremlin. Sometimes he would pick up an old lady he had spotted who was walking slowly and with difficulty or a small group of people waiting in the rain for the bus. Sometimes he would upbraid General Vlassik, the commander of his personal guard, for what seemed to Stalin excessive precautions. He wanted not to be isolated from the rest of the world but to be in a railway carriage "together with all others." Stalin was affable and had the common touch. He showed courage, particularly during the war.

During the war, he preferred to work at the dacha rather than in the Kremlin, even though there were no air-raid shelters at the dacha. During an air attack, he would sometimes watch the planes from the roof of the building. According to Rybin, Stalin did not panic in mid-October 1941 when German forward units had reached the suburbs of Moscow. While Beria gave orders to senior party officials for the evacuation of Moscow on the evening of October 15 and although Malenkov and Kaganovich also recommended the move to Kuibyshev, Stalin, in a

Kremlin meeting on October 16, announced that he had decided to stay in Moscow.[3]

There were riots in Moscow at the time, and shops were pillaged. According to Rybin, Stalin deliberately showed himself in various parts of the city and talked to people to give a boost to morale. Molotov was sent for three days to Kuibyshev to supervise the transfer of the foreign ministry, but he also confirmed in conversation with Rybin that Stalin had no intention of leaving the capital. On the other hand, Stalin's private plane and train were also kept in a state of readiness so that the generalissimus could leave in case of a change of mind at the last minute. When information was received that an unexploded mine or shell had landed not far from the dacha, Stalin joined the search party—yet another demonstration of personal courage.

As mentioned before, he traveled very little during the war or after. On his way back from the Teheran Conference, he stopped at Stalingrad and inspected the ruins. On a visit to Oryol in 1946, he walked the streets accompanied by hundreds of citizens. When they thanked him for having defeated the Germans, he replied modestly: "The people defeated the Germans, not I."

From the stories of his guards Stalin appears to have been a self-effacing, fatherly person. On various occasions he angrily protested having watched documentary films showing him in situations that had never taken place. When Beria and Malenkov argued that these scenes were "needed for history," he opposed them, saying: "Leave me alone with such history."

As he left for the Potsdam Conference, Stalin instructed Zhukov not to send guards of honor for his reception and to keep any ceremony to the very minimum. Beria's book on the history of Bolshevism in the Caucasus, which heaped praise on Stalin, was not written (as generally believed) upon Stalin's request; rather, it was written on Beria's initiative, because Beria wanted to ingratiate himself with Stalin.

In Stalin's living room there was a picture of Lenin in front of which a light was always burning, a ritual similar to that practiced by churches. In the adjoining room there was a bust of Lenin to which Stalin was so attached that it traveled with him whenever he had to leave Moscow.

Stalin was very hardworking, according to I. Orlov, another of his personal guards. He worked day and night, especially during the war;

usually he fell asleep only in the early hours of the morning, without even having undressed himself, in his gray military coat and his high boots.

Stalin aged visibly during the war; his hair became much grayer; in the years following the war, he suffered frequently from rheumatism, angina, and high blood pressure.

Yet with all the hard work and the sicknesses of impending old age, Stalin was a most considerate boss; according to Rybin, he never raised his voice. Because no member of his family lived with him, he often invited his guards for company and told them humorous stories of his life. At other times, he would ask for their advice, for example, what to do with the valuable fur that he had received as a present from Marshal Choibalsan of Mongolia. According to the same source, Stalin did not want to be surrounded by yes-men. About those who told him, "Whatever you command will be done," he said: "I do not need advisers of this kind." According to Orlov, he liked people to insist on their point of view if they were convinced that they were right.[4]

From other sources, information became available about Stalin's intellectual interests. In the year 1926, he composed a list for Tovstukha, his then secretary, to buy a personal library covering all major fields of human knowledge. He was particularly interested in historical literature, with special emphasis on Ivan the Terrible. But he also read historical textbooks, and from time to time he would send a short note to one of his favorite writers.[5] Because he had never systematically studied philosophy and felt the need to improve his knowledge, he was tutored for a period of time by Y. Sten, a philosophy professor who was the deputy director of the Marx-Engels Institute and one of Bukharin's followers. Stalin devoured newspapers. In 1936, he subscribed to no fewer than nine émigré Russian newspapers and periodicals from Paris, Prague, and New York— including *Vremya*, published in Harbin.

A number of sources, including some of the physicians treating him, have provided fairly detailed reports about his last days. On February 27, 1953, Stalin went to the Bolshoi Theatre to watch *Swan Lake*. The day after, Stalin saw a movie in the Kremlin, following which he invited Beria, Malenkov, Khrushchev, and Bulganin to his Kuntsevo dacha. They were served grape juice and fruits and left at about four in the morning. Stalin went to bed and told his employees and the guard that he would not need them. They, too, should get some sleep. Such instructions, we are told, were quite uncommon. During the following day (March 1), employees at the dacha heard no movement from his room, and at ten-thirty in the evening, their suspicion had grown to such an extent that they decided that someone should inquire. But they were so afraid to go to Stalin's room unasked that they postponed it until the mail had arrived.[6]

The messenger who went to Stalin's quarters found him prostrate on the floor; next to him was a watch and a copy of *Pravda*. He had not yet totally lost consciousness, but he could no longer speak. The guard called Ignatov, who had been recently appointed head of the KGB, but Ignatov was afraid of making any decision. He demanded that Beria be informed. The other members of the Politburo were also called.

The first to arrive were Beria and Malenkov. The idea of calling a physician apparently did not occur to them, or they were afraid to do so. Beria told the employees that there was no reason to panic, because, quite obviously, Comrade Stalin was just sleeping heavily. Only on the next morning at about nine o'clock did the first physicians arrive: "They were so agitated that their arms and legs trembled. They shook so much that they could not even take off Stalin's shirt; it had to be cut with a pair of scissors."[7]

The physicians diagnosed Stalin's condition as a burst blood vessel in the brain. An operation was ruled out, and when Beria told the doctors that they would be "personally held responsible for Stalin's life," it did not make them any less reluctant to take action. In all probability, such measures would have been ineffective, anyway.[8] The day after, Svetlana was called to the dacha, as was Vasili, who arrived drunk and shouted: "Scoundrels, they have killed Father."

A few minutes before Stalin's death on March 5, Beria approached Stalin's body and said: "All members of the Politburo are assembled here. Do say something, Josef Visarionovich . . ." But there was no answer.

Rybin says that there were rumors, above all in Georgia, that Stalin had been poisoned but that these were quite baseless. Stalin did not take good care of his health and hated to see doctors. He suffered from various illnesses in his later years, with symptoms such as dizziness. Irregular habits, such as eating dinner either early in the afternoon or late at night or not at all, may well have aggravated his condition.

Rybin's account and the evidence collected from others who worked for Stalin shows that they were faithful servants who were totally devoted to their boss. In their eyes, Stalin was a strict taskmaster but a great and good man, and their accounts are, no doubt, subjectively honest: It is as they remember it. But their views have been contradicted in detail as much as in general outline. If Major Rybin claims that no special precautions were taken in the Arbat to safeguard Stalin's driving along the street, Lev Razgon, who was living illegally in Moscow at the time, reports that the street was known as the Grusinian-Military Highway because secret police guards were positioned at virtually every entrance.[9]

A highly placed legal official who worked for the Soviet army characterized the Rybin account as rose-colored; the picture of amoral Stalin as a "simple" and honest man originated with people who were captives of the Stalin myth. How does one explain that the very same people who praise Stalin have the most negative recollections of his political associates, from Beria to Malenkov, from Voroshilov to Kaganovich?

Was Stalin a simpleton, a good man fallen among thieves, a tool of the bureaucracy that committed abominable crimes while keeping him in the dark? The real Stalin emerges from a review of the fate of the members of his family. Stalin was married twice, first to Ekaterina Svanidze. After her death, he married his secretary, Nadezhda Allilueva, in 1918. Nadezhda either committed suicide or was murdered in 1932. According to various rumors published under glasnost, Stalin and his wife had quarreled bitterly the evening before her death at a reception given by Voroshilov. Stalin either had killed her or drove her to suicide by his rudeness.[10] These rumors date back to 1932, and there is no way of corroborating them. The same is true with regard to Stalin's alleged liaisons (for example, with Rosa Kaganovich); they seem to belong to the realm of fantasy.

It has been reported that Stalin was deeply shocked by the death of his second wife; he visited her grave at the Novodevichi cemetery from time to time for many years.

That Stalin may have loved her in his own strange way did not prevent him from decimating her family in the purges. Her sister Anna was given a ten-year sentence in 1937; the sister's husband, the Chekist Redents, was shot in 1941. Another sister and a cousin (Ivan) were also arrested but survived the camps. The Svanidze clan fared equally badly. Stalin's brother-in-law (and personal friend) Alesha Svanidze was executed; his wife was given a ten-year sentence and died in prison. Alesha's son was arrested as a "relation of an enemy of the people" but returned from the camps in 1956. Maria Svanidze, Stalin's sister-in-law, also died in prison.[11]

Stalin had three children, but he took only limited interest in their lives—although enough to ruin them. Jakob Dzhugashvili was Ekaterina Svanidze's son. He was born in Baku in 1908. His mother died soon after from typhoid fever, and he grew up in the family of Ekaterina's older sister. In 1921, he went to Moscow to join his father. After graduating from school, Jakob went to Leningrad to work in an electric power plant but also enrolled in a workers' university. He then studied for an engineering degree in Moscow. Between 1937 and 1940, at the insistence of his father, he joined the artillery academy of the Red Army, from which he graduated in 1940; the following year, he joined the Communist party.

Relations with his father were bad; on several occasions he tried to commit suicide.[12] Stalin despised his son; he disagreed with most of Jakob's decisions, including the choice of his bride, Julia Meltser, a Jewish girl from Odessa. (She was arrested but released in 1943.) According to documents that have become accessible in recent years, Jakob was not an outstanding pupil at the military academy, but he was quiet and disciplined. Toward the end of his studies his performance improved; his work was described as accurate by his teachers, and he took an active part in the political work of the academy. His marks in Marxism-Leninism were worse than in all other subjects. He volunteered to go to the front when war broke out. From the beginning of the war, Jakob was the commander of a battery of howitzers in the Fourteenth Armored Division, with the rank of first lieutenant. On July 4, 1941, near Vitebsk, his unit was surrounded by advancing German troops, and he was taken prisoner.

The Germans used Jakob in their propaganda; thousands of leaflets were dropped over the Russian lines that stated that both Stalin's son as well as Molotov's had defected.[13] Therefore, any resistance was senseless; the leaflets also stated that Jakob was in good health and felt exceedingly well. There was also a short personal message to his father in which he said that he was well treated and would soon be sent to an officers' camp. The leaflets were first brought to Zhdanov, who forwarded them to Stalin.

From internal German documents discovered after the war, it appeared that Jakob Stalin behaved with dignity when interrogated by the Abwehr. He said that he considered it a disgrace to be a prisoner, that the war was by no means over, and that the Germans would never succeed in taking Moscow. He also said that he had talked with his father over the phone for the last time on June 22. Knowing that Jakob was about to leave for the front, Stalin said: "Go and fight."[14]

Jakob Stalin was kept in various officers' camps; he was on friendly terms with a group of Polish officers and, on one occasion, tried to escape with them. When the attempt failed, he was transferred to Sachsenhausen, a major concentration camp. After the battle of Stalingrad, Hitler suggested (through the Swedish Red Cross) an exchange of Jakob Stalin for Field Marshal Paulus. Stalin allegedly answered that a marshal would not be exchanged for a lieutenant.[15] Jakob might still have survived, because the Germans kept their prominent prisoners to the very end in the hope that some exchange could be arranged, after all. But he suffered from severe depression; he suspected what his fate as a "traitor" would be after the war. On April 14, 1943, Jakob entered the neutral zone near the outer perimeter of the camp; he knew, of course, that anyone who did so would be shot. According to one version, the suicide attempt followed a brawl between him and several British officers who shared a room with him. Jakob is said to have asked to see the commander of the camp, and when his request was refused, he ran toward the barbed wire, shouting "Shoot me!"

Jakob Dzhugashvili became the antihero of a bizarre novel published under glasnost by an obscure writer named V. Uspensky.

The book is entitled *Secret Adviser to the Leader*, and it was composed in the Pamyat tradition, with Trotsky as Stalin's evil genius.[16] There was a new twist to the story, however, inasmuch as Jakob becomes the lover of Nadezhda, his stepmother, in the novel. *Secret Adviser* was perhaps intended to counteract Rybakov's *Children of the Arbat*; it caused both indignation and amusement. In a country in which information has always been accessible only to a privileged few, rumors have always been particularly important, and at least some people are always ready to believe them, however farfetched or absurd.

Vasili Stalin, born in 1921, was Nadezhda's son, and although Stalin did not see him often, he preferred him to Jakob. He grew up in the Zubalovo dacha, went to a Moscow school, and then became a student in the Red Army aviation school, from which he graduated in 1940. During the war, he served mainly in the inspectorate of the air force. He also reportedly took part in twenty-seven combat missions over enemy territory and shot down one enemy aircraft, even though, following the capture of Jakob, Stalin had strictly forbidden him to participate in combat missions.[17] At the age of twenty-six, Vasili was made a major general. One year later, he became commander of the Soviet air force in the Moscow district. By 1949, Vasili was a lieutenant general. Following his failure organizing an air force parade in 1952, Stalin gave Vasili a public dressing down, calling him incompetent and a fool, demoting him and sending him back as a student to the air force academy.

While Jakob was apparently a decent man, no one ever spoke well of Vasili—not his classmates, his teachers, whom he terrorized, his fellow officers, or those serving under him. The annual reports about Vasili could hardly have been worse. In January 1945, it was said that he utterly lacked self-discipline. He was accused of beating some of his subordinates. He had little authority as a leader, and his private life was "incompatible with what was expected of a commander of a division." Considering that these comments referred to Stalin's son, a great deal of courage was obviously needed to be so outspoken. But the comments did not affect his subsequent career, until the father realized the true worth of his son.

Three weeks after Stalin's death, Vasili was thrown out of the armed forces without the right to wear the uniform, which was tantamount to a dishonorable discharge. He had been a heavy drinker since an early age and was involved in countless scandals and accidents. Arrested in April 1953, he spent the following years in and out of prison and in exile. His letters to the leadership remained unanswered, but Khrushchev received him in 1960. According to Svetlana Stalin, they kissed and wept; all was forgiven. Vasili got an apartment in Moscow and a dacha not far from the capital; he was reinstated into the party and his medals were returned. But by April 1960, following yet another traffic accident involving a foreign embassy, he was again in prison. Having received an eight-year sentence, he was released in late 1961 because of bad health. He lived the last months of his life in Kasan alone; his two wives and his four children (two of them adopted) had left him well before. He died in March 1962. His tombstone in Kasan bears the inscription "To the only one"—given by his third wife.[18]

One of Stalin's grandchildren, Alexander Burdonski, was interviewed by a Moscow newspaper in October 1988. Born in 1941, he was four years of age when his mother left Vasili; she was not permitted to take her children. They could meet again only after Josef Stalin's death. Alexander became a moderately successful producer at the Moscow Red Army Theater. When asked how he reacted to the revelations at the Twentieth Party Congress (when he was fifteen), Alexander said that for the outside world he was a Stalin—and the telephone did not ring for a long time. Yet, in actual fact, many of his mother's friends had been in the gulag, and she had been in constant fear of being arrested for many years. He and his sisters became *persona non grata* in school and had to be transferred to another institution.[19] Thus, the Stalinist heritage affected even some of his grandchildren.

But Stalin also had his admirers among his grandchildren, of whom there were eight. One of them, Josef (Svetlana's son), worked as a physician in Moscow; his sister Katya, a geologist, lived and worked in Kamchatka in the 1980s. The greatest Stalinist of them all was the eldest, Evgeni Dzhugashvili, Jakob's son. In his lifetime, Stalin had never shown any interest in five of the eight, including Evgeni, who was born out of wedlock. Evgeni was sent to a military school and rose to the rank of colonel, teaching at the Frunze Academy. He said he admired Josef Visarionovich for all he had done for his country and took a very dim view of the de-Stalinization campaign.[20] Stalin's policy was the only possible way to move ahead with both the industrialization of the country and the collectivization of agriculture. He bitterly criticized Volkogonov for stating that after Trotsky had been exiled from the country only a few Trotskyites had remained behind. This was a falsification of history; there had been many. It was absolutely necessary to continue the fight.

The fate of Svetlana is well known in the West. But not much was known about her in the Soviet Union prior to glasnost. Only then did Soviet citizens learn that she had been a good pupil at school, with a pronounced inclination toward literature. Her father took a certain interest in her work, but when she wanted to study literature, he disapproved of her choice, insisting on the study of history at Moscow University. He also disapproved of the choice of her first lover, the well-known filmmaker Aleksei Kapler. For the first time in her life, Svetlana was beaten by her father, and Kapler went to the gulag.[21] According to a Soviet author, her attitude toward her father was quite critical. She realized that her father "was not in the mold of the new Soviet man, which, according to theory, should have emerged from the Revolution."

In 1957, she changed her name to Alliluyeva; she was married first to G. Moroz, a classmate of hers at the university. Later she married Yuri Zhdanov; still later, she married an Indian citizen, and in 1967 she left the Soviet Union and went to the United States. Her subsequent pere- grinations and marital problems, her attempt to resettle in the Soviet Union in 1984, her quarrels with her two older children, from whom she had been separated for seventeen years, are now common knowledge among Soviet citizens. Once she had been the symbol of happiness, of Stalin's love for children in general and his own daughter in particular, of his tenderness. The unhappy fate of his children speaks for itself. But could his offspring have led a normal life in the Soviet Union, or indeed in any other society?

There are intriguing similarities in life-style between Stalin and Hitler, much less so between these two and Mussolini. This subject will preoc- cupy us later on; suffice it to say that both came from poor families. Although Hitler had a profession of sorts, Stalin had none; instead, he was a professional revolutionary virtually from the day he had to leave the theological seminary in Tbilisi. Neither was interested in money; they could get what they wanted in any case. Volkogonov states that Stalin left few earthly possessions when he died. Hitler by comparison told the workers at the Krupp factory in March 1936, "I am perhaps the only statesman in the world without a bank account. I have no shares, nor am I a co-owner of any enterprise."[22] If Hitler, with all his flair for drama and grand entrances, lived relatively simply, so did Stalin; commentators have frequently used the term "ascetic" to describe their life-styles.

Other contemporaries were less impressed by Stalin's alleged asceticism. They included Mikoyan's son, who knew him from a close angle. Stalin's dinners, he reports, often turned into drunken orgies; in addition to the two opulent Moscow dachas, he kept six more at the Black Sea and in the Caucasus.[23] True, Hitler's "dacha" in the mountains, the Berghof near Berchtesgaden, was spectacularly located, but the furniture and the lay- out were petty bourgeois. Both thought themselves irreplaceable; both despised the bureaucracy. Hitler would have liked to destroy the higher officer corps, as Stalin had done, but doing so was impossible while the war continued. The Nazi satraps did not have to fear for their lives, only for their jobs, but the net result was the same as in Moscow—a permanent jockeying in order to curry favor of the supreme leader.

Hitler and Stalin were first-rate tacticians, and both were underrated for a long time by outside observers and their comrades alike: Trotsky continued to refer to Stalin's "mediocrity" until the very end. Both utterly lacked scruples, were masters of perfidy and deceit, and were among the most brazen liars of all time. Stalin, we are told, never raised his voice and only seldom lost his temper, in contrast to Hitler, whose outbursts of rage were notorious and whose conversation often consisted of a few obiter dicta between moody silences. Yet both could be exceedingly charming toward men and women alike, and although they were tyrants, they were not necessarily tyrants vis-à-vis their domestic employees. It was said about Stalin that while he did not hesitate to destroy two-thirds of his Central Committee and most of his military leaders, he did not dare to dismiss a certain domestic serving him, even though he strongly disliked her. Hitler and Stalin distrusted orthodox medicine; whereas Hitler believed in all kinds of fads, Stalin asked for pills and potions from Poskrebyshev, who had once trained as a *feldsher*. Hitler and Stalin were both thought to be homosexual by some analysts, but the evidence is unconvincing; their sexual urge seems to have been limited; unlike Mussolini, neither Stalin nor Hitler flaunted their sexual prowess.

They certainly were male chauvinists; the place of women, as far as they were concerned, was in the kitchen (and, in Russia, also in the factory)—certainly not in the higher echelons of party and government. Neither Hitler nor Stalin showed any interest in their families; their stage was the world, and it left no time for domestic concerns. The women they seem to have truly loved—Angelica (Geli) Raubal in Hitler's case and Nadezhda Alliluyeva in Stalin's—both committed suicide. Hitler and Stalin preferred male to mixed company (Stalin more so than Hitler), and they felt themselves more at ease among comrades younger in years. Both liked to watch movies at night, but so did Churchill. Both were men of vision—immoral, perverted, and ultimately infeasible. In contrast to mere gangsters, however, they were not in politics to get wealthy, nor were they in the condottiere tradition, like Mussolini. They had a grudging respect for each other but none for the democratic leaders of other countries. Both pretended to be annoyed by the cult around them, although both enjoyed it thoroughly.

The comments of people who knew Hitler make strange reading for the student of Stalin's personality. "He wanted to be known as the man of steel," wrote Albert Speer.

> Hard men enjoyed his respect, soft people were never in his favor . . .
> Hitler literally turned day into night; his fear of solitude was striking, he
> expected his entourage to remain with him until he went to bed. . . . His
> meals were taken with grotesque irregularity. . . . His sociability was un-
> real, forced and self-deceiving. . . . He absolutely lacked any feeling about
> family life, the name of his stepbrother Alois Hitler could never even be
> mentioned in his presence. . . . No one in the vicinity of Hitler stood a
> chance of developing into a personality in his own right. . . . He was in no
> sense mentally ill, rather he was mentally abnormal, a person who stood
> on the broad threshold between genius and madness. . . . His dominant
> characteristic was his will to power. . . . Why was he not killed? In ret-
> rospect the elimination of such a dangerous despot appears to have been
> necessary and possible. But at the time such an act should have been
> carried out, it seemed disastrous and impossible. . . . The very measures
> which the [German] people found especially oppressive, the ones that gave
> rise to the saying—if the Führer only knew . . .—were those that Hitler
> had personally ordered. . . .

All these observations, taken from a book of memoirs on Hitler, fit Stalin as well as they do the Führer. Yet the same leaders could turn on their charm as far as visitors and friends were concerned. If Stalin invited the old lady walking with difficulty in the street to join him in the car, Hitler stopped an unknown man walking in pouring rain and gave him his own raincoat.[24] He had his occasional violent fits of rage, but only in the presence of a few courtiers. Even someone who knew him well, like Speer, wrote many years later: "Never in my life have I met a person who so seldom revealed his feelings, and if he did so, instantly locked them away again."

To point to these striking common patterns is not to belittle the great differences between the two men. They were heirs to different traditions, ideologies, and political cultures. Hitler was a spellbinder who owed most of his success to his public speeches both before and after 1933. Musso-lini was one of the greatest artists of twentieth-century propaganda. Stalin was a less-than-mediocre speaker in a language that was not his native tongue; his impact was strongest in a small circle that he dominated absolutely. In contrast to Hitler, Stalin seldom appeared in public. Hitler's life-style was that of a bohemian turned man of action, Stalin was more calculating than the Führer. Stalin's interests were broader than Hitler's; as a good Marxist, he knew that economics was important, and toward the end of his life Stalin established himself not only as a military genius but also as the foremost linguist, historian, philosopher, and economist of his time. Hitler's ambitions were in another direction: He thought of himself as an inspired town planner and architect.

The question of Stalin's sanity has become a major subject of discussion under glasnost. Some experts maintained that the Soviet Union had been ruled by a madman for many years; others argued, on the contrary, that while he had certain obvious character deficiencies, he did not rave; his behavior at least until the end of the war was purposeful, and his personality was rather primitive.[25] There were frequent references to his paranoia, which became worse with age, his frequent *zamknutnost* ("withdrawnness"), his asocial character, and his megalomania. Parallels were drawn with Ivan IV.

Stalin utterly lacked scruples (the Freudian superego), and he was totally convinced that he was always right and the only person farsighted and determined enough to lead his country. But such convictions, coupled with cruelty and vengefulness, do not necessarily amount to a psychosis, a true mental disease, according to the definitions in modern textbooks of psychiatry. Almost all the experts agree that Stalin understood what he was doing and that he was responsible for his actions. He had a good deal of self-possession and was never actually delirious.

Nevertheless, Stalin was, of course, not "normal" in any meaningful sense. He was a psychopath. His condition became more pronounced with age, perhaps as the result of somatic processes (atherosclerosis). Many stories related by experts point to a condition more severe than mere eccentricity. One concerns a native Georgian, Sergei Kavtaradze, whom Stalin had known since his youth. Kavtaradze was arrested, like so many others, but in the middle of the war Stalin remembered him and ordered that he be brought to his dacha for dinner. He greeted him in a very friendly way and asked Kavtaradze what he had been doing of late. "I was in a camp," Kavtaradze answered. Stalin answered that it was unwise to pick such a time to be in a camp. ("You know a war is going on.") Why did he not rejoin the foreign ministry? And so the conversation became ever more amiable until Stalin suddenly drew nearer to him, looked into his eyes, and said, barely audibly: "But you did want to kill me, after all . . . ?" Another story concerns Voroshilov, whom Stalin, toward the end of his life, thought to be a British agent. He gave an order to keep him out of meetings of the Politburo. But he added that if Voroshilov would beg very nicely, he could be admitted, after all. Vannikov, a young protégé of Stalin's, became people's commissar at a very young age but was arrested during the purges and found guilty of high treason. Yet once the war had broken out, Stalin sent an emissary to prison and ordered Vannikov to compose a memorandum concerning his thoughts with regard to the organization of the war economy. Within a few weeks Vannikov was back at his ministerial desk. There were many other totally irrational and inconsistent actions when Stalin was in his fifties, well before old age and infirmity set in.

It is difficult, in summary, to write of Stalin's private life because there was so little of it once he had arrived in the Kremlin, nor was it clear where the public sphere ended and his private life began. As one of Hitler's confidants wrote:

> He carried on official business in the midst of his private life. . . . Since he imposed upon himself so enormous a burden of work, he had to handle it after his own fashion, which meant by highly personal methods. That is why he did not—as he so often said of himself—have any private life. . . .[26]

The same is true, broadly speaking, of Stalin.

9. The Companions-in-Arms

In Stalin's lifetime there was widespread belief outside the Soviet Union that despite all the adulation, the *vohdz* ("leader") was something akin to a *primus inter pares* among the Soviet leadership. No one doubted that his position was preeminent, but it was frequently assumed that those around Stalin in the top echelons of the party and the government were also men of stature, that Stalin had to take their opinions into account, that he had to maneuver to get his way, and that he could not act against their consensus. True, knowledgeable observers had always doubted the supposition that Stalin's power was based on consensus. Yet in spite of the revelations under Khrushchev, one could still find in the West references to alleged struggles for power in the Politburo, to "Stalin beleaguered" by dissenting rivals, and so on.

Many foreigners had met Stalin during wartime and a few thereafter, and the more astute among them had, of course, realized that the other Soviet leaders accorded him deference without example. But other Westerners, misled by rumors or by mirror imaging, firmly believed that important decisions were taken by majority decision in the Politburo, even though the Politburo had virtually ceased to exist at the time. Sometimes Stalin would deliberately add to the confusion by invoking the Politburo as an obstacle when rejecting certain Western proposals. If Churchill told him that certain ideas would be unacceptable to the House of Commons, if Roosevelt said that Congress would disagree, it must have seemed an obvious repartee. It was less obvious why it should have been believed.

Western observers have always found it difficult to understand totalitarian politics. Hence, the reports in the late 1930s about the moderate Hitler finding himself under pressure from radical Goering and aggressive

Ribbentrop. In actual fact, Hitler was under as little pressure as Stalin; the true seat of power was Hitler's secretariat, not the cabinet, and the same was true with regard to Stalin. It took a long time for these facts of political life to be accepted in the West, and only under glasnost were the misconceptions about the mechanism of power under Stalin finally laid to rest.

It had, of course, not always been like this. But since the mid-1930s all power was concentrated in Stalin's hands. Some members of the Politburo would be delegated to carry out specific tasks, and for years Stalin went through the motions of asking for their opinion. But they could not be certain from one meeting to the next whether they were still holding their job and what their chances for survival were. There was a jockeying for position—Malenkov would intrigue against Zhdanov, for example—but none of them had a decisive influence on the shaping of the policy of their country. The only effective limit to the absolute power of the ruler was his limited ability to monitor events and give instructions. And because he needed time to sleep, eat, drink, travel from the Kremlin to his dacha, and for other elementary functions, as well as an occasional hour or two of rest, it follows that he had to concentrate on important affairs of state and that less important ones were ignored.

There were certain differences between the state of affairs in Nazi Germany and the Soviet Union. Hitler's main interest was foreign and military affairs; he interfered fitfully only in social and economic policy and in ideological and cultural matters, in great contrast to Stalin, who did so on a wide range of issues. The Nazi and Fascist satraps had also to obtain the agreement of Hitler (and Mussolini) for important policy decisions. But as far as their tenure was concerned, they could feel more secure, and if they disagreed with a decision, they felt they could sometimes raise objections, albeit cautiously and tactfully.

Such behavior was unthinkable in Moscow. Stalin had surrounded himself with carefully handpicked yes-men, all younger than himself (except Kalinin, a mere figurehead), second- or third-raters who could be relied upon to carefully keep to themselves any ideas of their own. They were neither very clever nor (with one or two exceptions) very stupid. They could be trusted blindly to obey him. Like medieval retainers, they owed all they had to the *seigneur*, who could withdraw his patronage at any moment and thus cause their immediate downfall. They were, without exception, either weak or dishonest; no one of elementary decency would have lasted a day in such surroundings. There was no room for friendship or even sincere cooperation under the circumstances, for they could not trust each other. Nor could hate and rivalry be openly displayed, for a certain team spirit was expected. Stalin's court was a hothouse of deception and dissimulation; the only safe policy was to pay constant homage to the supreme leader, to try to anticipate his thoughts, and, if possible, to suggest new ideas to him in such a way that it would appear that they had been fathered by Stalin himself. But because Stalin was not stupid and had an excellent memory, even this was not at all easy.

One can only guess as to the thoughts of his associates. The older ones, like Molotov and Voroshilov, had been with Stalin since his rise to power. They wholly identified themselves with him; they were his creatures and had no higher aspirations. Their loyalty was absolute, even though it was mixed with a good deal of fear. They had no dignity or self-respect; if Stalin kicked them, they would even more assiduously lick his boots. The attitude of the younger ones was more complicated either because they did have ideas of their own (like Khrushchev and Voznesensky) or because, like Beria, they were unmitigated cynics who, like the master, believed only in power. Among Stalin's close associates there were aggressive scoundrels like Zhdanov and Kaganovich and more likable ones like Kalinin and Mikoyan, who, in other times and surroundings, might have been perfectly normal and decent public officials. Kalinin wept when he signed the many orders for arrest, but he signed them all just the same.[1]

Mikoyan is known to have protected a few people when it was not too risky. But he was the head of the Politburo subcommittee that signed the order that Bukharin, Rykov, and the others were to be arrested, tried, and shot. He knew, of course, that they were innocent, and he could have opted out of the vicious circle of giving orders to kill. But his ability to do so came at a price that was too high for him; he preferred his own survival to the survival of others. Most of Stalin's comrades-in-arms were quite blameless in their private lives: They had no known major vices and loved their spouses and children. They lived very well, although not extravagantly, like Goering, nor did they keep expensive cars, like Brezhnev. Most of them probably never wrote a check in their lives, and they had no time to spend money in any case. Molotov was a model citizen in private life, but so was Himmler. There was nothing flamboyant about anyone in Stalin's retinue; it would have been very dangerous to stand out. Because Stalin's comrades-in-arms had acquired a pronounced sense of self-preservation, they made themselves as inconspicuous as possible.

A Soviet historian writing during glasnost has observed that Stalin's aides worked very hard and some died young. The first part of the observation is correct; most of them worked long hours under the irregular habits of a boss who liked to call them in the early hours of the morning, causing further inconvenience. But in contrast to the Nazi leaders, of whom only Hess lived to a ripe old age, Stalin's henchmen were a living refutation of the allegedly destructive impact of stress on physical health. Except for those few who died relatively young (Zhdanov and Sherbakov) or those who were shot, Stalin's men were distinguished by longevity. In their nineties Molotov and Kaganovich could be seen walking the streets of Moscow; Budyonni died in his ninetieth year, and Voroshilov almost attained the same age. Mikoyan, Bulganin, Malenkov, and Suslov all died in their eighties; Khrushchev and Poskrebyshev, in their seventies. Thus, the wages of sin were not death but a long life as all-Union old-age pensioners.

The renewed fascination with Stalin under glasnost extended only to a limited extent to his aides. The younger generation barely knew their names and had no idea about their historical merits or demerits, nor did they greatly care. If the issue of Stalin's comrades-in-arms did come up, it was mainly because they figured in the sidelines in the many publications about Stalin. This led to a question about why the names of various places that had been renamed after them should not revert to their original names. There was Kalinin and Kaliningrad, and the question arose whether time had not come to rename Kirov (formerly Vyatka), Kirovabad, Kirovgrad, Kirovakan, Kirovsk, etc. Kirov had not been involved in the terror; in fact, he may have been a victim, but the question arose whether the whole practice of renaming cities did not belong to an age that had come to an end. Some right-wing eccentrics, such as the painter Ilya Glazunov, even began to refer to Leningrad as St. Petersburg, but this was an exception.

Although a great deal was known about Stalin, the background of his "true soratniks" ("companions-in-arms," the obligatory term for many years) was largely unknown. There had been some biographies of Voroshilov both before and after Stalin's death, but they contained little substantive information. Mikoyan had written an autobiography that was published (with major cuts) under Brezhnev.[2] Molotov had also worked on his autobiography, but no one wanted to touch it.[3] As for the others, the only available sources were little booklets from the Stalinist era and some books published in the West, which ranged from the uninformed to the fantastic and ridiculous. Most of the essential facts were simply not in the public domain. Roy Medvedev made a brave effort to compose a series of sketches of Stalin's henchmen; they were originally published in the West and, later, under glasnost also in the Soviet Union as "documentary accounts"; Anton Antonov-Ovseenko collected much material about Beria, and this, too, began to appear after 1987.[4] These short profiles were mainly based on stories told by surviving old Bolsheviks; some stories no doubt were true, but others were, in all likelihood, untrue, half true, or embellished. With glasnost, more evidence came to light, and a somewhat more detailed picture emerged.

Molotov

Molotov, more than anyone else, was Stalin's true shadow. He had begun his political career well before 1917, but his outstanding characteristic was not revolutionary fervor. He was an efficient, totally reliable yes-man who perfectly understood even a slight gesture or an unfinished sentence by the boss and acted accordingly. He was a member of the party secretariat since 1924; he later became "prime minister" and, still later, foreign minister. He remained the man closest to Stalin, even though his wife was arrested and sent to the gulag. A year or two before his death, Stalin began to suspect Molotov of being an American or British agent; he could not quite decide which. Molotov was no longer invited to meetings of the Politburo, and, in 1952, he lost his seat in the Presidium (as the Politburo was renamed). There is reason to believe that Molotov would have been shot had Stalin lived for another year or two. This did not prevent him from believing until the end of his days that Stalin had been the greatest genius in all history; his devotion to Stalin was unbounded.

At Stalin's funeral he was the only one to weep, and his short speech could hardly be understood:

> We can be proud that for the last thirty years we have lived and worked under the guidance of Stalin . . . and we will always remember what Stalin taught us right up to the end of his days. . . . The whole life of this inspired fighter for communism, illuminated by the sunshine of great ideas, is a vital and life-affirming example to us all.[5]

He was truly a man after Stalin's heart. At the Politburo meeting in 1937 he shouted at Bukharin: "If you don't confess, you'll only prove that you are a Fascist agent." Two years later, when addressing the Supreme Soviet, he would say that whether one accepted or rejected Nazism was a matter of one's political view, but it is "both senseless and criminal to wage a war for the liquidation of Hitlerism." Yet two years later, when the German ambassador left, having handed him the declaration of war, an aggrieved Molotov said: "Truly, we have not deserved this. . . ." His name appears on thousands of memoranda calling for the execution of wholly innocent people, including cases about which Stalin had perhaps not yet made up his mind.

After Stalin's death, Molotov was reunited with his wife. She, too, was an unregenerate Stalinist; the stay in the camps and the interrogations had done nothing to shake her beliefs. She was to retain her privileges in later years, when Molotov gradually lost his position and eventually his party membership as well. Under Chernenko, Molotov's party membership was restored. Unfortunately, there is no verbatim record available of the meeting between these two senior citizens—the one half deaf, the other barely able to talk.

During the last years of his life, Molotov continued to receive writers and historians, such as Ivan Stadnyuk and Feliks Chuev, particularly from the pro-Stalinist wing of the party, who came to consult with him in connection with their work on the 1930s and the war years. His views had not changed. He referred to Khrushchev as "that criminal"; when interviewed about the purges and the terror, he said that the number of victims was no doubt exaggerated. In any case, the situation was "complicated," and the international constellation demanded "constant vigilance." For this reason, formal procedures could not always be followed, but the leadership had always acted in accordance with the will of the party and the people.[6] "In such an enormous country like the Soviet Union you cannot make an omelet without breaking eggs," he said. True, he disagreed with Stalin on some minor issues, and it was also true that in 1952–53 there had been the danger that he would be arrested and executed: "I was prepared for everything. . . ." When he was asked whether it was not horrifying that old revolutionaries like him should pay with their lives for crimes they had not committed, his standard, emphatic answer was "There are no revolutions without victims. . . . All the rest are bagatelles."[7] When asked whether the party might not have pursued a different course of action under Kirov, he replied with contempt: "Kirov? A mere agitator. . . ." He idolized Stalin and told Chuev shortly before his death in November 1986, "I do not know what would have happened to us but for him."[8]

Soviet historians will continue to discuss the Molotov phenomenon for a long time. He had clearly persuaded himself that every revolution involved many sacrifices; that is, sacrifices by others. If he accepted the arrest of his wife without complaint, it was not because he thought it an inevitable precondition of the victory of communism but because he was afraid for his own life. His was not the psychology of a fanatic who thought that Stalin was always right; in conversations he made it clear that once Stalin was in power no one would dare contradict him. Fear and a slave mentality were the psychological mainsprings beneath the apparently arrogant and uncompromising old Bolshevik, "the man of iron," the "hammer" (Molotov)—an image carefully cultivated over the years that continued to impress not a few of his countrymen and even some foreigners.

"Klim" Voroshilov

Voroshilov was the only one of Stalin's comrades-in-arms who at one time had a substantial cult of his own. He became the people's commissar of defense (a position in which he remained for fifteen years—longer than anyone else) and then a member of the Politburo in 1925. During the civil war, he had shown personal courage and the qualities of a leader. His subsequent appointments were quite unwarranted, but the propaganda machine created an elaborate legend around the "first marshal"; it made him a military leader of genius, a far-sighted warlord. He became an idol and father figure for millions of Soviet children, second only to Stalin. Pictures showing him and Stalin (Gerasimov's *Guarding Peace*, which won him the Stalin Prize in 1941) or *Voroshilov and Gorky* (V. Svarog) could be seen in millions of Soviet offices and homes.[9] They exuded confidence, the feeling that the defense of the country was in trusted hands. When Voroshilov died in 1969, he had received a record eight Orders of Lenin—more than any World War II commander, more than Stalin, who received a mere three or four—and this despite the fact that he had never won a single battle.[10] Even after his death highly laudatory biographies continued to appear,[11] and, in 1988, at the height of glasnost, a Moscow publishing house brought out a big poster of him with the following inscription: "In every line of work you ought to be honest, skillful, and conscientious."[12]

This revered figure of the Stalinist era was not only a man of massive stupidity but also of great duplicity. His incompetence became known with the first thaw; the memoirs of the World War II marshals and generals all referred to him with contempt. He was lost when involved in the intricacies of modern warfare and was eventually shoved off to assignments where he could do least harm. Less known was the part he had played in the destruction of the commanders of the Red Army. To quote Volkogonov:

> He [Voroshilov] did not have the inhuman capacity of work of Kaganovich, the brains and the cleverness of Molotov, the caution and circumspection of Mikoyan; he was in other respects inferior to the other members of the Politburo. But Stalin needed Voroshilov precisely because of his legendary image that had been created around the "leader of the Red Army." The general secretary was certain that the people's commissar would not hesitate to support him. And Stalin was not mistaken when the hour of the bloody purge came. Together with the general secretary, he set light to the stake on which the military commanders were to be burned.[13]

It goes without saying that Voroshilov did not defend his marshals and generals, who, only the day before, had been his closest associates. He volunteered to name new candidates for the firing squads and, generally speaking, acted well beyond the call of duty. Mention has been made of the contemptuous way in which he had returned Bukharin's last letter, a desperate call for help. He behaved exactly in the same way toward the many appeals that reached him from military commanders, who, invoking past friendships in the army, had implored him to take care that their families did not starve.

The great majority of senior personnel in the ministry of defense and the general staff became overnight "Fascists" and "Trotskyite spies." This kind of language was not just for outside consumption; in internal correspondence, too, Voroshilov referred to the victims as "scoundrels" and "dogs." He issued orders that were transmitted to the military districts "to arrest and punish in the most severe way."[14]

Reading these documents raises various questions: Did Voroshilov not fear that by implicating so many of his collaborators he was undermining his own position (for it tended to show that he had not displayed sufficient "Bolshevik vigilance" in the past)? Perhaps he felt that his own life could be saved only by absolute obedience to the general secretary and extra zeal. If so, his calculation proved to be right in the end.

There were other puzzling questions: What did his comrades expect when they sent him these last appeals before their death? Whence these illusions about the true character of this "commander of the army of world revolution"?[15] They must have thought that there was some feeling of human decency in Voroshilov's character, and they could not have been more mistaken.

Kaganovich

In the early and mid-1930s, Lazar Kaganovich had been one of the men closest to Stalin. Later, his position weakened, and he barely survived in the Politburo.[16] Born in the Ukraine, the son of a poor Jewish cobbler, he had joined the party in 1911; he played a modest role in the revolution and in the civil war. His rise to power began when Stalin became general secretary in 1922, at which time he was made deputy in charge of appointments to party offices. In the years that followed, he became party secretary in the Ukraine and, later, in Moscow. He played a role in the collectivization of agriculture and was prominently involved in the organization of Soviet transport and heavy industry. He was a hard worker and a severe taskmaster, although not unpopular except with those who had the misfortune to work closely with him.

Although unswervingly loyal to Stalin, his relations with the other members of the Politburo were not good. In later years, they tended to ignore or even boycott him, all the more reason for Kaganovich to tie his own fate even closer to Stalin. His enthusiasm to "purge" his closest collaborators was unbounded; the percentage of victims in the chief administration of transport and heavy industry, headed by Kaganovich, was higher than anywhere else except the military. In addition, he was sent to the Donbas, to Ivanovo, to the northern Caucasus, and other parts of the country to prod local leaders to intensify the terror, which he did with his usual energy and lack of scruples. When Stalin told him that there was evidence against his older brother, Mikhail, the people's commissar of defense industry, Kaganovich is said to have answered: "What has to be done ought to be done." Mikhail Kaganovich committed suicide during interrogation.

The details of Kaganovich's crimes became known after the Twentieth Party Congress, some and were added under glasnost. His role had been as bad as that of the other members of the Politburo, and there would have been no reason to single him out except that he had the misfortune of surviving his erstwhile colleagues. After Molotov's death in 1986, he was the only one still alive; as a result, he became a most convenient target for Pamyat and other supporters of the extreme Right. They were willing to forgive Molotov and Zhdanov, who had been, after all, Russian patriots. They found mitigating circumstances for everyone else, even for Stalin, who had made Russia strong again and had liquidated the old-guard Bolsheviks, whom they considered antipatriots and internationalists.

For Kaganovich, the Jew, there were no such excuses. He became a demonic figure of truly gigantic dimensions—Stalin's evil spirit (together with Trotsky), out of all proportion to the real role he had played. The anti-Kaganovich party seemed not particularly bothered by the great number of people who had perished in the purges. But the fact that some old churches and other historical monuments had been destroyed when Kaganovich was Moscow district secretary was unforgivable, part of a satanic plot against the Russian people. That Kaganovich had not acted alone but under the supervision of Stalin and in collaboration with the whole Politburo mattered little.[17] The "hang Kaganovich" campaign became so vociferous that Roy Medvedev, no friend of any of Stalin's old associates, felt himself obliged to write yet another essay in which he noted that although the builder of the Moscow metro had been a great scoundrel, he had not been the only one or the greatest of the butchers.

Malenkov

Born in 1902, George Malenkov was one of the youngest of Stalin's aides. He played a prominent role in the purge of the Moscow party organization, and his rise to power dates from that purge. He belongs to the generation that benefited directly from the slaughter of the old Bolsheviks. A Central Committee secretary, Malenkov ended up in the Politburo, widely regarded at one time as Stalin's chosen successor. Yet, of all the leading figures, he was the palest one, almost entirely lacking personality. Despite the proximity to Stalin, he did not succeed in creating a power base of his own and remained a lightweight who was overthrown within a year after the death of his master. He lived on for another thirty-five years, much of the time in a comfortable apartment in the same house on Moscow's Frunze embankment in which Kaganovich lived. Unlike some of his colleagues, he felt no inner urge to write his memoirs. When he died in early 1988, his family decided not to seek any publicity.[18]

Mikoyan

Of Stalin's henchmen, Anastas Mikoyan was probably the most sympathetic. He was the great survivor; his career spanned fifty-five years, from Lenin's days to the Brezhnev era, "from Ilich to Ilich," as the saying went. He played an honorable role at the Twentieth Party Congress, the only leading figure to give Khrushchev full support in launching the anti-Stalin campaign.

In 1926, he became the people's commissar for internal and external trade and, at the age of thirty, a member of the Politburo. Like all other members of that body, he took part in planning the terror campaign. His signature appears on many death warrants, and he was sent on a special mission to Armenia to give additional impetus to the purge in his native region as well as in Georgia.

In contrast to Molotov, Kaganovich, Malenkov, and the others, he was a considerate boss and is known to have helped some victims of the purge. But when Stalin asked him to participate in the preparation of the show trials, he did not hesitate for a moment. He formulated the resolution at the plenary meeting of the Central Committee in February 1937 in which the NKVD was given a free hand to deal with Bukharin, Rykov, and Tomsky. True, Bukharin had also written in his letter to Voroshilov that he was "terribly glad" that the "dogs had been shot," referring to the murder of Zinoviev and Kamenev: Why judge Mikoyan more harshly than Bukharin?

Mikoyan's son Sergo (named after Ordzhonikidze) addressed this question many years after the event. He admits that his father had become an accomplice in murder, even though his signature was a mere formality. What was the alternative? Even if he had committed suicide, his family would still have been killed. At the time, Mikoyan had five sons aged eight to fifteen. His younger brother was a well-known aircraft designer; the MIG is named after him. According to Sergo Mikoyan, mitigating circumstances can be adduced; above all, it is impermissible to apply today's "normal" standards to the events of 1937. Mikoyan's suicide would not have saved anyone; on the contrary, it would have caused the death of people who otherwise survived. Sergo Mikoyan concludes that his father was not an angel, but then, few angels can be found on earth at any given time.

This, in brief, is the case for the defense. More mitigating circumstances can be found for Mikoyan than for the other members of the leadership in 1937–38. But he was still an accomplice to mass murder.[19]

Beria

Lavrenti Beria has attracted more interest under glasnost than any of Stalin's other associates, partly as a result of Abuladze's film *Pokaianie*: The main villain was quite obviously fashioned after Beria. Beria has been regarded as the chief hangman for many years and has been the source of countless scandals. No other member of the Politburo had shot a leading Communist in his own office.[20] No other had the head of his personal guard procure and kidnap pretty young women in the streets of Moscow.[21] In brief, Beria was a colorful criminal, not a mere desk murderer like Molotov.

His initial career as senior NKVD official in Transcaucasia was slow. But Stalin had an eye on Beria because of his zeal; Beria had liquidated all of Stalin's early enemies in Georgia. He was also the grossest flatterer of the crowd; according to a book he wrote (or, to be precise, a book that was written on his instructions), Bolshevism in the Caucasus was Stalin's own creation—at the age of nineteen. By the mid-thirties, Beria's name was well known in Moscow. Even the court painters began to pay attention to him. Kolkov's picture *Voroshilov and Beria Inspect Georgia's Tea Plantations* was shown in the Tretyakov Gallery. He shared the brazenness of his boss: Stalin and Beria had Ordzhonikidze's older brother shot and his younger brother arrested. When Ordzhonikidze committed suicide (or was killed), Beria was appointed head of the state commission to commemorate him.[22]

In 1938, Beria replaced Ezhov as head of the NKVD and, at this point in his career, became an integral part of Soviet history because the NKVD served as a state within a state. Precisely for this reason, most of the details of his crimes remain undocumented; the archives of the security organs remain closed.

Antonov-Ovseenko and others have collected evidence about Beria from survivors, but much of it is, by necessity, hearsay; for a reasonably detailed account of even his main crimes, one may have to wait a long time. On June 26, 1953, Beria was arrested in the middle of a meeting of the Politburo. Khrushchev pressed a button, and six officers, led by Zhukov and Moskalenko, entered the room and arrested Beria.[23] Once Stalin was dead, the instincts of survival got the better of the members of the Politburo; the military were only too willing to obey despite the presence of two NKVD divisions in Moscow. The mystery is not why the arrest took place but why they had not dared to act earlier.

The list of Stalin's main cohorts—those who would have been arraigned before a tribunal if there ever had been a Soviet Nuremberg tribunal—is, of course, much longer. No mention has been made of Khrushchev, Bulganin, and Suslov. They were members of Stalin's entourage; so were Zhdanov, Andreev, Shkiratov, and others. There is no room to discuss all their roles as they emerged under glasnost, but mention should be made of two of Stalin's assistants who were particularly close to him. One was Poskrebyshev, his secretary, yet another "man without qualities." Poskrebyshev headed Stalin's chancery, the true seat of power. Compared with Bormann, Hitler's chief assistant, Poskrebyshev was far less powerful; he rarely expressed an opinion. His assignment was to bring order into the flow of paper to and from Stalin's office, and he kept Stalin's list of appointments. He was a bureaucrat with a phenomenal memory, an important quality in precomputer days; through him, Stalin kept abreast of developments in many fields.[24] Unlike Bormann, he would not dream of making decisions or interpreting Stalin's views. Nevertheless, many lives depended on whether this letter carrier submitted a certain paper at the right time or whether he delayed it. Poskrebyshev rightly feared that sooner or later he would be liquidated by Stalin because he knew too much. During the last year of Stalin's life, Poskrebyshev fell from grace; but for the death of the dictator, he might have been a victim of the next purge.

Several years earlier, Stalin had Poskrebyshev's wife arrested and sent to the gulag; she was the sister of the wife of Trotsky's son Sedov. Poskrebyshev tried to interfere on her behalf, but Stalin allegedly told him that he was powerless to intervene.

Finally, Lev Mekhlis, a native of Odessa and, although a Jew, a favorite of the supreme leader's. Mekhlis was, at various times, editor-in-chief of *Pravda*, the people's commissar of state control, and the head of the political administration of the Red Army, with a rank of colonel general. Stalin used Mekhlis as one of his chief hatchetmen, and he acted as one of the main instigators of the purge. During the war, as a result of interfering with the decisions of the military experts, he reportedly contributed to some military setbacks. According to Konstantin Simonov, he did not lack personal courage but tended toward hysterical outbursts. Simonov reports a telephone conversation between Stalin and General Kozlov, who commanded the Crimean front. Kozlov complained that Mekhlis prevented him from carrying out his job, whereupon Stalin told Kozlov that he was obviously more afraid of Mekhlis than of the Germans, which was not how a senior commander should behave.[25]

Mekhlis died two years before Stalin; because he was equally unpopular among military and civilian leaders, Mekhlis would not have survived long after Stalin's death. Being of Jewish origin, which he tried to hide as well as he could, he became one of the favorite targets of the extreme Right under glasnost—a villain greater than Ezhov, Molotov, Voroshilov, or even Stalin himself.

These then, in briefest outline, were the posthumous fates of Stalin's closest comrades-in-arms. While the leader was alive, he had towered over those surrounding him, as had Hitler and Mussolini. This did not change after his death. Once, these had been names to conjure with, although their real power had been far more limited than widely believed. Since the late 1950s a veil of silence had enshrouded them. Following three decades of silence, interest in them has sharply declined. If there has been some renewed interest in these figures under glasnost, it has been merely a reflection of the continuing fascination with their erstwhile boss.

10. The "Cult of Personality"

Extreme instances of hero worship can be found in distant periods of history and in certain primitive societies. A more recent phenomenon, such as the cult of Stalin, has been rarer, and it has been insufficiently studied. The nearest in character were the cults of the Führer and Il Duce and Maoism in China.

Most students of Stalin's life agree that the decisive date for the beginning of the cult was the fiftieth birthday of the leader in December 1929. On this occasion, Stalin was celebrated in the Soviet newspapers in a way and at a length quite without precedent in the history of Bolshevism. As one of Stalin's leading biographers wrote: "No ink can transcribe the systematic stimulation inaugurated on the occasion of Stalin's fiftieth birthday and prolonged since in a crescendo of adulation, artificial veneration and adoration."[1] If ink could not transcribe the quality and the extent of the adulation, how to do justice to the celebration of his sixtieth birthday in 1939? And those who thought that the cult could not possibly be intensified any further beyond the level of 1939 had to revise their judgment with Stalin's seventieth birthday in 1949.

The attitude of dictators toward their birthdays has varied considerably. In Hitler's case even his forty-fourth birthday, the first after coming to power, was the occasion of public celebrations. This practice became even more pronounced on the occasion of his forty-fifth and forty-sixth. His forty-ninth birthday, on the eve of the war, was a major affair of state, although not remotely as fulsome and far-reaching as Stalin's the same year.

Mussolini, on the other hand, forbade the Italian newspapers even to mention his fiftieth birthday in 1933, not out of modesty but because he was afraid of becoming old and wanted to appear ageless.

The pomp and circumstance of 1929 was later compared with the modest celebration of Lenin's birthday in 1920. It was confined to a meeting of old comrades in Moscow, with speeches by Trotsky, Zinoviev, and Kamenev, resulting in a small book of less than a hundred pages. Lenin left the meeting early, finding it unnecessary and embarrassing.

But it is also true that almost as soon as Lenin had come to power the deification of the leader began, and "religious associations, symbols, and attributes were made use of to introduce Lenin to the country in which he had seized power."[2] Less than a year after the Revolution, Zinoviev made a speech that became the first official biography. It said that "he was truly chosen from among millions. He is a leader by the grace of god. This is the true figure of a leader such as are born only once every 500 years."[3] Zinoviev did not believe in God, and therefore his invocation of the deity should be taken with a grain of salt. The "500 years" were, no doubt, also an arbitrary choice; a thousand years, as in Hitler's case, would have been far more appropriate. But what matters is that a Lenin cult, *in statu nascendi* existed in the lifetime of Vladimir Ilyich, even though there is every reason to believe that he regarded it with distaste. As another person close to Lenin put it: "I believe that Lenin, who could not stand hero-worship and who rejected it by every means, understood and forgave us in his last years."[4]

Lenin was a Marxist and, his personal predilections quite apart, he knew that worship of a leader was simply not becoming to a Marxist party, with its stress on the all-important role of the masses and, of course, on objective circumstances. But the Lenin cult continued in any case, culminating in the establishment of the mausoleum as a manifestation of immortality, pharaonic influence may well have been involved: The decision to build a mausoleum came a little more than a year after the opening of Tutankhamen's grave, which had received enormous attention all over the world.[5]

The Byzantine and Russian origins of the Lenin and Stalin cults remain to be studied. According to Byzantine political theory, the emperor was, ex officio, like God. For the Russian peasant of the eighteenth and nineteenth centuries, the tsar was not God but his representative on earth. Great respect has been paid to all tsars, good and bad, and especially among the courtiers, there had been a tendency toward systematic adulation. But even the simplest muzhik knew that above the tsar there was someone even more powerful, and there had never been a cult of the ruler even approaching the intensity of Stalin's.

Stalin pretended not to like the cult. Thus, he upbraided I. M. Shatunovsky in 1930, who had written about his "devotion" to Stalin, which, Stalin claimed, was "not the Bolshevik way." Said Stalin, "Have devotion to the working class, its party, its state. That's needed and good. But don't mix it with devotion to persons. . . ."[6] He is reported to have rejected the title Generalissimus during the war, arguing that it would not add any authority to that which he already possessed. It is certainly possible that certain excesses by overeager lackeys offended his taste. The "cult" was created not because Stalin had instructed his secretaries: "Go out and praise me." Rather, it was an interaction between what Stalin thought proper and necessary and the eagerness of his assistants to please him, to curry his favor. And it is quite likely that both Stalin and his lackeys were genuinely convinced that this was what the country needed. They probably thought that the Russian people needed an individual, not an abstraction (the party) or a dead man (Lenin) to inspire them. Given the general cultural level of the country and the autocratic political tradition, their basic assumption may well have been right.

Stalin could, of course, have stopped or at least restrained the adulation had he wanted to do so. One of the first to emphasize this was Louis Fischer, an American journalist stationed in Moscow for many years. In the early days of the cult, after the Sixteenth Party Congress (June/July 1930), he wrote:

> A good friend might also advise Stalin to put a stop to the orgy of personal glorification which has been permitted to sweep the country. Daily, hundreds of telegrams pour in on him brimming over with Oriental supercompliments: "Thou art the greatest leader . . ." and the like. Three cities, innumerable villages, collectives, schools, factories and institutions have been named after him. . . . If Stalin is not responsible for this performance he at least tolerates it. He could stop it by pressing a button.[7]

But no good friend talked to Stalin, and no button was ever pressed.

The next major stage in the development of the cult was a letter written by Stalin and published in the journal *Proletarian Revolution*. The issue at stake was of no particular topical consequence—the correct interpretation of one of Lenin's writings—but the intention was to show that once

Stalin had spoken, all discussion had to end. He was not only the general secretary and supreme leader but also the highest ideological authority, an equal to Marx, Engels, and Lenin, with whom, from now on, his name was always associated.

At the same time, orders were given to rewrite the history of the Communist party in such a way as to show that Stalin had never been wrong and that he had played a central role in the events of 1917. This teaching process went on for a number of years and culminated in the *Short Course* of late 1938, which became the bible of the cult. As a best-selling author, Stalin eclipsed the other classics of Marxism-Leninism. In 1932–33, 7 million copies of the works of Marx and Engels were published and 14 million of Lenin's. During the same period, 16.5 million copies of Stalin's works were printed, even though his literary output was far smaller. But this was only a modest beginning. By 1949, 539 million copies of Stalin's work had appeared; 36 million copies of the *Short Course* alone were printed. A mere election speech from 1946 produced 19 million copies in 58 languages.[8]

The whole style of party and public life became different. From the Seventeenth Party Congress in 1934 (the "Congress of the Victors") onward, Kirov declared that Stalin was the greatest leader of all times and nations, and the ovations on this occasion, as on all subsequent appearances of Stalin, befitted a leader of such stature. The ovations became almost as long as, and certainly stormier than, the speeches. He was not a man but a titan, and his authority was invoked on every occasion, whether in education, philosophy, economics, literature, music, sports, Oriental studies, physics, or legal studies.

The new constitution of 1936 became known as the Stalin constitution, even though it had been prepared by a group of people, including "enemies of the people" such as Bukharin and Radek, rather than the "father of the peoples," perhaps his most frequently used unofficial title.

In addition to Stalingrad, other cities were named after him—Stalino, Stalinabad, Stalinsk, Stalinaoul, Stalinogorsk. Pictures of Stalin appeared in the tens of millions in every office, school, hospital, and in many homes. Even the most banal statement made by Stalin had to be repeated endlessly: "The cadres decide everything." "We Bolsheviks must master technique." "The Soviet Union, an agricultural country, is developing into an industrial country." For the poets, he was "the sun," "the master of our hearts," the only source of inspiration of artists and scientists alike, the greatest, the only, teacher of historians, economists, and philosophers. Leonid Leonov, a highly esteemed writer at the time, wrote that the day would come when all mankind would revere him and history would recognize him as the starting point of time, not Jesus Christ. Whereas the Byzantine emperors had merely been illustrious, victorious, pious, or triumphal, such flattery was deemed insufficient for Stalin. As a writer in *Izvestiia* declared: "Writers no longer know with what they can compare you, and our poets have no longer sufficient pearls of language to describe you."[9]

But this was a feeble excuse. Even if they had temporarily run out of epithets, the writers had to think of new ones or slightly modify the old ones. On Stalin's sixtieth birthday, Voroshilov had written on "Stalin, the creator of the Red Army." Ten years later, his task was easier; he wrote of "Stalin, the war leader—genius of the Great Fatherlandic War." Kaganovich had written in 1939 about "the great constructor of the machinery of history." In 1949, he turned to the future: "Stalin leads us to the victory of communism." He was joined by Molotov with the relatively restrained title "Stalin and his leadership," and by Beria ("the great inspirator and organizer of the victories of communism"), Poskrebyshev ("the beloved father and great leader"), Kosygin ("Our achievements we owe to Stalin"), Khrushchev ("Stalin's friendship of the peoples—the guarantee of the invincibility of our fatherland")—and virtually everyone else among Stalin's paladins.[10]

But the cult was by no means restricted to sycophants catering to the taste of semiliterate masses. The old party leadership, which should have known better (and knew better), did their share and more than that. Bukharin and Rakovsky, Kamenev and Rykov, and many others not only recanted but did their utmost to flatter Stalin in public and private. Radek wrote in *Pravda* in 1934 that Stalin was Lenin's best pupil, the model of the Leninist party; "bone of its bone, blood of its blood," he personified the entire historical experience of the party.

Among the intellectuals and artists, the cult was by no means restricted to Kazakh and Kirghiz bards extolling the virtue of the leader in extravagant Oriental terms. Virtually everyone participated, poets and playwrights, composers and moviemakers. Some went much further than others; one of the most extreme performers was the former émigré Count Aleksei Tolstoy, a cynic who wrote that Stalin thought of everything and knew everything. But among the members of the committee to commemorate Stalin's seventieth birthday, we find not only Lysenko's name but also that of Shostakovich. Among the poets who, on one occasion or another, paid tribute to the leader were not only the professional hacks but also Pasternak (who wrote a poem for *Izvestiia* following Bukharin's advice), Akhmatova, Isaac Babel (who advised his fellow writers to study Stalin's use of language), Leonov, Tikhonov, Fedin, above all, Sholokhov, and virtually everyone else. There was, of course, a world of difference between Fadeev, Simonov, and other officials and such non-Communists as Pasternak or Akhmatova, who had been persuaded that if they referred to Stalin in some form or another, they might not be arrested or one of their close relations might be released from prison or a camp.

It was the same in every discipline, however remote from politics. And if a few courageous men and women did get away without writing a poem, novel, or play; composing a song or a symphony; writing a book on the Middle Ages or biology or astronomy, without ever referring to the wise father of the people, chances were that they were not sufficiently prominent to arouse suspicion and resentment.

But there were also a great many, perhaps the majority, who genuinely believed that Stalin was a great leader and that without his wise guidance, the country, facing so many threats at home and abroad, would be lost.

To understand the Stalinist cult, a comparison with other contemporary dictators may be called for. In some ways, the central role of the two Fascist leaders was far more natural: their movements had largely been created by them, and their ideology rested on the leader principle (*Führerprinzip*). It took three to four years in Germany and Italy for the cults to reach full blossom. But, already in 1933, there were poems in the German media that God had sent a savior, that springtime was here at last. True, no German city was named after Hitler, and no Italian after Mussolini, but everyone implored them to become honorary citizens. Flags and greenery and pictures of Hitler adorned houses in even the smallest village. There were countless pictures and busts of Hitler and speeches saying that "in the personality of Hitler, a millionfold longing of the German people has become reality."[11]

Hitler was hailed as the greatest authority on architecture and the stage and later as the greatest military leader and diplomat as well. But there was no attempt to extol him also as a writer or a scientist of genius or as a master of philosophy, economics, and historiography. The German greeting ("Heil Hitler") became the official form of address, replacing "Good morning" and "Sincerely yours." On every occasion, Hitler's popular origins were stressed: "He came from the people and remained with the people." A common soldier in World War I, his kindness, gentleness, and fatherly attitude were always emphasized, as in Stalin's case. If Stalin was the "man of steel," Hitler was a "rock in the sea." Hitler was modest, simple, frugal, and loved children; at the same time, he was a titan, a hero without comparison. As in Stalin's case, it was frequently pointed out that he worked for his people even while others slept. Barbusse wrote that the new Russia worshiped Stalin, "but it is a worship created by a confidence that has risen wholly from the bottom."[12] The same motive was used not only by Goebbels, a propagandist of genius, but also by Hitler's bitter enemies, the Social Democratic intelligence service. *Sopade Berichte* reported as early as February 6, 1935, that "enthusiasm was enormous. . . . People can be forced to sing—but not with such enthusiasm. Trust in Hitler's political talent and honest intentions is getting even greater, just as generally Hitler has again won extraordinary popularity. He is loved by many. . . ."[13]

If the identity of Stalin, the party, and the people was emphasized daily in the Soviet Union, Goebbels always belabored the same theme: "Never in the history of all time has one man united in his own person as he [Hitler] has the trust and feeling of belonging of an entire people."[14] Both Hitler and Stalin initially regarded the cult mainly as a device to foster the integration of party and people, as an instrument for the stupefaction of the masses.[15]

But gradually their innate megalomania, reinforced by their political victories, seems to have persuaded them that the cult was not just a political-educational necessity but a natural expression of the true state of affairs. Constant repetition of their greatness came to persuade them that they were all that their lackeys proclaimed them to be.

The Stalinist cult was more pervasive than the Hitler cult both quantitatively and qualitatively. Having been chosen by providence to lead his country, it did not matter to Hitler whether he was also the ultimate arbiter in all things cultural. In any case, Hitler was bored by the humanities, knew little about science, and because he did not think highly of intellectuals in the first place, their acclaim was for him a matter of indifference.

While Stalin was alive, virtually no biography was published except a short "political biography" written by a committee toward the end of his life. The same is true with regard to Hitler. The reason was not so much the innate modesty of the leaders but their belief that no biography could possibly do them justice. In Mussolini's lifetime, no less than 400 books about Il Duce were published—most of them, admittedly, biographies for the use of schoolchildren and quite a few in verse.[16]

Mussolini was predestined, elected, called by God and history. As the prophet Isaiah had predicted the coming of Jesus, so had Dante announced the coming of Il Duce. He was also the new man, the greatest man who ever lived, or at least the highest incarnation of the Italian race. His stature was so much greater than that of ordinary mortals. He was alone and sad; he could and should not be measured by ordinary standards. He was a colossus, a titan, a cyclops, a giant. He was infinite, like the sky or the ocean, and for this reason it was impossible to describe or define him.

If Stalin in his teens was already the leader of the Caucasian Bolsheviks, Mussolini was first the *capo dei ragazzi* in his native village, later the "young lion of the Romagna." His father was a true proletarian—a blacksmith, not a drunken cobbler, as in Stalin's case. Whatever Mussolini did, he was always the first—reading books, as an army recruit, as a teacher, as an agitator facing the police; his thought was so concentrated that his nose often bled as a result. He became the greatest soldier of World War I, and he shed his blood for his country. In the dark postwar period he appeared as the only sane man amid madmen and fools. Mussolini's somewhat unorthodox sex life is not mentioned, and his socialist past is ignored, as are the early terrorist activities of the Fascists.

Once in power, he soon revealed himself as not only a genius but the greatest genius. Like Stalin, he was frequently compared to an eagle. He was a collective representation of the finest attributes of the Italian nationality and embodied revival of imperial Rome. His knowledge was unmeasurable, encyclopedic, and universal; like Stalin, he was considered omniscient and omnipresent.[17]

Mussolini was the greatest journalist who ever lived and always wrote the full truth. But he was even greater as a speaker. When he made a speech, it was not only great but also beautiful, and the youth of Italy was called to learn by heart at least sections of his speeches. He created a new style and was the greatest poet, musician (he played the violin), and artist. Like Hercules and the centaurs, he had a limitless capacity for work. He virtually never slept. He was a champion swimmer, flier, horseman, fencer, driver, cyclist, and so on.

His most frequent title was *Salvatore d'Italia*, "the Savior." But his historical mission transcended Italy; it was worldwide: He was the engine of the century, the voice of history pointing the road to all of Europe. Furthermore, the masses loved him; he was identical with the people: *Tu sei tutti noi*. He was infallible, greater than Caesar, Augustus, Napoleon, and throughout the years, more and more attributes of God were attributed to him. If Gori, Stalin's birthplace, became a place of pilgrimage, so did Predappio, where Mussolini was born. Many pregnant women looked at Mussolini's picture, hoping that their sons would be like him; the blind could see again when Il Duce embraced them; those who kissed his hands could die in peace.

These examples must suffice to give a general idea of the quality of the Duce cult. But as so often in Italy, there was a far cry between words and reality. The books quoted did not appear in millions of copies, and if Christ stopped at Eboli, the Mussolini cult stopped well before. Like Stalin, Mussolini felt he could trust no one; he knew that many of the leaders, the *gerarchi*, had been stealing left and right. But he was reluctant to dismiss them, for he feared that the new appointees would steal even more. When he was prime minister in 1926, he held six ministries out of thirteen, and in 1928, eight. When he was overthrown in 1943, he still kept five. His distrust, his wish to concentrate power, and his incompetence as an administrator caused virtual paralysis whenever he left Rome. Like Hitler and Stalin, he believed that he was greatest as war leader; he had always wanted to prove that he was greater than Napoleon.

Although Mussolini's sway over the masses was boundless, at least until the outbreak of the war, those close to him had much less respect and less fear than those surrounding Stalin. The same was true with regard to large sections of the upper class and the intelligentsia. Enthusiasts were free to praise Mussolini (or Hitler), but there was no compulsion to do so.

Hitler and Mussolini were masters of the spoken word; they were able to manipulate the masses with their speeches, whereas Stalin was anything but a great orator. Therefore, his achievement seems even greater because in his case there was no direct communication; the cult came about and was maintained as the result of administrative-bureaucratic machinations engineered from a back room. But it also shows that it must have fallen on fertile ground; otherwise, it could not possibly have had such a great and lasting success. [18]

Thus, despite all the similarities, there are also striking differences between the cult of the leader in the Fascist regimes and the Stalinist cult. Neither Poland nor Hungary, neither East Germany nor Czechoslovakia, produced their Stalins—and it is doubtful whether Stalin would have tolerated any such competition even on a local scale. The situation in Asia was different. There was an immense Maoist cult; indeed, in some respects the deification of Mao went even further than Stalin's, especially during the cultural revolution. Seven hundred million copies of the little red book were circulated, dwarfing even Stalin's *Short Course*. Lin Biao stated that Mao was immortal; other leaders announced that he would live at least 10,000 years. The population of China was told that they had the incredible good fortune to live under the shadow of such a great tree. Mao's swim in the Yangtse River was treated as a turning point in world history. He was not only the greatest Marxist of all times; he was the greatest genius who had ever lived. He had never been mistaken, everything he said was the truth, every statement he uttered was worth 10,000 sentences (of everyone else). Newspapers featured a quotation from Chairman Mao every day in heavy black print so as to distinguish it from the rest of the news.

Mao was, of course, aware of the cult; the initiative of his aides seems to have been even more marked than that of the Kremlin. As the chairman told his old acquaintance Edgar Snow, he did not particularly like it, but then the Chinese people had always been accustomed to looking up to their emperor. We know from other sources that Mao regarded himself the last of the great emperors. There had been a Sun Yat-sen cult in the 1930s: three bows before his portrait and the observance of three minutes of silence in school every Monday. In contrast to Stalin, Mao had natural charisma, and he was the leader of the party and supreme military chief for a much longer period than Stalin. But when he died, most educated Chinese seem to have believed that he had stayed on some twenty years too long at the helm. The military were openly saying that he did not really understand much about modern warfare.

Specific for Maoism were the thaumaturgic effects of his teachings. Having studied Chairman Mao's writings, Chinese doctors restored sight to the blind, restored limbs that had been severed, made deaf mutes hear and speak, and resurrected the dead. [19] The speeches and writings of Mao made it possible to wipe out snails, to collect night soil more effectively, and to prevent frostbite.

The ovations in Beijing were as thunderous as in Moscow: "excited faces turned to Chairman Mao, like sunflowers to the sun. . . . Dear as are father and mother, Chairman Mao is dearer." Many wrote on the flyleaf of their treasured red books: "At 7:30 p.m. November 14, 1967, I met Chairman Mao, the Red Sun that shines most brightly in our hearts." Or, "Oh, Chairman Mao, your kindness is taller than the sky, deeper than the ocean, and brighter than the sun and moon. It is possible to count the stars in the highest heaven, but it is impossible to count your contributions to mankind."[20]

There was a Ho Chi Minh cult in Vietnam, but it went not remotely as far as the Stalin or Mao cults. Ho had no ambitions in the ideological field, and he positively disliked the quotation mongery that had spread in the Soviet Union and in China. He would not have approved of the mausoleum that was built for him six years after his death. The one Communist leader whose cult possibly surpassed the Soviet and Chinese was Kim Il Sung; even four-year-old children in North Korea have to study the abbreviated version of his official biography.

The Stalinist cult could be explained, albeit with some difficulty, in the context of Byzantine influences in Russian history, the low level of Soviet political culture in the 1920s and 1930s, and other such factors. But how does one explain that distinguished Western intellectuals also contributed to the cult when it was at its height? The question figured prominently in the writings of ideologues of the extreme Right, who argued that the participation of such Communists or fellow travelers as Barbusse, Rolland, Shaw, Feuchtwanger, and Einstein showed that it had been a worldwide phenomenon "from Madrid to Shanghai" rather than a specific Russian feature. The intention of the line of argument was obvious: If the cult was worldwide, the Russians would have no particular reason to be embarrassed, perhaps there was even no need for explanations. But the same questions about the naïveté of Western fellow travelers were also asked among the dissidents: for example, in Yuri Dombrovsky's satirical novel *The Faculty of Unnecessary Things*. It continues to intrigue many in the West and East.

What could be the explanation? Henri Barbusse, a physician by profession, had been converted to pacifism by World War I. He joined the

Communist party in 1921, and his writings about the Soviet Union cannot therefore be taken as the work of a nonpolitical Western intellectual. He visited the Soviet Union in 1934 to collect material for a biography of Stalin that appeared a year later. In fact, he was presented to the Western public as a "personal friend of Stalin's"[21] even though he had seen the dictator only once for a few hours at his dacha. The book is an incredible paean from its very beginning—"In this country, if the cobbles in the street could talk, they would say: Stalin"—until the very last sentence, which is often quoted: "The finest part of your destiny is in the hands of that . . . man who also watches over you and who works for you—the man with a scholar's mind, a workman's face, and the dress of a private soldier."

This biography became something of an embarrassment even while Stalin lived. It was too crude for Western consumption, and the only thing that can be said in mitigation is that for the better part it might not have been written at all by Barbusse.[22]

The case of Romain Rolland is more complex. A lifelong pacifist and a writer of greater stature than Barbusse, he had become very sympathetic to the cause of communism, mainly because of his revulsion vis-à-vis fascism. He was twice received by Stalin, and his public statements were positive, even flattering. Russia was a symbol of world progress, Stalin and his comrades were motivated by a social ideal of justice and "panhumanism" that is "more idealistic than human dreams."[23] He found Stalin accessible and unpretentious and quoted him—"modesty is the ornament of the Bolshevik"—trying to refute André Gide's report about a new cult of personality in the Soviet Union.

But in private letters and diaries there are frequent references to the "cult," which show that it angered him. Rolland referred to Stalin's maliciousness, sadistic sense of humor, and paranoid policies. He intervened for Victor Serge, who, as a left-wing writer, was arrested years earlier in the Soviet Union, but, in all other cases, his attempts to get prisoners released were unsuccessful. Yet his public utterances remained those of an uncritical fellow traveler. The Soviet Union, where more than a million of his books had been translated, received him as a "glorious friend" (Bukharin's words), but the non-Communist Left accused him of having been effectively "Stalinized."[24]

In 1988, the leading Soviet Rolland scholar, Tamara Motyleva, tried to answer the questions frequently put to her under glasnost: Why had

Rolland, the great humanist and moralist, kept silent under Stalin? Had he not known? Motyleva had been one of the few to gain access to Rolland's archives in Paris in 1967, and she quoted from letters and diaries, some hitherto unknown. It appeared that Rolland had been perfectly aware of the terror and the all-pervasive fear and suspicion. He had considered the idolization most damaging, whether it concerned Stalin or Hitler or Mussolini. But he said, "I do not defend Stalin, but the Soviet Union, whoever would be its leader."[25]

Motyleva's explanations were of interest, but they hardly helped to explain the psychological riddle. For if Rolland believed that any negative comment about the Soviet Union would have been grist for the Fascist mills, he could still have kept silent. Instead, he knowingly lied.

Like Rolland, Lion Feuchtwanger never belonged to the Communist party and had not subscribed to Marxist doctrine, perhaps not even to socialism, but in the 1930s he became the fellow traveler par excellence. He visited the Soviet Union in January 1937 at the height of the terror. It has been surmised that his famous book was commissioned as an answer to André Gide, whose long essay, published after a visit the year before, had caused considerable damage to the Soviet Union among Western intellectuals,[26] even though, read fifty years later, it is difficult to understand the indignation it caused among the Communists. Gide had seen only a small part of the truth, and he did not reveal all that he had seen. But Feuchtwanger was invited (by Mikhail Koltsov) well before Gide's return, and for all one knows, there was no casual connection between the two trips, even though Feuchtwanger referred to Gide on more than one occasion.[27] Feuchtwanger was very popular in the Soviet Union; most of his books had been translated, and some had been made into movies. He had written for *Pravda* and was on friendly terms with several Soviet writers, such as Koltsov and Sergei Tretiakov, both soon to be executed. Feuchtwanger did not comment on the disappearance of his friends. He found that although the citizens of Moscow still faced some "minor inconveniences," such as housing, which was a little cramped, Soviet society was content, or—more than that—happy. It was unfair to charge it with conformism, as had Gide; they were genuine patriots and liked their leadership. There was more purposeful cohesion in Moscow than anywhere else in the world. They knew that their country would inevitably become even more prosperous.

Moscow 1937 attained much notoriety because of its defense of the trials. Feuchtwanger said he was absolutely convinced that the confessions were genuine and that they had not been extracted by violent means. Feuchtwanger conceded that although he was convinced of the guilt of the prisoners, he had not found a completely satisfactory explanation for their behavior in court. Perhaps this was a question of cultural lag. He also found the Stalinist cult ("exaggerated and partly tasteless") difficult to understand, even though it was doubtlessly genuine. Stalin had told him that Soviet workers and peasants had been too busy to acquire sophistication; in some cases, the exaggeration might be the work of recent converts to his cause who wanted to show their faithfulness by excess enthusiasm. Stalin had to do something about the Trotskyite menace, and "history cannot be made with the gloves on." But Stalin was utterly determined to lead his country along the path to democracy:

> Read any book or any speech of Stalin's, look at any portrait of him, think of any measure which he has taken for the purposes of the construction. It at once becomes clear as daylight that this modest, impersonal man cannot possibly have committed the colossal indiscretion of producing with the assistance of countless performers so coarse a comedy, merely for the purpose of holding a sort of festival of revenge with Bengal lights to celebrate the humiliation of his opponents.[28]

Only unreasonable people or those who think that the means dishonor the end could believe that the trials were "arbitrary and terrorist." The air that one breathes in the West is stale and foul, in contrast to the invigorating atmosphere of the Soviet Union, where a "sober ethics" prevailed. Feuchtwanger's book appeared within a few months, in a Soviet edition of 200,000, almost unheard of in those days.

Fifty years later, the book had become a curiosity, and Soviet readers wondered how an experienced writer, a student of the human psyche, had been deceived by Stalin and by the performance in the House of the Unions, where he had attended the Piatakov-Radek trial. How could he have believed with "childish naïveté" the fairy tales dished up at the very time that the terror was reaching its apex? How could he have believed that the "boss" disliked the cult but was powerless to do anything about it?[29]

Soviet authors tend to exaggerate the political and psychological sophistication of Western fellow travelers such as Feuchtwanger: Their knowledge of Soviet affairs, of the whole context and background, was limited; they did not know the language and were at the mercy of translators. They were wined and dined, flattered and well paid for their books; it was only human that they should react in a friendly way to the overwhelming hospitality. But there was also a political consideration that this "unselfish bard of Stalinism" had in mind: The main enemy was Hitler and fascism, and under those circumstances, any criticism in a book written mainly for Western readers was making a united front against Nazism more difficult. [30]

This explanation was correct—in part. For there was a moral pathos in Feuchtwanger's book that tends to prove that he genuinely believed in the Stalinist propaganda. This was no mere "holy lie" to defend the Soviet Union against its detractors. Feuchtwanger seems to have been persuaded that he was writing the truth, the whole truth. Nothing would have happened to his reputation among the Communists or even to the sale of his books in the Soviet Union had he decided under one pretext or another to decline the invitation to Moscow. Instead, Feuchtwanger returned "bearing witness" (his own words), and Soviet historians are finding it impossible to decide whether he was genuinely deluded or whether he was lying because he was convinced that it was in the best interest of the Soviet Union and because he saw Hitler as the main enemy.

Among the other outstanding fellow travelers of the 1930s, the names Webb, Shaw, and H. G. Wells are mentioned most often. As far as the cult is concerned, their cases are quite different. None of them visited the Soviet Union after 1934, and their interest was basically in the Soviet system rather than in Stalin's rule. Shaw had been to Moscow and found Stalin a good listener; he thought that the adulation of the boss (*"pontifex maximus"*) was more than a little ridiculous. But like the Webbs and many others, he also believed that Stalin was not the "sort of person" who wanted arbitrary personal power.

In any case, Shaw had a weakness for dictators; his attitude toward Mussolini in the 1920s had been quite positive, and Wells, too, had not been guiltless in this respect. Shaw, always the gadfly, found Marxism quite ridiculous; on the other hand, he liked Trotsky as an intellectual, and he never thought that Mussolini had engaged in murder. The value of Shaw's political comments were therefore problematic from the Soviet point of view.

Wells's real interest in things Russian was limited; he was preoccupied with the future of mankind in general and saw striking parallels between Stalin's Five-Year Plans and Roosevelt's New Deal. He was not unaware of the autocratic element in Soviet politics and told the Webbs that they had underrated it in their work.[31] Soviet authors, trying in later years to understand the blindness of so many prominent Western fellow travelers, often overlooked the fact, blatant in the case of the Webbs, Shaw, and Wells, that their toleration of the Stalin cult rested on the assumption that the Soviet Union was basically still a Third World country, even before the term had been coined: Democracy was well and good, but only once a certain stage of development had been reached—and even then, only to a limited degree.

These visitors to Moscow were elitist "totalitarian democrats," in Shaw's words. Stalinism and the cult appeared a little grotesque, like some Indian or African cult. But who were they to judge what Russia needed at the present stage of its development?

Others, like Heinrich Mann and Arnold Zweig, genuinely persuaded themselves that Stalin was a great humanist, a good man (like Henry IV of France in Heinrich Mann's novel), that the Moscow trials had been just, and so on. Some of them lived to recognize that they had been mistaken; most persisted in their beliefs.

Their delusions cannot possibly serve as an alibi for Stalin's Russian admirers, such as Maksim Gorky, for instance. Gorky, it will be recalled, had been hostile to Lenin and the Bolsheviks in 1917–18; later he moved to his Italian exile. But from 1928 on, he began to revisit the Soviet Union with increasing frequency. He was given the highest honors; Nizhni Novgorod was renamed "Gorky," and Stalin wrote that Gorky's *Death and the Maiden* was better than anything Goethe had ever written. Gorky, on the other hand, joined the official chorus against the "traitors and wreckers," beginning with Shakhty and the trial against the Industrial party. He visited Solovki Island and the White Sea Canal, which were constructed using the labor of political prisoners, and gave these "great educational projects" his seal of approval. He referred to Stalin as "the boss," Lenin's legitimate heir; he provided the regime with needed slogans: "With whom are you, masters of culture?" "The humanism of the proletariat." "If the enemy does not surrender, he will be destroyed."[32]

True, Gorky was not altogether happy about what he saw and how he was treated. He was less than enthusiastic about the renaming of Nizhni Novgorod; he even felt that he was used by the GPU and the Stalinist propaganda machine. He was unhappy about the inferior quality of his literary output during the last decade of his life, and he intervened on behalf of some writers, such as Pilnyak and Zamyatin, who were in disfavor.[33] Gorky kept his doubts and reservations to himself; as far as the Soviet public was concerned, he enthusiastically endorsed Stalin and Stalinism.

The Gorky tragedy was another example for the *trahison des clercs*; in this specific case, it happened to a great writer at the end of his career, in indifferent health, who was aware that his creative powers were failing. But there is sufficient evidence that Gorky was quite aware to his last days what went on around him, and he certainly knew his Russia infinitely better than the Rollands and the Feuchtwangers. Suspicions about the circumstances of his death were voiced under glasnost; the full truth about the last months of his life may never be known.

Under glasnost, Soviet writers were able for the first time to openly confront the cultural shambles left by Stalin. Some spade work had been done during the Khrushchev era, but at that time only half truths could be revealed and half measures taken. Where to start the clearing of the Augean stables? The *Short Course* of the party history had been the chief propaganda document, the bible of the cult of the individual.[34] Written in 1937–38 by a committee headed by Knorin (soon to be shot), Pospelov, and Yaroslavsky, it was to Soviet history and philosophy what the trials were to Soviet politics.

The *Short Course* was edited 301 times in subsequent years, and translated in sixty-seven languages; 42,816 million copies were distributed. One short chapter (about dialectical and historical materialism) was written by Stalin himself, who took a close interest in the preparation of the book and acted as editor. The book was neither better nor worse than other histories written in the 1930s.[35] But it became something akin to canonic law, and it monopolized the field, virtually putting an end to the writing of Soviet history and philosophy. Editing the manuscript, Stalin, to his credit, deleted some of the most ludicrous exaggerations concerning him personally. But what remained was still a flagrant perversion of the historical truth.

Thus, the impression was created that Lenin had received from Stalin the permission to publish *Iskra*, the first Bolshevik periodical, even though Lenin had not even heard of Stalin at the time. Or to give another example, the Prague Conference of 1912 became an event of absolutely crucial significance not because any decisions of particular importance were made on this occasion but because Stalin was co-opted as a member of the Central Committee.

The cleaning of the stables was bound to affect not only the master himself but various *dei minorum gentium*, the little Stalins and the idols of the period, such as Aleksei Stakhanov, the hero of Socialist labor, and Pavlik Morozov, the symbol of total loyalty. On August 31, 1935, as a Donetsk coal miner, Stakhanov had allegedly drilled 102 tons of coal in six hours, about fifteen times the normal output in a single shift. After his remarkable feat, he was feted for years throughout the Soviet Union, and his name was given to the movement of shockworkers throughout the country who established the record. He was transferred to Moscow, and then nothing was heard of him anymore.

The truth emerged in stages. First it became known that he had died in 1977, a bitter man and a drunkard. He had been needed only as a symbol, not as a living person. When he had fulfilled his purpose (and he seems not to have been very good as a symbol), he was dropped from his desk job in Moscow and disappeared.[36] Soon after, the news emerged that the record had been achieved under suspicious circumstances: He had been helped by two other miners, all other work had been stopped in the coal mine, and a whole gang had performed auxiliary services.[37]

The truth about Stakhanov provoked not only approval but also bitter criticism: Had the Stakhanov movement not made a major contribution to the industrialization of the country? Would the Five-Year Plans have succeeded but for this initiative? The debate brought about further revelations: Most, if not all, "records" of the Stalinist period had been spurious. Thus, a milkmaid named Persialtsev in a kolkhoz near Moscow had achieved an output of 2,000 liters of milk per cow in 1935 and of 4,500 liters the year after. A nationwide movement was started to "storm the 3,000-liter level." And what good had it done the country at large? Fifty years later, the average output per cow in the Soviet Union was still 2,400 liters. Quite obviously, records could be achieved only under special conditions.[38]

The story of Pavel Morozov concerns not minerals or animals but human beings. It is the story of a tragedy that took place in a small village in Sverdlovsk district when a fourteen-year-old boy and his nine-year-old brother were killed by inhabitants of the village, including members of his own family.[39] Pavlik, the only member of the Komsomol and "agitator" in place, had informed the police that Trofim, his father and chairman of the collective farm, had kept some wheat in reserve instead of delivering everything to the government and that he engaged in other illegal activities, such as selling (or giving away) ration forms with the stamp of the local soviet. Whether Trofim was engaging in black-market dealings or whether he tried to help poor people affected by de-kulakization, or both, may never be established because the transactions took place within a small circle of people. Because of the information received from the son, Trofim got a ten-year sentence and disappeared in the gulag, never to return. The children were killed by irate relatives, who in court expressed regret that they had not burned the corpses. They were executed.[40] Pavlik's mother, who had divorced her husband earlier on, survived.

Pavlik Morozov became the idol of the Komsomol in the 1930s and 1940s, a young Communist saint who had given his life for the cause of communism. Stalin supported the Morozov cult in every possible way; Lenin, after all, had said that every Bolshevik should be a good Chekist, and informers were needed in the 1930s more than ever before. The whole system of control rested on the presence of informers—wives against husbands, children against parents, friend against friend.

In the post-Stalinist era, Pavlik Morozov's fame paled; gradually he became an antihero. The most that a high Soviet legal official could say under glasnost was that the trial against Pavlik's father in 1932 had not been a show trial, that the historical context (of collectivization and de-kulakization) had been a very different one from the one prevailing fifty years later; many legal depositions in the Morozov file bore not a signature but a fingerprint. As for the moral issues involved, the legal authority said, every contemporary has to provide his own answer.[41] However, Pavel Morozov also had his defenders. Laudatory articles appeared in official organs, and the Komsomol leadership passed a resolution in 1989 confirming an earlier (1955) decree that inscribed Morozov's name in the Komsomol roll of honor.[42] At the very same time, Yunost, a monthly literary magazine vaguely connected with the Communist Youth League, published a well-researched, devastating article on the Pavlik Morozov myth, arguing that it was based on invention from beginning to end.[43] In brief, the party line on the historical role of this young martyr has broken down.

The plague of informing was all-pervasive: the biographer of Marshal Zhukov revealed that he was deeply shocked when he discovered under glasnost a letter of denunciation written by his hero. It was dated January 1938, addressed to Voroshilov, and dealt with a speech in 1917 (!) in which Marshal Egorov, the deputy defense minister, had allegedly called Lenin an adventurist.[44] Karpov argues that such a letter could no longer harm Egorov, who had been dismissed from his job the year before. This seems not to be quite true because Egorov was dismissed only in February 1938. But even if there were such "mitigating circumstances," the incident still shows that the writing of such letters was a commonplace affair, the rule rather than the exception. Following the revelation of this discovery in the archives, Zhukov's daughters had the marshal's signature submitted to graphological analysis; the experts maintained that a forgery had been committed.[45]

In Stalin's lifetime, there was no escaping the all-pervasive presence of the cult. A reader opening the magazine *Iskusstvo* (*Art*) in January 1950 would encounter an article (to pick an example at random) on the exhibition in Moscow on "Joseph Stalin in Graphic Arts." One of the prize exhibits was a picture by F. Shurpin, awarded the Stalin Prize in 1948.

> On a bright early morning Comrade Stalin is seen walking in the vast collective farm fields with high-voltage power transmission lines in the distance, wearing a white tunic with his raincoat over his arm. His exalted face and his whole figure are lit with the golden rays of springtime sun. One recollects verses by the people's poet Dzhambul: Oh, Stalin, the sunshine of springtime is you. . . . He walks confidently toward the new dawn. The image of Comrade Stalin is the triumphant march of communism, the symbol of courage, the symbol of the Soviet people's glory, calling for new heroic exploits for the benefit of our great motherland. In this image are immortalized the features of a wise, majestic, and at the same time amazingly modest and unpretentious man who is our beloved leader. . . .[46]

It will be recalled that Stalin only visited a farm once, and this had been twenty years earlier, when they had not yet been collectivized. During the whole war, only once had he been anywhere near the front line, and only for a few hours, whereupon he quickly informed Churchill and Roosevelt and apologized for not being able to answer their messages earlier because his presence with his troops was so urgently needed. The place of a war leader is not in the front line (Hitler did not visit the front, either), and there is no cogent reason why Stalin should have wasted his valuable time inspecting kolkhoz fields even in spring sunshine. What matters is the false pretense, the utter mendacity, that permeated so deeply every aspect of public life.

Even during the last years of his life, when his place in the life of his country was firmly anchored, when all superlatives had already been exhausted, and when no further exaggeration seemed possible, he still had to make his mark as the leading philosopher, economist, even linguist, of the era.

What Lysenko was to Soviet biology, Mitin, Yudin, Pospelov, and a few others were to the social sciences. They were the official interpreters of Stalin's sayings. These young professors-agitators of the 1930s had somehow wormed their way into Stalin's entourage and become his academic secretaries. They would get orders to compose a new party program in eight to ten days (1939) or to prepare a purge in the natural sciences.[47] Quite literally, they exploited corpses, the corpses of their colleagues—that, incidentally, did not impede their career even after the boss had died. They plagiarized shamelessly; thus, the entry "philosophy" in the first edition of the *Great Soviet Encyclopedia* was signed "Sten." Sten, who had been Stalin's private tutor in philosophy, belonged to Bukharin's circle and was shot in the 1930s. But the article survived; in the next edition, it appeared under the signature of Mark Mitin.

These men (and a few women) became members of the Academy of Sciences, heroes of socialist labor, Stalin (and state) award winners; they were greatly honored under Khrushchev and Brezhnev, even though their only merit was to have built up the boss into a great philosopher. True, not all philosophers kept silent in the post-Stalin period of 1953–86, but even they could not utter more than a few cautious words of dissent.[48] By and large, these sciences were still dominated in the post-Stalin period by the same people who had been the recognized leaders in Stalin's lifetime.

In 1952, Stalin published a long essay entitled "The Economic Problems of Socialism in the U.S.S.R." It is not entirely clear to this day why this essay was written or who wrote it. The subject had some distant connection with the current problems of the country, even though it contained nothing that was new, startling, or important—nothing that could not have been said by thousands of candidates or aspirants of economic science.

Ostensibly, Stalin's articles were triggered by four letters he had received by a not very well known husband-and-wife team of managers, Vladimir Venzher and Alexandra Sanina, who were greatly surprised to get an answer to the questions they had asked and to others they had never raised. (They lived to tell their story under glasnost.) That Stalin received thousands of letters every month, was, of course, not the real explanation why the aging and ailing leader's fancy was suddenly struck.

It is even more difficult to explain Stalin's foray in the field of linguistics in 1950, a time when the Soviet Union faced immense problems both on the home front and in foreign policy, the year of the outbreak of the Korean War. And the "father of the peoples," concentrating all power in his hands, found time to study some of the problems preoccupying Soviet linguists and to write not just one article but three.[49] True, he had a tutor, the academician Arnold Chichibaba from Tbilisi, who explained to him the intricacies of "Marrism," named for Nikolai Marr (1865–1934). Marrism was a kind of Japhetite theory concerning the origins of certain languages that had become, not least owing to Stalin's support, the leading doctrine in the field from the late 1920s. It now came under fire because of Stalin's intervention. Stalin had a certain interest in the topic, having written on nations and nationalities in his earlier years, but he was still an amateur, and not a gifted one. In his article, there was not a single new idea, and some of his assertions, such as the idea that the dialects of Kursk and Orel were the basis of the Russian language, were simply embarrassing.[50] The only likely explanation would be Stalin's aspiration during his last years to enter history not only as a great political leader, diplomat, and warlord but also as a theoretician the equal of Marx and Lenin.

Stalin intervened wherever an opportunity offered itself. He told the then heads of the writers' organization who should get a first-class Stalin Prize, who should get a second-class or third-class prize, and who should get none at all.[51] In February 1947, Eisenstein, one of the great filmmakers of all times, and Nikolai Cherkasov were summoned to the Kremlin to receive orders on how to remake the movie *Ivan IV*. The tsar was very ruthless, Stalin said, "but you must show that it was necessary to be ruthless." One of Ivan's errors, said Stalin, was that he had failed to cut down five large feudal families. Had he wiped out these families, there would have been no "Time of Troubles."[52] Ivan the Terrible was not terrible enough. When Eisenstein asked whether there were, in addition, specific instructions in regard to the film, Stalin replied that he was not giving instructions; his was merely the reaction of a spectator. But it soon appeared that he had some detailed "suggestions"—concerning, for example, the way the tsar was catching flies. Zhdanov complained that the tsar's beard was too prominent, whereupon Eisenstein promised to trim it.

Under glasnost, the Stalin cult in architecture was derided for its plans for monumental neoclassic buildings and projected statues of Lenin and Stalin 100 meters high (or even higher) because the heads of these statues, given the Moscow climate, would have been quite literally in the clouds.[53]

In his wartime exile, Bertolt Brecht had once told a young fellow émigré (Henry Pachter), "Stalin? In fifty years everyone will have forgotten about him." Fifty years later, Brecht's prediction seemed premature, to say the least. Even in his own lifetime, Stalin had become a prominent topic of Soviet folklore. True, most of it was synthetic, pseudofolklore. The various *skazki* and *noviny* were commissioned by the authorities. A good example was the story of Ivan, one of three brothers who left home in pursuit of his fortune. He is heading east, for a wonderful country he has heard about. He finds it difficult to enter because its borders are well guarded but eventually succeeds and is met by a gracious people who show him a city filled with miracles and introduce him to the person who made these miracles possible—a friendly man with a mustache who wears a soldier's boots and smokes a pipe.[54]

True, after Stalin's death his name was dropped, but the goal of Soviet folklorists remained essentially what it had been in the 1930s.[55] Under glasnost, a new kind of folklore has made its appearance—legends, myths, *pritchy* ("parables"), and even "folklore of the intelligentsia" about Stalin that could not be published earlier and that had been collected by some unafraid enthusiasts.[56]

If, as George Bernard Shaw claimed, the art of government is the organization of idolatry,[57] then Stalin was the greatest statesman of the twentieth century—indeed, of modern times. Stalin wanted not only the adulation of contemporaries but also of posterity; seen in this light, he has been much less successful. In St. Paul's Cathedral in London, the son of the builder had an inscription engraved that states: *Si monumentum requiris, circumspice* ("If you would see the man's monument, look around"). It is a fitting epitaph for Stalin.

11. Stalin as Warlord

Whereas Stalin emerged as the great victor from World War II, Hitler went down to defeat together with a Reich that was to last a thousand years. Stalin and the Soviet military victory became for years more or less identical in popular belief. The view prevailed that only because of Stalin's relentless willpower and his wise leadership was the Soviet Union prepared when war came in 1941. He did, of course, make mistakes, but they counted for little because in the end the Soviet armed forces defeated Nazi Germany and Japan.

As the years passed and as it became possible to talk and write more freely about the war, this view was increasingly questioned. Under glasnost, searching questions are being asked concerning Soviet foreign policy in the 1930s and vis-à-vis Germany in particular. The wisdom of the German-Soviet pact of August 23, 1939, is being questioned, as is the general conduct of the war following the Nazi invasion of June 22, 1941.

Stalin was anything but a consistent anti-Fascist. According to his speeches and those made by Molotov in 1939–41, ideology was not really important in international relations. That Italy was Fascist had not prevented normal relations between Moscow and Rome; Britain and France were mistaken if they thought that the Soviet Union would "get the chestnuts out of the fire" just to please them—that is to say, that the Soviet Union would get involved in a war with Nazi Germany. Stalin's defenders have argued that given the policy of appeasement vis-à-vis Hitler that ultimately led to Munich, he had no alternative but to play out one imperialist camp against another, thus gaining valuable time for strengthening Soviet defenses.

That appeasement had many supporters in Britain and France goes without saying, but it is not sufficient to absolve Stalin from responsibility. His misjudgments date back to the period before Hitler's rise to power, to the constant attacks against "social fascism," that is, social democracy, which was considered an enemy worse than the Nazis. As Ernest Genri, who had served the Soviets in both Berlin and London before the war, wrote many years later:

> Unity of action in the working-class movement was becoming a matter of life and death for the anti-Fascists. Stalin did not understand that at all. Or did he not want to understand it? Many Communists in various countries perceived this theory [of social fascism] as unexpected and almost incomprehensible, but obeying the usual party discipline, they carried out instructions. . . . The possibility of preventing the Nazis' accession to power was lost.[1]

There is, of course, no certainty that a united front of the Left (and the center) would have prevented Hitler's rise to power. But it was never even tried. True, Stalin realized in later years that a popular-front policy was needed, but by the time he reached this obvious conclusion, it was too late. In some countries the Left had already been defeated; elsewhere suspicion vis-à-vis the Communists had grown so deep as to prevent true collaboration. In any case, the popular-front strategy lasted only for a short time and was abandoned as the Soviet-German rapprochement began.

It was not just a question of tactical maneuvers or even long-term strategy. There was, as far as Stalin and his close collaborators were concerned, a deep-seated hostility toward the Western powers, an "anti-Western syndrome" in the words of a Soviet historian. To put it bluntly, they slightly preferred Hitler to Churchill, Roosevelt, and the French leaders. The Western countries were considered to be the true enemies of the Soviet Union, whereas the attitude toward Nazi Germany was far more equivocal. If Stalin had more respect for Hitler than for the Western leaders, the same is true with regard to Hitler's appraisal of Stalin: "Stalin, too, must command our unconditional respect. In his own way he is a hell of a fellow. . . ."[2] This Hitler stated on July 22, 1942, in the middle of the war; Hitler never talked in similar laudatory terms about Churchill or Roosevelt.

Stalin overestimated British and French hostility toward the Soviet Union—and also the ability of the status quo powers to inflict damage on the Soviet Union if they wanted. He underrated the aggressive character as well as the military power of Nazism.

Under Stalin, the Soviet Union developed a political system that resembled, in certain important respects, the Fascist regimes. To state this fact and to emphasize that the similarities were not superficial was for a long time considered a base calumny in the Soviet Union, and it was also thought to be bad form in many Western circles. It is one thing to equate the Soviet system of the 1930s with Nazi Germany, which is ahistorical and of no help in understanding either. It is another proposition to point to parallels such as the one-party system, the crucial role of the leader, the important function of the secret police, etc.[3] and to conclude that the two systems were probably more similar to each other than to the "plutocratic democracies." These similarities have preoccupied many Soviet authors for a considerable time; Vassili Grossman's great novel *Life and Fate* is based on this problem, and, under glasnost, the issue is almost freely discussed.

As a Soviet commentator stated, there were no major ideological differences between Hitler and Stalin in 1939, only conflicting imperial battles of the two empires that could easily be satisfied if the bill was paid by their neighbors. What ideological differences could exist between Beria and Himmler, between Rosenberg and Vyshinsky?[4]

Such statements may appear too emotional and extreme to cautious historians. There were, as a matter of fact, important ideological differences, but they were not decisive as far as foreign policy was concerned. In any case, it was not just a question of political and social convergence as a theoretical proposition. Even the most hardheaded realpolitiker in the West did not regard Stalin's Russia as a very attractive potential ally. Or, to put it more bluntly, "In the eyes of many Westerners, the reputation of the Soviet Union was for a long time lower than that of Hitlerite Germany."[5]

As a result of the Stalinist purges, the images of the Red Army had plummeted. The political consequences were enormous. For the French general staff, Russia had ceased to be an ally on whom one could rely. For either the Soviet generals were guilty of the charges against them, in which case the Soviets could no longer be trusted with any secret, or they were innocent, in which case one had to draw the conclusion that Russia was ruled by madmen.[6] The massacre of the Soviet officer corps had an enormous impact on potential allies and enemies alike. Whereas the Germans had been very much impressed by Russia's military preparedness until the mid-1930s, the appraisal of Soviet military power after that date was more and more negative: Stalin had weakened the Red Army for many years to come, in the words of the German military attaché in Moscow. As Marshal Vasilevsky was to write in later years: "But for 1937, the Second World War and the attack in 1941 might not have occurred at all. . . ."

There could be no two views inside the Soviet Union on the impact of the purge of the Red Army command. Nevertheless, Stalin's decision to conclude a nonaggression pact with Nazi Germany finds supporters even under glasnost. In fact, the official party line continued to assess the pact favorably. As Gorbachev said in his speech on the seventieth anniversary of the Revolution:

> It is said that the decision made by the Soviet Union to conclude a non-aggression pact with Germany was not a very sound one. Maybe so, if one is led not by harsh reality but deals with it on the level of abstraction and speculation, removed from the context of time. Under the circumstances, the problem confronted us approximately as it did in the time of the peace of Brest Litovsk: whether or not the country would remain independent, whether socialism would survive. We succeeded in postponing the conflict with the enemy, a conflict in which there was only one alternative: to prevail or to go under.[7]

Those defending Stalin's decision adduce a number of reasons. They claim that the Soviet leadership genuinely wanted to reach an agreement with the Western powers, but there was no such willingness on the part of Paris and London. Second, the Soviet Union succeeded in preventing a war on two fronts that it would have had to fight in 1939. Third, it made the emergence of a common anti-Soviet front (including both the Axis powers and the Western nations) impossible. Fourth, it created the basis for a common front between the Soviet Union and the West in 1941 that had not existed in 1939. And finally, the Soviet Union gained a breathing spell of almost two years to prepare itself for the armed conflict.[8]

True, the advocates of the pact now admit that certain mistakes were made. It was not necessary to sign the friendship treaty of September 28, 1939, or to insult the Poles in various speeches after their defeat (Molotov's reference to the "friendship between Russia and Germany that had been sealed in [Polish] blood"). It was indefensible to forcibly return to Germany leading German and Austrian Communists who had sought exile in the Soviet Union.[9] Many foreign supporters of the Soviet Union opposed the pact, which they regarded as unnatural, but (it is argued) they did not know what the Soviet leaders knew. Seen in retrospect, the establishment of a common anti-Nazi front with France and Britain in 1939 would have been preferable; it might have prevented aggression and World War II. If such an agreement was not reached, it was not the fault of the Soviet Union, which had negotiated in good faith, whereas in the case of the Western allies, the narrow, egoistic class interests proved to be an insurmountable obstacle.

How much truth is there to these allegations? There was not much enthusiasm among Western leaders to sign a military pact with the Russians (less among the British than the French), and the reasons for this hesitancy have been noted. Stalin seemed neither a good bet nor an attractive ally. But they wanted to stop Hitler, and they needed a counterweight to Germany. The options were still open in August 1939 when Stalin, under pressure from Hitler, decided to call off the talks and give Germany a free hand against Poland, thus unleashing World War II. As a Soviet historian has put it:

> It is true that the talks proceeded with difficulty in a zigzag fashion, but they did nonetheless proceed, and this flickering flame had to be maintained come what may. It was at this complex moment that the Soviet leaders lost their sense of realism and restraint. They ostentatiously signed the fatal pact with Germany, which essentially meant the rejection of further talks with Britain and France. In the spring and summer of 1939 the Soviet leadership acted sensibly, maintaining contact with the Western powers and with Germany and keeping both doors open. But unfortunately it shut the wrong door. . . . That Hitler was in such a hurry to sign the pact meant that the other side should have, conversely, taken time to think about the motives for this haste and should have displayed the utmost caution. . . .[10]

Yet another Soviet historian, while claiming that the pact was ultimately "forced" on the Soviet Union, admits that the repression of dozens of experienced diplomats had a negative effect on Soviet foreign policy and that Voroshilov had no diplomatic experience at all. He notes that the replacement of Litvinov by Molotov also influenced Western public opinion, as did the Stalinist purges.[11]

Those who justify the pact in retrospect argue that the Soviet side could not be sure that Hitler would indeed attack Poland. But this claim stretches one's imagination beyond any reasonable limit. After all, Hitler had written Stalin that there might be an "explosion" about Poland any day. A secret protocol had been signed concerning the division of Poland and of Eastern Europe in general. True, Soviet official spokesmen claimed up to 1989 that no copies of the secret protocol had been found in Soviet archives. Yet they did not maintain that such a protocol did not exist, merely that one should suspend judgment until one could be absolutely certain on this point. By that time some Soviet newspapers had already published the text.[12]

The issue of the "special protocol" accompanying the Soviet-German friendship treaty—that is, the deal made between Stalin and Hitler to carve up Eastern Europe—became a major bone of contention inside the Soviet Union. In the Baltic republics, countless articles were published claiming that it was ridiculous to deny facts known to the whole world, and there were even mass demonstrations in this regard.[13] But Soviet government spokesmen continued to cast aspersions on the authenticity of the protocol, and they had the support of Gorbachev, who made an official statement on the subject at the Congress of People's Deputies in June 1989. Eventually, two commissions were appointed in Moscow to deal with the affair: one by the party Central Committee, the other by the Congress of People's Deputies, and an unofficial emissary (Lev Bezymensky) was sent to Bonn and London to do research in the archives. Professional historians had known for a long time that the original protocol had been destroyed following Ribbentrop's orders toward the end of the war. But several copies existed. Furthermore, most of the maps dividing Eastern Europe signed by Molotov and German officials had survived, as well as the negotiating notes of the German embassy in Moscow and other wholly conclusive evidence, including Stalin's signature.[14] There was great psychological resistance in Moscow to accepting the facts in this case (as in the case of Katyn), even though there could not have been any reasonable doubt.

It is true, to repeat once again, that the Western powers proceeded with excessive caution in their talks with the Soviet Union in July and August

1939, but they still wanted to negotiate, whereas Stalin broke off the talks. The other arguments used by Soviet historians cannot be taken seriously. The danger of a war on two fronts was largely mythical. No one in Japan wanted to attack the Soviet Union except some junior hotheads in the Kwantung army. Japan was totally preoccupied with China, having swallowed more than they could digest during the previous two years. If they had been eager to invade the Soviet Union, they would have done so after June 22, 1941. But they refrained from invading Siberia simply because they believed that Japan should expand in a southward direction. Nor is it at all certain that Hitler would have attacked the Soviet Union in the autumn of 1939 (or the summer of 1940) except for Stalin's willingness to sign the pact. As Hitler said in a secret speech addressing the heads of the Wehrmacht on November 23, 1939, Germany could attack the Soviet Union only after the threat in the West had been removed.[15]

The next argument also belongs largely in the realm of fantasy. There was no danger that all the "imperialist" powers would make common cause in a war against the Soviet Union. This specter had haunted the Soviet leadership throughout the 1920s, but in 1939 it was less true than ever before. Given Hitler's almost boundless ambitions, a collision between Germany and the "saturated" Western powers was inevitable. Stalin may not have understood this, but his misjudgment can hardly be used fifty years after the event as a mitigating factor. It is more likely that, as a Soviet author has put it, the "anti-French and anti-British syndrome of Stalin and his immediate entourage caused enormous harm to Soviet foreign policy at the time, and emotions, not sober political calculations, gained the upper hand. The confrontationist spirit so pervaded all actions of the Soviet leadership that it prevented it from seeing with open eyes its own interests and determining in a realistic way where the enemy was. . . ."[16]

Last, the most important question: To what extent did the Soviet Union gain time to strengthen its defenses? Was it in a better position in June 1941 to face a Nazi attack than a year or two earlier?

The number of Soviet soldiers grew from 1.9 million in 1939 to 5.4 million on June 22, 1941, but most of their equipment was not new: Only about half of the tanks for the tank divisions had been delivered, and, of these, less than one-fifth were recent models. The same was true, broadly speaking, of the Soviet air force. Furthermore, many airports were not in working order. Neither Soviet communications nor transport met the exigencies of modern warfare.[17] On the other hand, the German forces were in no position in 1939 to attack the Soviet Union. Hitler had altogether 110 divisions at his disposal, of which almost half had to be kept in the West in case of an attack by France. The mechanized divisions in the East had enough fuel and other supplies for a war of very short duration, such as against Poland. Anything more ambitious would have ended in disaster. Neither the German air force nor the navy was ready for a major, prolonged war against the Soviet Union; there was no plan for such a campaign. Hitler's position twenty-one months later was considerably stronger; he could dispose of 152 divisions for the attack against the Soviet Union, not to mention the availability of several dozen divisions from other countries.

How does one explain (in the words of a Soviet military author writing under glasnost) that regardless of the existence of a strong industrial base in the Soviet Union and the presence of talented designers, the weaponry of the Nazi army was so superior?[18]

One of the reasons adduced is that, for several years prior to the attack, Germany had converted its economy to the production of modern weaponry, and "this the Soviet Union could not do for foreign political, economic, and other reasons." Soviet defense expenditure, which had been 25 percent of the total budget in 1939, rose in 1941 to 43 percent of the state budget.[19] These figures tend to cast doubt on the reasons for the delay in Soviet mobilization allegedly responsible: That the Soviet Union was in various respects inferior to the German military machine pertains mainly to qualitative inferiority. It is true that, as Soviet authors argue, between 1939 and 1941 German forces acquired the equipment of thirty Czech divisions, that in France alone they captured 5,000 tanks and armored personnel carriers as well as 3,000 aircraft, and that they could outfit ninety-two divisions with motor transport seized in France. Furthermore, the German stocks of raw and semifinished materials grew immensely.

All this shows that the German high command benefited more than the Russians from the twenty-one months gained as the result of the nonaggression pact of August 1939. Stalin no doubt assumed that the war in the West would last much longer; such misjudgments have frequently happened in military history. But they cannot be offered as evidence for Stalin's good judgment and farsighted statesmanship.

There still is a case that can be made in favor of the nonaggression pact, but it is not the one advanced by Gorbachev in 1987 or by some other Soviet authors. It could be argued that, after the bloodletting of 1937–38 the Red Army command needed breathing space so that new commanders could be promoted and gain experience. But this consideration did not weigh heavily in Stalin's calculations; the purge continued in the defense industry, and the damage in the army command could not be rectified within a few months or years. The head of military intelligence was changed six times between 1936 and 1940, and, during 1940, the chief of the general staff was replaced three times (Shaposhnikov, Meretskov, Zhukov, and again Shaposhnikov). Military reforms were launched, stopped again after a few months, and then reversed. As the commander of the navy wrote in a memorandum to the people's commissar of defense about the situation at a certain plant:

> It is the sole plant where the designing, development, and manufacturing of naval artillery are concentrated. [At the present time] the situation is catastrophic, since, as the result of incorrect leadership and the arrest of virtually all the leading workers in the design bureau . . . as well as a number of workers in the plant management and shops . . . the plant is almost completely demoralized.[20]

Alternatively, it could be argued that although the treaty with Hitler cost the Soviet Union much goodwill in the West, this was ultimately of less consequence than the gain of space and time: Not only did the Soviet Union survive the Nazi onslaught, but Communist regimes were established throughout Eastern Europe. Without the outbreak of a world war, the Soviet Union would not have made such great advances. Only because of the war did the Soviet Union emerge as a military superpower; there was no other way to export the Soviet system. This is a weighty argument, but it ought to be carried to its logical conclusion. At what cost was victory achieved, what were its international consequences, and how firm were the gains made in Eastern Europe, from a perspective of fifty years? What were the long-term moral and political repercussions of the transformation of the Soviet Union into an imperial power whose security rested on the force of arms rather than on the power of its ideology?

Mention had been made of Gorbachev's comparison between the non-aggression pact of 1939 and the treaty of Brest Litovsk twenty-one years earlier. It will be recalled that the Bolsheviks split three ways at the time: Bukharin and some other left-wingers claimed that it was the duty of the

Soviet government to fight on; Lenin argued that there was no alternative but to sign the treaty; and Trotsky, who took a "centrist" position, launched the slogan "Neither war nor peace." Eventually Lenin prevailed, and the treaty was signed.[21]

At the time of the nonaggression pact of 1939, Trotsky was the only main principal of Brest Litovsk still alive. When the parallel was suggested to him, he emphatically rejected it: The young Soviet republic had no alternative in 1918 but to sign; it capitulated because it faced a much stronger enemy. It had not a single battalion at the time that could be thrown into battle. The pact between Hitler and Stalin, on the other hand, was concluded despite the existence of a strong Soviet army; its purpose was to give Hitler a free hand to invade Poland, which was to be subsequently divided between Germany and the Soviet Union. "What kind of analogy is this?"[22] Commenting on the Brest Litovsk treaty two years after the event, in his famous essay on "The Infantile Disorders of Left-Wing Communism," Lenin had made a similar point: It was one thing to surrender one's money (or passport or car) to a bandit in order to survive; this was a compromise that no sensible human being would reject. It was another kind of compromise to join the bandit, to give him arms and money in order to divide the loot. The pact of August 23, 1939, belonged, no doubt, to the latter kind of compromise. It could still be explained on the level of realpolitik: The territory gained as a result was to stay part of the Soviet Union. But the Brest Litovsk treaty is still not a good precedent to justify the pact of 1939.

That Stalin failed to take seriously countless warnings concerning an imminent German attack in 1941 had been known even well before glasnost. The issue was never in doubt, and though glasnost has brought some new revelations, it did not substantially affect the general picture. Some Western authors have maintained, on the contrary, that Stalin was preparing an attack against Germany and that the German offensive surprised him in the midst of those preparations.[23] Much emphasis was put on a (secret) speech made by Stalin during a visit to the Frunze Military Academy on May 5, 1941. Under glasnost it has become known that he had indeed said on this occasion that one ought to be ready for the "unconditional destruction of German fascism."[24] It was also true that on the eve of the war a Soviet army memorandum had been prepared mentioning a "just and offensive war." Lastly, Soviet forces near the border were deployed in an offensive fashion and for this reason found it difficult to redeploy facing the German attack. But all this evidence amounts to very little for the simple reason that Soviet preparations for any war were nowhere near completion and Stalin could not have attacked even if he wanted to.

II

The "Great Fatherland War" has been the central event in Soviet postwar consciousness. It was celebrated in countless novels, plays, poems, movies, and television documentaries as well as in thousands of books, encyclopedias, and innumerable articles dealing with specific aspects and operations. But the official historiography, and there was no other, dealt predominantly with the latter period of the war, that is, 1943 onward, when Soviet armed forces were on the offensive. The grave setbacks of the first eighteen months were seldom discussed except perhaps by novelists. The deeper reasons were usually ignored, the real facts and figures were not known or could not be used, and certain topics were not dealt with at all.

These issues included the fate of the Soviet prisoners of war, of whom there had been many millions, and the price the Soviet Union had to pay for its final victory. In some respects, the military historians were permitted to make greater concessions to historical truth than their civilian colleagues, for virtually all the military leaders were rehabilitated. In other crucial respects they could not, or would not, publish the true facts relating, for instance, to the military balance of power in 1941 and after. The manpower and equipment of the Germans and their satellites was always exaggerated; in a comparison of the number of tanks, for example, the Russians counted only their tanks of recent production.

A bitter debate over the state of Soviet military preparedness on the eve of the war began in 1988–89. Some observers argued that the Soviet Union had always had more tanks than Germany. It produced 7,000 in 1941 compared with the 3,500 that were produced in Germany. During 1942, more tanks were produced in the Soviet Union than in Germany during the entire war.[25] One writer noted that the Soviet Union led the world in the training and deployment of parachute troops and commandos and that Soviet aircraft was also not inferior to that of the Germans, as was frequently stated.

In the final analysis, the decisive factor was leadership and strategic doctrine (or the absence of it) rather than the largely mythical Soviet inferiority. The opponents in this debate claimed that Soviet tanks and airplanes existed largely on paper; the sixty-one Soviet tank divisions (as compared with thirty-one German) were grossly understrength because most of the tanks allocated to them had not actually been delivered.[26]

The pattern of searching questions would persist. Thus, a young civilian expert investigated the preparation for war made by the Soviet air force.[27] On the basis of painstaking research, he found that everyone agreed on the number of German war planes that had been designated for the June 1941 attack (about 4,000). There were wide divergences in regard to the number of Soviet planes, however. According to all estimates, the Russians outnumbered their foes. According to Marshal Zhukov, some 17,700 war planes had been delivered between January 1, 1939, and June 1941. Even if many were not the most recent model, there still existed substantial Soviet superiority even after 1,000 planes on the ground had been destroyed by the Germans on the first day of the war. The writer continued: Had not the British shown during the battle for Britain what could be achieved against an enemy superior in numbers? What was the reason for the poor performance of the Soviet air force not only during the early phase of the war? These and similar questions had been ignored by the official military historians prior to glasnost, and even after there was a marked reluctance to delve too deeply into these questions.

When glasnost came, the criticism of Stalin's foreign policy (the rapprochement with Germany) and his refusal to believe that Germany was about to attack spread to other, more fundamental strategic issues: Why the enormous losses? Why a layman's unwillingness to take advice, especially during the first year and a half of the war? Why the absence of a basic (defensive) strategic doctrine in the prewar period?

Most of the attacks come from civilian writers, and none was more outspoken than the novelist Astafiev: The majority of Soviet historians, including the editors and authors of the *History of the Fatherland War*, had lost the right to use the holy word "truth"; their hands were unclean, their thoughts dirty. Astafiev, a Russian patriot second to none, had taken part in the war and had been severely wounded, but the war in which he had fought (he said) was not the one described in the history books.[28]

Such attacks are emphatically rejected by the leadership of the armed forces as well as by the military-historical establishment: Mistakes had, of course, been made; they happened in every war. But the mistakes had been the result of the purges of 1937 as well as the perfidious, sudden attack of the German forces that caught the Red Army unaware.

But even the purge was described in a curious way: It was said that a "considerable number" (not the overwhelming majority) of commanders had been dismissed (or removed) but had been later rehabilitated and the "mistakes had been corrected."[29] A reader unfamiliar with the true state of affairs was bound to reach the conclusion that Tukhachevsky and the others had taken early retirement in 1937, devoting their time to hunting, fishing, playing with their grandchildren, or perhaps writing their memoirs.

In a similar vein it was claimed that the civilian critics who now argued that the price of victory had been far too high and who criticized the conduct of the war either were not familiar with the true facts or were seeking to undermine the prestige of the Soviet armed forces.[30]

This argument was undoubtedly the decisive one; no institution wants to admit mistakes, even if committed in the distant past, and the army was no exception. The same was true, a fortiori, of the military historians responsible for the publications during the Brezhnev era. To admit that they had been wrong would have been to deny their life's work.

Many books written by leading Soviet marshals, generals, and admirals of World War II had been published in the 1960s. Subject to both self-censorship and outside censorship—especially after Khrushchev's fall—they had been less than candid with regard to the military situation before and after June 22, 1941. The generals had been afraid of Stalin, remembering what had happened to their predecessors in 1937–38. Konstantin Simonov writes that "to say aloud that Stalin was wrong, that he commits mistakes, could mean that even before leaving the building you find yourself going to have coffee with Beria." Naturally, the Soviet commanders preferred to have their coffee in their own offices, and it is difficult to blame them even in retrospect. Nor is it surprising that confessions of this kind could be published only years after Simonov's and most of the marshals' deaths.[31]

True, some military authors took a more cautious "centrist" line: They conceded that there was a need for reexamining the early period of the war. Mistakes had been committed inasmuch as the precious experience of Hitler's victories (blitzkrieg) had been ignored. But it was still wrong to assign blame only to Stalin and Voroshilov. If there had been an erroneous concept, it had also been advocated by Zhukov and even Tukhachevsky and Egorov.[32] If everyone had been (partly) wrong, then no one should be signaled out for blame; in any case the mistakes should not be overemphasized because their results were not fatal.

Significant changes in this respect occurred only during the summer of 1988. From this date on, basic criticism of Stalin was no longer limited to civilian historians; instead of "mistakes," writers now referred to crimes, and the "cult of the individual" became "Stalinism."[33] A writer in *Krasnaia Zvezda* noted that the Soviet leadership did not have the faintest notion of what was happening at the beginning of the war; hence, the crazy order on the evening of June 22, 1941, to launch an immediate counterattack. The former people's commissar of the navy, Kuznetsov, was quoted to the effect that on the eve of the war the Soviet Union had no clear military doctrine.[34] Volkogonov, previously deputy head of the political directorate of the armed forces, said in an interview with a Finnish journal that Stalin had made a cardinal error; when drunk with power, he had given Finland an ultimatum, assuming that Finland would immediately bow to his demands.[35]

Severe in particular were the strictures of Nikolai Pavlenko, a professional military historian and former lieutenant general, as well as those of V. Kulish, yet another military intellectual.[36] That Stalin found also his defenders goes without saying, but after 1987 they, too, were on the defensive. Their argument was no longer that Stalin had been the greatest strategist of all times but that it was unfair to make him the only scapegoat for the Soviet defeat in the early stages of the war.

Certain specific issues that earlier on had been out-of-bounds for historians now became major bones of contention. None was more crucial than the question of the price that had to be paid for victory by the Soviet Union. Stalin had initially tried to play the role of the *"tertius gaudens,"* but as Soviet experts pointed out, their country suffered more than 20 million victims, whereas the United States had 405,000 fatalities, Britain had only 375,000, and even the Germans suffered only a fraction of the Russian losses.[37]

How does one explain this disproportionate loss by the Soviets? As a young historian who became a pioneer in this field noted: "People want to know. It is a question that agitates not only the veterans but also the young generation now that human beings have become the basic value and the main aim of our society."[38]

The basic facts are briefly as follows: During the war some 30 million Soviet soldiers fought an army less than half its size. Much of the time (some authors claimed) the Soviets were also superior in the quantity of their equipment. Soviet historians had not previously conceded this; it was not, for instance, revealed prior to 1988 that the Soviet Union had more tanks than the Germans at the outbreak of the war. If only some were of recent production, the same was also true for the other side.

Could the enormous losses perhaps be explained as the result of the surprise achieved by the Germans during the first months of the war, when the Soviet armed forces were unprepared? Between the date of the invasion and the end of 1941 the Germans and their allies lost some 250,000 soldiers, whereas the number of Soviet losses was 730,000, a ratio of 1 to 2.8. (During the same time, almost 4 million Soviet soldiers became German prisoners of war; by early 1942, only 1.1 million of them were still alive.) However, the ratio between German and Soviet losses between January 1942 and mid-1944 was even more unfavorable from the Soviet point of view; it was closer to 1 to 5.

Even during the last year of the war, when a second front was already in place and the Germans were in constant and often disorderly retreat, the ratio was 1 to 1.7. Thus, surprise alone cannot possibly explain the huge disproportion in losses after the first few months of war. The losses in material were equally striking. At the outbreak of the war 10,000–11,000 Soviet tanks were facing 4,300 German tanks, and 12,000–15,000 aircraft were facing some 5,000 German. Although the German planes were superior in quality, the tanks were not. Yet the Soviet rate of loss was 3.5–4.0 to 1 during the first months of the war. In mid-1942 it was 9 to 1 in tanks, and even in early 1944 it was still 2.7 to 1. There is another possibility mentioned by Sokolov: The Soviet losses in material during the first period of the war were indeed very heavy, including 8,000–10,000 aircraft, many destroyed on the ground. But the disproportion in losses of tanks and aircraft between 1942 and 1944 must have been exaggerated, probably as the result of false production reports by the defense industry about tanks and planes that never reached the front line. In fact, German defense industries produced slightly more tanks during the war than the Soviet; aircraft production was also higher by about 1 to

1.8. Only in the production of guns and minesweepers did the Soviet defense industry have a clear advantage. These figures are greatly at variance with those given by Shlykov (mentioned above). It is amazing that forty years after the end of the war authentic figures still remain absent.

Two figures stand out: Whereas the Soviet Union lost about 11 million people on the battlefield, the Germans and their allies lost 3 million. Second, "virtually the whole prewar Soviet army was destroyed by 1942" (Sokolov). However, the Germans had seriously underrated the ability of the Soviet Union to draw on further human reserves; thus, by the time of Stalingrad, a new army had come into being.

Which raises the crucial question: How does one explain the immensely high losses except with reference to the ineffectual conduct of the war? Blind obedience prevailed over common sense; an order had to be carried out however senseless or even suicidal. "Fear of authority was stronger than fear of death; there was a chance to survive an attack but none to be acquitted by a military tribunal."[39] Frequently, Stalin insisted on offensives on special symbolic occasions, Kiev had to be taken on November 7, Berlin on May 1. Although during the war a new generation of talented leaders and experienced soldiers emerged, the losses were still unacceptably high, which was primarily the fault of the supreme leader, that is to say, Stalin, who was commander in chief, people's commissar of defense, and virtually head of the general staff and the State Committee for Defense.

Some Soviet and Western writers have argued that if Stalin alone was responsible for the heavy losses of 1941 and 1942, he must be allowed the credit for the amazing successes of 1944.[40]

It seems a fair proposition, but it is in part a non sequitur. Whereas during the first eighteen months of the war Stalin conducted the war more or less single-handedly, the situation changed with the preparation of the counteroffensive in the fall of 1942. Stalin became far more attentive to the advice given by the military leaders, and his advisers became bolder and more daring in resisting him—within limits.[41]

The general debate over Stalin's role as a war leader was begun by a civilian, the academician Samsonov. His critique was based, broadly speaking, on the following points: Stalin's unwillingness to accept information about the impending conflict in 1941, his misjudgment concerning the main direction of the German attack in both 1941 and 1942, his decapitation of the Red Army in prewar years, and his desire to conduct the war single-handedly despite having only hazy notions about military affairs:[42] "I am convinced that Stalin was not a leader of genius or a great military leader, if only because he committed mistakes that had tragic consequences."

At the same time, Samsonov agrees that after the autumn of 1942 Stalin learned some lessons. He began to rely on the knowledge of the professionals, he familiarized himself with the experience of contemporary warfare, and he played an important role as commander in chief and head of the State Committee of Defense.

Such criticism of Stalin provoked much protest—from simple citizens to novelists and professional military historians. Ivan Karasev, a truck driver, suggested that Stalin's name should be engraved in gold for his great merits. The writer Ivan Stadnyuk, a former army colonel, argued that Samsonov in his writings in earlier years had taken a much more favorable view of Stalin's leadership. Vasili Morozov, the author of the fifth volume of the official, award-winning history of World War II, claimed that both objective and subjective factors had been involved in the temporary setbacks in 1942.[43] One such objective factor was that the Germans could deploy ninety divisions in the attack aimed at reaching Stalingrad and the Caucasus in 1942 and that the Soviet command had no equal force to oppose them. But this argument is not convincing in the light of the memoirs of Marshal Vasilevsky, published in 1988. According to Vasilevsky's memoirs, 900,000 German soldiers attacking in the south on June 1, 1942, faced 1.7 million Soviet soldiers.[44] In brief, the Germans had no numerical advantage.

Gorbachev paid handsome tribute in 1987 to Stalin's "enormous political will, purpose, and persistence and the knowledge to organize and discipline people that he had shown during the war" as one of the factors that led to final victory. But in actual fact his leadership seems to have been much less impressive. In the final analysis, Stalin's defendants are left with the *tu quoque* argument. If they had praised Stalin even after his death, especially during the Brezhnev era, so had everyone else— historians, playwrights, and novelists, albeit in varying degrees. This was undeniable; the party line of the 1953–88 era had been based on the careful selection of facts and the suppression of others. If a historian like Samsonov had the courage to admit that much, he should have been praised for his honesty rather than blamed for his inconsistency.

Even under glasnost there is considerable resistance to placing the blame for the events of 1941–42 where it belonged.[45] Exceptions were made, however, in the treatment of specific cases. A few examples should suffice. Thus, on July 22, 1941, army general D. G. Pavlov and four other generals serving under him on the Western front were shot, having been found guilty by a military tribunal of cowardice, inactivity, lack of administrative ability, intentional disorganization of troops, and the surrender of arms without fighting. An investigating committee appointed in 1956 found many shortcomings in leadership but reached the conclusion that none of the accusations had been true and that the "trial" had been "instigated by Stalin and the Beria gang with the aim to deflect from themselves the responsibility for insufficiently preparing for and repelling the attack of the enemy."[46]

These are damning accusations, but there existed such controversial issues as Order 270 of August 16, 1941, and Order 227 of July 28, 1942. These orders had been kept secret throughout the postwar period and could not be quoted in the literature on the war, even though they had been read out at the time to every soldier. Order 270 stated that every officer and soldier who was taken prisoner of war was to be considered a traitor and enemy of the people; their families were to be subject to repression and at the very least deprived of food rations. There is no doubt that the order was issued at a critical moment, but it still seems indefensible because of its indiscriminate character. Hundreds of thousands of soldiers became prisoners either because they ran out of ammunition or were cut off or wounded. Why punish them and not those responsible for their plight? Among those responsible were the very people who signed the order, namely, Stalin and Molotov, the apostles of collaboration with Germany, who rejected the information about the impending attack, and the incompetent Voroshilov and Budyonni.[47] (Zhukov also signed it but probably had no alternative.)

Order 227 was issued at an even more desperate juncture in the course of the war. This order ("not one step farther back") pointed out that in the preceding months the Soviet Union had lost 70 million civilians, now in enemy hands, and much of its industrial and agricultural production. The belief had gained ground that further retreats were not possible without causing irreparable damage. On the southern front, in a fit of panic, Rostov and Novocherkask had surrendered without serious resistance. Hence, the call to fight to the last drop of blood; hence, the threat of draconian punishment to be meted out against anyone retreating without permission. Special units were to be established in the rear of "unstable divisions" to shoot to kill in the case of panic and disorderly retreat.

There have been more than a few cases in history in which military leaders have applied extreme measures in desperate situations to save their armies. Seen in this context, Stalin's Order 227 can perhaps be justified. But again, as in the previous year, Stalin bore a great measure of responsibility for the catastrophic state of affairs and the low morale that existed. In November 1941 he had said that the German armies could continue fighting for (at most) six to nine months. On May 1, 1942, his order of the day announced that the Red Army would achieve not only the liberation of all Soviet territories from the Hitlerite scoundrels during the year but also the "final destruction of the German Fascist army." After the experience of 1941, Stalin must have known that this was a wholly unrealistic perspective; yet by misleading his own people about the balance of forces between the two sides, he contributed to the panic that spread over some parts of the front during the summer of 1942. Order 227 certainly helped to impress on the Soviet armed forces the seriousness of the situation, since they had been told only three months earlier that final victory was more or less around the corner.

It was not the first time that withholding the bitter truth had caused panic in the Soviet ranks. Perhaps the best-known example, which could not be mentioned for decades in the Soviet literature, was the Moscow panic of October 16, 1941. On that day, most of the factories and shops, as well as public transport, had suddenly ceased to function. Almost all the ministers and hundreds of thousands of private citizens left the city, although the forward enemy columns were still 100–120 kilometers away.[48] But rumors about a major Soviet defeat near Vyatka, where some 600,000 Soviet soldiers had been encircled by the Germans, had spread in the capital. Zhukov had reported to Stalin that German tanks could suddenly appear in the Moscow region, and this, too, had somehow become known. As the result of withholding information from the population, the view gained ground that the situation was even worse than it actually happened to be.

It was during this critical period that Stalin reportedly put out feelers to induce Hitler to make a separate peace. According to these reports, which have become known under glasnost, he was willing to give Hitler the Baltic republics, Moldavia, and apparently also parts of White Russia and the Ukraine. The sources agree that contact was made by way of the Bulgarian envoy in Moscow, Ivan Stamenov. According to one source, Beria was the go-between; according to another, Molotov saw the Bulgarian diplomat in Stalin's presence. The same source reports that the Bulgarian envoy, who had a higher opinion of the Soviet capacity to resist, refused to act as a go-between, and nothing became of this trial balloon.[49]

To return to the initial question: How does one assess Stalin's role as a warlord and compare him with other civilian war leaders such as Hitler or Churchill? One cannot address the issue as yet with confidence; certain facts have yet to come to light. One knows as yet infinitely less about high-level decision making in the Kremlin during the war than in any other country. To quote a leading Soviet authority, so far there has been no serious research on how the supreme organs of Soviet power functioned during the war: that is, the State Defense Committee, Stalin's headquarters, the general staff, and the party Central Committee. "The style of leadership of the country and the armed forces and the relationship between leaders have not been studied, even though this had far-reaching political and military repercussions. In the circumstances then existing, the incorrect judgments and mistakes committed by Stalin could not be corrected in time or challenged by other members of the supreme leadership, but usually they were not even noticed."[50]

There are many observations and comments in the memoirs of military leaders and people's commissars who worked closely with Stalin during the war. But they were written during a period in which freedom of expression was still quite limited.[51]

These comments are of interest, but they must still be subjected to critical analysis. One example should suffice. When Konstantin Simonov asked Marshal Konev many years after the war how the Red Army would have performed but for the massacres of 1937–38, it emerged that Konev had a low opinion of Blyukher, who (he thought) was very much past his prime and who would have acquitted himself no better than Voroshilov and Budyonni. Nor did he think highly of such leaders as Egorov and Kork, Dybenko and Belov, men with only mediocre ability who were steeped in the civil war tradition and were not prepared for the exigencies of modern warfare. He thought highly only of Uborevich

among the supreme command, and to a somewhat lesser degree of Tukhachevsky and Yakir, gifted war leaders with certain weaknesses.[52]

Such speculations are legitimate, but they do not lead very far. The
relatively junior commanders of 1937–38, such as Konev, Zhukov, and
Rokossovsky, were also unprepared for the kind of warfare they were soon
to face; they grew in experience, competence, and stature as they fought.
The same, for all one knows, might have happened to the commanders
who were murdered. Tukhachevsky and Belov would have been forty-
eight in 1941; Yakir would have been forty-five. Even the oldest in the
group, Egorov, was four years younger than Stalin. If Stalin learned
during the war, they, too, could have. Furthermore, it was, of course,
not only the loss of the marshals and the generals but also of many
thousands below them in rank—the divisional and regimental commanders, the best and the brightest—who were missing in 1941–42.[53] Not all
of them would have emerged as great leaders, but many would have
acquitted themselves well. Those who had the good fortune to survive
and prove themselves in the war, the Zhukovs and Konevs, are probably
not entirely unprejudiced in their judgment.

The generation of 1941 had initially believed in the omniscient role of
Stalin, but with the outbreak of the war and the ensuing disasters, their
belief was undermined. That Stalin tried to assign blame to the military,
refusing to accept any responsibility, claiming that he had been misled,
only strengthened their doubts. Konev witnessed Stalin in a state of near
hysteria during the beginning of the battle for Moscow (October 1941),
when the commander in chief called the Western front and referred to
himself in the third person: "Comrade Stalin is not a traitor, he is an honorable man, his only mistake is that he believed the cavalry generals too
much, he is doing everything to put right the situation that has occurred."
To Konev, Stalin's outburst was a manifestation of utter confusion.[54]

Zhukov commented on Stalin as a war leader during different periods
in accordance with the political situation. He wrote in his memoirs that
at the beginning of the war Stalin had only a hazy notion of military
affairs. Later on, in conversation with Simonov, he said that Stalin's
professional knowledge was inadequate not only in the beginning of the
war, but until its very end. Stalin found himself more comfortable facing
strategic questions because they were closer to his natural habitat—
politics.

What General Halder, German chief of staff during the war, wrote about Hitler applies, to some extent, to Stalin as well: Useful solutions for military questions are not the monopoly of the professional soldier. As Moltke had said long ago, the basic principles of wartime leadership do not go beyond elementary common sense. Hitler did have useful ideas; at times, in fact, he was right when his advisers were wrong. [55]

General Jodl relates that Hitler was the creator of modern weaponry for the army. It was due to him that the 75-millimeter antitank gun replaced those of lesser caliber. The modern German tanks, such as Panther and Tiger, were developed through his initiative. A self-confident civilian could more than hold his own when confronting the generals in military decision making, and what was true with regard to Hitler applied also to Stalin.

But Hitler believed that his gambling would always pay off; he lacked elementary patience and usually belittled the risks and the strength of the enemy. He did not accept what was militarily possible; as a war leader, Hitler subordinated his actions to the fanatical politician: He did not know where to stop. Stalin shared some of these weaknesses but not others. He had patience and did not like to gamble. Nor was he devoid in most cases of intelligence and common sense. Many of his instructions were correct and justified. [56] Elsewhere Zhukov noted that at least up to the Stalingrad battle Stalin would occasionally ask questions following reports given to him that revealed he had not even an elementary grasp of the issues involved. Later, his understanding seems to have improved.

The evidence that has emerged from the memoirs of military commanders working closely with Stalin is contradictory, and a great deal of work remains to be done before making a fair assessment of his role as supreme military commander.

That Stalin was not a fool goes without saying. He immersed himself totally in affairs of war and was a hard worker. That he did not understand military tactics, as Vasilevsky put it, was probably not of great consequence in a commander in chief. After the first eighteen months, his belief in military experts was largely restored; he was far more willing to listen and accept advice. But once he had made up his mind, there was no way to make him change it. He went through the motions of asking his advisers whether they agreed with him; but they would seldom offer a dissenting opinion at this stage, because they knew that it was fruitless and potentially dangerous to disagree with the boss. Despite his many wrong forecasts, his belief in his infallibility was not shaken. Some Soviet commanders report that Stalin admired people who contradicted him and had the courage of their convictions. But there are few, if any, known cases in which the career of a general or marshal was fostered as the result of contradicting Stalin. And there are many cases known to have resulted in tragedy. Generally speaking, Stalin greatly preferred to work with people known to him; he distrusted new faces.

If Hitler lost the war, it was not because of Stalin's superior military leadership but owing to a variety of objective and subjective factors: The Soviet Union was neither Poland nor France. It was a much bigger and more populous country. By mid-summer of 1941, Hitler had overextended himself. His aims were no longer commensurate with Germany's strength. The Soviet Union had a much larger army than the other countries that had been defeated by Hitler, and it also had a military tradition and experience of long standing. The distances, the poor roads, and the climatic conditions also helped defeat the Germans, as did the courage and the steadfastness of the Soviet soldiers, once they had recovered from earlier setbacks. Stalin's leadership and that of his marshals did play a role, but not a decisive one. The odds were so heavily against Hitler that the Soviet army, together with its allies, would have won the war unless they had shown massive incompetence. Stalin did not flinch in adversity; he was not a defeatist, as were some of the French leaders. Like Hitler, he did not give up in the face of major setbacks. And so eventually he led his country to victory, but at a price, for which the Soviet people had to pay for decades, that was, in all probability, unnecessary.

12. Why Stalin?
A National Debate

For a long time Communists were reluctant to use the term "Stalinism," and some shun it even now. "Marxism" and later "Leninism" entered the Russian vocabulary as well as the global political dictionary, and "Trotskyism" became a generally accepted term. But the use of "Stalinism" was forbidden in the Soviet Union (Stalin opposed it) and was frowned upon by most Russian party leaders—even under glasnost. About a year after he had come to power, Gorbachev said in an interview that the term had been "coined by our enemies," which was incorrect.[1] The crucial question, of course, concerned not authorship but essence: Had Stalin not established in many respects a political system *sui generis* and therefore worthy of a name of its own?

The answer to this question seems obvious, but the coyness in the ranks of the Soviet leadership persisted. Undeterred by their continuing silence, a heated debate on the causes, origins, and essence of Stalinism developed during glasnost among Soviet playwrights, philosophers, psychologists, historians, sociologists, and the public at large. Although certain aspects of Stalinism can be understood only with reference to the personality of the leader (which is also true with regard to Hitler and Mussolini), it is even more obvious that the system did not develop in a vacuum. It had historical and ideological roots; conditions existed that made the rise and victory of Stalinism possible in the first place. It is unlikely (to put it cautiously) that an outlandish system, which was alien to Russian mentality and tradition and totally opposed to the Bolshevik doctrine and practice, would have generated so much enthusiasm, lasted for so long, and found supporters even decades after the demise of its founder.

Before turning to the debate that engulfs the Soviet Union under glasnost, we ought to review, even if briefly, the Western discussions of Stalinism that preceded by decades those in the East. Generations of Western students of the Soviet Union had pondered issues such as the relationship between Lenin and Stalin. Had Stalin deviated, or was his system merely the continuation of Lenin's work, "full-blown Bolshevism"? There was no agreement on these issues, but a great deal of spadework had been done studying the historical precedents of Stalinism and considering their implications. Many of the ideas expressed by Soviet authors under glasnost were quite familiar to Western and Soviet émigré students, such as the Mensheviki, who had discussed them from the 1930s onward.

For the left-wing Russian émigrés, the most reprehensible feature of Bolshevism was its antidemocratic character. This belief predated Stalinism; it predated even 1917; Trotsky in 1904 and Rosa Luxemburg in 1918 had expressed fears that Lenin's concept of the vanguard party would lead to a more or less permanent dictatorship, with power passing from the party to the Central Committee and ultimately to one ruler. Russian Social Democrats saw these fears confirmed with a vengeance over the years.

The great majority of nonsocialist émigrés were baffled by Stalin's system. Some still believed that Stalin was only pretending to be Abdul Hamid (the most murderous of Turkey's last sultans) and that, in reality, he was a closet Trotskyite waiting to export his revolution.[2] Others believed that Stalinism was simply a specific Russian form of fascism or, to be precise, a halfway house on the road to fascism.

Nikolai Berdiaev, the philosopher who was exiled from the Soviet Union and has become posthumously popular in Moscow under glasnost, wrote in 1937:

> Stalin is a leader-dictator in the contemporary Fascist sense of the word. . . . Stalinism, that is to say Communism of the construction period, is being imperceptibly transformed into a peculiar sort of Russian fascism. All the characteristics of fascism are inherent in it—a totalitarian state, state capitalism, nationalism, "leaderism," and a militarized youth. . . .[3]

Some regretted and others welcomed it, but the belief that Bolshevism and fascism had a great deal in common gained ground among many observers, unless they happened to be Communists or Fascists, in which case they rejected such analogies out of hand.

Even the earlier shedding of the internationalist features of Bolshevism had caused much interest among the émigrés. Various National Bolshevist and Eurasian circles warmly welcomed these trends, as did the Smena Vekh group, which welcomed post-Leninist Bolshevism because it made Russia a great power again; not a few of them decided to return. But these developments date back to the 1920s rather than the 1930s, well before the full blossoming of Stalinism.

Stalin was widely welcomed in the West in the early days. The older generation of experts, such as Bernard Pares in Britain and Samuel Harper in the United States, who had not sympathized with the revolutionary Left in the first place, found more to admire in Stalin than in Lenin or Trotsky. Lenin (as they saw it) had been a wild revolutionary anarchist and a destroyer, whereas Stalin stood for rebuilding the country, discipline, and order. They found in early Stalinism—and not without reason—traditional Russian elements that were familiar to them. For Western statesmen like Winston Churchill, who had watched the rise of Lenin and Trotsky with apprehension and loathing, it was easier to find a common language with Stalin, who stood for the normalization of conditions and apparently did not believe in the doctrinal nonsense of exporting revolutions. Even to the Nazis, Stalin appealed more than the leaders of the 1917 Revolution, partly because he liquidated the Bolshevik old guard but also because they saw in him the victory of the national idea over the internationalist elements. However, in view of the geopolitical conflicts between Germany and the Soviet Union and the Nazi designs to expand in Eastern Europe, a lasting détente between these regimes seemed impossible.

True, the purges and the terror inside the Soviet Union during the 1930s gave rise to new doubts; perhaps the regime was not as normal and stable as many had assumed. But not a few outside observers preferred to suspend judgment; perhaps there had been conspiracies, after all? The Soviet Union became again an enigma, a conundrum, a mystery, and one of the most frequently quoted phrases in the editorials was that no one could really know what was happening in the Soviet Union; there were only varying degrees of ignorance.

During World War II, the Soviet Union was the ally of the Western powers; the heroic stand of the Soviet army seemed to justify Stalin's policy. E. H. Carr, a lifelong student of Russia, wrote that it was Marshal Stalin who, "consciously or unconsciously usurping Woodrow Wilson's role in the previous war, once more placed democracy in the forefront of Allied war aims" (*The Soviet Impact on the Western World*). Such extravagant misreadings were by no means exceptional at the time. Even experts who knew Russia well, such as the sociologist Nikolai Timasheff, reached the conclusion that the victorious Stalin was in full retreat on the domestic scene toward more normal, traditional patterns of society and policy.

The wartime alliance was followed by the cold war, and if in earlier years there had been a reluctance to look too closely at the Soviet regime and to draw far-reaching conclusions, such inhibitions disappeared in the early 1950s. According to the new consensus, Stalinist Russia was not just a ruthless dictatorship but a totalitarian regime very similar to the Fascist regimes (a one-party system, with a single leader, a binding ideology, a monopoly of terroristic control by the police, and all-pervasive propaganda). Some Western observers, such as Hannah Arendt, at one time went further and virtually equated Nazism, fascism, and Soviet communism; others, pointing to important differences among these regimes, favored a more cautious approach. In later years, the totalitarian concept was severely criticized by the revisionist school (which is discussed in more detail below), which claimed: first, that the concept was a brainchild of the cold war; second, that it was quite misleading with regard to post-Stalinist Russia; and, third, that it had probably never been quite true, even under Stalin. Only the first assertion is of relevance in the present context. Although the totalitarianism concept gained many supporters during the cold war, its origins are in the 1930s among left-wing émigré social scientists from Germany, and it was probably more widely used by the Left among Marxists, such as Trotsky, than by the Right.

Even during the height of the cold war, however, there were wide differences of opinion among students of the Soviet Union. It may be sufficient to point to the work of two of the most influential authors of the period, E. H. Carr and Isaac Deutscher. Although not uncritical of Stalin and his system, on the whole they took a positive line toward him and his system. Although he had caused much suffering, in their eyes the benefits that accrued to his country from his policies far outweighed the damage. Seen from a larger perspective, the suffering would be forgotten, whereas the achievements would remain. Who could say with any assurance that there had been any other approach but Stalin's to modernize a country as backward as the Soviet Union? Among Western students of the Soviet economy, there were not a few who, although admitting that an enormous price had been paid for Stalin's policy, believed that any other approach might not have given such tremendous results within such a short time frame.

Other major issues that preoccupied Soviet experts in the West concerned the origins of Bolshevism. Russia alone among the major European countries had known only short periods of relative freedom in its history. Russian intellectuals from Cha'adaev, Belinsky, and Herzen onward had been among the most merciless critics of the lack of freedom that had prevailed in Russian society throughout the centuries. It was therefore not by accident that historians (such as R. Pipes and T. Szamueli) were looking for the origins of the new serfdom in the old, whereas others (such as Besançon, but also Solzhenitsyn) faulted the Russian revolutionary movement, or at least its more extreme wing, for the wrong turn that Russian history had taken. It was not difficult to find fascinating parallels between Ivan IV (Ivan the Terrible) and Stalin, a subject that, as has been mentioned, was of great interest to Stalin himself. No one but the blindest Russophiles could possibly deny the absence of a democratic tradition in Russian political life.

But this did not, per se, produce a wholly satisfactory explanation for the rise of Stalinism. People and societies change, especially over long periods; although the Swiss and the Swedes had once been among Europe's most martial peoples, this was no longer the case in the nineteenth century or in the twentieth. That most Russians had been either masters or serfs until the 1860s did not necessarily offer a full and satisfying explanation for the state of affairs 100 years after the emancipation of serfs, even though it was certainly one factor to be taken into account.

Another historical debate that preoccupied Western students during the last decade was the question of continuity or discontinuity between Lenin and Stalin, that is, between early Bolshevism and full-blown Stalinism. It was argued that even early in the rule of Lenin, the author of *What Is to Be Done*, the origins of dictatorship could easily be detected. After reading Lenin, Plekhanov, wrote:

> The congress constituted by the creatures of the Central Committee amiably cries "Hurrah!" It approves all its successful and unsuccessful actions, and applauds all its plans and initiative. Then, in reality, there would be in the party neither a majority nor a minority, because we would then have realized the ideal of the Persian shah.[4]

This was a fairly accurate description of party congresses under Stalin: Instead of democratic socialism, Asian despotism had prevailed. According to this line of thought, there was a (more or less) fundamental continuity, a straight line, leading from Lenin to Stalin. All major policies were usurped from Lenin, who had provided the basic assumptions of Stalin's system. Seen in this light, Stalin was, as he always claimed, Lenin's legitimate heir. Indeed, one could go even further back in one's search for roots, for the idea of the "dictatorship of the proletariat" had not been invented by Lenin but first appeared in Marx, albeit in a rather nebulous way. For Marx had never made it clear what "dictatorship of the proletariat" implied, how long it was to last, or who would rule in the name of the proletariat.

Most leading scholars of the 1950s and 1960s believed with Merle Fainsod that out of the (Leninist) totalitarian embryo had come "totalitarianism full blown," and they agreed with Adam Ulam that "after its October victory, the Communist party began to grope its way toward totalitarianism"; the only outstanding problem was what character and philosophy this totalitarianism was to assume.[5] Thus, Stalinism appeared as the logical and inevitable sequel to Leninism.

The opponents of the continuity concept argued that although Bolshevism had contained the seeds of Stalinism and totalitarianism, this did not mean that Stalinism was bound to succeed it. Bolshevism had been strongly authoritarian but not totalitarian; quantitative changes, to use Marxist terminology, had resulted in qualitative change. In the early years, Bolshevism, according to the same sources, had not been monolithic; only Stalin's victory made it so. But for Stalin, the NEP might have continued, another economic development model might have been adopted, and the terror of the 1930s would not have taken place.

This line of thought was of particular interest because it is very close to the Gorbachev approach under glasnost: Leninism had basically been a good idea, only to be perverted by Stalin, who presented himself as its legitimate heir.

Some Western historians explained Stalinism with reference to certain trends that had taken place in the Soviet Union in the 1920s and 1930s, such as the transformation of both the working class and the bureaucracy by the influx into the cities of petty-bourgeois elements from the countryside. Others noted the emergence of a new class, which was antiegalitarian, conservative, and vitally interested in the preservation of the status quo. It was not, however, readily obvious whether these trends indeed had a major effect on the rise of Stalinism, whether they simply happened concurrently, or whether they were in part initiated by Stalin's policy rather than vice versa.

Most of the theories of Stalinism mentioned so far, both those maintaining that Marxism-Leninism was bound to lead to tyranny and those arguing that there was no such inevitability, regarded Stalinism as an aberration, a moral and political disaster despite its great contribution to Russia's development as a global power. Communism, as they saw it, had appeared on the historical scene not with the promise to create the stronger battalions, not even to outproduce capitalism, but, above all, to fulfill a desire to create a society more free and more just than any of those that had ever existed. This endeavor had clearly ended in failure. Some Western observers believed that the system created by Stalin could be reformed; others thought that the deformations were incurable. Both sides agreed that the "Soviet experiment" (as it was called in the 1920s and 1930s) had resulted in a society far removed from that which was originally envisaged.

In the 1970s, a new "revisionist" approach emerged mainly among the younger generation of Western social historians and political scientists that took a more positive line toward the effects of Stalinism. If the older generation had been influenced (as the revisionists argued) by the cold war experience, the revisionist view showed traces of the post-Vietnam mood in the United States, of New Left doctrines, and of similar manifestations of the *Zeitgeist*. To point to these influences does not necessarily detract from their intrinsic value. The decisive criterion is, of course, always whether they present a realistic and helpful approach toward the subject they try to investigate. There was a global revisionist fashion at the time: Revisionism in the Soviet field coincided with similar trends in recent German historiography, in particular, with regard to the Hitler era. There was a fascinating parallelism in their conclusion: Both schools argued that ideology and politics had been given excessive attention. Both argued that the extent and the effect of terror had been exaggerated and that objective social trends (such as mobility, the function of the bureaucracy, etc.) had been underrated. Both argued that Hitler had been, overall, a weak leader and that the importance of an embattled Stalin had also been exaggerated. Much of the time, he had not been in control.

Some revisionist social historians dealt predominantly with the revolutionary period (1917–21); their work is of no relevance here. Others addressed Stalinism by trying to view (and analyze) Soviet society not from above but from below: dealing with problems of social structure, hierarchical stratification, mobility, interaction, or with empirical studies of a certain geographic area. Such studies show that there were striking similarities in, say, the management of a hotel, a tailor shop, a kindergarten, or a veterinarian's practice in a town in the Soviet Union, in Nazi Germany, or in the United States in 1940 (or 1989). That such similarities existed had never been in doubt, but what did they tell us about the specific character of societies, about life in the Soviet Union under Stalin, in Nazi Germany under Hitler, and in the United States under Franklin Roosevelt? Alas, not very much.

One spokesman for the "revisionists" argued that the phenomenon of large-scale upward mobility needs to be incorporated into our interpretation of Stalinism because the Stalinist regime claimed, and almost certainly received credit for, enabling members of the lower classes to improve their social position.[6] This is an observation of some significance in assessing the popularity of Stalinism while it lasted—and even after the death of the leader. But was Stalin really more popular among the higher echelons of the *nomenklatura* than among the backward elements of society? There certainly were more pictures of Stalin found in the 1980s in working-class quarters or in the cabins of taxi and truck drivers than in the dachas of the nomenklatura. In any case, it was not a crucial issue, because upward social mobility (or the rise of a meritocracy) could be found in various countries and societies: socialist, capitalist, and mixed—even Fascist. A critic of the revisionist school stated their weakness harshly but not unfairly:

It reminds me of a historian who chooses to write an account of a shoe factory operating in the death camp of Auschwitz. He uses many documents and does not falsify the material; he decides not to use all available sources and dismisses the testimony of survivors as "biased." Instead, he concentrates on factory records. He discusses matters of production, supply, and marketing. One might even say that he adds something to the wealth of human knowledge, yet he altogether misses the point. He does not notice the gas chambers.[7]

At times, it would appear that the revisionist approach to the Soviet field attempted to write history with the policy aspects carefully kept out—and this on a subject that could not possibly be divorced from politics. At other times, on the contrary, it seemed that one set of political beliefs (unstated but very powerfully present) had simply replaced another.

It was the historical misfortune of revisionism that it appeared on the scene at the least auspicious time; namely, on the very eve of glasnost. The ink had hardly dried on the articles and books that argued one should not exaggerate the importance of the terror, although perhaps some tens of thousands (at most, some hundreds of thousands) had perished, when Soviet sources mentioned millions of victims and some even dozens of millions. Soviet publications from 1986 onward focused on the great fear that had prevailed from top to bottom, on mass starvation, on the moral climate of the Stalin era, the Byzantine "cult," the pervasive denunciations. In short, they did exactly what the revisionists had rebelled against, deriding "moral judgment" and "polemical excesses." The patience of Soviet writers for a minute analysis of bureaucratic tensions, of social mobility, and other such topics was strictly limited. Instead, they wrote about tyranny, even about totalitarianism. If a Western historian had argued as recently as 1983 that judging Stalin was an exercise in "moral imperialism," such views could be heard in the Soviet Union under glasnost only from neo-Stalinists, and even they would usually put their case more cautiously.

The revisionists could argue that Soviet writers were too emotional in their approach, that they lacked the distance and perspective needed by true academic observers, that the historical sources were not complete and entirely trustworthy. Furthermore, revisionists could draw some comfort from the fact that as we shall show, not all Soviet writers joined in the damnation of Stalin and Stalinism: But this was not jocund company to keep. . . .

II

The Soviet debate on the origins of Stalinism preoccupied literary figures and philosophers well before historians and sociologists addressed the subject: A more daring spirit prevailed in the literary magazines than in the "party sciences"; furthermore, many Soviet historians were not qualified by training and experience to deal with topics that had been out of bounds for decades. The Soviet debate took little notice of earlier Western discussions on Stalinism, largely, no doubt, because Soviet intellectuals were not familiar with these exchanges.

Nor was there apparently much interest in Western comments on Stalinism among Soviet conservatives. Thus, Volkogonov, a middle-of-the-roader, observed that in the final analysis only Russians could or should write about the recent history of their country because only they would do it with their lifeblood; Roy Medvedev, for once, seemed to share this view. Many Soviet authors believed that the Stalinist phenomenon had been so distant from the political-social experience of Westerners that they would find it difficult, if not impossible, to understand it. Or, as Alexander Zinoviev put it, "All the concepts of the Western Sovietologists should be thrown into the dustbin if you want to understand something . . ."[8]

Once the debate on Stalinism was under way, all kinds of conflicting interpretations were voiced. One of the most frequent was the attempt to explain Stalinism with reference to the character of the great leader or, alternatively, some basic policy decision that had been taken in the 1920s, such as collectivization of agriculture or the decision in 1923 to suppress inner-party freedom. But with all the attention placed on Stalin's personality, such interpretations were found wanting, if only because they did not explain the positive reception to Stalinism. Nor was it very helpful to stress the debt Stalin owed to Trotsky, from whom he had allegedly borrowed many basic ideas, or to Eugen Dühring (Kapusta), or to point to the integration of individual Mensheviki in the Communist party in the 1920s (Otto Latsis) or to the change in the social composition of the party in the 1920s. Even if true, these explanations were no more helpful than the studies proving that Hitler had derived some of his ideas from obscure pre-1914 thinkers in Vienna and Munich, such as Lanz von Liebenfels.

The crucial issue was, of course, not so much the provenance of these ideas but why they fell on such fertile ground. There were frequent references to the "administrative-command system" in the Soviet Union and the hypertrophy of the bureaucracy. But these were merely extreme manifestations of trends that could also be detected in many other countries. They offered no satisfactory answers as to the specifics of the Stalin phenomenon.

The historical interpretations that sought explanations in the Russian and Soviet past were, in many ways, the most promising. But they also faced great problems: If Stalinism was a perversion of Leninism (according to the party line), then Soviet history had taken a wrong turn after 1923—which effectively closed the door to more searching investigations that might consider the possibility that Stalinist roots might be found, wholly or in part, in Leninism and perhaps even in Marxism.

The Psychology of Stalinism

Among the glasnost writings on Stalinism, those dealing with its psychological profile and its impact on the Soviet people are of special interest. As a noted Soviet philosopher put it: "The love of prohibitions and the belief in their omnipotence is in our bloodstream." It is part of the siege mentality, a concept that has played an important role in the attempts to explain Stalinism. Such an ideology needs, above all, the presence of an enemy against whom one must defend oneself, an enemy either wholly invented or altogether indistinct. This desire for prohibitions can be historically explained: It makes life easier inasmuch as the individual no longer needs to think for himself. But it also means that the person who supports the prohibitions, even if he (or she) lacks power, may feel himself closer to those in power than those against whom the decrees are directed.[9]

Another philosopher noted that the attitude of many adults toward Stalin reminded him of the attitude of children in an orphanage (detdom) toward their parents: Intellectually they may know about the tragic consequences of the cult of the "great father," but their hearts reject the insight. The father may be guilty or not, but he is still the father. Hence, the father syndrome and its corollary, the orphan syndrome. A children's poem of the 1930s was quoted as an illustration describing the plight of a little girl lost in the forest and threatened by the gray wolves. She was so afraid she could not move: "But Mummy, darling Mummy, Stalin knew about my plight. The gates of the Kremlin open, someone carefully lifts me like Father and embraces me like Father, and suddenly I was very happy again. And who was this, do you guess?"[10] The father-orphan syndrome (we are told) has deep roots; the fairy tales of childhood tend to persist into old age. It is an infantilist streak but one against which it is almost impossible to argue on a rational level.[11]

Yet another analyst has provided an ambitious theoretical framework in an attempt to establish whether the Stalin cult was just a case of conformity or of servile worship. The author reaches the conclusion that compulsion alone cannot explain the cult, nor does conformity or demagogy. In the cult, there is a central religious element, the belief in a godlike being equipped with superhuman qualities (omnipotence and omniscience). The Christian God is replaced by a pagan god—the atheist Stalin—which is tantamount to regression from the Christian concept of all-embracing love and general human values, which are too abstract for the pagan mind. Instead, one dominant factor emerges: the "class approach." In this quasi-religion, everything is permitted—murder, denunciation, terror, and repression—as long as it serves the great father. Everything non-Soviet is, a priori, hostile.[12]

The consequences of the cult of the pagan god do not end at this point. The cult removes one of the great achievements of Christian (monotheistic) religion; namely, the concept of the individual's inner moral control. Formerly, the individual had no right to kill even an enemy; now this becomes permissible or even imperative if it is done for Stalin against the class enemy. Furthermore, following the theory of cognitive dissonance, the individual has to justify (rationalize) his behavior to achieve a maximum of harmony: "If Stalin is great, I am small, a mere nothing. If he is the sun, then I am mere dust." The individual loses his identity in the state of servitude; group thinking takes over and provides various psychological comforts. It releases the individual from the responsibility for social and ethical decisions. Even if a person should be confronted with obvious instances of glaring injustice, there are various ways to rationalize them. Perhaps the pagan god is not responsible but his human aides, such as Beria or Vyshinsky, are. Or, alternatively, arguments, such as "I alone can change nothing" or "Perhaps all this is necessary for reasons I don't know and don't understand." Such descriptions of the psychological mechanisms underlying the cult are persuasive. But they do not explain why such regression should have happened in twentieth-century Russia during the attempt to build a socialist society.

These questions can be answered only within the historical context.

Can Stalinism be explained by the specific extremism of the Russian revolutionary movement? Very much so, according to Aleksander Tsipko, a philosopher and author of a long historical-philosophical investigation into the origins of Stalinism.[13] Tsipko's critique concerns not only the left-wing elements inside the Communist party in the 1920s whose ideas Stalin eventually appropriated. The extremism goes back much further into the nineteenth century—to Bakunin, on the one hand, with his belief in the joy of destruction, but also to the father of Russian Marxism, Plekhanov, who preached that the old Latin adage *salus respublicae suprema lex* also applied to the contemporary revolutionary movement. The success of the Revolution was the supreme law, the supreme morality overriding all other considerations.

The danger of the transformation of a democratic-socialist movement into a military and bureaucratically centralized system with unlimited power for the individual at its helm was invoked in the nineteenth century by thinkers like Bakunin and Lavrov. But these warnings were disregarded; instead, contempt for law and legal norms prevailed among the intelligentsia. At the same time, a concept of human nature emerged that was influenced more by Rousseau than by Marx and Engels: hence, the idealization of the working class on the one hand and the emergence of all kinds of fantasies and romantic utopias on the other. Thus, there existed a belief that a classless society could be built without trade and market relations, without peasants and a middle class. According to Tsipko, Stalin was far closer than the skeptical Lenin to the majority of the Communist party, who genuinely believed that fundamental social change was possible and would result in the building of a new, ideal society.

Tsipko sees the origins of Stalinism in the belief of the Bolshevik old guard that the working class and, a fortiori, its vanguard, the party, were always right (Kamenev). Furthermore, the character of the peasantry was considered fundamentally petty bourgeois, and, last, the moral level of the Revolution was measured by the number of victims and the measure of destruction. However, the nonproletarian classes, which were regarded as an impediment on the road to a better future, constituted no less than 80 percent of the population. As Tsipko sees it, there is much in common between the Slavophiles (and their descendants, the Russian right wing of today) and the extreme revolutionaries: their disdain for bourgeois society, positivism, common sense, and patient daily work. Both shared a messianic belief in tomorrow and had only contempt for the present state of affairs. Both lacked a feeling of realism; the dreams and passions of the revolutionary situation became the norm of life. Nothing is more contemptuous than normal life: "the quiet philistine happiness."

Such a mood may have existed elsewhere, too, but it was particularly dangerous in Russia, which lacked a counterweight to left-wing radicalism, where the desire prevailed to live in a world of fantasy in which human thought and will know no limits, in which fairy tales became reality. True, the maximalism and the romanticism of the revolutionary intelligentsia had its uses at turning points of history; without dreamers, there would have been no October 1917.

But the majority of those who brought about the miracle of the Revolution had no sufficient understanding of its creative aims. Thus, an excess of revolutionary enthusiasm became an end in itself and led to an increase in violent suppression and injustice and "ultimately to a policy of national self-extermination."[14] The analysis concludes with a psychological portrait of the revolutionary dogmatist, his cult of impatience, his total unwillingness to consider reality, and the details of daily life.

Many of these observations seem obvious, but it ought to be recalled that analyses of this kind could not have been voiced before glasnost.

This interpretation raised questions such as whether the Russian revolutionary intelligentsia was indeed particularly vulnerable to infantile attitudes; elsewhere, such as in Cambodia, there had been manifestations of the most destructive extremism, although in the context of a very different tradition. Perhaps ultrarevolutionism was growing not on the basis of a specific political culture but, rather, in its absence.[15] If Stalinism had its roots in Marxism, the neo-Marxists claimed that this had happened only in the way that cancerous cells need a living organism to develop—a parasitic growth in a weak organism. Tsipko correctly pointed out that it was wrong to accuse Stalin of being a counterrevolutionary breaking with the traditions of the revolutionary proletariat (Trotsky's "Thermidor"); Stalin had built socialism in accordance with the Marxist doctrine of his time. Many of his ideas about industrialization, for instance, can be found in Preobrazhensky's writings and, before that, in Lenin, Marx, and Engels. Hence, the conclusion that "we shall never expel the slave in ourselves unless we educate ourselves to healthy skepticism even with regard to certain conclusions drawn by Marx and Engels."[16]

If Tsipko made some critical remarks about Marx and Lenin, they did not go very far, nor were they specific, except, by implication, that perhaps Marxism-Leninism had placed too much emphasis on the nature of a class-based society to the detriment of all other factors.

Two other writers went considerably further in their widely discussed essays on Stalinism, for example, Igor Kliamkin, a philosopher by training, and the economist Vasili Selyunin.[17] Kliamkin's thesis is, very briefly, that developments in the Soviet Union since 1917 were more or less inevitable. Once the leadership opted for the noncommodity, nonmarket approach, there were no barriers, no checks and balances, against a progressively stronger despotism. Kliamkin also deals at great length with a topic frequently neglected by students of Stalinism—namely, that it was genuinely popular and, to a certain extent, remained so even after the death of the dictator. There were broad strata in both the village and the city that, because of the patriarchal structure of life (mainly in the village) or because they could not adjust to the NEP (or later on to perestroika), needed a system of social defense and a feeling of security. To a considerable extent, Stalinism provided just this. True, similar trends existed in other countries, but in most places they remained marginal phenomena, whereas in the Soviet Union they became the prevailing system.[18]

Whereas Tsipko stresses Marx's humanist approach (and blames Russian intellectuals for having misinterpreted him), Kliamkin notes that Marx advocated a noncommodity approach and that such a system could be maintained only by coercion. Furthermore, the Russian intelligentsia developed their own models of the future society (populism and industrial feudalism) quite independently of Marx. That critics discovered in Kliamkin certain similarities with Hajek's concept of the "road to serfdom" did not bother him; he had never read Hajek in the first place.[19] He argued, like other writers, that comparisons with fascism might throw some light on the specifics of Stalinism in view of the totalitarian character of both systems.[20] He also stressed certain features in the Russian historical tradition (the "national character") that contributed to the emergence of character; among the examples given is the fanatical tradition manifested by the seventeenth-century "Old Believers": The total rejection of the state as the Antichrist could turn into an equally blind deification of the state.[21]

Kliamkin's articles were considered so unorthodox that there was considerable resistance against their publication, and they appeared only following strong pressure exerted by Sergei Zalygin, editor of *Novyi Mir*. Kliamkin argued that his critics (such as Tsipko) knew perfectly well that Trotsky had opposed forcible collectivization of agriculture, yet tended to put the blame on him and other old Bolsheviks. He strongly urged not to try to overcome Stalinism by using Stalinist methods. He was not pessimistic about the future. Even though there was tremendous resistance against a real confrontation with Stalinism, a return to Stalinism seemed impossible because a dictatorship of this type could not solve a single major issue facing the Soviet Union.

Although Kliamkin's interpretation of Stalin moved further away from traditional Marxist patterns than most, critics noted, with some reason, that his concept left little room for historical accident. But Stalin's personality was, of course, just such an accident, and although Kliamkin's argument about the inevitability of coercion and tyranny might well be accurate, the specific manifestations of Stalinism were not foreordained. Nor is it to belittle Kliamkin's reasoning if one contends that some of it was not new. It had been voiced almost 100 years earlier by Pyotr Struve (then under the influence of Marxism) in debates about an exchange economy, commodity production, and the future of the market in Russia. Struve criticized the populists who thought that Russia could do without them, and he was attacked in turn by the young Lenin, who believed that capitalist development in Russia would somehow be artificial.

Vasili Selyunin is one of the most daring and original thinkers of the glasnost era. His most famous essay, "Istoki" (The Origins), opens on a personal note: a visit to the village in which his mother had been born and lived until shortly before her death. His visit triggers thoughts about the underlying causes of Russia's economic backwardness, including the absence of an essential precondition of industrial progress—namely, the freedom of the worker to choose the work he wanted.[22] Selyunin notes that a few days after the Bolsheviks had come to power, on November 10, 1917, a decree was published in which speculators were declared "enemies of the people"; three months later, another signed by Lenin announced that speculators would be shot at the scene of their crime. Selyunin says that given the conditions of the time, this meant that any sale of any commodity, however small the quantity, was banned. It has been the custom to explain these draconic laws with reference to hunger and general destruction. But, in actual fact, it was a matter of ideological principle: As long as commodity production and the market were not stamped out, the victory of the Revolution could not be assured; therefore, it still remained a mere "bourgeois revolution."

These concepts led by necessity to a war communism and to the perpetuation of dictatorship and servitude. Selyunin mentions that Lenin considered the kulaks the most savage, even bestial exploiters who ought to be liquidated. Thus, the ground was laid for the destruction of the kulaks as a class ten years later.

The roots of the evil, seen in this light, should be traced back well beyond Lenin to the constant state tutelage over the economy, beginning with Peter I, who had nationalized virtually all economic activities. The power of the state bureaucracy with regard to the management of the economy was always much larger in Russia than in the West; hence, it is wrong to consider Peter's reforms as "Western." Private property never had a real chance in Russia; the bureaucracy was always the decisive factor.[23] Hence, Selyunin's pessimistic views regarding the future of perestroika: Unless the bureaucracy was destroyed or its power greatly cut, either by a revolution from above or below, true reform had no future.

Once the taboo concerning Leninist doctrine had been broken by Selyunin, others followed suit.[24] True, the usual circumlocution was still used ("command-administrative" or "bureaucratic system") instead of Stalinism, but it was conceded that Stalin's system had its roots in Lenin's views on the nature of socialism, as a state monopoly over the means of production. Whereas Selyunin had juxtaposed the (relative) freedom of the NEP to the lack of freedom of war communism, the historians from the Marx-Engels Institute drew attention to the narrow limits of NEP democracy.[25] The NEP contained strong elements of authoritarian control, and the democratic elements had little support from below. Thus, the passing of the NEP did not provoke a major outcry; to the "collective leadership" that ruled the country after Lenin's death, the adoption of repressive means came quite naturally; they were unaccustomed to rule by democratic means.

Stalin and the Russian Right

Stalin, needless to say, has his defenders even under glasnost, and some have stated their beliefs quite openly, in particular to Stalin's role as a wartime leader. In not a few novels, movies, and history books during the late 1960s and 1970s, Stalin had appeared as a great leader of the people, and some authors stuck to their guns even after doing so had become less fashionable.[26] The memoirs of the marshals and generals published under Brezhnev had many positive things to say about Stalin's wisdom and resolution. The neo-Stalinists could also point to the fact that some of the writers who have bitterly attacked Stalin's competence under glasnost had been writing in a different vein earlier on. Such tu quoque attacks did not add anything to the historical debate, instead, they tended, at least in the eyes of some, to create doubt about the integrity of anti-Stalinists who had not always been anti-Stalinists.

It was less easy to find mitigating circumstances for Stalin as a political leader in the 1930s, but it was still attempted. Some basic motives recur in all the pro-Stalin writings, above all: "You must not look at 1937 through the eyes of fifty years later." Kaganovich used this argument when he was excluded from the party in 1962.[27] Molotov did, as did just about everyone else. Why should one not examine the horrors of the 1930s with the benefit of hindsight? The reasons: because Hitler had come to power, because war seemed imminent, because it was not a normal situation. This argument does not explain in what way the Nazi danger (which neither Stalin nor Molotov fully appreciated) could be averted or diminished by decapitating the Red Army. It does provide an answer in some other respects, however. Extraordinary measures had to be applied to push forward industrialization so that the Soviet Union would be prepared for the coming trials. To achieve this aim, Stalin's approach was the only possible one.

This argument had been used grosso modo by not a few Western writers, most prominently by Carr and Deutscher, and it persisted in some circles even under glasnost. True, excesses had been committed, and Stalin bore the responsibility for them, but in the overall balance, Stalin's achievements were greater than his failures. Furthermore, there was reason to believe that overeager (or treacherous) assistants should be made responsible for the excesses. A variety of explanations were presented, ranging from "Stalin was the prisoner of the bureaucracy" to "Trotsky provoked Stalin" to the "secret police chiefs misled and duped him," thereby exploiting his innate tendency toward suspicion.

Survivors of the Stalinist period reminded the public that for many people the 1930s had been a period of happiness and enthusiasm, when a feeling prevailed that great things were being achieved. A typical representative of the generation that "made it" under Stalin was Ivan Aleksandrovich Benediktov, who became the people's commissar of agriculture in 1938 at the age of thirty-five, remained in key government positions for many years, and eventually served as ambassador to India and Yugoslavia (1959–70).[28] Among the main points made in Stalin's defense are the following: Promotion under Stalin was by merit only. Many very young people (such as Voznesensky, Ustinov, Kosygin, Tevosian, and Vannikov) were appointed to key positions in their early thirties—and proved themselves. Thousands of innocents suffered, but the overall number has been grossly exaggerated; the general atmosphere was not one of fear, repression, and terror but of a mighty wave of revolutionary enthusiasm, of pride in country and party, and of belief in the leadership. Decisions taken at the top were far more democratic than generally believed; Stalin was not an extremist, but on the whole a fair and reasonable man. In fact, Khrushchev's style was more autocratic than Stalin's. As for the murder of the Red Army leadership, there is reason to believe that they plotted not against Stalin but against Voroshilov, who they thought was not equal to his task. Such behavior would not have been tolerated in any country. As for Lysenko, again, his merits were greater than his shortcomings, and he had nothing to do with the arrest or the execution of his opponents.

If Stalin was such a good judge of men and promoted only the most capable, Benediktov was asked, irrespective of his own predilections, how does one explain the appointment of such individuals as Vyshinsky or Beria? Well, some of these men had a Menshevik past (a fact that cannot have been unknown to Stalin), and, in any case, no one is infallible; after all, Lenin also appointed Trotsky, Kamenev, and others to responsible positions.

Benediktov and other men of his generation had an answer to all, or almost all, painful questions concerning the Stalinist era. Theirs is the version of the victors and the survivors. Psychologically, such a justification of their life's work is by no means surprising; from postwar memoirs of the surviving Gauleiters and other high dignitaries of the Third Reich, there emerges a very similar picture: The 1930s had been a time of great enthusiasm, of national unity and pride, of belief in the leadership, and of a historical mission; young people had been given chances like never before, and so on.[29]

An account provided by M. I. Malakhov about the fate of his generation conveys a general picture very similar to that given by Benediktov:

I am amazed how we had the strength for all that. When did we sleep and eat? And when did we find time to love, to rejoice, and to raise our cultural level? Our Komsomol girlfriends also combined work, studies, and social affairs and still managed to very pretty, sweet, modest, kind, and loving. And they were able to manage at home, too, without shirking any kind of work. And how chaste the relationships were among the young women and men! We were afraid to offend our young girlfriends with awkward advances, immodest words, or crude behavior. . . . At night we slept soundly, for we were tired from our hard and intensive labor, and we did not lie awake listening for the knock on the door. What's more, the door to the house was seldom locked, for it was always open to our friends and neighbors, and thieves had no use for our poor possessions. These days it is acceptable among young people if everything is not just so at home or at work to write, to demand, to complain to all levels of authority. In my time such things simply could not be; there was no one and nowhere to complain to. . . . There were perhaps some people "overzealous" in their demands on themselves and their comrades. It was considered shameful to visit restaurants; divorce was condemned, as were unofficial marriages and modish or ostentatious clothing. On the other hand, high value was put on labor, knowledge, friendship, patriotism, social activities, discipline, and proletarian internationalism. Narcotic addicts and prostitutes were simply unheard of in our working milieu, and drunkenness and absenteeism were punished severely. . . . Our life was not idyllic. There were many hardships; there was hunger and cold, the destruction of basic tools and equipment as the result of the civil war. There was an acute ideological war and sabotage and wreckers (yes, wreckers: these were not figments of the imagination of state authorities suffering from acute paranoia). . . . We wanted universal knowledge. We studied philosophy and literature. We were interested in scientific innovations. We delved into politics; we learned to know music and the fine arts, everything that our family and school could not give us.[30]

The writers of the memoirs had been enthusiasts; their beliefs were genuine; they were idealists—like many young SS men and Blackshirts. But they still served a bad cause. Their explanations help little to understand why they believed in policies that were often inhuman and absurd.

Why the abdication of independent, critical thinking? The reminiscences of the old Stalinists try to show that life under the leader was much more satisfactory than frequently believed and that, in any case, there was no alternative then and probably is none now.

The nationalist interpretation of Stalinism differs from that of the orthodox Communist on one essential point: It does not look back with nostalgia to the 1930s. It regards Stalin as a monster and Stalinism as a national disaster.[31] However, it does not see any basic difference between Stalin and other members of the Bolshevik old guard; in fact, Stalin appears in a better light because he put an end to the cosmopolitan, internationalist, "Russophobic" political and cultural orientation of old-guard Bolsheviks like Bukharin and Lunacharsky and, a fortiori, Trotsky, Kamenev, and other rootless cosmopolitans who dominated the extreme Left from the beginning. Their attitude toward Lenin is, of course, basically hostile, but this hostility could not be openly expressed, even under glasnost. Nor do they have any sympathy for Marx, except perhaps on the occasions when Marx attacked the Jews. Naturally, the references to Dostoevsky, Tyutchev, and the Slavophiles are far more frequent in the writings of the Russian nationalists than are references to Marx or Lenin.

The attitude of the Russian party toward Stalin could perhaps most accurately be characterized as anti-anti-Stalinist; it found its first, comprehensive definition in a long, hostile review of the most widely read anti-Stalinist novel of the glasnost era; namely, Rybakov's *Children of the Arbat.*[32] Kozhinov was known during the 1970s as one of the most eloquent and erudite spokesmen of the Russian party. In his wide-ranging essay published in 1988, he was far more outspoken than on previous occasions. Among the basic points he made are the following: The Stalinist cult was by no means the result of his own intrigues or those by some dubious sidekicks; it was a global phenomenon, *tout court*, that prevailed from Madrid to Shanghai. This cult seized the masses and became a powerful material force. As evidence for his thesis, Kozhinov cites a speech by Dolores Ibarruri (La Pasionaria of Spanish civil war fame), Feuchtwanger's book about Moscow in 1937, and a few other leading Western fellow travelers.

Kozhinov strongly dislikes the exclusive emphasis accorded the victims of the purges of 1936–39. After all, more people perished during the civil war and, in particular, as the result of the collectivization of agriculture.

The purges mainly affected party militants who had helped promote Stalin and his cult. As a poet belonging to Kozhinov's cohort expressed it: "The Arbat souls do not want to know how a Russian priest and a lowly Kulak were freezing to death in Narym [one of the main gulags]. They had a happy childhood, while somewhere in the Volga region cannibalism occurred. . . ."

Time and again Kozhinov and other nationalist spokesmen stress the non-Russian character of Bolshevism—the prominent part played by Jews, Latvians, Armenians, Georgians, and other foreigners in the revolutionary movement and in the party and state for many years after the Revolution. These foreigners had no feeling for Russia. They did not understand it and frequently hated it; their only interest was to use the Soviet people as cannon fodder for the world revolution. For Russian patriots, there is no reason to mourn the fact that so many of them died as the result of the terror.

According to Kozhinov, it is historically quite wrong to see in Stalinism a specific Russian (or "Asian") phenomenon. Fascism, after all, prevailed in Europe rather than in Asia. Peter the Great, often regarded as Stalin's most prominent precursor, took his inspiration (and his assistants) from Europe, whereas his victims were all Russian. As for Ivan the Terrible, he was no more cruel, having killed fewer of his subjects than Erik XIV of Sweden, Charles IX of France, or Philip II of France. In any case, there never was an Ivan IV cult in Russia. Generally speaking, the Russian political tradition was much more humane and less violent than the European; even during the most severe repression (1908–10), a mere 3,000 people were executed—much less than in Paris in either June 1848 or during the Paris Commune.

Kozhinov concludes that proving Stalin an evil man does not explain anything. The essence of the matter lies in the "powerful global force" that transformed Stalin into a human god who could destroy or send to a camp whomever he wanted. Stalin (on the authority of Ilya Erenburg) considered himself a faithful Communist, the pupil who continued Lenin's work. The real tragedy is that the greatest periods of human history (such as the Renaissance) are also the ones in which the most people are killed.[33]

It is an eloquent and, in parts, original interpretation, but it does not survive critical examination. There is no historical law that demonstrates that the greatest periods of history are also the bloodiest. In any case,

Russia in the 1930s cannot by any stretch of the imagination be compared with the Renaissance.

Nor is the thesis concerning Stalinism as a global force persuasive. The 1930s were a period of major setbacks for communism outside Russia; that the French Communists attracted some voters, that the Spanish Republicans fought Franco, and that the Chinese Communists launched their long march to Yenan had nothing to do with Stalin. True, leaders of Communist parties would pay respect to Stalin in extravagant terms; they had to do so because they needed Soviet political and financial help. They conformed with Soviet practices, but they had not invented them. Some Western fellow travelers paid tribute to Stalin for a variety of reasons—because the alternative, as they saw it, was Hitler; because they thought that it was not the right time to criticize the Byzantine-Asiatic political practices of a backward country, and so on. Western fellow travelers, to their lasting discredit, swallowed many of the lies of Stalinism. But most of them had to swallow hard, and their compliance came not as the result but in spite of the "cult."

Kozhinov is on safer ground when pointing to the emergence of Fascist dictatorships in Italy and Germany in the interwar period; the relapse to barbarism was not confined to Eastern Europe. But the spokesmen of the Russian party mention fascism only in passing, and rightly so from their point of view. Any deeper investigation would show that with all their differences the dictatorships were in some ways "birds of a feather." To argue that Stalinism was the specific Russian form of international fascism (as Berdiaev and others had done) would not be acceptable to Russian patriots.

Kozhinov's defense of Stalin is that of a (great) Russian nationalist, but the same arguments have been used in other quarters. The Georgian writer Levan Khaindrava was a victim of the terror, and he does not deny that Stalin was the "curse of the Georgians," that he engaged in the genocide of his own people.[34] About 10 percent of the population was "repressed" between 1921 and 1951. However, the author still dislikes the "anti-Stalin bacchanalia," and he uses many of the arguments of the Russian Right and the neo-Stalinists. The crimes attributed to Stalin were mostly committed either by his predecessors or his contemporaries. Kirov, Ordzhonikidze, Bukharin, and others were not mild, inoffensive figures; many foreigners thought highly of Stalin; the military historians who attacked him in the 1980s had praised him in the 1950s. Stalin, in brief, was a giant, and those who deride him do so either because they or their families suffered under Stalin. Such an emotional approach, however subjectively intelligible, is a poor guide in the search for an understanding of a global historical phenomenon. The Georgian writer does not join Kozhinov in his search for the "real culprits" (i.e., Trotsky and other Jews) but, on the contrary, is deeply convinced that much of the enmity toward Stalin stems from the inability of Russians to forgive Stalin, that he, the son of a small people, headed an enormous country and led it to victory.[35]

The right-wing Russian interpretation of Stalinism is chiefly preoccupied with refutations: Stalinism was not a Russian phenomenon in view of the presence of so many aliens in leadership positions. How true is this allegation? There were many non-Russians in the Bolshevik leadership in the early days. But then Russia was a multinational empire, and the minorities were even more oppressed than the rest of the nation. The idea that some foreign conspirators could have ruled the country for any length of time against the wishes of the overwhelming majority of its inhabitants is far-fetched. It is based on a conspiracy-theory-of-history approach, which engages in the search for unlikely culprits instead of the obvious ones. Thus, the roles of Lenin and Stalin, Molotov and Voroshilov, Zhdanov and Ezhov, Bukharin and Rykov, Malenkov and Brezhnev, the descendants of Russian nobility, Russian workers and peasants, and Orthodox priests and Kuban Cossacks are ignored; instead, Trotsky and Kaganovich are elevated to positions of superhuman, demonic power.

The anti-Semitic interpretation of recent Russian history goes back to the Black Hundred, the extreme right-wing political movement that came into being in the early years of the century. The idea that the Russian revolutionary movement was masterminded by Jews and, to a lesser extent, by other foreigners and masons was widely propagated among the extreme Right in the Russian emigration. Through these circles, it became part and parcel of official Nazi doctrine: "Soviet Judaea" was the bulwark of the Elders of Zion. A whole literature came into being: Books were created that consisted mainly of long lists of names and photographs purporting to show that all Jews were Communists and all Communists were Jews, that Bolshevism was not a political movement at all but the attempt of world Jewry to dominate mankind.[36] Many of the "facts" were false: Lenin was not of Jewish origin, as alleged, nor was Kerensky, and

Stalin had no Jewish wife. Krassin and Kollontai came from old Russian aristocratic families; neither Safarov (an Armenian) nor Tomsky, neither Manuilsky nor Unschlikht nor Beria, neither Shvernik nor Marshal Blyukher, neither Lashevich nor the composer Shostakovich, were of Jewish origin, as maintained in the Nazi literature. The technique of these race researchers was simple: Everyone with a name that sounded a little unfamiliar to them was made Jewish. And because they did not know much about names, a Latvian (Ratchaitak) or a Tartar (Mustafin) could easily be suspected as a Jew. In some cases, photographs served as evidence. Thus, Tomsky, the trade-union leader, looked suspicious to them; in Professor Hans Guenther's standard textbook on race, Tomsky's picture appeared with the caption "Near Eastern race." In light of the execution of so many Jewish Communists in the purges, it became difficult to maintain that Jews were actually ruling Russia through their chosen instrument (Stalin). But it could still be argued that Kaganovich was the real master and Stalin a mere puppet, a theme that first appeared in the Nazi literature fifty years before Kozhinov and his friends.[37]

Nazi authors proclaimed that the day would come when the people of Russia would overthrow Jewish rule, that the racialist idea would eventually prevail in Russia, as in all other countries. Russia had been ruled for much of its history by foreigners. But at present a mighty upsurge of the Russian national ideal was taking place, and the dictatorship of Judeo-Marxism over the Russian people was about to end.[38]

Thus, Nazi doctrine paved the way for the articles that would appear in the late 1980s in journals such as *Nash Sovremennik* and *Molodaia Gvardia*.[39] But only up to a point: Those Nazi writers who had announced the impending victory of the national ideal in the Soviet Union and the end of Soviet Judaea were bitterly attacked for ideological backsliding by their more radical colleagues, who claimed that because the Slavs were racially inferior, there could be no real national renascence in the Soviet Union. They would not be able to transform their system into a true national state.[40]

At this point, the Russian far Right had to part company with Nazi doctrine. They could accept whatever the Nazis had to say about the ruling Kaganovich clique, about the hangman Matvei Berman (but not his bosses Dzerzhinsky and Menzhinsky), and about Jewish Communists in general. But they could not possibly agree that the great Russian people belonged to an inferior race.

That Jews constituted a high percentage of the Bolshevik leadership during the first decade after the Revolution is a well-known fact. (However, of the fifteen members of the first Soviet government, thirteen were Russians, one was Georgian, and one was a Jew.) In Moscow, Jews constituted 11 percent of the state bureaucracy in the 1920s; in Leningrad, 9 percent ; the percentage was higher in the Ukraine and lower in other parts of the union.[41] They had been persecuted in tsarist Russia; therefore, they tended to join the radical antiestablishment parties—the Mensheviks to an even greater degree than the Bolsheviks. However, most leading Jewish Bolsheviks belonged to the opposition to Stalin and were eliminated during the 1920s. More perished during the terror of the 1930s; by 1940, Kaganovich was the only (and last) member of the Politburo of Jewish origin. And he, too, was no longer a central figure after 1938. Whether Stalin was an anti-Semite or not is a question that can be endlessly debated; Stalin disliked and distrusted Jews; most of them were removed from the upper echelons of the party leadership, the army, the foreign ministry, and the police during his rule. Toward the end of his life, Stalin prepared a comprehensive pogrom that might have resulted in the deportation of many, perhaps most, of the Jews from European Russia.

However, it is also true that Stalin hated and despised people in general, that almost every nationality in the Soviet Union suffered to some degree, that a handful of Jews remained in his entourage all along, that a few received Stalin Prizes and similar distinctions even at the time of the worst anti-Semitic outrages. If he was an anti-Semite, his anti-Semitism was not so much "biological-scientific" as Hitler's but, rather, political-psychological and instinctive. However, the whole issue is not of central importance with regard to an understanding of the Stalin phenomenon. Jews neither "made" Stalin, nor were they his main target.

Foreigners have played a considerable role in Russian history. Even more often, they were blamed for all that had gone wrong. They frequently had to serve as a lightning conductor. If there is a global phenomenon, it is this search for the "hidden hand," the "dark powers," rather than the international character of the Stalinist cult. A case can still be made (and is made by some) that all the trouble in Russia began with the defiance of authority (the church, the monarchy, and, generally speaking, the existing order of things) that had developed over the centuries on the part of the intelligentsia. Such an approach must logically lead to the denunciation of revolutionaries and even reformists in Russian history—from Radishchev and the Decabrists to Belinsky, Herzen, and the radical intelligentsia of the late nineteenth century. As a rule, such charges cannot be made openly even under glasnost, but they are quite frequently made by implication.[42] They amount to the propagation of an ideology diametrically opposed not just to Leninism but to the Enlightenment and all the values of the nineteenth-century Russian intelligentsia. Such views may still have considerable attraction for sections of the ruling class, and it is not at all surprising that attempts are made to bring about an amalgam of certain Bolshevik (Stalinist) tenets with beliefs directly opposed to them.

Racialist doctrine cannot explain Stalinism, nor does the "class approach," that is to say, unadulterated Marxism. Otto Latsis, Roy Medvedev, and others have argued that Stalin was not a Marxist; he merely pretended to be Lenin's faithful pupil. The results of Stalin's activities were horrible not because of Lenin's principles but because he betrayed them.[43] Nor do these Marxists accept that the Revolution was premature inasmuch as it was bound to lead to massive violence.

Latsis argues that Russia was not Gandhian India, that nonviolence was not a viable political approach, and that the revolutionaries had suffered the repressive violence of the tsarist authorities for many years. According to the same logic, a wrong turn was made only when Stalin introduced a regime of terror at a time when he could have managed without it, when the formation of a new socialist culture and consciousness had appeared on the agenda.

Stalin's main crime, according to this interpretation, was that he wanted too much economic progress too quickly. The lower the level of development of a country in which a revolution occurs, the greater the receptiveness of adventurous promises and the greater the number of people willing to believe that major changes that require persistent work over many years can be achieved overnight. In these circumstances, the leaders carry an enormous responsibility to keep the party on a realistic course. Lenin lived up to this task; Stalin did not.

Otto Latsis, the author of this interpretation, was among the leading liberals under Brezhnev and became a deputy editor of *Kommunist* under Gorbachev. But it is by no means certain that in a relatively undeveloped country the working class is more adventurously inclined than in the highly industrialized countries in which revolutions have not taken place.

Even if such adventurism existed, would it be the decisive political factor? Finally, many of Stalin's policies had nothing to do with the rate of economic development; if many leading factory managers were shot, it was unlikely to increase production, nor was it intended to do so.

Latsis's interpretation is shared by Gavriil Popov, the editor of Voprosy Ekonomiki, but with one important reservation. The antipragmatic idea of "administrative socialism," with its emphasis on total centralization, goes back not to 1929, the year of the great turning point, but to the second program of the Communist party of the Soviet Union, which was adopted in 1919, less than two years after the Revolution. This program led by necessity to the emergence of a state based on physical power, the army, and the political police, a state no longer in need of mass support. This orientation prevailed while Lenin was the undisputed leader of the party, well before Stalin had taken over.[44]

It has been argued by some that Stalin was the "ideal leader expressing the interests of Soviet bureaucracy," pushing aside and subjugating the working class.[45] Some have even gone further and argued that under Stalin the bureaucracy became a real class in the Marxist sense, the true owner of the means of production.[46] Subsequently, the "socialist bureaucracy" created the state and the society in its own image, and its ideal was socialism run like a military barracks and by the command-administration system. For good measure, in view of its Bonapartist character, Stalinism could also attract other sections of the population, such as the Lumpenproletariat.

These attempts of "class analysis" have been rejected by other authors as of little help.[47] True, Stalin imposed his will on the party and effectively broke its power by using the bureaucracy to this end. But the bureaucracy was no more immune to purges and liquidation than others. The majority of the middle and higher echelons of many ministries were decimated. Nor was the average bureaucrat, or the bureaucracy as a whole, the owner of the means of production in any meaningful sense. They "owned" the economy no more than sailors owned the ships. They were permitted to sail on them as long as they faithfully executed the commands they were given from above. S. Andreev fully recognizes the emergence of the bureaucracy as an exploiting class in socialist society, but he rightly concludes that Stalin and his apparatus were not part of this class. The attempt to explain the mainsprings of political power in the Soviet Union under Stalin mainly (or solely) with reference to class interest and the ownership of the means of production is as unconvincing as similar attempts concerning power under Nazism. Neither Beria nor Himmler fit into these schemes.

The Marxist approach is perhaps of some help in identifying the social strata that had a specific interest in supporting the Stalinist system, but even this is only helpful within narrow limits. For, like fascism, Stalinism derived its support from many strata of society, high and low. Like fascism, it was as much a political-psychological-cultural phenomenon as a socioeconomic one.

That Stalin was not Marx and Lenin's legitimate heir has been argued by Trotsky and many other Marxists in the West and East for many decades; but is this a question of crucial importance? In the party, as constituted at the time of Lenin's death, Stalin had overwhelming political support for his style and his aims. There is no reason to dispute his subjective honesty when he proclaimed his undying loyalty to Lenin.

It is, of course, perfectly true that the Russian revolutionaries suffered under tsarism, that violence begets counterviolence, and that a nonviolent political party stood not the slightest chance of seizing power in 1917. But it was equally unrealistic to assume that a party that had established its dictatorship by violent means, systematically destroying all other political forces from the very beginning, could suddenly (or even gradually) transform itself into a democratic force, establishing a new, more progressive democracy. The specific paranoid character of Soviet rule between the late 1920s and 1953—that is, Stalinism—may have been a historical accident. But the general trend of development was in accordance with how communism in Russia seized power. To assume that it could have developed in a different way, that it could have moved away from repression toward political freedom and democracy within a few years or a few decades, is to disregard historical experience. There is nothing specifically Marxist in a "voluntarist" and "idealist" point of view that in the final analysis puts most of the blame on the "betrayal" and the crimes of a single individual.

The reluctance among many Russians, especially of the older generation, to come to terms with the Stalinist phenomenon is psychologically not surprising.[48] As in postwar Germany, there is a tendency to argue that the old days were not remotely as bad as believed by later generations, that the regime was universally supported, and that, in any case, the worst excesses were planned and carried out by foreigners. In a similar way, the neo-Marxists will continue to believe that Stalin crossed his Rubicon not with the murder of the tsar's family or even the deportation of the kulaks, but only when he began to exterminate the old Bolsheviks.

All these arguments contain some grains of truth, but they fail to go to the roots of the Stalinist phenomenon. The essence of Stalinism will be debated for a long time to come, and even among those willing to accept uncomfortable truths there will not be unanimity on its interpretation in the foreseeable future. Some will see the root of the evil in Lenin's disdain for political freedom; others will find the origins further back in the Russian political tradition of autocracy and in Russia's political backwardness at the time of the Revolution.[49]

Sixty years after the rise of fascism, forty years after its demise, there is no unanimity about its origins, why it prevailed for a time, and how power was exercised in this regime. Even though fascism seems in some ways easier to interpret, its ideology was certainly less complicated. It is not a matter of unearthing new sources on Stalinism and studying them. Some interesting material will probably still be discovered. Whether it will shed much new light on Stalinism is doubtful. Even about Stalin's state of mind we shall probably not know much more twenty or thirty years from now. It is more a matter of pondering the existing evidence than searching for new sources. That there will be no unanimity about Stalinism in the near future should not unduly discourage us; there is no unanimity about the French Revolution even now, 200 years after the event. Having eliminated the false facts and assertions, we know, broadly speaking, what Stalinism was not.

Stalinism certainly had this in common with other totalitarian movements of the age: It generated enthusiasm among sections of the population, it acted as a spur to the careers of a generation, and it maintains its advocates long after the great leaders have passed away. But for the country at large, it was a disaster despite industrialization and military victories. The full extent of the disaster came to light only after Stalin's death. One historian had expressed the hope that, properly cleansed by history, the good side of Stalinism would survive, much as the achievements of Napoleon and Cromwell had survived at the time. But this detergent theory of history seems out of place in regard to Stalinism. The developments that took place under Stalin's rule concerned not the surface of Soviet society but its essence. Stalinism, in all likelihood, will retain its believers and advocates in the years to come; to study their motives and the strength of their political support is a legitimate endeavor.[50] But historical interpretation will mainly be preoccupied with other questions: How much of a disaster was it? Where are its roots? Did alternative policies exist? Finally, on a more speculative level, how can Stalinism be eradicated?

13. Memorial and Its Opponents

The process of de-Stalinization in the Soviet Union has been long and complicated because there was no radical break with the past. Although most of Stalin's victims have been rehabilitated, this has often been done grudgingly. The process of de-Stalinization reversed itself for long periods, frequently lapsing into an emphasis on the merits and achievements of the late "leader of the peoples" rather than focusing on his crimes. Only since the advent of glasnost has there been a systematic, if slow, attempt to do historical justice to Stalin's victims

De-Stalinization refers to a variety of things: It concerns free and unfettered research into the Stalinist period of Soviet history, the publication of documents and books hitherto banned, the cleansing of the Augean stables of Soviet historiography, the screening of uncensored movies, and the staging of plays on life under Stalin. Before glasnost the furthest limits of de-Stalinization were reached with the publication of Solzhenitsyn's *One Day in the Life of Ivan Denisovitch*, in *Novyi Mir*—a great sensation in its day but no more than a fleeting glance into a *universum*, the very existence of which had been denied earlier on.

Compared with the first thaw, the revelations of 1987–90 are truly astonishing, and it is difficult for outsiders even to begin to understand the shattering effect they have had and the passions they have provoked. But de-Stalinization implied, of course, much more than the destruction of old myths and the rewriting of history books. It meant eradicating the spirit and habits of a whole epoch that were deeply ingrained in the political and social life of the country, a gigantic task likely to take not months and years but decades and generations, an endeavor bound to face great resistance.

It meant not just expressing pity and regret for Stalin's victims but com-

259

memorating them in a fitting way, comparable to the victims of the Nazi terror in Germany and other countries. It meant naming not just the victims but also the informers, the hangmen and all those involved in working the repressive machinery, including those who had given enthusiastic support to shooting the "mad dogs." It referred not just to a few long-dead secret police officials but repentance and mourning on a national scale. Some public figures insisted that such moral cleansing was imperative, but the general public response was not overwhelming at first.

Establishing the historical truth and commemorating the victims even in a modest way was a prerequisite for more far-reaching changes, and it is to this that we shall turn next. The first initiative to establish a monument in honor of the victims of Stalinism came in 1986 from a small group of young people, mainly located in Moscow. The members of this group collected signatures, and by spring of 1988, they had collected some 30,000–50,000. Yuri Afanasiev remembers:

> By June 1988 when the Nineteenth Party Conference met, they had collected 54,000 signed petitions. They gave them to me and Elem Klimov [head of the moviemakers' union], as conference delegates, to deliver to the Presidium. I personally carried the huge bags to the conference hall. They were very heavy, and it was very hot. There was a break in the proceedings, and all the delegates were milling around in the halls. I shouted, "Make way, make way! These are petitions to the Presidium— petitions for a monument to Stalin's victims." You can imagine the reaction. I took the bags right to the conference tribune. And as you know, Gorbachev endorsed the idea on the last day of the conference.[1]

The idea was neither radical nor novel; Khrushchev had made a similar proposal at the Twenty-second Party Congress but had encountered stiff opposition. The de-Stalinization of 1986 encountered similar resistance on the part of the authorities. The collectors of the signatures were harassed by the police and, from time to time, taken to local militia headquarters. True, the 1988 plenum of the Central Committee endorsed the proposal to establish a monument, but harassment of the activists continued,[2] even though Memorial (as the group came to be called) had, in the meantime, received the support of leading members of the Soviet intelligentsia, including Andrei Sakharov, who became its president, as well as Evtushenko, Rybakov, Yuri Afanasiev, Vasili Korotich, Roy Medvedev, Ales Adamovich, Grigori Baklanov, Dmitri Likhachev, and others. The unions of architects and filmmakers were the first public organizations to join; the writers' union followed with considerable delay. The organization established a small office in Moscow.[3] In November 1988, in the framework of a "week of conscience," an exhibition took place showing designs for a memorial complex. A similar exhibition took place in Leningrad in April 1989. *Ogonyok, Moscow News,* and also, to a certain extent, *Literaturnaia Gazeta* and *Sovetskaia Kultura* bolstered the initiative by providing publicity and asking for donations to finance the activities. Eventually, following some preparatory meetings, a foundation conference took place in Moscow in January 1989 with 500 delegates representing small and large groups from more than 100 cities throughout the Soviet Union. On January 28, 1989, Memorial published its statutes and applied for legal status, according to Soviet laws. But the authorities were in no hurry to comply. At the same time, the first issue of a Memorial publication, the *Vedomosti Memoriala,* appeared in a minuscule edition (5,000 copies), opening with Anna Akhmatova's poem "Requiem."

In letters to the Central Committee and to Gorbachev in person, Memorial asked for support for its activities. The proposed activities included not only the building of monuments in Moscow and other parts of the country but also the establishment of a museum, a research center, and a library. The writers noted that such initiatives would make an important contribution to the democratization of society, quite apart from giving expression to the mourning of the whole country.[4]

Support for Memorial came from individuals, some of the descendants of victims, and from others who had not personally suffered but were shocked by the revelations. Some cultural clubs, connected with leading Moscow institutions, provided a venue for Memorial meetings; the Komsomol organization at Khimki, a Moscow suburb, donated much of the money needed for the "week of conscience."[5]

Some suggested monuments in various parts of the Soviet Union, especially on the main campsites in northern Russia and Siberia.[6] Others put the emphasis on the collection of documentary evidence, but local museums reported that they received little help from the authorities.[7] A sociologist proposed that Lefortovo, one of the main Moscow prisons, be turned into a museum, another suggested Butyrka.

Everything there should be reconstructed exactly as it was: The conference room of the Military Collegium, the execution cells, the offices of Beria and Avakumov, and a multitude of other technical "premises," the outfitting and interiors of which are familiar only to forensic experts. The evildoers' waxworks should be arranged in such a way as to reconstruct the sinister ritual.[8]

The writer argued that such "naturalism" was necessary because the memory of the crimes should live on, for if evil deeds are forgotten, so are the victims: "A strong emotional shock is needed to knock us out of our smug complacency and to make us aware of our responsibility for the future." Many other suggestions were made concerning the site and the character of buildings and other commemorative sites.

From the very beginning differences of opinion came to light regarding the character, organization, and activities of Memorial—differences between radicals and moderates, between Moscovites and militants from other parts of the Soviet Union. The radicals, among them the early militants, many of whom were concentrated in Moscow, suggested that the society should not limit its activities to the Stalinist period. Concentration camps had existed in the 1920s as well, and there had been show trials well before 1936. The establishment liberals, on the other hand, as well as representatives from outside Moscow (Leningrad and Sverdlovsk, for instance), suggested that activities should be limited to what was politically feasible. Some delegates to the early Memorial meetings, for example, those from White Russia, suggested that there was a danger that Moscow would dominate a country-wide organization. Under such circumstances, was it not preferable to refrain from establishing a national network and instead rely on local initiative? Most candidates, however, considered this a setback to the whole idea.[9]

The indifference of authority did not diminish; no help was given in Moscow, and outside the capital there were incidents of open repression. The most famous such case took place in Minsk in October 1988: Units of the militia were mobilized in a major operation to disperse a mass demonstration called by anti-Stalinist activists to commemorate the local victims of the terror of the 1930s and 1940s. This scandal was widely reported in the Moscow newspapers and ultimately backfired; with a delay of some nine months, the White Russian leadership was subjected to criticism for its lack of enthusiasm for glasnost on the part of *Pravda* voicing the views of the Politburo.

Applications to the authorities for requests of details about the fate of relatives were not welcomed. When Grant Gudasov of Baku asked the republican prosecutor whether he could see the file concerning his father, he was told: "This is expressly prohibited. Imagine all those illegally repressed having access to criminal cases. They list the names of investigators, witnesses, judges. This would unleash an all-Union massacre. . . ."[10]

The response to the Memorial initiative was more pronounced in some outlying regions, including the Baltic countries and the Ukraine, whereas in Russia proper there was little support. There was no tradition in the Soviet Union of citizens' initiatives.

If Memorial was so lacking in influence, how does one explain the unrelenting hostility of the authorities? There were the usual suspicions of the bureaucracy vis-à-vis any movement, however small, not under its control. True, attempts were made to gain control and to squeeze out the militants with whom the Memorial idea had originated. Thus, the daily newspaper *Trud* charged the movement with "isolationism": Why did it not include the "broad popular masses" through trade unions, womens' organization, and the Komsomol?[11] But these mass organizations had shown no interest and taken no initiative.

The real reason for the antagonism of the authorities had less to do with the "elitist" character of Memorial than the fear that its leaders wanted to go much further in rejecting Stalinism than thought advisable and safe by the party leadership. Thus, to give but one example, the three national-front organizations of the Baltic countries (the Lithuanian Sayudis, the Latvian Duma, and the Estonian Council of Deputies) published in May 1989 a common resolution on the "crimes of Stalinism" that was quite unacceptable to the Moscow leadership. It stated that a "totalitarian regime" had been established in the Soviet Union in the 1920s based on merciless state terror, the consequences of which could be felt until the present. The resolution demanded legal condemnation of the crimes of Stalinism and bringing those responsible to trial. It insisted that the Supreme Soviet acknowledge that the system of state terror was tantamount to genocide with regard to the Baltic peoples, that compensation be paid to the victims out of the Soviet state budget, and that the organizers and executors of the genocide (such as the secret police) be subjected to legal prosecution similar to the Nuremberg tribunal investigating crimes against humanity.[12]

The idea of a Nuremberg tribunal dealing with Stalinism rather than with individual Stalinists was widely discussed in the Soviet Union following the publication of several articles in 1988. Those articles noted that individual NKVD interrogators, such as Khvat (who had dealt with the academician Vavilov) Boyarsky, and Grishaev (who had been in charge of investigations in 1948–53), were still alive and that some interrogators had not even been pensioned yet. Irate letters from readers demanded that the statute of limitations not apply in such cases. (According to Article 48 of the Russian criminal code, the decision to apply the statute of limitations in the case of crimes punishable by the death sentence is in the jurisdiction of the court.) Soviet law does not in principle provide for legal actions against the dead (Article 5); hence, the conclusion drawn by some writers that a trial would be impossible.[13] However, the legislator left certain loopholes so that, in theory, a trial against Stalin might not have been impossible. If it was feasible to rehabilitate individuals posthumously, it should have also been possible to sue them, even if they could no longer be punished. But what would have been the political value of a legal action of this kind? There has been dissent among the committed anti-Stalinists along these lines. Some, like Elena Bonner (Sakharov's wife), have categorically opposed any legal sanctions, stressing that for the moral recovery of the Soviet people it was imperative to declare the mass repression illegal; for the sake of humanism and charity it was desirable to refrain from legal persecution.

Others have argued that a Nuremberg tribunal was necessary; only a legal verdict would make de-Stalinization irreversible.[14] Yet another school of thought, voiced by writer Ales Adamovich and philosopher Yuri Kariakin, suggests that the question of juridical responsibility should be decided by a popular referendum.

Those who proposed a tribunal along the lines of the Nuremberg trials were probably aware of the legal, moral, and political difficulties involved. But there was no chance, in any case, that the party leadership would have permitted any such action. It might have resulted in declaring entire institutions (such as the NKVD) criminal and, by necessity, would have raised embarrassing questions about the responsibility of party and state authorities.

The party leadership found it difficult enough coping with two much less ambitious assignments: the rehabilitation of Stalin's victims and the renaming of cities, villages, and institutions. In October 1987, following a resolution by the Central Committee, a commission was founded "for the additional study of materials relating to the repression that occurred in the period of the thirties, forties, and early fifties." This committee consisted of several Politburo members, including Yakovlev and Chebrikov, heads of Central Committee departments, and Smirnov, director of the Marx-Engels-Lenin Institute. Although it was claimed that the commission's work would not "take place in isolation," the public was not represented, nor were its meetings made public except by short official communiqués.

The chairman of the commission gave his first interview one year after the committee was founded.[15] When asked in what way this commission was different from those set up after the Twentieth Party Congress (1956), he pointed to the fact that their work had been cut short prematurely and that they had not dealt with "unjustified repression" that had occurred prior to 1936. The rehabilitation process had been selective and episodic, and the earlier commissions had not dealt with more general issues. Thus, the existence of various espionage and sabotage "blocs" and "centers" had not been questioned.

The new commission proceeded by instructing the Soviet prosecutor's office to investigate individual cases, which were then submitted to the Supreme Court, or with regard to posthumous reinstatement in the party, to the Central Committee Control Commission. Solomontsev announced: "As yet we do not know of any cases of archival material having been removed, but we have encountered archives, including party archives, that are in a mess." According to his evidence, the committee was not only preoccupied with the fate of prominent party officials but also with individual workers and peasants; it had judicially rehabilitated 636 people in one year, including a concrete worker and other ordinary laborers. This was not a very impressive figure considering the total number of victims.

Elsewhere, no greater priority was given to de-Stalinization. According to a spokesman of the military prosecutor's office, only 40 people were investigating applications for rehabilitations; 500 had been dealing with such applications during the years following Stalin's death. If the staffing remained the same, it would take 150 years to finish the job. . . .[16]

But there was a more startling statement to come. When asked about the fate of the perpetrators of the repressions and about the statute of limitations, Solomontsev answered:

> With regard to those instances of violations of socialist legality in the thirties, forties, and early fifties that have been revealed, the culprits have already been punished through criminal, legal, and party channels. It is obviously not a secret to everyone that V. S. Avakumov, M. N. Ryutin, A. G. Leonov, V. I. Komarov, M. T. Likhachev, L. L. Shvartsman, and other former leaders and personnel of the U.S.S.R. Ministry of State Security were sentenced to death for fabricating investigation materials. . . .[17]

Solomontsev also said that the guilt of Stalin was truly monstrous but that the guilt of the leaders does not detract from the responsibility of voluntary informers or obedient executors of the immediate violations of socialist legality, of those who supported and blindly fulfilled the inhuman orders and perpetrated the tyranny. He also made it known that there were still a number of circumstances concerning the Kirov murder that should be clarified.

On subsequent occasions, the communiqués from the commission investigating the crimes were slightly more explicit. One example was the decision to reinstate (on June 21, 1988) party membership to Bukharin and others accused (with the exception of Yagoda) at the third Moscow show trial.[18]

However, the impression was created that the commission not only pursued its task with less than breakneck speed—which could be justified—but also that it dealt with only a tiny number of cases and that it apparently assumed that the others would be dealt with on the local level. Those persons who had been instrumental in carrying out the terror were apparently considered outside its purview.

It was indeed no secret that six collaborators of Beria had been executed soon after the fall of their patron. But the very suggestion that this meant that "the culprits have already been punished" was, of course, grotesque, and it pointed to the limits of the second wave of de-Stalinization. Even more amazing was an interview given by V. Pirozhkov, deputy head of the KGB. When asked how many hangmen had been brought to trial, he answered that 1,342 NKVD officials had been sentenced for severe violations of socialist legality, including Beria, Ezhov, Kobulov, Frinovsky, Agranov, Avakumov and others.[19] But Ezhov, Frinovsky, and Agranov had been executed by Beria in 1939 not because of their crimes but because they knew too much, and Beria and his cohort had been put to death as British spies rather than because of their complicity in the regime of terror. With equal justice, the speaker could have argued that some 20,000 secret-police officials had been killed during the purge (1936–39). But this had nothing to do with justice, socialist or otherwise, or punishment for crimes that they had committed.

Although the rehabilitation of individual victims of the Stalinist terror gave rise to a great deal of debate, the question of renaming cities, villages, streets, factories, and universities generated no less heat. The practice of naming cities after monarchs (sometimes during their lifetimes) predated the Revolution; the names of Empresses Catherine and Elizabeth in particular had been given to several towns. But after the Revolution of 1917, doing so became much more frequent: Taldom became Leninsk in 1921, Gatchina was renamed Trotsk in 1923, Petrograd became Leningrad in 1924, and Tsaritsyn in 1925 became Stalingrad. The practice reached its apogee under Stalin, but it was by no means discontinued after his death. Thus, Naberezhnie Zhelny became Brezhnev; Ustinov and Suslov were also commemorated in a similar way. These changes were not inexpensive: It was estimated that renaming a city the size of Kirov would cost 150 million rubles, and it would cost 100 million for Kalinin—the cost of building several new suburbs.[20] When it was decided to restore the old name, the same amount had to be spent again.

In some cases, there were several changes. Thus, Lugansk became Voroshilovgrad in 1935, then Lugansk again under Khrushchev, again Voroshilovgrad under Brezhnev, and will soon, no doubt, revert to its old name. Rybinsk became Shcherbakovsk (under Stalin), then again Rybinsk, and later Andropov, whereas Elisavetgrad was named first Zinovievsk, later Kirovo, and finally (?) Kirovgrad.

In such cases, many millions of rubles had to be spent, and the residents were, of course, never consulted. Furthermore, the naming of streets and institutions led to a uniformity that amused some and annoyed others: Why should the streets all over the Soviet Union have more or less the same names? Why should local traditions be disregarded?

After the Twentieth Party Congress, Stalin's name disappeared; he had been preceded by Beria, and he was followed by Molotov (the city of Molotov again became Perm), Kaganovich, and other close companions.

However, the names of other leading representatives of the Stalin cohort, such as Zhdanov, Kalinin, and Voroshilov, persisted much longer. Even under glasnost, the city of Tver is still Kalinin, and Leningrad University is still named after Zhdanov, the scourge of Soviet intellectuals, as was Mariupol in South Russia and the Taganka district in Moscow. This caused bitter complaints from many residents of the cities, regions, and streets; they resented being identified with individuals who had been found guilty of crimes against the Soviet people. True, there were some who opposed yet another change. Stalingrad, after all, had entered world history, for better or worse, under that name, and references to the "battle of Volgograd" sounded unfamiliar.

The debate was spreading: Why should five out of sixty-nine Soviet universities be named after Gorky, who, with all his merits, had never attended one? Why had the time-honored city of Nizhni Novgorod been renamed Gorky, even though the real name of the writer was Peshkov and despite the fact that he had never favored a memorial of this kind? Why not give back Kuibyshev its old name (Samara)? And why have Kirov's name all over the Soviet Union, including the old city of Viatka, not to mention the Baku Institute of Parasitology, of Balneology, and so on. Why had the old city Gzhatsk been renamed Gagarin after the first cosmonaut who had been killed in an accident?

It appeared that a majority of concerned citizens favored the return to the old names, even though it involved considerable expense and not all the old names had been particularly beautiful or time-honored—as in the case of new cities or streets.[21] The practice that had prevailed for so many years smacked of the Stalinist era, and there were widespread feelings that it should be discontinued.

The need to come to terms with the past and to commemorate the victims of the Stalinist era manifested itself in many different ways. In some regions, local initiatives gained much support. A Latvian journal began to publish excerpts from Dmitri Yurasov's famous lists of victims.[22] In Moscow, after prolonged resistance, it was announced that Solzhenitsyn's *Arkhipelago Gulag*, that encyclopedia of the camps, would be published. (Large sections of it appeared throughout 1989 in *Novyi Mir*.) In Lithuania, a retrospective exhibition covering Stalin and the Stalinist era was shown, and in Karaganda local residents began to explore the history and geography of one of the biggest camps, the Karlag complex.

A meeting took place with members of the local branch of Memorial and veteran members of the organs of the MVD (Ministry of Internal Affairs), who had done guard duty in the camps in the 1930s and 1940s. One of the latter shouted that writers of defamatory articles on the camps should be shot, and there was some applause. Others claimed that the inmates of the camps had been criminals and not political victims. No one remembered cases of inhumane treatment, food had been plentiful, medical care excellent. If one believed these witnesses, conditions had been similar to those of a holiday resort. True, some people had died, but then, others had died outside the camps.[23]

The most traumatic recollections that emerged were not those published by government commissions but the artless accounts of simple, sometimes semiliterate people. When asked in his interview about the place of burial of the victims, Solomontsev had said that this was one of the most painful aspects of the terror but that in most cases it was virtually impossible to give an answer. A Moscow popular weekly published a letter from a woman describing how, in 1937–38, clouds of fine dust had covered the neighborhood of the cemetery of Don Monastery (one of the biggest and most famous in Moscow) and how she and her friends had stopped playing in the neighborhood. There were similar letters relating to other crematoria that had worked day and night.[24] Groups of young local historians throughout the Soviet Union reported that they had tried to find the graves of various individuals but without success. They had met with comrades from the KGB but received no answer. At the same time, mass graves were discovered all over the country. In many cases, their existence had been known, or suspected, for a long time, but no one had dared to ask searching questions before glasnost.

On Moscow television, a letter by one Ivan Efimovich Movchan, aged eighty-four, was read. He had joined the Komsomol and become a private in the NKVD in 1928. He told how he had participated three times in executions, in April 1934 and in July 1938. Groups of 29 and 39 people had been shot at the Solomenski cemetery in Kiev and in Babi Yar, which later became the execution site of 90,000 Kiev Jews. As Movchan recalled:

I shot four people; we covered them with earth and then went to town. I was then very proud because I thought I had done this for the party and for Comrade Stalin. I now know that I shall die soon, and I want it to be known where those executed have been buried. I know that at least 200 rest there. I do not give my address; I want to live out my allotted span quietly. I have no one in the world. My wife died ten years ago, my son was killed by evil people, and I don't know where my grandchildren are. God will judge me. Nowadays everyone repents, and so do I. Good people do forgive me.[25]

The attitude of the authorities in these, as in other cases, ranged from indifference to actively covering up the crimes that had been committed. Not all bureaucrats were heartless people, and there is reason to assume that at least some were as shocked as the rest. But there were objective difficulties; many files had indeed been destroyed, and it was no longer possible to reconstruct individual cases—there simply had been too many victims.

But there were also political considerations militating against devoting too much thought, time, and resources to uncovering all the traces of Stalin's crimes. Some of the considerations had been articulated by Gorbachev soon after his appointment as general secretary: The crimes had been horrible, but too intensive a preoccupation with the past was unhealthy at a time when all efforts should be directed toward building a better future. There should be a limit to delving into the past, because the memories were too painful, and they could only bring the party and some of its institutions (such as the NKVD) into further disrepute. But the party was no longer the same, nor was the NKVD (KGB). There were no arbitrary arrests, show trials, or mass executions anymore. What if a few people in their eighties or nineties were apprehended who had been involved in the executions? In what way could one punish people with one foot in the grave? Furthermore, there was the danger that the exclusive preoccupation with the darkest chapter in Soviet history would deepen internal divisions at a time when unity was needed more than ever before.

This, in briefest outline, was the case against too much publicity for Stalin's victims. However tragic their death, there was no way to bring them to life again. To students of German history after 1945, the arguments will sound familiar.

But there was also more extreme rejection, the denial that crimes had taken place, or assertions that the executions had been justified. A retired Kharkov prosecutor named Ivan Shekhovtsov tried seventeen times to bring court actions to restore the honor and good name of Josef Stalin. The eighteenth time, he almost succeeded inasmuch as the Sverdlovsk regional court in the city of Moscow agreed to deal with Shekhovtsov's action against the well-known White Russian writer Ales Adamovich, who (he claimed in an article in *Sovetskaia Kultura*) had been guilty of criminal libel.[26] The line taken by Shekhovtsov during the trial was that because there were no documents proving that Stalin had ever committed a crime, he must not be vilified. On the other hand, the victims of the Stalinist period from Bukharin to the academician Vavilov, had all admitted their guilt. According to Shekhovtsov, anti-Stalin hysteria was engulfing the country, and with the help of foreign radio stations, the anti-Stalinists were systematically undermining the prestige of the Soviet system.[27] Adamovich was accompanied in court by two leading figures of the glasnost movement, the historian Polikarpov and the philosopher Kariakin. Kariakin called Shekhovtsov a victim of the Stalinist period, which greatly offended the man from Kharkov. Shekhovtsov did not deny that there had been repressions during the civil war, when orders were given to wipe out whole villages. There had been, he said, more repressions under Lenin than under Stalin, and he thought Tukhachevsky guilty. He did not give credence to the Politburo resolutions concerning the rehabilitation of the accused in the Moscow trials.[28]

Shekhovtsov was a member of the legal profession, and as far as he was concerned, only documents counted; all the rest was hearsay. For this reason, he did not accept the verdict against him by the Moscow court but went to a higher court that again turned him down.[29] Even after that, he continued to believe in the justice of his cause.

His real motivation was, of course, political. He knew that there had been hecatombs of victims. But just as old-style history books had always argued, "No documents—no history," Shekhovtsov claimed "no *corpus delicti*, no crime." The Soviet government had not given access to the relevant files in the Marx-Engels-Lenin Institute, let alone in the KGB archives, and this policy played into the hands of the neo-Stalinists.

Shekhovtsov did not cut an impressive figure in court. He was not a demagogue; he spoke haltingly and not always coherently. Yet he had many supporters in court and outside; posters were displayed against glasnost and perestroika and for the restoration of Stalinist methods.[30] Enterprising cooperatives sold plastic Stalin busts for fifteen rubles.

In Georgia, Lt. Gen. Irakli Dzhordzhadze established an international association to honor Stalin, who had been, in his view, a leader of enormous merit. Whereas he had assured the victory of communism, the leaders who followed him had betrayed his heritage and were leading the country back to religion and capitalism. The general had been a contemporary of Stalin's son Jakob; they had trained in officers' school at the same time. His association counted 1,513 members in early 1990.[31]

The Shekhovtsov-Dzhordzhadze phenomenon was not per se surprising; it is easy to point to similar reactions in Germany and Italy and also in post-Franco Spain: The defendants of the old order always had some support. In the Soviet Union there were probably more of them precisely because there had been no radical break with the past and because the government had not given unqualified support to the campaign against Stalin.

Memorial faced opposition not only from the authorities and from the upholders of the old order; it also encountered opposition among certain sections of the intelligentsia, in particular the right-wing circles and their mouthpieces. There had been some resistance against Abuladze's film *Pokaianie* (Repentance) in 1987, even though the target of this film had been Beria, rather than Stalin, and Beria, in contrast to his master, had few supporters. The anti-Memorial chorus was swelling in 1988–89, and countless essays with titles such as "A Memorial—to Whom?" appeared in such literary journals as *Moskva*, *Molodaia Gvardia*, and *Nash Sovremennik*. They took the anti-Stalinists to task for their alleged desire to engage in selective rehabilitation and for sensationalism and besmirching the good name of the Russian people.

Vladimir Soloukhin, a well-known village writer who had done much during the 1970s to make old religious customs again respectable, published an open letter "Why I Did Not Sign That Letter."[32] He explained that he felt inner resistance to signing a manifesto referring to the "victims of Stalinist repression" without any further clarification. Soloukhin's arguments amounted to the following: The memory of the victims of Stalinism was certainly to be kept alive, but the same was true with regard to the many who had lost their lives before Stalin. He referred to the crimes committed by the Cheka, the forerunner of the NKVD and KGB, as attested by Ivan Bunin and by Korolenko.[33]

And what about the victims of 1929, when millions of totally innocent peasants were transplanted to the naked tundra to die of starvation or freezing? What of the ten million victims in 1933, when in the Ukraine, the Kuban, and in the Volga region parents had eaten their children because of a man-made hunger?

Why should the commemoration be limited to the *House on the Embankment,* ignoring the victims in other parts of European Russia—the north, Siberia, Central Asia, and so forth?[34] Was it right not to mention the murder of the family of the tsar (including four young girls, a boy, several women) that had also been an illegal act? And what of the million cossacks who had been killed during the civil war? What of the 320,000 Orthodox priests who had disappeared between 1917 and 1919? The victims of the 1930s should be remembered, but it was neither right nor moral to relegate the other victims to oblivion.

Soloukhin's critics would point out that he had not always shown such moral sensitivity; when Pasternak had been branded an enemy of the people following the publication of *Dr. Zhivago* in Italy, Soloukhin had not hesitated to sign a letter joining the campaign against him. Soloukhin would answer that this had been a different period, and it did not invalidate his arguments.

Soloukhin's case rested on two assumptions: that the members of Memorial were faithful Leninists who cared only about leading party members who had perished in the 1930s and to whom the fate of millions of others was a matter of indifference.

Although some of the leading members of Memorial were perhaps neo-Leninists, this was not true for the majority, and even the neo-Leninists had sufficient compassion to remember the victims of the terror. Second, and more important, Soloukhin's refusal to sign the manifesto rested on the assumption that most of the victims of the 1930s had been important Communists, Stalinists who had been instrumental in the murder of earlier victims. In fact, for every resident of the "house on the embankment" who was executed, there were thousands of workers, peasants, minor officials, and simple people who were not members of the party but were also put to death.

The Soloukhin case showed that in some circles a tremendous amount of bitterness, even hatred, had accumulated against the generation of old Bolsheviks who had caused so much misery to the Russian people. Stalin had killed many Jewish commissars, and such a man could not have been wholly evil, even if for every such commissar there had been a hundred purely Russian victims. Thus, there was less hatred and bitterness against Stalin than against his prominent victims.[35] It is not certain whether these circles would have signed an appeal even if it had called for commemorating all victims since November 1917, including the tsar and all the grand dukes and patriarchs, for those initiating the appeal belonged to the wrong party. They were liberals and internationalists, and there were too many non-Russians among them.

If the Soloukhin letter was written in a spirit of a certain restraint, both in substance and in form, this was not so with regard to the stream of anti-Memorial literature emanating from the organs of the extreme Right.[36] There was much venom in these outpourings; sometimes it was implied, or even stated, *expressis verbis*, that the fate of the victims of the 1930s (in particular, the old Communists among them) had been well deserved, even though they had been killed for the wrong reasons. For example, some asserted that it had been wrong to rehabilitate the Bukharins and Zinovievs in view of the crimes they had committed against the Russian people. Because a great many crimes had indeed been committed during the civil war by both sides, it was not difficult to single out certain episodes in the history of the "Red Terror," such as the killing of hostages, indiscriminate executions of members of the upper and middle class, and the expulsion of leading members of the old intelligentsia.

As Vasili Bondarenko put it: "In front of our eyes the myth of 1937 as a particularly cruel year collapses. We know about Zinoviev's bloody deeds in Leningrad, about Sverdlov's horrible orders that brought an ocean of blood on the Cossacks."[37] Seen against this background, Stalin was no more than a minor, if grotesque, figure.

The opposition to the anti-Stalinist campaign of the 1980s came from two groups, between which there seemed to be basic differences of opinion: the neo-Stalinists on one hand and the Russian nationalists on the other. The neo-Stalinists were atheists; their enthusiasm for the old church, the precollectivization village, the traditions of the tsarist army, and the White Army forces in the civil war was strictly limited. At the same time, they realized that much of the old doctrine was no longer valid. The nationalists, on the other hand, had to accept that even if the Revolution of 1917 had been a most unfortunate event, it could no longer be undone. If so, Stalin had been the lesser evil—unlike Lenin and Trotsky, Bukharin and Zinoviev, *e tutti quanti*, his policy had aimed to make Russia again a great power. Above all, he had ruthlessly stamped out the radical internationalist elements that had dominated Soviet policies until the mid-1930s. On this basis, a general understanding among the divergent antiglasnost forces could be reached. Only time would tell whether this coalition would last, nor was it certain how much support there was in the country for views of this kind. But even if public opinion polls indicated that support for Stalin had sharply declined between 1985 and 1990,[38] much of the essence of Stalinism was not yet dead. As the policies of glasnost and perestroika run into growing difficulties, a revival of the nationalist neo-Stalinist forces, perhaps under some refurbished populist slogans, seems by no means excluded.

The Memorial initiative remained the prerogative of a small minority except in the non-Russian regions of the U.S.S.R., where it was frequently national in inspiration. As one of the secretaries of the group said in an interview: "People are reluctant to join; they ask themselves who will be in power tomorrow?" Even in early 1990 the group had not been officially registered by the authorities, who did recognize, however, a breakaway group from Memorial that called itself the Association of Victims of Repression, which seemed to be politically more expedient.[39]

And yet, despite their limited efforts and the lack of support by the authorities, Stalin and Stalinism have been widely discredited under glasnost, which was almost entirely the achievement of writers, poets, playwrights, and filmmakers. To write the history of intellectual de-Stalinization is to write the history of Soviet intellectual life after 1986. It is the story of Abuladze's *Pokaianie*, of Akhmatova's "Requiem," of Tvardovsky's poems, of Grossman's *Life and Fate*, and of Rybakov's *Children of the Arbat*, of the novels by Bek and Pristavkin and the recollections of Razgon, Zhigulin, Evgenia Ginzburg, and others, as well as the political-philosophical essays published during that period. They were read by many millions, the poems were often learned by heart, the articles discussed by young and old. Their impact was not limited to the Moscow intellectual scene; much of it, through radio and television (including such films as *Vlast Solovetskaia*) reached the last village.[40]

In 1989 a Soviet literary journal published *Everything Is Flowing*, a philosophical novel by Vasili Grossman that had been written in the late 1950s. The writer had finished it shortly before his death in 1964. It read, inter alia:

With Stalin's help such revolutionary categories as dictatorship, terror, the rejection of bourgeois liberties—all those things that Lenin had considered temporary, transitory expedients—were transformed into the permanent basis of Soviet life, became its essence, and were absorbed into Russia's historical thousand-year continuum of lack of freedom. All the pitiless traits of enslaved Russia, Stalin gathered unto himself. In his unimaginable ferocity and cruelty, in his unbelievable falsity and treachery, in his talent for playing the hypocrite, in his cherished resentments and his vengefulness, in his crudeness, rudeness, humor—behold the Asian tyrant. . . .

Some will detect a certain embellishment of Lenin's views in these lines, but this hardly affected the general thrust and the impact of Grossman's writings. Such comments caused great anger among both the extreme right wing and the neo-Stalinists, for reasons that we have tried to explain. But others were induced to rethink the history of their country. The very fact that someone had dared to express such views about the once-infallible Stalin was a guarantee that, like Akhitophel, Stalin had fallen, never to rise again. The cult had been based on the assumption that no one would dare to question it. Once this taboo had been broken, once Stalin's deeds became the subject of public discussion, his cause was lost.

14. Conclusion: Forty Years After

"Call no man happy, but only lucky, until he is dead." The Greek sage might have added that a few decades more often provide an even better perspective.

In 1949, when Stalin celebrated his seventieth birthday, a noted historian of the Soviet Union pondered his place in history. There seemed to be little doubt, having led his country through its greatest war and surmounted the immediate difficulties of demobilization and reconstruction, that Stalin stood at the pinnacle of his own and his nation's power. Our historian was a distant admirer of Stalin, and yet he felt a little uneasy: Stalin's work was still too plainly subject to the distorting lenses of excessive propinquity. And thus he reached the conclusion, reluctantly perhaps, that Stalin's place in history was not yet fixed, nor would it be for a generation to come: "Had he carried forward the experience of the Revolution of 1917 to its triumphant conclusion, destroyed it altogether, or twisted it out of shape?"[1] Given E. H. Carr's generally positive attitude toward Stalin and Stalinism, this was an astonishing revelation of prescient skepticism at a time when friends and foes alike were overawed by Stalin and tended to see in him one of the greatest and most successful statesmen of modern times; his achievements seemed monumental, gigantic, likely to last forever.

Since then, forty years have passed, and views have radically changed not only in the West but even more strikingly in the Soviet Union and the countries under its influence. More often than not Stalin is regarded as one of the great criminals of all time, his lifework a near total failure. True, there are no final verdicts, subsequent generations will reexamine Stalinism, accents may be put differently, and mitigating circumstances will be adduced. But another radical reassessment still seems unlikely, for the perspective of 1990 is infinitely better than that of 1950. Only now is it possible to assess the consequences of Stalin's policies: a widespread belief that the country has entered an impasse and that only a radical break with the past will lead to a better future. There is a feeling of shame that so many of Stalin's subjects became active or passive accomplices in crime.

True, the Soviet Union has become a superpower, and its armed forces are among the strongest in the world; the territories under its control have expanded, and its sphere of influence has increased. This has brought pride to some but not greater happiness. On the contrary, the expansion has implanted the seed of disintegration, of a resurgence of nationalism directed against Moscow. Above all, Stalin has been a failure on his own terms. His great aim was to lead his people to communism as he understood it, and he was wholly convinced that only he had the wisdom and the determination to guide his flock. Today communism in all its varieties is discredited; it has become a synonym for servitude and inhumanity. Stalin has done more to bring into disrepute the ideology he believed in than the books and speeches by anti-Communists all over the globe.

Some diehards still believe in him, and a few young people also, mainly in order to shock their elders; Hitler, too, has his admirers, and it is only natural that Stalin should have his. They argue that while Stalin was alive everything functioned, there was plenty of food, public order and discipline were perfect, people were radiantly happy, except perhaps a few enemies of the people. It was only after his death that decay set in. But even if this were true, it would not acquit him of the responsibility for what happened after 1953. For a responsible statesman makes provision for his succession, training heirs to continue his work. Stalin's successors were not traitors; they grew up in his school and by and large kept to his style of work.

It has also been said that Stalin's policies were eminently suitable for his period, with the rapid development of heavy industry, the state-of-siege mentality, and the harsh dictatorship in general, but that new approaches were needed for the postwar world. But even if this were true, it would not carry much weight, for Stalin's policies were so deeply ingrained that they made change, a more or less smooth transition, virtually impossible. For the problem facing the Soviet Union after Stalin was not just the change of economic priorities or of political institutions;

the real issue was how to change the mentality of a people who had been indoctrinated not to think for themselves, not to take initiatives.

Since glasnost, Russians have not stopped talking about Stalin, and new light has been shed on his rule, more, admittedly, on how his subjects felt about him than about his motives. Some ghosts have been laid to rest, some questions resolved: He was not a weak dictator, not indecisive, not a closet democrat acting as chairman of the Politburo. True, the style of the Stalin of 1950 was not the one of twenty years earlier, when he still pretended to listen and when, on occasion, opposition made him change his tactics.

In later years there was no pretense of collective leadership, and even the Politburo had virtually ceased to exist. Stalin was not a beleaguered, embattled leader, as some thought at the time. He was not a pawn in the hands of "extremists" like Molotov and Zhdanov. His satraps existed not in their own right but entirely depended on his goodwill. They were interchangeable, and the reason even more of them were not executed was that with advancing age Stalin disliked new faces around him.

In other respects his personality still remains a riddle. There was a streak of madness, especially paranoia, in his mental makeup that became progressively worse with age. But there was also extreme cruelty and mendacity in his character, and it is difficult to outline with any certainty the borderlines between rational calculation, evil, and madness. Some of his actions were perfectly rational, even though, like all humans, he tended to be mistaken from time to time without ever admitting it. Stalin's conviction in 1941 that Hitler would not attack belongs to this category of errors. Such an error might have been committed by other leaders, a major, near-fatal mistake, but still an understandable miscalculation. Or, to give another example, Stalin's misjudgment of the direction of the German summer offensive of 1942. As a result, the Soviet reserves were concentrated where they were not needed, and it took a long time to shift them to the south. Similar mistakes were committed by other war leaders with more experience than Stalin. Another example is the pact with Nazi Germany in August 1939, which is justified by party spokesmen and historians to this day: There was, they claim, no alternative. This is quite true if one takes, say, January 1939 as one's point of reference: Having led the Soviet Union into political isolation, having decimated the officer corps of the Red Army, the Red Army was no longer considered much of a threat by its enemies or much of an asset by its potential allies. Under these conditions, having foreclosed other options, a case of sorts can perhaps be made in favor of the pact, even though eventually Nazi Germany benefited more from it than the Soviet Union. Seen in a wider historical perspective the pact was, of course, anything but inevitable.

Some of Stalin's mistakes were the result of doctrinaire narrowmindedness, for instance, the manner in which the collectivization of agriculture and industrialization were effected. Stalin realized correctly that given the uncertainties of the international situation, the establishment of heavy industry as a base for a modern army was urgently needed. He was right in assuming that not many years were left to accomplish that task. The way he did it was hardly the most effective; in the case of Soviet agriculture it was a disaster. But again, it could be argued that he was by no means alone in his misjudgments—many party leaders gave him fervent support. Some of Stalin's actions, however grotesque or inhuman, can still be rationally explained. If he was convinced that only he was capable of leading his country through the confrontation with dangers at home and abroad, it follows that he had to eliminate potential rivals. One could even explain against this background the Stalin cult—at least up to a point.

Beyond this point certain aspects of Stalin's behavior defy rational comprehension. A survivor of Stalin's last great purge tried to explain the behavior of the dictator with reference to his general mental makeup, the pathological traits in his personality and the psychophysiological consequences of arteriosclerosis. Yet with all this, the writer, a distinguished medical man, reaches the conclusion that rationally it is impossible to understand the purpose of the staging of the "doctors' plot."[2] A reviewer noted that the assumption of normal human behavior was not perhaps the correct starting point in this case.[3] Perhaps so; madness, too, has a logic of its own, and the study of abnormal behavior is a legitimate subject. But it is also clear that at this point we cross the line between the realm of near certainties and probabilities to hypotheses and speculation.

Stalin was a man totally devoid of conscience; Pascal once remarked that men never do evil so completely and cheerfully as when they do it from religious conviction—or, it should be added in a postreligious age, from political conviction. Since in Stalin's case personal ambition and ideological conviction coincided, the question of conscience never arose.

He was a great man because the stage on which he performed was so great. Any actor on this stage was bound to be powerful and important unless, like Hitler, he managed to destroy the stage in the end.

Some latter-day well-wishers have argued that, though a villain, he was a tragic figure and that a Shakespeare would be needed to do him justice. There are some superficial similarities between the bard's villains and Stalin: Shakespeare's are great deceivers, murderers, driven by ambition, accomplished plotters and dissimulators, from Richard III and Claudius to Iago—always pretending to be the honest man—to the murderers in Macbeth. But Stalin lacked the stuff that the great writer needs to make a great villain. The passion, the imagination, the demonic qualities, even his madness, seemed always under control. Nor did he ever face tragedy in his career; he went, it seemed, from success to success and died more or less peacefully in his home. In brief, his was not the material from which tragic heroes or great stage villains are cut.

Later generations of young Germans have failed to understand Hitler's magic; to them the little man with the ridiculous mustache and the hysterical speeches was more an object of amusement and bewilderment than of fright, something like Charlie Chaplin's *Great Dictator*.

Russian attitudes toward Stalin have been different, even with the benefit of hindsight. A Soviet writer has blamed the Russian intelligentsia for, while hating Stalinism, not having learned even now to hold it in contempt, to laugh about the boorishness and insignificance of Stalin and his entourage, about his speeches and articles, which were nothing but window dressing.[4]

It is perfectly true that Stalin was not a well-educated man, and some of his comrades-in-arms were even less so. Many of his sayings, which became winged words and were repeated ad nauseam, were utterly trite and in some cases outrageously stupid. But Dr. Batkin also tells us that Stalin, like Hitler, will be remembered two and three thousand years from now more vividly than the great people whom he destroyed. One ought to be careful with predictions covering the next two thousand years, but for the time being and the near future, the statement seems correct. Such a villain is not a figure of ridicule.

Support for Stalin is likely to remain greater than for Hitler because of the Soviet victory in the war. Hitler, as Vasili Grossman noted, was "great" while he was winning, and Stalin was winning much longer. Stalin persuaded his countrymen that there was no alternative but the "harsh measures" he used. Perhaps not that much persuasion was required; perhaps Stalin's style was more attuned to the prevailing mood of his party and country than his rivals. These questions remain to be investigated in greater detail.

In some respects, the study of the Stalinist period is only at its beginning, one example of which is the Ukrainian famine of 1933, a catastrophe that caused the death of millions of people. Until glasnost this dark chapter in Soviet history remained a taboo zone for historians, but in 1988–89 it became a central issue in public debate. There was unanimity with regard to the extent of the disaster and the identity of the main culprits, above all, Stalin, but also Postyshev, his main lieutenant in the Ukraine, as well as Molotov and Kaganovich, who were sent there on special missions.

There was no such unanimity with regard to the causes. Some Ukrainian historians and writers maintained that it was a carefully planned action meant to "pacify" (that is to say, punish) the Ukrainian people because they were too prosperous, too independent, and because they showed insufficient enthusiasm for the collectivization of agriculture. The Ukraine had been an exporter of grain, but in 1932 there was a sudden decline in agricultural production and the Soviet government found itself deprived of much-needed revenue in foreign currency.[5]

That the famine had not been the result of a natural catastrophe was never in doubt; 1932–33 were not years of drought. And there is also unanimity that, generally speaking, the policy of collectivization was an unmitigated disaster. But the punishment thesis has not been proved. There seems to have been no plan to destroy Ukrainian agriculture and to cause the death of millions of people. One tends to underrate the extent of the foolishness and incompetence of the leadership and, perhaps even more importantly, the fanaticism and lack of moral scruples of the dictator and his emissaries, who believed that all difficulties could be overcome if only sufficient toughness was shown and pressure applied. The year 1933, after all, also witnessed widespread famine in Central Asia and the Kuban region. If so, can it be shown that there was a specific anti-Ukrainian motive in Stalin's policy?[6] The question will be discussed for years to come.

It is easier to assess Stalin's role in building up Soviet industry in the 1930s, in preparing his country for war, and in leading it to victory. That Stalin's strategies for the economic development of his country were the only feasible ones cannot be seriously maintained; other countries made greater progress at less cost. But were his strategies the only practical ones given the conditions? There is no convincing evidence to this effect; Stalin's genius was to make it appear that he had no options. But Russia was a big country, rich in resources, vast in territory and population. True leadership would have shown itself in mobilizing these resources for victory rationally and effectively with regard to economic development as well as to war. Under another leader the growth rates achieved in the Soviet Union in the 1930s might have been smaller, but this might have been compensated by higher quality. In any case, many of the new factories and the coal and iron mines fell into German hands in the first weeks after the German attack—in which Stalin had not believed. He built up the Red Army and at the same time destroyed its leadership and paralyzed it by his amateurish interventions. His achievements seemed breathtaking to contemporaries, as did Hitler's; it was the era of the strong men, the "iron will," the "decisive measures," the "steely nerves." But what he gave with his left hand, he took away with his right. It was said about King Midas that everything he touched turned to gold and about some other historical figures that everything they touched became ashes. Stalin had the touch of Midas—his achievements seemed to be enormous, but only for the historical moment. As the years passed, it appeared that the gold was dross, the achievements not lasting. It was not exactly a house built on sand, but it resembled more a giant prison than a palace of culture and leisure, a house in which no one felt comfortable.

To savor the full flavor of the Stalinist period and to realize the enormous distance between promise and fulfillment, one ought to immerse oneself in biographies such as Barbusse's, published in 1935, or reports from Moscow such as Feuchtwanger's, which appeared in 1937. Or perhaps, even more appropriately, one should watch one of the Soviet movies that were so popular at the time, such as *Tsirk*,[7] the story of a U.S. circus performer, played by the leading Soviet star of the period, Liubov Orlova. Being the unmarried mother of a little black child, she is ostracized in America. She is afraid that reaction in the Soviet Union will be the same. But much to her surprise and gratification, everyone is exceptionally nice to her and the baby. Solomon Mikhoels, the leading Jewish actor, sings "My beloved little black baby" in Yiddish, and the film ends in an apotheosis, the May 1 demonstration in Red Square, with big Stalin pictures carried by enthusiastic and radiantly happy young people. Everyone sings the hit song of the film, the "Song of the Fatherland," *Shiroka strana moia rodnaia*, which was to become something like the second national anthem of the Soviet Union in succeeding years, with the refrain "There is no other country in the world in which people breathe so freely. . . ." For many years it was the signature tune of Radio Moscow; it is still widely quoted today, as a bitter comment on the mendacity of the Stalinist era.

Mikhoels, a cosmopolitan "enemy of the people," was killed by the secret police in a dark street in Minsk. The attitude toward blacks is not now what it was fifty years ago, to put it mildly, and the procession with the pictures of Stalin provokes reactions ranging from amazement to hilarity. Some misfortune or other befell virtually everyone connected with the making of this film, but the strangest, in retrospect, involved the man who composed the song that made the movie famous, Isak Duna-evsky. In a recently published letter to a friend, he wrote on the occasion of Stalin's seventieth birthday:

> Stalin appears to be the greatest human being of our era. We do not find in the history of mankind a similar example of the greatness of a person, of depth of popularity, of reverence and love. We ought to be proud that we are his contemporaries and his collaborators, however minute our role in his actions. How often do we forget—and this goes particularly for the young generation—that we breathe the same air as he does, that we live under the same skies. How often do people shout: "Dear, beloved Stalin"— and then they turn to their own affairs and behave meanly at work or in their relations with others. Coexistence with Stalin demands from his contemporaries boundless purity and devotion, belief and will, moral and social heroism. [8]

These lines were not written for publication; they are from a private letter. They were wholly sincerely meant and are therefore all the more difficult to understand. Dunaevsky was an honored citizen in his country, recip-ient of some of its highest awards, and had every reason to be grateful to Stalin. But he lived in Moscow, not in a remote village. He moved among the intelligentsia. He was not a young enthusiast; he knew what happened to so many of his friends and contemporaries. He was a Jew and aware of the campaign against the "cosmopolitans." And yet he wrote about Stalin in terms that in other times and countries would have been thought extravagant even when addressed to a saint. It is difficult to think of comparable admiration and devotion to a leader who, after all, was only mortal.[9] During one of the many "roundtables" that have taken place under glasnost, one of the participants said that the most horrible aspect of the truth was that the "heart of the matter was not Stalin but—us." In the light of such case histories it is difficult to dismiss such comments out of hand.

The German example shows how difficult resistance is once a totalitarian regime has been installed, with its agencies of repression in full control. The time to resist modern tyrants is before rather than after the seizure of power. The absence of any organized resistance can be explained once the NKVD was in full control. It is far more difficult to understand the genuine admiration for Stalin personally. It is unfair to blame a whole people for not having risked their lives in a hopeless struggle against the dictatorship. It is legitimate to express amazement in the face of so much popular enthusiasm for an inhuman regime.

One facet of Stalin's heritage was lasting: the political system that he left to his country—the character of leadership, the values of society, public opinion, and the general mentality.

Hitler and Mussolini were defeated in the war, and for this reason there was in their countries a radical break with the past. Stalin prevailed, and therefore the break with the past was infinitely more difficult. How could one expect the Dunaevskys to burn the shrines at which they had been praying for so many years? Many Soviet citizens had been brainwashed to such an extent that the true character of their society had escaped them. In their enthusiasm they failed to see the constant lying, the all-pervasive informers, the widespread envy, the arbitrary bureaucratic rule, the stifling cultural oppression, the general fear, the hostility between nationalities.

There is the temptation to assign all the blame to one man or, alternatively, to belittle his importance and to blame the "system."[10] This was the case with Hitler and Mussolini, and it is now happening with regard to Stalin. True, up to a point Stalin was an accident. Had there been no Stalin or had he died in the early 1930s, his place would have been taken by one of the other leaders, Kirov, perhaps, or Molotov, Ordzhonikidze, Voroshilov, or Zhdanov—perhaps even a collective leadership. We have been accustomed to thinking of these men as second-raters, which, in fact, they were. But nature and politics do not suffer a vacuum; another leader or leadership would by necessity have assumed power. Perhaps a leader of the right-wing opposition or one of the marshals would have emerged as the leader of the Soviet Union, but it is much less likely.

In what way would their policies have differed from Stalinism? The extremes of bloodshed and cruelty would have been prevented; there would have been a cult of the party but less of the leader. There is every reason to believe that such a leadership would have successfully resisted the Nazi invasion, and there is equal reason to assume that it would gradually have run out of steam, as Stalinism did. The Marxist-Leninist inspiration would have become less and less important, and it would have given way to a nationalist-populist ideology. There would have been more political and cultural freedom, albeit considerably less than in other developed nations. In the socioeconomic sphere the leadership would have faced, grosso modo, the same problems as Khrushchev, Brezhnev, and Gorbachev.

Seen in this light, Stalin did make a difference not only for the millions whose lives were cut short and their families but for the whole nation. But even in Stalin's absence there would have been a one-party bureaucratic command system, that is to say, a dictatorship moving toward a crisis as the shortcomings of the system became manifest. The world revolution would not have come to its aid, Communist regimes might have emerged (or been imposed) in other countries, but they would not necessarily have followed the Soviet lead, if they could only help it.

To deny Stalin's importance runs contrary to historical experience, nor is it sensible to put all the emphasis on social and economic changes that took place under his leadership. ("The Stalins come and go, but the social and economic changes remain—and lead to political change.") True, perhaps, in a perspective of centuries; in reality, the relationship between political and economic change is infinitely more complex. Many other countries were industrialized in Stalin's lifetime; all over the world a process of urbanization was taking place. There is no reason to assume that the Soviet Union alone would have been an exception. But the political consequences differed enormously. The "objective trends," in short, cannot account for the specifics of the Stalinist system.

To recognize Stalin's political importance is not to say that all that happened over a quarter of a century occurred owing to the evil genius of one man and one man only. The system could not have functioned but for the hundreds of thousands of little Stalins who served it. Nor does it explain how Stalin could attain total power in the first place. Some

German patriots have claimed that Hitler and Nazism were a "traffic accident" in the course of German history; others have argued that fascism was a phenomenon that appeared all over Europe and that Hitler's movement managed to seize power in Germany only because of bad luck and some historical burdens, such as the Versailles Treaty. Russian patriots, in broad symmetry, have claimed that Bolshevism was a foreign importation, Marx and Trotsky were Jews, Lenin and Bukharin déraciné Russians.

But Stalin was no more a Jew or a freemason than Mao or Tito, or an antipatriot; on the contrary, he restored time-honored Russian traditions and expanded Russia's borders. Stalinism was not a universal phenomenon "from Madrid to Shanghai." There were specific reasons for its emergence in Russia; however unpleasant the truth, it has to be faced.

The search for the roots of Stalinism takes us back into Russian history and also to a reexamination of the character of Bolshevism. That the democratic tradition in Russian politics has been weak cannot be seriously denied. Autocracy had deep roots in the country; so had the radicalism of the Russian intelligentsia. The interaction of these elements did not make a development toward a democratic order impossible, but it made it very difficult indeed.

This, broadly speaking, is the core of the Kliamkin thesis, the near inevitability of the course of recent Russian history. The concept is in many ways persuasive: Authoritarian repression led to a violent revolution. The Leninist seizure of power in a backward country was bound to lead not to freedom and a progressive society but to something akin to the Stalinist system. This thesis has been contested, and it is, of course, true that the course of history is never wholly predestined; the element of accident, of good or bad fortune, can never be wholly ignored. But for Lenin's presence in October 1917, the Bolsheviks would not have made their coup, and it is quite likely that if they had missed this opportunity there would have been no second chance. Whether this would have been a loss to mankind can be endlessly discussed, and this is also true as to whether Leninism was or was not embryonic Stalinism. There is no serious doubt that Leninism was authoritarian in character and that under Stalin the repression was greatly intensified. Historians deal with probabilities, and seen in this light, it seems unlikely that Leninism would have become more democratic after the death of its founder and leader. The Bolsheviks wanted to stay in power, they saw themselves as a beleaguered avant-garde in their own country, they considered it treason to make far-reaching concessions to those who did not share their convictions. Under these circumstances, radical policies were far more likely to be adopted than moderate ones. The Stalinist excesses of terror and the absurdities of the "cult" were perhaps a historical accident, but tyranny would have prevailed in any case. Stalinism, in brief, was not inescapable, but it was the most likely outcome, much more so than Bukharin's victory, let alone a resurgence of social democracy. Whether one should define a non-Stalinist Communist regime (Stalinism minus the absurdities) as strongly authoritarian or totalitarian might be of great interest to the catalogers among the political scientists but not to many others. In any event, the radical alternative prevailed, and not, a Marxist would say, by accident. It also happened to be more popular than a more moderate regime would have been in view of the propensity of both party and country for strong rule.

But why should Russia have gone her own way, rejecting freedom and more democratic avenues toward modernization? Were these really the long-term consequences, as sometimes claimed, of Byzantium, the Mongol yoke, and the Tartar invasions? If Russia was not in the European mainstream, it is even less true that it belonged to Asia. Such issues will be reexamined for a long time to come, but it is by no means certain that to these last questions of history (as of philosophy) there will ever be generally accepted final answers.

The Soviet debate as to why Russia developed as it did, and not like France and England, has had its parallel in the German discussion about its *Sonderweg* or in the idea of American exclusivity: Why did modernization not proceed smoothly in Russia as in Germany? Why were liberalism and democracy rejected for so long? These questions do not bother the Russian right wing because, as they see it, Russia developed its own values and way of life and it had nothing to learn from the decaying West. But they remain crucial questions, and a variety of answers have been given to them over the years. Some put the emphasis on geographic location: Germany, located in the very center of Europe, was exposed to pressure from all sides. Liberty, as some nineteenth-century political philosophers had maintained, could prosper only if outside pressure did not exceed a certain degree—which may account for the democratic tradition of Iceland and perhaps even of Britain. But if Germany was under pressure as a "country of the middle," so was Russia as Europe's flank, the glacis most exposed to invasions from the East. In any case, the danger of such invasions no longer existed after the sixteenth century, when Russia's expansion to the East was under way.

Germany, like Russia, had no successful revolutions in her history, and the political regimes were more authoritarian and state directed and controlled than in the West. The middle class was less politically powerful in Germany and Russia than in the West, and in Russia, a largely agrarian country, it was also less numerous. Political parties were less influential in Germany than in Britain, France, and the United States, and in Russia they did not exist at all before 1905—and were of no great consequence thereafter. But there are no purely economic reasons for economic backwardness and belated development, just as there are no obvious geopolitical reasons, and thus the debate about deviations from the (Western) norm. If the authoritarian state and the bureaucracy were stronger than society in Russia as in Germany, if dictatorships based on a single party emerged, the reasons were manifold and in part intangible: Some assigned responsibility to Luther and his unquestioning acceptance of secular authority, others on the Thirty Years' War and its ravages, which set back Germany for a century. Yet others would regard the twentieth-century disasters as mere traffic (or industrial) accidents for which there was no accounting. A madman appeared on the scene and hypnotized the people. Russia had no Luther, but it labored with the Byzantine tradition. There was no Thirty Years' War, only the *Smuta*, the interregnum of the early seventeenth century. Its traditional social and political structures withstood the attempts at innovation and reform. But whether all this was predestined, we do not know; there is no satisfactory explanation, not even a persuasive paradigm.

In their attempts to come to terms with the Stalinist heritage, Soviet thinkers even under glasnost face certain obstacles. In 1986 caution was still advisable, but in the following year it became perfectly safe to curse Stalin in even the strongest terms, and, a fortiori, his comrades-in-arms. But Stalin and Stalinism, unlike Aphrodite in the classical legend, had not sprung from the foam of the sea. Stalinism had political, social, and intellectual roots, and it cannot be understood without reconsidering its links with Marxism and Leninism. This is not easy even now, despite greater intellectual freedom.

Mention has been made of the important role played by the books of Vasili Grossman, written around 1960, published in 1988. Grossman's

Life and Fate and *Everything Is Flowing* were the first works outside samizdat that confronted such issues as the common ground between Nazism and Stalinism, the weakness of the democratic tradition of the Russian people, and the nondemocratic essence of Leninism. If they had been published a quarter of a century earlier, their impact would have been even greater, but this was of course impossible in view of the political constellation at the time. When they finally appeared, they were still read by millions and their influence was considerable.[11]

A reassessment of Marxism has been undertaken by some daring spirits in the Baltic republics, and after 1988 also by some Moscow critics. They do not make Marx responsible for Stalin's totalitarian state, but they find fault with Marxist-Leninist ideology, which became a dogma in the Soviet Union and guided Stalin and his party. Seen in historical perspective, Marx and Engels correctly analyzed the weaknesses of capitalism but ignored its strength; they ignored, or underrated, the importance of democratic freedom, the staying power of nationalism and religion. They did not appreciate sufficiently the role of the cultural heritage, the family, and many other factors of society; most political trends, in fact, except the class struggle. They thought they had provided a scientific underpinning to socialism, yet they were, in fact, the last and greatest of the utopian socialists, as events during the century after their death were to show.[12]

Attitudes toward Lenin have widely diverged under glasnost. While Solzhenitsyn, not handicapped by the rules confining historians, has described him as one of the most evil men who ever lived, Russian nationalists inside the Soviet Union have found positive aspects in Lenin very much in contrast with his cosmopolitan followers. The official party line has sponsored a "back to Lenin" movement with the result that his writings have been even more frequently quoted than before; only the quotations have changed. However, it is also true that by 1990 a stage was reached in which open attacks against Lenin and Leninism in the streets of Moscow, in the media and even the Supreme Soviet were no longer an extraordinary event.[13]

The liberals, too, have been divided: some are trying to make the historical Lenin more human. They have inaugurated a Lenin cult of their own, putting some of their own unorthodox ideas into Lenin's mouth. Other liberals, on the contrary, have pointed to the weaknesses and inconsistencies of Leninism. Lastly, the neo-Stalinists have reacted with vehement indignation against any attempt to discontinue the Lenin cult. A prominent Soviet actor suggested in a television program that the mausoleum should be closed and Lenin reburied in a suitable site. Yuri Kariakin, in a speech to the Congress of People's Deputies in June 1989, made the same suggestion. In response, the Marx-Engels-Lenin Institute reportedly received many calls to the effect "to us the mausoleum is more than sacred." The editor of Lenin's works reminded the public that workers had claimed in 1924 that it was essential that "Ilych remains with us physically." Lenin's niece, a professor of Marxism-Leninism commented: "I often go to Lenin's mausoleum. When I am with Ilych, I cannot hold back my tears. Whenever I am there, I see around me a multitude of people who have come to see a leader and person to whom everyone feels close."[14]

If feelings of this kind are still widespread (which is not certain), de-Leninization will not be sanctioned, which points to the limits of de-Stalinization even today. It is one thing for heretical intellectuals to voice unorthodox views about Lenin and even Marx; it is another, far more difficult matter for the party leadership to break with its past. True, certain basic truths have been accepted, at least by the more enlightened members of the leadership, such as the realization that revolutionary violence should not be idealized, that impatient attempts to speed up sociohistorical developments are bound to lead to disaster, and that throughout history no one ever succeeded in building a better society through violence.

On the occasion of the two hundredth anniversary of the French Revolution, a member of the Politburo was sharply critical of the practice of committing crimes in the name of a better future, referring to a "stream of blood covered with the roses of tragic illusions." A Soviet historian noted on the same occasion that the terror of the French Revolution was its undoing and that the guillotine set the rights of men back by a hundred years.[15]

But at the same time orthodox Politburo members refused even to use the phrase "Stalin's crimes"—it was always the "personality cult" to which reference was made. The orthodox complained that a campaign had been launched to slander everything dear to the hearts of the Soviet people.[16] There was the conviction among the top party leadership that de-Stalinization had gone much too far and that it ought to be stopped. Yet there were diehards like Nina Andreeva, the outspoken militant from Leningrad who had attained fame in 1988 by suggesting that "our media are slandering Stalin." Andreeva was a pioneer of the new "Russian ideology," a mixture of Stalinism and anti-Marxist views held tradition-ally by the extreme Right.[17]

For how long has the cause of socialism been set back by Stalin? Perhaps by a century or more; socialism is a concept covering a great variety of political doctrines and approaches, and as the Scandinavian experience has shown, it has not always been the road to serfdom. That a particular extremist brand of socialism failed in an underdeveloped country does not necessarily mean the final bankruptcy of all shades of socialism, just as the sad state of affairs in many Third World countries does not mean that the death knell is ringing for capitalism. Inside the Soviet Union cross currents may prevail for a long time to come: On the one hand, a violent backlash is taking place against socialism, tout court, the reaction against economic even more than political failure; the same is true for most Eastern European countries. The great majority of people want a well-functioning welfare state, life without constant shortages and standing in lines. But the ideal is not America; they cast their admiring eyes to the mixed economies of Western and northern Europe.

There is also a section of the population with a vital interest in the perpetuation of the status quo. They may no longer believe in Marxism-Leninism, but they fear that a freer political and economic system would not work in their country. The party of tradition, or order and discipline, has not fought its last battle, and the outcome of the struggle may not be clear for a long time to come. Perhaps it is true that, as one Soviet historian (M. Gefter) put it, "Stalin died only yesterday"; the emancipa-tion from Stalinism, its institutions and its mentality, is only just begin-ning. To eradicate the Stalinist heritage means a cultural revolution, changes much deeper than political and economic reform. History teaches that such revolutions are rare in the annals of mankind and that they are never accomplished in a short time.

Commenting on a documentary shown on Soviet television in 1989, a Soviet critic wrote:

How on earth could people live in the hell of Stalin's rule? But they did. They worked, built dams and factories, sang songs, danced, celebrated national holidays, starved to death, languished behind barbed wire, and praised Stalin, even as they faced the firing squad. Life went on. Some of them executed peasants, others demanded death sentences for the "enemies of the people," still others reproached themselves for failing to comprehend the grandeur of Stalin's ideas. Why did they live like this? (L. Likhodeev).

An answer has been attempted by another Soviet writer: The young generation of the 1930s accepted Stalin precisely because it was young, idealistic, and enthusiastic. It had nothing but hope and belief in its country and the ideas of a great Communist brotherhood. It was certain that the Soviet Union was in the vanguard of humanity and that the great future would come very soon. This dream was the only thing they had; it formed the essence of their lives and gave them the strength for their sacrifices and victories. And they forced themselves to accept the terror for the sake of a dream that seemed almost within reach (Anatoli Makarov).

There is truth in these words, which remind the historian of modern Germany of the idealistic and enthusiastic generation of 1933. One of them wrote in later years:

National Socialism offered all that a young man in his most secret and proudest imagination could desire—activity, responsibility for his fellows, and work with equally enthusiastic comrades for a greater and stronger fatherland. It held out official recognition and careers that had been unthinkable before; while on the other side there were only difficulties and dangers, an empty future and doubts in the heart.[18]

True, not everyone in the Soviet Union (or in Germany) was young and idealistic in the 1930s. There were not a few careerists; there were frightened people, and massive, mendacious propaganda had succeeded in the deindividualization of large sections of these generations.[19]

What, then, was Stalinism? Any definition is bound to simplify a complex phenomenon. It was the building of socialism in a single country—as Stalin understood it. But a statement of this kind raises more questions than it answers. It was the revolution from above in a relatively backward country to carry out the party program. It was the extinction of whatever inner-party democracy and popular initiative had still existed in Lenin's times. In the course of time, the style of government became more and more dictatorial and idiosyncratic and the controls from above as absolute as physically possible. The early internationalism was gradually replaced by a doctrine consisting of Communist, nationalist, and populist elements. Lastly, Stalinism was shaped to a very large degree by Stalin's sinister personality. Seen at a perspective of several decades, the achievements of the system were modest, the misery caused enormous; it will take a long time to eradicate it altogether. There can be no forgiveness for Stalin and those who helped to operate his system: To pardon the oppressor is to deal harshly with the oppressed.[20]

How will the transition from Stalinism to democracy proceed? The Soviet Union is now passing through uncharted waters, for there has been no precedent for the peaceful transformation of a totalitarian into a democratic political system. Seen in historical perspective, the transition to democracy from the much milder forms of authoritarian rule has been difficult enough. If in a totalitarian regime everything is forbidden that is not permitted *expressis verbis*, under authoritarianism everything is, broadly speaking, permitted but politics.

In what stage of development is the Soviet Union at present? In the economic sphere, the advance is unmistakable, certainly on the legislative level. In the spiritual sphere, to quote a Soviet commentator, "we have practically passed over to guided democracy during the last three years."[21]

But such freedom does not yet exist in politics. In the view of some Soviet commentators, there is yet another stage to be passed between authoritarianism and freedom, which they define as (Communist) liberalism.[22] The liberals are willing to consult the people with regard to their decisions, but they are not willing to surrender power. As far as they are concerned, everything is permitted that does not bring about a change in the power structure. Criticism is free but not independent action. Such "liberalism" is more vulnerable than its precursors and will succeed only if it defends society against the totalitarian and authoritarian temptations and fosters the growth of a democratic consciousness.

This concept of the transition to democracy seems persuasive, but it is by no means foreordained. Just as Stalinism effectively froze Soviet society for decades, it is possible that the Soviet Union may not move for a long time beyond the guided-democracy stage, an enormous advance compared with Stalinism but as yet a far cry from democracy.

How much longer will Stalin and Stalinism preoccupy us? Similar questions were asked with an undertone of impatience in Germany about Hitler and Nazism in the 1950s and 1960s. The answer surely is, as long as its last traces have not disappeared. Paradoxically, the official lack of willingness to make all the historical sources available will prolong the Stalin debate. As there is only limited access to these sources, uncertainty is bound to continue and further revelations certain to be delayed. It could well be that Stalin was innocent of some of the crimes of which he has been accused—the murder of his second wife, of Kirov, or of Ordzhonikidze. But as there can be no independent investigation under present conditions, there can be no definitive answer to these and many other questions. But it is also true that if we knew all the historical facts, the debate on motives, on alternatives, and on consequences would still continue, and the heritage of Stalin would be with us for a long time.

New Light
on the Moscow Trials

From the reports of the Politburo Commission (1989)

Introduction

Mention has been made repeatedly of the special commission appointed by the Politburo "for further study of materials pertaining to the repressions of the 1930s, 1940s, and early 1950s," to give it its full title. Reports referring to various trials were published in 1989, together with background material prepared by the party Central Control Committee and the Marx-Engels-Lenin Institute. The following excerpts from some of the most important reports cover the first and second Zinoviev-Kamenev trials (1935 and 1936), the trial of the Red Army leadership (1937), the Radek-Piatakov trial, and the Bukharin-Rykov trial (1938). These reports contain much interesting new material; they are based on documents in the archives of the Central Committee, the KGB, and the archives of various legal institutions. To a considerable extent they are based on the interrogations of surviving NKVD officials between 1956 and 1964 that were not published at the time. However, the reports leave a great many questions open, intentionally or because essential source material has disappeared. Thus, they do not shed much light on the criteria according to which Stalin and his aides selected their victims. Frequently, reference is made to torture, physical violence, threats, etc., but seldom, if ever, is it specified what kind of torture, physical or mental, was used. Such squeamishness in an official document is surprising; it is unlikely that these details were not provided when the interrogators and torturers gave evidence after Stalin's death. There seems to be no intention for the time being to give full access to, let alone to publish, the documentary evidence pertaining to the Stalinist terror. Under the circumstances, these Politburo commission reports will remain of considerable importance for all students of Soviet history even though a "digest" of this kind cannot possibly replace detailed and independent studies based on full and unfettered access.

The reports, excerpts from which appear below, were originally published in *Izvestiia Ts.K. KPSS*, 4, 5, 7, 8, and 9, 1989. Most of the material was translated by Paul S. Triolo.

The "Moscow Center"

In December 1934, there was absolutely no basis for the arrest of G. E. Zinoviev, L. B. Kamenev, and other persons implicated in the Moscow center case. Their arrest marked the beginning of the implementation of a scheme to use the assassination of Kirov to politically discredit and physically eliminate former opposition figures by charging them with organizing, preparing, and executing this crime. The charge that the former members of the "Zinovievist" opposition planned and organized the murder of Kirov was based on the fact that the murderer, L. V. Nikolaev, had allegedly been a partisan of Zinoviev's at one time. Yet there were no documentary or other materials that supported this contention. The notion that Nikolaev belonged to the Zinovievist opposition came from Stalin. It was conceived and brought to life through an investigation and trial as a result of direct pressure on his part. Appearing at the February–March 1937 Central Committee plenum, in his concluding remarks, N. I. Yezhov reported on the conditions under which the investigation of Kirov's murder was continuing and how at the initiative of Stalin the investigation was directed along the lines of charging the former members of the Zinovievist opposition in this crime. An excerpt from this speech (quoted from an unofficial record) follows:

YEZHOV: Now, Comrades, permit me to make several remarks. Would it have been possible to prevent the murder of Comrade Kirov based on materials and information that we have? I assert that it would have been. The blame in this matter lies wholly with us.

Would it have been possible after the murder of Comrade Kirov and during the investigation to expose the Trotskyist-Zinovievist center? It would have. We did not expose them; we overlooked them. The fault in this case is mine personally; they evaded me, deceived me. I had no experience; I did not even have a whiff of it.

First, Comrade Stalin began, as I now recall, and called Kosarev and me and said, "Look for the assassin among the Zinovievists." I should say that the Chekists did not believe this and in any case were looking elsewhere, along the lines of a foreign source.

Second, I am not excluding that based on precisely this line, it was necessary to collect all the material available to the secret-political section and all the intelligence, because it provided a direction, contained many facts, and with regard to which it would have then been possible to expose and prove the direct participation of Zinoviev and Kamenev in the murder of Comrade Kirov. These materials were not seized upon.

It is not by chance, it seems to me, that the first time it was quite difficult to repair relations with the Chekists under our control. They did not want to give evidence for the investigation. Comrade Stalin had to interfere in this affair. Comrade Stalin called Yagoda and said, "Take care, we will muzzle you."

What was the result? The result concerning the case of Kirov, then, due to narrow bureaucratic considerations—and here and there, for some people, due to political considerations, for example, Molchanov—was that we had such preconceived notions. The bureaucratic considerations indicate that, first, the CC suddenly gave control to organs of the Cheka. People could not in any way stomach this. And a large fraction of the fault for the fact that the center was not exposed then and for the murder of Kirov lies at the feet of these narrow-minded bureaucratic antiparty workers, even though they are staunch Chekists. . . .

In addition, in a confrontation between Bukharin and Radek in the Central Committee on January 13, 1937, in the presence of Stalin, Bukharin stated that on the second day after the assassination of Kirov, Stalin called him and L. Z. Mekhlis and told them that the murderer Nikolaev was a Zinovievist. Stalin did not deny that this meeting took place and only clarified that the conversation had occurred upon his return from Leningrad, where he had gone to head a commission investigating the circumstances of Kirov's assassination. However, there was no objective information concerning Nikolaev's membership in a Zinovievist opposition, and Stalin's assertion was unsubstantiated. Nevertheless, on December 8, 1934, arrests began of former Zinovievists implicated in the case. Kamenev and Zinoviev were arrested on December 14, 1934.

A letter from Zinoviev to Stalin, written during a search of his apartment, testifies to the fact that this new arrest was totally unexpected, because they did not feel any sort of guilt. The text of the letter follows.

At present (December 16 at 7:30 P.M.) Comrade Molchanov and a group of Chekists have come to my apartment and are conducting a search.

I tell you, Comrade Stalin, honestly, from the time when by instruction of the Central Committee I returned from Kustanai, I did not take a single step, did not say a single word, did not write a single stroke, did not have a single thought, that I would keep from the party, from the Central Committee, or from you personally. I thought only of one thing: how to earn the confidence of the Central Committee and your personal confidence and what to do so that you would put me to work in some way.

I have nothing besides the old archives (all that has been accumulated over more than thirty years, including the opposition years), and there can be nothing else.

I am guilty of nothing, nothing, nothing before the party, before the Central Committee, and before you personally. I swear to you by all that may only be held sacred for a Bolshevik, I swear to you by the memory of Lenin.

I cannot imagine that there could be suspicions against me. I implore you to believe this, on my word of honor. I have been shaken to the depths of my soul.

This letter of Zinoviev's was sent to Stalin by Yagoda. Stalin left it unanswered. At the time, Stalin had already advanced the version blaming Kirov's assassination on Zinovievists. In Leningrad, Moscow, and other cities there were mass arrests of former members of the Zinovievist opposition.

Stalin closely monitored the investigation on the case of the Moscow Center, receiving a daily copy of the proceedings for the interrogations of those who had been arrested and accounts concerning the depositions of defendants at court sittings, and he listened to the reports of Yezhov, Agranov, Vyshinsky, and others who were conducting the investigation on the case; they submitted the texts of the most important and crucial documents to him for approval.

Starting with the version that Nikolaev belonged to the Zinovievist opposition, the NKVD operatives, deputy procurator of the U.S.S.R.

Andrei Vyshinsky, and the investigator dealing with the most important cases, procurator of the U.S.S.R. L. R. Sheynin, all took part in an investigation of these matters, and then individuals at the Supreme Court of the U.S.S.R,. who had considered the cases, started down the road of falsification and distortion of the real facts and circumstances, artificially associating the tragic event of Kirov's murder with the imaginary anti-Soviet activity of the former Zinovievist opposition, activity allegedly carried out under the leadership of a center located in Moscow.

As a result of an examination of materials in party archives and the archives of organs of the KGB, no data were discovered concerning the fact that Nikolaev had joined with any sort of opposition group, including a Zinoviev group.

As is well known, according to the initial plan, Zinoviev and Kamenev were to be tried in a single case along with Nikolaev and others. However, the effort to establish a link between the cases was not successful. On February 3, 1935, at a strategy session, the deputy head of the NKVD, Ya. S. Agranov, concerning the course of the investigation of the cases that had arisen in connection with the murder of Kirov, stated: "We have not succeeded in proving that the 'Moscow center' knew about the preparation for the terrorist act against Comrade Kirov."

Further falsification of the case occurred at the court session. The trial was held using a simplified procedure. The defendants did not have their rights explained to them. The court personnel did not carry through the functions of justice because the nature of the crimes of the defendants and the type of punishment to be administered had been determined beforehand. The defendants were required, "for the purpose of strengthening party unity," to come forward publicly for self-exposure and confess to the anti-Soviet activity of all members of the former Zinovievist opposition.

The former NKVD official A. I. Katsaf, who escorted Kamenev to the trial, indicated during an interview in 1956 that in his presence, immediately prior to the opening of the court session, an aide to the head of the secret-political section of the NKVD, A. F. Rutkovsky, who had conducted the investigation of the case, turned to Kamenev with the following words: "Lev Borisovich, believe me, your life will be spared if you corroborate your depositions in court." To this Kamenev replied that he was guilty of nothing. Rutkovsky then said to him: "Consider this. You will be heard by the whole world. This is necessary for the world." Apparently, therefore, Kamenev declared in court: "This is not a juridical process but a political process." A. S. Kuklin said to the court: "Before yesterday I did not know that I really was a member of the center. It was only yesterday that I heard from Zinoviev that I was a member of the center." None of the other defendants gave concrete facts in their depositions, facts that would have provided a basis for their confession of guilt in the conduct of underground anti-Soviet activity.

Hence, all those charged in the case of the so-called Moscow center, who in the past had been members of the Trotskyist-Zinovievist opposition, had, by the time of their arrest in December 1934, broken with it, and the party organs and organs of the NKVD had no information available concerning either their anti-Soviet or antiparty activity.

It has been established that the "Moscow counterrevolutionary Zinovievist organization" and the Moscow center never existed. In the period between 1928 and 1932, the accused had maintained personal connections and during meetings had held discussions on political questions; in a number of cases they had expressed critical opinions about the difficulties the country was experiencing and, in relation to the measures taken by the party and government, had also manifested hostile attitudes toward certain party and government leaders, particularly Stalin. These conversations do not constitute a crime.

The notion that the murder of Kirov was carried out by members of the Zinovievist opposition was put forward by Stalin in order to take reprisals against the former opposition figures, primarly the Zinovievists. In connection with this, the NKVD organs unlawfully arrested Zinoviev, Kamenev, and other individuals who in the past had shared the views of the opposition. In attempting to prove the participation of the latter in the assassination of Kirov, the investigatory and judicial personnel falsified materials of the inquiry and permitted the most grave breaches of legality in the process of the preliminary and judicial investigation. As a result of this, all the defendants in this case groundlessly confessed their guilt and were condemned.

The CPSU CC Politburo Commission Dealing with Additional Study of Materials Associated with Repressions That Occurred in the Period of the 1930s and 1940s and the Beginning of the 1950s:

The "Anti-Soviet Union"

From this time on, the investigation of the Trotskyists took a new direction. Active work began on the fabrication of a case concerning the "union of the Trotskyist-Zinovievist center." How it was conducted and who directed it may be discerned from the appearance of Deptuy NKVD Director Ya. S. Agranov before a meeting of the most active members of the NKVD that was held March 19–21, 1937 (quoting here from an unofficial record):

AGRANOV: I want to discuss the matter of how the investigation dealing with the Trotskyist-Zinovievist terrorist center can be successfully set on a reliable track.

Yagoda and Molchanov have taken an incorrect antiparty line in this matter. Molchanov has definitely attempted to curtail this case, as in April of 1936 he was still stubbornly contending that the exposure of the terrorist group of Shemelev, Safonov, and Olberg, associated with I. N. Smirnov, could be limited, that this was in fact the Trotskyist center, while all the others had no relation to this matter. . . . Molchanov tried to discredit and slow down investigations dealing with the matter of terrorist organizations that had been exposed by the Leningrad and Moscow directorates. . . .

In this situation, the complete disclosure and liquidation of the Trotskyist gang would have been frustrated had it not been for the interference of the Central Committee (Stalin) in the case. He intervened in the following manner. . . . On my return after illness, Yezhov summoned me to his dacha. It must be said that this meeting had a conspiratorial air. Yezhov passed on Stalin's instructions on the errors permitted by the investigation on the matter of the Trotskyist center and instructed me to take measures in order to expose the Trotskyist center and clearly reveal the unexposed Trotskyist gang and the personal role of Trotsky in this matter. Yezhov raised the question in such a way that either he himself would call a strategy meeting or would interfere with me in this matter. Yezhov's instructions were concrete and give a correct initial thread to the disclosure of the matter.

It is precisely due to the measures taken on the basis of these instructions of Stalin and Yezhov that the Zinovievist-Trotskyist center was exposed. However, the development of the investigation on the basis of new information has been far from smooth. First of all, there is the blind but stubborn resistance of Molchanov, who has tried to curtail this case. It was necessary to refer to very important materials that were possessed by the NKVD directorate for the Moscow oblast in connection with the depositions of Dreytser, Pikel, and E. (Esterman). This made it possible to shift the investigation onto new tracks.

In fact, after the conversation that took place between Yezhov and Agranov, the latter personally took part in investigatory work on the creation of a case dealing with the "united center." On July 23, 1936, Agranov, in the presence of the responsible NKVD operatives A. P. Radzivilovsky, G. M. Yakubovich, and P. Sh. Simanovsky, personally conducted a reinterrogation of two previously arrested individuals, the former Trotskyist E. A. Dreytser and the former Zinovievist P. V. Pikel, and managed to obtain from them "depositions" concerning the fact that the united center of Trotskyists and Zinovievists was formed on the basis of terror.

That the depositions obtained by Agranov from Dreytser and Pikel were false and forced is indicated by the statements apropos of this by Agranov himself and by the deputy head of the NKVD directorate for the Moscow oblast, A. P. Radzivilovsky.

In a declaration in the name of Yezhov on December 20, 1936, Radzivilovsky reported that the Trotskyist E. A. Dreytser had been brought to Moscow for interrogation in May 1936, while the Zinovievist P. V. Pikel was arrested somewhat later. Here Radzivilovsky writes: "Exceptionally heavy work over the course of three weeks on Dreytser and Pikel led to a situation wherein they began to provide depositions." When the depositions of Dreytser and Pikel were reported to Yagoda, he, as Agranov reported in 1937, wrote "untrue" on the depositions concerning the existence of a Moscow Trotskyist-Zinovievist center, while on the depositions concerning the fact the Dreytser had allegedly received a directive from Trotsky dealing with the murder of party and government leaders, he wrote "falsehood" or simply "false." Yezhov also spoke of this at the February–March 1937 Central Committee plenum, when he declared that Yagoda considered the depositions of Dreytser, Frits-David, M. I. Lurie, and all others to be rubbish and wrote on the proceedings of the interrogations: "rubbish," "nonsense," and "impossible."

Despite the manifest groundlessness of the depositions obtained from Dreytser and Pikel, they were used as the basis for the creation of a case on the united center. As Agranov reported, "This made it possible, by including a number of new operatives in the investigation, to put the case on new tracks." Shortly after this, the investigation "obtained" the necessary confessional depositions from all the accused.

The appearance of Yezhov at the February–March Central Committee plenum in 1937 also testifies to the circumstances concerning the appearance of the case on the united Trotskyist-Zinovievist center presented above. There he stated (quoted from an unofficial record):

YEZHOV: When the investigation of this case had just begun . . .
STALIN: What case?
YEZHOV: The case involving the exposure of the Trotskyist-Zinovievist united center, which began at the end of December 1935. (The first report was in 1935.) In 1936 it began to expand somewhat, and then material was first presented to the Central Committee, and as a matter of fact, the real purpose in presenting these materials to the Central Committee, as is now being revealed, was, since they were on the trail of an emissary of Trotsky, and then discovered the center in the person of Shemelev, Esterman, and others, the purpose was to generally curtail this case. Comrade Stalin correctly realized that there was something wrong in this case and gave instructions to continue it and, in particular, had the Central Committee appoint me to monitor the investigation. I had the chance to observe the entire conduct of the investigation and must say that all along Molchanov attempted to limit the investigation: He tried to represent Shemelev and Olberg as lone emissaries and to conduct and conclude the proceedings or trial only on this basis. Completely impermissible was that all the depositions that had been given to the Moscow oblast [NKVD] by Dreytser, Pikel, and Esterman, namely, the principle instigators, were completely ignored, and the discussions involved such things as: How is Dreytser linked with Trotsky? What is his connection with Sedovy, with Berlin? What nonsense, what rubbish, etc. In a word, the discussions were undertaken in this spirit, and nobody wanted to link

either Dreytser, Esterman, or Pikel with this entire matter. Such were the sentiments.

Appearing at the above-mentioned meeting of the most active members of the NKVD, Yezhov indicated that the arrests of these persons had occurred in the absence of materials on their criminal activity and that "the investigation was forced to be limited by the fact that it put pressure on the person arrested and squeezed information from him." And, as he expressed it, those who were arrested "were forced to be dissidents."

It has been established that during NKVD investigations unlawful coercive measures were used against those arrested for the purpose of obtaining confessions of criminal activity. The methods used by the investigators in the interrogations and the means used to obtain false depositions have become evident from the numerous declarations that the arrested individuals wrote during the investigations.

Thus, after his first two interrogations, on Janaury 27, 1936, V. P. Olberg wrote the following declaration to the investigator:

> After your last interrogation of January 25, I was seized by a terrible and agonizing fear of death. Today I have calmed down somewhat. It seems that I could slander myself and do everything if only it would put an end to the torture. But I am obviously unable to slander myself and state a deliberate falsehood, namely, that I am a Trotskyist, an emissary of Trotsky, etc. I arrived in the Soviet Union on my own initiative; now, in prison I understand that this was madness, a crime. I bitterly regret it. I am unhappy not only for myself but for my wife and my brother. Now I understand just how wrong this step was, namely, my arrival in the U.S.S.R. through false information and the concealment of my Trotskyist past.

On the following day, Olberg returned with a new declaration in which he stated: "I beg you to summon me today. Among other questions, I want to give the names of people who could confirm my innocence of the incriminating charges."

No examination was done of these declarations, and they were kept secret from the court. Olberg began to confess his guilt to all the subsequent charges brought against him during the interrogations.

On May 8, 1936, as a sign of protest against the investigatory methods, I. N. Smirnov announced a hunger strike, which lasted thirteen days.

V. A. Ter-Vaganyan, protesting against his groundless arrest, twice announced hunger strikes and then cut his own finger and wrote in blood: "Comrade Berman, I beg you to send all my letters to Stalin and Yagoda. Having lost hope that you will keep your word, I will stop drinking for 12 hours." In the letter to Stalin he wrote that he had decided to end his life by suicide:

> I am charged with using terror. They charge me with participating in the preparations of terrorist groups based on the depositions of people who directly participated in this affair. These people are guilty of slander, base, vile and brazen slander; their slander is easy to see through, it does not require great effort to reveal it, and the motive of the creators of this lie is transparent. Nevertheless! I am powerless against this blatant false-hood. . . . I swear, by the sacred memory of Lenin, I have never had any relationship with terrorist speeches or the affairs of counterrevolutionary bandits and cannibals. . . .

This letter of Ter-Vaganyan's was not brought to the notice of the court, and on August 10, 1936, after a review of the accusatory findings, nine days prior to the start of the trial proceedings, Stalin included Ter-Vaganyan among those accused in the proceedings as being one of the active organizers of the united Trotskyist-Zinovievist center.

A. N. Safonova, the former wife of I. N. Smirnov, who appeared in this case as a witness (she was later convicted for Trotskyist activity), in her explanation on June 14, 1956, to the U.S.S.R. KGB and U.S.S.R. procurator, reported that she and the others accused gave false depositions during the investigation and during the trial. She points out that during the interrogations NKVD operatives used methods of moral coercion and demanded depositions on criminal activity, which were allegedly re-quired in the interests of the party. Safonova said that "we were obligated to the chief [Stalin] to answer for the murder of Kirov, we had to provide false depositions, not only I, but all the others who had been accused." Along with this, she reported that the investigator threatened her by declaring that if she persisted in refusing to provide a deposition he would see to it that her sister was arrested and her children exiled and would use methods of physical coercion on her. The investigator, reported Safo-nova, stated that she must corroborate the depositions that she had given regardless of whether they were true or not, because that was what the party required. "Hence, in the preliminary investigation," wrote Safonova, "and in the trial this was reinforced by the presence of foreign correspondents, and all of us, realizing that the latter could use our statements to harm the Soviet state, could not speak the truth."

As a result of the investigators' actions, declared Safonova, her depositions, and also the depositions of S. V. Mrachkovsky, G. E. Zinoviev, L. B. Kamenev, G. E. Evdokimov, and V. A. Ter-Vaganyan, which they had given in a previous investigation and at the trial, were 90 percent inaccurate.

The methods that were used by the investigator are strikingly clear from a declaration of L. A. Shatskin, written on October 22, 1936, to Stalin. Shatskin was arrested on the charge of belonging to the united Trotskyist-Zinovievist center. In the declaration he stated that he had been presented with the very serious charge of participation in a terrorist conspiracy, a charge of which he was innocent. Shatskin wrote:

> Not disputing the legality of the suspicions of the investigator and realizing that the investigation could not take my word for it, I always considered, that the investigation should carefully and objectively verify the available, and in the words of the investigation, the proper, depositions. In fact, the investigation deprived me of even the elementary possibility of refuting the false depositions. The leitmotif of the investigations was: "We will compel you to confess to terror, and if you refuse, you will depart this world."

Later, Shatskin writes:

> Here is how they interrogated me. My principle investigator, Gendin, composed a four-page text of my deposition on terror. (He included in it conversations between myself and Lominadze, about which he had nothing, including false information; there could be no information.) In the case of a refusal to sign this deposition, I was threatened with being shot without a trial or, after the fifteen-minute formal meeting with the Military Board in the office of the investigator, during which I was to be limited to only the one-word answers yes and no, with organized beating in the criminal chamber of the Butyrsky prison, with the use of torture, and with the banishment of my mother and sister to the Kolmsk region. Two times I was not allowed to sleep through the night "until you sign." Moreover, during one solid twelve-hour interrogation at night, the investigator commanded: "Wake up, open your eyes!" and brandished his fists in front of

my face. "Wake up! Take the pen! Sign!" etc. I by no means cite these facts in order to protest against them from the point of view of abstract humanism, but I wish only to state that with such measures, after several dozen interrogations, the greater part of which were devoted to cursing, a human being may be reduced to such a state that it is possible for false depositions to emerge. More importantly, however, of the interrogations: The investigator demands the signing of the deposition in the name of the party and in the interests of the party.

By the fall of 1936, falsifications of the interrogation proceedings became more brazen. A system of composing show records of proceedings was introduced: After a number of interrogations, a record was drawn up in the absence of the person who had been arrested; it was printed on a typewriter and in this form was given to the accused to sign. On March 3, 1937, at the Central Committee plenum, Yezhov declared (quoting from an unofficial verbatim record): "I should directly state that such a practice did exist: first a record of the proceedings was given to the accused to sign; it had first been reviewed by the investigator and then transferred to the authorities at a higher level, and important records of proceedings even reached the people's commissar. The people's commissar issued instructions and stated that it was necessary to record things in a certain manner, and then the records were given to the accused to sign."

All the investigators were obliged to become familiar with a large quantity of confessional depositions on terror and on this basis to form their own "correct consciousness." A conception of terror was "hammered" into the consciousness of all the workers. Systematic suggestions concerning the danger, allegedly on all sides, threatening the life of Stalin created a tense situation that grew with each passing day. Yezhov directly conducted monitoring for the investigation on the case of the united center, went to interrogations, and as they said at the time, "tightened the screws." Those who were arrested were subjected to long periods of nighttime interrogation. At the persistent demand of Yezhov, an investigation was not to be carried out using "kid gloves," and he insisted that one should "not stand on ceremony with the Trotskyists."

In fact, A. Ya. Vyshinsky played a provocative role during the investigation of cases. At the meetings, manifesting the utmost severity in relation to the investigators, he was called upon to obtain direct depositions from those arrested. During an analysis of the depositions he required more strict political conclusions and generalizations, and in essence, the falsification of cases.

The "Parallel Center"

For political reprisals against objectionable individuals it was not sufficient for Stalin to falsify the accusations against them. It was important that the Soviet people and world public opinion should believe unquestioningly in these charges. The open trials served this purpose; those accused had to confess to the most monstrous crimes against their party and country. In the offices of the NKVD investigation, detailed scenarios were worked out for the behavior of the accused in court. They were frequently indoctrinated with the idea that by unmasking themselves they would help the party in its struggle against international Trotskyism and against the designs of domestic and foreign enemies. And it ought to be said that many of the accused eventually accepted these "rules of the game" and behaved according to the scenario that had been worked out. In this regard, Karl Radek's letter to his wife is quite characteristic.

Knowing that the letter would be read by the interrogators (who may have dictated it in the first place), Radek quite transparently gave to understand what was the true value of the "unexpected" and "intolerable" admissions that he had to "confirm" in court. A draft of this letter has been preserved in the archives; it is dated January 20, 1937:

> During the next few days there will be the trial against the Zinoviev-Trotsky organization. I have asked for a meeting with you so that what will happen in court should not come as a shock to you. Listen to what I shall tell you and don't ask any questions. I have admitted that I was a member of the center, that I participated in terrorist activities and about links with the German and Japanese governments, and shall confirm this in court. It is useless for you to say that such admissions could not be extracted from me by either violence or promises. You know that at the price of such admissions I would not buy my life. . . . It means that this is the truth. If this truth is intolerable as far as you are concerned, then try to remember me as you knew me.
>
> But you have no reason or the right to put any doubt whatsoever concerning the truth as it will be established by the court. If you think it over carefully, you will understand that in view of what will happen in court,

and in particular the international part of the revelations, I had no right to hide the truth from the world. Whatever will happen in court, you ought to live. If I shall live, you will have to help me. If I shall die then you will have to help the country through some useful work. But you should know that whatever happens, I never felt as closely linked to the cause of the proletariat as I do now. . . .*

In the CPSU Central Committee Politburo Commission for Further Study of Materials Pertaining to the Repressions of the 1930s and Early 1950s:

The "Military Organization"

The affair of the "military people"—that is how the world press described the trial of military leaders in the Red Army that took place in the summer of 1937 in Moscow—had far-reaching and tragic consequences. The mass repressions in the army conducted by J. V. Stalin and his entourage on the eve of World War II inflicted great harm on the Soviet armed forces and the entire defense capability of the Soviet state.

The internal political situation in the country during the latter half of the 1930s and the exacerbation and extension of the repressions were rooted in J. V. Stalin's suspicions regarding the major military leaders whose authority among the people and in the army had been supreme ever since civil war times. Their deep professionalism, independence of opinion, and their criticism of those promoted by J. V. Stalin, namely, K. Ye. Voroshilov, S. M. Budennyy, G. I. Kulik, Ye. A. Shchadenko, and others who failed to understand the need to create a modern army, caused irritation, suspicion, and definite misgivings that the army might waver in support of the course that he—Stalin—might pursue. Hence, his desire to remove all the waverers from the army, all those who caused J. V. Stalin and his entourage even the slightest doubts.

The "discovery" by NKVD organs during the latter half of the 1930s of a so-called anti-Soviet Trotskyite military organization was totally unexpected by the Soviet people, who were accustomed to seeing M. N. Tukhachevsky, I. E. Yakir, I. P. Uborevich, and others as major military

* *Izvestiia Ts.K. KPSS*, 9, 1989, pp. 42–43.

leaders of the glorious Red Army whose names were known to everyone.

Most military people of various rank and position who were declared enemies of the people had rendered great services to the land of the Soviets and the Communist party. Many of them had participated in the Great October Socialist Revolution, been active fighters for Soviet power, selflessly defended it during the years of foreign intervention and civil war, and had fought in the ranks of the Red Guards and Red Army since they had been created. Most of them had trod the path from organizers and commanders of independent units and formations to commanders of armies and fronts, had grown into major political and headquarters workers, and become the pride of the Soviet armed forces.

During the latter half of 1936 the arrests started among command personnel of the Red Army. Under the leadership of and with the direct involvement of N. I. Yezhov, NKVD organs started actively to gather various provocative testimony against a number of military leaders. Thus, from the deputy director of the Chelyabinsk "Magnezit" Plant, E. A. Dreytser, to chief of construction on the Karaganda-Balkash railroad line, S. V. Mrachkovsky, to chief of the cotton administration in South Kazakastan, I. I. Reyngold, and other former "participants" of the so-called parallel Trotskyite center, testimony was "extracted" about the existence of a military Trotskyite organization in the army. According to that testimony, the group included, in particular, the deputy commander of the Leningrad Military District, V. M. Primakov, and the Soviet military attaché, V. K. Putna. All this testimony—extremely contradictory and not exactly instilling trust—was obtained by using unlawful methods.

Arrested on August 14, 1936, Corps Commander V. M. Primakov had been held in the Lefortovo prison in Moscow for nine months; he refused to admit that he was guilty. Several statements from V. M. Primakov are preserved in J. V. Stalin's archives, in which he protested his illegal arrest. However, V. M. Primakov was unable to withstand the cruel ordeal, and on May 8, 1937, in the Lefortovo prison, he wrote the following statement to N. I. Yezhov:

> For 9 months I have refused to speak about the affair of the Trotskyite counterrevolutionary organization. In this refusal I have resorted to such insolence that even in the Politburo before Comrade Stalin I continued to refuse to speak and tried in every possible way to mitigate my guilt. Com-

rade Stalin was right when he said "Primakov is a coward, for to refuse to speak in such a matter is cowardice." In fact, for my part this was cowardice and false shame for the purpose of deception. I now state that when I returned from Japan in 1930, I made contact with Dreytser and Putna with Mrachkovsky and started Trotskyite work about which I shall provide full testimony for the investigation.

It can been seen from this document that J. V. Stalin himself took park in the interrogation of V. M. Primakov, and yielding to the solicitations of the investigation and pressure from J. V. Stalin, V. M. Primakov set out on the path of deception and self-slander. Already at the interrogation on May 14, 1937, naming his "accomplices," he had reported the following about I. E. Yakir: "The Trotskyite organization thought that Yakir was most suitable for the post of people's commissar to replace Voroshilov. . . . They thought that Yakir was a strictly clandestine Trotskyite and allowed that he, Yakir, was linked personally with Trotsky and would possibly carry out top-secret independent tasks unknown to us."

Continuing the "treatment" on V. M. Primakov on May 21, 1937, the NKVD organs managed to obtain from him "his own testimony" that M. N. Tukhachevsky, who had links with L. D. Trotsky, led the conspiracy. In addition, at this interrogation, V. M. Primakov named forty eminent Soviet workers as participants in a military Trotskyite plot in the army. In particular, he offered testimony that compromised eminent military figures such as B. M. Shaposhnikov, S. S. Kamenev, Ya. B. Gamarnik, P. Ye. Dybenko, S. P. Uritsky, and others.

Corps commander V. K. Putna was arrested and subjected to a night of torture and interrogation. On May 14, 1937, he was transferred from the prison hospital at the Butyrka prison to the Lefortovo prison, where he was interrogated throughout the night. As a result, V. K. Putna provided testimony about M. N. Tukhachevsky and other eminent military workers as participants in a military anti-Soviet Trotskyite organization.

The methods by which this kind of "testimony" had been obtained became known later. In his examination in the procurator's office on June 3, 1955, former NKVD worker V. I. Budarev testified that during the period of the investigation of the cases of V. M. Primakov and V. K. Putna it was known to him that those persons offered testimony about their involvement in a plot after they had been beaten in the Lefortovo prison and that he himself, on instructions from A. A. Avseyevich [an associate of the NKVD Special Section—editors's note], had sat for hours with V. M. Primakov, preventing him from sleeping, and that he was still doing this before V. M. Primakov admitted his guilt.

In December 1962 the former U.S.S.R. deputy minister of state security N. N. Selivansky reported in the CPSU Central Committee as follows: In April 1937 the Putna and Primakov cases were passed to Avseyevich. Using brutal and cruel interrogation methods Avseyevich forced Primakov and Putna to provide testimony about Tukhachevsky, Yakir and Feldman. The testimony of Putna and Primakov served as the foundation for the arrest in May 1937 of Tukhachevsky, Yakir, Feldman and other major military workers.

In his explanation to the CPSU Central Committee in 1962 A. A. Avseyevich, who had conducted the interrogations of V. M. Primakov and V. K. Putna, said: "Like many other associates, I had to work within the NKVD Special Section during 1937 and 1938, that is, during the period of the mass arrests of military workers, and take part in the interrogations, and also in the beatings of those arrested. . . . At the interrogations Leplevsky (the chief of the U.S.S.R. NKVD Special Section) formulated the questions and answers, and then the names of those whom Primakov had named were inserted in the record.

"Primakov's testimony about a large group of military workers was formulated in this way."

New arrests of eminent military workers took place in mid-May 1937. Those arrested included the chief of the Frunze Academy, Army Commander 2nd Rank A. I. Kork, and Corps Commander B. M. Feldman, who had been appointed deputy commander of the Moscow Military District.

During the first interrogations of A. I. Kork, who was arrested on the night of May 14, 1937, he denied involvement in anti-Soviet activity, but on May 16 his resistance was broken, and he signed two statements addressed to N. I. Yezhov. A. I. Kork reported that he had been recruited into a rightist organization by A. S. Yenukidze* and that the military rightist organization also included a Trotskyite military group made up of Putna, Primakov, and Turovsky.† M. N. Tukhachevsky was supposedly also connected with the rightist organization. A. I. Kork wrote further

---

*A. S. Yenukidze worked as a U.S.S.R. secretary.
†S. A. Turovsky was an army inspector.

that the group's main task was to effect a military coup in the Kremlin and that he led a military organization of rightists headquarters people for the coup made up of himself (A. I. Kork) along with M. N. Tukhachevsky and V. K. Putna.

Corps Commander B. M. Feldman was arrested on May 15, 1937. In his statement he requested that he be able to familiarize himself with the available material in the investigation, and he expressed his readiness to provide testimony concerning that material.

When he presented the record of the interrogation to J. V. Stalin, V. M. Molotov, K. Ye. Voroshilov, and L. M. Kaganovich on May 20, 1937, N. I. Yezhov asked them to discuss the question of the arrest of "the remaining participants in the plot" named by B. M. Feldman.

The "remaining participants in the plot" who had not been arrested at that time were M. N. Tukhachevsky, I. E. Yakir, R. P. Eydeman, and other commanders. They were arrested after May 20. In the records of B. M. Feldman's interrogations on May 19, 21, and 23, 1937, more than forty army commanders and politial workers were named as participants in the military Trotskyite organization.

M. N. Tukhachevsky was arrested on May 22, 1937, the same day as the chairman of the Society for Assistance to the Defense, Aviation and Chemical Construction of the U.S.S.R. [Osoviakhim] Central Council, R. P. Eydeman. I. E. Yakir was arrested on May 28; I. P. Uborevich, on May 29.

The arrests of M. N. Tukhachevsky and I. E. Yakir were preceded by measures along the line of the People's Commissariat of Defense. They were basically as follows.

On May 9, 1937, K. Ye. Voroshilov sent a letter to the All-Union Communist Party (of Bolsheviks) Politburo confirming new appointments. On May 10, 1937, the All-Union Communist Party (of Bolsheviks) Politburo adopted the following: "The following appointments are confirmed: (1) marshal of the Soviet Union Comrade A. I. Yegorov as first deputy people's commissar of defense; (2) commander of the Leningrad Military District Commander 1st Rank Comrade Shaposhnikov as RKKA chief of General Staff; (3) commander of the Kiev Military District Army Commander 1st Rank Comrade I. E. Yakir as commander of the Leningrad military district. . . . (8) marshal of the Soviet Union Comrade M. N. Tukhachevsky as commander of the Volga Military District, relieving him of his duties as deputy people's commissar of defense."

On May 13, 1937, the above was entered into the record book, and J. V. Stalin personally received Marshal M. N. Tukhachevsky in the Kremlin. No material can be found in the archives concerning the conversation between J. V. Stalin and M. N. Tukhachevsky.

There is no adequate data on how M. N. Tukhachevsky comported himself on the first day of his interrogation by the NKVD. Either no record was kept of M. N. Tukhachevsky's first interrogation, or they were destroyed during the investigation. However, individual documents from the investigation that have been preserved indicate that during the initial stage of the investigation M. N. Tukhachevsky denied involvement in a plot.

A statement by B. M. Feldman may serve as confirmation of M. N. Tukhachevsky's behavior during this period; Feldman said that M. N. Tukhachevsky denied everything. There is also a statement from M. N. Tukhachevsky dated May 26, 1937, about confrontations with V. M. Primakov, V. K. Putna, and B. M. Feldman.

Archive materials from the investigation show that the behavior of M. N. Tukhachevsky, that is, denying involvement in a plot, was very short-lived. Every measure was applied to break his resistance. The investigation of M. N. Tukhachevsky was led directly by N. I. Yezhov, and the interrogators used were G. M. Leplevsky, Z. M. Ushakov, and others.

On May 29, 1937, N. I. Yezhov interrogated M. N. Tukhachevsky. As a result of that interrogation, "direct testimony" was obtained from M. N. Tukhachevsky: "Back in 1928 I was recruited by Yenukidze into a rightist organization. In 1934 I had personal contacts with Bukharin, and I had espionage links with the Germans from 1925, when I traveled to Germany for training and maneuvers. . . . During a trip to London in 1936, Putna arranged a meeting for me with Sedov [the son of L. D. Trotsky— editor's note]. . . . I maintained clandestine links with Feldman, S. S. Kamenev, Yakir, Eydeman, Yenukidze, Bukharin, Karakhan, Pyatakov, I. N. Smirnov, Yagoda, Osipyan, and a number of others."

During the process of studying the M. N. Tukhachevsky case, brownish spots were found on some individual pages of his testimony. The conclusion of the U.S.S.R. Ministry of Defense Military Medical Administration Central Forensic Medical Laboratory of June 28, 1956, states the following: "Blood was found in the spots and smears on pages 165 and 166 of case file no. 967581. . . . Some of the blood spots are in the shape of an exclamation mark. Blood spots of this shape are usually found when blood drips from a subject when moving or when blood drips onto a surface at an angle. . . ."

Corps Commander R. P. Eydeman, arrested on May 22, 1937, simultaneously with M. N. Tukhachevsky, was taken to the internal prison of the U.S.S.R. NKVD and on the following day was transferred to the Lefortovo prison. On May 25 a statement appeared from R. P. Eydeman addressed to N. I. Yezhov in which he reported his agreement "to help in the investigation" to discover crimes. To judge from its outward appearance (the uneven handwriting and the gaps in the letters and words), this statement was written in a state of nervous shock.

At his examination on July 4, 1956, in the procurator's office, former deputy chief of an NKVD section Ya. L. Karpeysky testified that he had taken part in the investigation in the R. P. Eydeman case. He explained that in addition to himself, G. M. Leplevsky and V. S. Agas had also interrogated R. P. Eydeman and that "with regard to Eydeman, before my arrival threats and even physical measures had been used to influence him. It should be taken into account that during Eydeman's interrogation peoples' cries and groans and noise could be heard from neighboring cells. . . .

"After a day or two I . . . summoned Eydeman for an interrogation in the Lefortovo prison. This time Eydeman behaved somewhat strangely, responded to the questions in an irrelevant manner, listlessly, and was distracted by extraneous thoughts, and when he heard the sound of a running motor, Eydeman said: 'Aircraft, aircraft.' I did not write up the record of the interrogation but later reported that Eydeman was in a strange state and that his testimony should be verified. . . . After that Agas interrogated him."

On May 30, 1937, a confrontation was arranged between A. I. Kork and I. P. Uborevich, who had allegedly joined a rightist-Trotskyite organization. Objecting to A. I. Kork, I. P. Uborevich stated the following: "I categorically deny that. It is all lies from start to finish. I never had any conversations whatever with Kork about counterrevolutionary organizations."

But I. P. Uborevich's "direct testimony" was absolutely essential, and this testimony was dragged out of him by force. Former U.S.S.R. NKVD worker A. A. Avseyevich gave evidence as follows: "In May 1937, at one of the meetings, the aide to the section chief, Ushakov, told Leplevsky that Uborevich was unwilling to offer testimony. At the meeting, Leplevsky ordered Ushakov to use physical methods on Uborevich."

Soon after that, I. P. Uborevich signed two statements addressed to N. I. Yezhov. He also signed the record of the interrogation, admitting his guilt.

J. V. Stalin personally dealt on a daily basis with matters concerning the investigation of the "military plot." He received the records of the interrogations of the prisoners and N. I. Yezhov almost daily, and also the deputy people's commissar, M. N. Frinovsky, on May 21 and 28, and he was directly involved in the falsification of the charges.

Shortly before the start of the trial, a meeting took place in the U.S.S.R. NKVD Special Section at which G. M. Leplevsky gave instructions to interrogators once again to convince those under investigation to confirm their testimony in court and to say that an "admission" in the court would mitigate their fate. The interrogators who had fabricated the case accompanied their own defendants into the court, staying with them in waiting rooms, and they were also present in the courtroom. On the day before the trial the prisoners were summoned by Leplevsky, who stated that the trial would begin on the following day and that their fates depended on their behavior in court.

On June 11, 1937, the Special Judicial Hearing of the U.S.S.R. Supreme Court opened in Moscow to consider the case regarding the charges against M. N. Tukhachevsky and the others. After the reading of the indictment, in response to questions from the chairman of the court, all of the defendants entered a plea of guilty. Subsequently, complying with the demands of the NKVD workers, they confirmed in court the main testimony that they had given during the investigation.

Here are some of the factors that characterized the course of the trial:

In accordance with the intentions of the organizers, I. E. Yakir's statement during the trial was to "prompt" the line of behavior for the other defendants, namely, to unmask the attempts by L. D. Trotsky and Fascist states against the U.S.S.R. Here, M. N. Tukhachevsky's role in the plot was to be emphasized in every possible way. However, when V. K. Blyukher tried to concretize the preparations for the defeat of the Red Army's air force in a future war and asked a question about this, I. E. Yakir replied: "I cannot tell you anything plainly except what was written for the investigation." In response to a question from the chairman of the court about how the wrecking was expressed with respect to military training, I. E. Yakir answered evasively: "I talked about this in a special letter."

M. N. Tukhachevsky did not confirm some of the charges in court. When I. P. Uborevich started to deny guilt in wrecking and espionage, the court cut short his examination and after a recess of an hour moved on to the examination of other defendants.

Under examination in court, I. E. Yakir and I. P. Uborevich denied the charges of espionage. Thus, in response to a question from P. Ye. Dybenko—"When did you specifically begin espionage work for the German General Staff?"—I. E. Yakir replied: "I never did personally and directly start that work."

When P. Ye. Dybenko asked I. P. Uborevich "Did you engage directly in espionage work with the German General Staff?" I. P. Uborevich responded: "I never did that." In response to V. V. Ulrikh's question "Do you confirm that you have been involved in anti-Soviet activity since 1932 but that your espionage activity, which you regard as anti-Soviet, started much sooner?" M. N. Tukhachevsky replied: "I do not know if it could be regarded as spying. . . ."

During his examination in the court R. P. Eydeman was asked three questions.

The fate of the defendants had been decided beforehand. In 1962 former secretary of the court I. M. Zaryanov reported: "Ulrikh informed J. V. Stalin about the course of the trial. Ulrikh told me this, and he said that he had instructions from Stalin to impose the death sentence—execution by firing squad—on all of the defendants."

The Bukharin Trial

The execution of reprisals against the former leaders of "right deviationism" was made complicated for its organizers by the circumstance that N. I. Bukharin and A. I. Rykov at the time had not been expelled from the party and had not had criminal proceedings brought against them, while both were candidate members of the Central Committee of the AUCP(B) (All-Union Communist party [Bolsheviks]) and were widely known as major figures in the party and state. Therefore, before creating a criminal case against them, steps were undertaken to compromise them politically in the eyes of the party and people and turn public opinion against them. To this end, unjustified attacks on them appeared in the press, using falsified and tendentiously selected facts concerning their past activity. Thus, on October 28, 1936, a lead article was published in *Pravda* in which Rykov was falsely depicted as a Menshevik hanger-on who had come forward in 1917 on the appearance of V. I. Lenin in the court of the provisional government. Protesting against this attack, Rykov appealed to Stalin with a personal letter on November 4, 1936. In his own letter to Stalin on December 2, 1936, Bukharin also expressed his protest against the slanderous attacks contained in the article published in *Pravda* concerning matters at the Academy of Sciences and requested that Stalin personally accept the letter and explain why this negative reputation was being created around him (Bukharin). Stalin, however, paid no attention to these letters.

A "theoretial work" by N. I. Yezhov recently discovered in the party's Central Committee archives is a testimony to the fact that Stalin and Yezhov spared no effort in trying to link the leaders of "right opportunism" with the supporters of Trotsky and Zinoviev. This work, entitled "From Factionalism to Open Counterrevolution," directly sets forth a version of the contact of the Trotsky-Zinoviev block with the center of the "right," namely, Tomsky, Bukharin, and Rykov. Yezhov began work on this manuscript in 1935, shortly after the murder of Sergei M. Kirov, and at this point he had already formulated (one might say a priori) accusations concerning the terrorist intentions of the former members of the opposition. At the request of Yezhov, Stalin personally edited this "work" and made comments and recommendations as appropriate, corrections that were fully taken into account by the author during further work on the manuscript. While purporting to be an analysis of the "counterrevolutionary" activity of the Trotsky-Zinoviev faction and other opposition groups, the work, by the intention of the author, was in fact to be a document for the liquidation of all former oppositionists and those whose views differed from Stalin.

Although in 1936 no information had been obtained concerning illegal terrorist or organizational activity by Bukharin and Rykov, the investigations began consistently to obtain just such evidence from all those who had been arrested. During such inquiries, all legality was flouted, and such prohibited methods as blackmail, intimidation, persuasion, and promises, as well as direct physical coercion, were widely used.

Thus, in September of 1936, G. G. Yagoda presented Stalin with the records of the proceedings for the interrogations of E. F. Kulikov and A. V. Lugovy-Livenshtein with evidence on Tomsky, Rykov, and Bukharin. The cover letter noted that

> the deposition of Kulikov concerning the terrorist activity of the counter-revolutionary organization of the right is of particular interest. Of those named in the depositions of Kulikov and Lugovy, Matveev has been arrested and Zapolsky and Yakovlev will be arrested.
>
> I am requesting authorization to arrest Ya. I. Rovinsky, manager of the Union Tanning Market, and Kotov, chief secretary for social insurance for the VTsSPS (All-Union Central Council of Professional Unions).
>
> Uglanov, who was arrested in Omsk and has arrived in Moscow, is presently being interrogated.
>
> All the remaining members of the counterrevolutionary organization who have been named in the depositions of Kulikov and Lugovy have been identified for arrest.

On October 7, 1936, Yezhov, who had replaced Yagoda as the head of the U.S.S.R. People's Committee of Internal Affairs (NKVD), presented Stalin with the records of the proceedings for the interrogation of Tomsky's former secretary, M. Z. Stankin. He wrote:

> Stankin provided evidence concerning his membership and active participation in the terrorist organization of the right. . . . Stankin indicates that the militant terrorist group of Slavinsky, which also included Kashin and Voinov (former secretaries of Tomsky), contemplated the perpetration of a terrorist act against Comrade Stalin on the day of a ceremonial meeting at the Bolshoi Theatre on November 6, 1936.
>
> Stankin also indicated that he learned from Tomsky about the existence of the center of the counterrevolutionary organization of the right, which included Tomsky, Bukharin, Rykov, Uglanov, Shmidt, and Syrtsov. . . .

Later on, similar evidence was obtained from others who had been arrested. All such information was passed on to Stalin. For the period from September 1936 to February 1937 alone (i.e., from the moment of the arrest of Bukharin and Rykov), Stalin received nearly sixty records of interrogation of former "rightists."

That such evidence was extorted is clear from a statement sent to the Presidium of the U.S.S.R. TsIK (Central Executive Committee) in November 1936 by one of those who had been arrested, M. N. Ryutin:

At the present time, after the passage of nearly five years of a ten-year imprisonment, I have again instituted criminal proceedings against the NKVD due to the fact that, first, at present, individual phrases and expressions which I wrote at the time in illegal "documents" were interpreted by those conducting the investigation as calls to terror, and second, that right terrorist groups were supposedly formed and exposed on the basis of these documents. . . .

On the basis of all the above, which most profoundly confirms my innocence of all that they have charged me with, you will find that the charges are absolutely unlawful, arbitrary, and prejudiced, dictated exclusively by malice and the thirst to conduct a new and bloody reprisal against me. . . .

To all that has been noted here, I consider it necessary to add in conclusion that the methods themselves used on me during the investigation were unlawful and intolerable. They threatened me at each interrogation, screamed at me as though at an animal, insulted me, and finally, did not even allow me to give an explanatory written renunciation of the deposition. . . .

It is clear from books discovered in the NKVD archive that recorded events in the internal prisons of the U.S.S.R. NKVD GUGB (Main Directorate of State Security) from December 1934 to March 1937 that the former "rightists," who were delivered to Moscow from the camps, protested against the arbitrary nature of the investigations, continuously went on hunger strikes, and made attempts to commit suicide. A. N. Slepkov and M. N. Ryutin resorted to hunger strikes on many occasions. Slepkov tried to commit suicide several times. Ryutin tried to hang himself. L. A. Shatskin, who in his own letter to Stalin reported that he was compelled in the supposed "interests of the party" to give false evidence on the terror, also protested against the arbitrary nature of the investigations.

The implementation of a directive dating from September 29, 1936, concerning regard for the former oppositionists, led to some of the most flagrant distortions of socialist legality. Thus, the NKVD of the Kirghiz SSR proclaimed a socialist competition for the purpose of "successfully dealing with the problem of crushing the right-Trotskyist and other anti-Soviet organizations." An order of the republic NKVD "concerning the results of the socialist competition between the Third and Fourth Departments of the NKVD UGB (Directorate of State Security) for February of 1938" stated that

> the Fourth Department had more than one and a half times more arrests for the month than the Third Department and unmasked 13 more spies and members of counterrevolutionary organizations . . . ; however, the Third Department passed along 20 cases to the Military Board and 11 cases to the Special Board, while the Fourth Department had nearly 100 more cases (not including outlying districts) completed by its own staff. . . .

As a result of the perversions of legality that were permitted, thousands of innocent people were arrested and convicted on groundless charges.

After the generation of these new depositions, the question of Bukharin and Rykov was taken before a party Central Committee plenum, which took place December 4–7, 1936. At the plenum, Yezhov presented the document "Anti-Soviet, Trotskyist and Rightist Organizations." Using, as has now been established, false depositions taken from those who had been arrested, including L. S. Sosnovsky, E. F. Kulikov, V. A. Yakovlev, and V. A. Kotov, he accused Bukharin and Rykov of forming an alliance with supporters of Trotsky and Zinoviev and charged them with complicity in terrorist activity.

During his own appearance at the plenum, Bukharin denied all the accusations brought against him. He asserted: "There is not a shred of truth in all the slander that has been heaped on me here. I had one confrontation with Sokolnikov. . . . In fact, I even asked him to state that we had never had conversations on political matters, that he speaks from the words of Tomsky—Tomsky, who by that time had ceased to exist. . . .

"In regard to Sosnovsky, Comrades, I have written several times: Why have you not arranged for me to face my accusers? Not once have I had a conversation with Sosnovsky about general political matters, nor did we speak about any platform of Ryutin's. I have not read Ryutin's platform myself, because only one single time, at the behest of Comrade Stalin, was it pointed out to me. I did not see it; I was not even familiar with it before this. . . .

"I would never deny that in 1928–29 I led the opposition struggle against the party. But I do not know how to convince you that later on I absolutely had not the slightest idea about any of sort of common goals nor any platforms nor any 'centers.'. . .

"They say there is some sort of center of the right. I swear that I have not seen Uglanov for many years now. I don't know whether he is alive or dead or where he is, and I have absolutely no idea where on the face of the earth he might be.

"I assure you that, whatever verdict you bring, whatever decision you make, I always, up to the very last minute of my life, I always will stand for our party, for our leadership, for Stalin. . . ."

At the plenum, Rykov stated: "I assert that all the accusations against me are false from beginning to end. . . .

"Kamenev has testified at the trial that each year right up to 1936 he was seen with me, and I asked Yezhov, so that he would know, where and when I had been seen with Kamenev so that I could somehow refute this falsehood. They said to me that Kamenev could not be asked about this, but now it is impossible to ask him—he has been shot. . . .

"I met very rarely with Tomsky over the course of the last two years. With Bukharin, I am not sure, but it seems I last saw him in 1934. . . . In recent years we never discussed political questions. . . ."

On December 7, 1936, on the working day of the Central Committee plenum, Bukharin sent Stalin a declaration, "To All Members and Candidate Members of the AUCP(B) CC," with which he requested that all participants in the plenum familiarize themselves and which he requested to be put on the record verbatim. In this declaration, he expressed his outrage at the enormity of the accusations made against him and wrote that when adopting a political evaluation in the form that it emerged from in the report and debates, the investigatory organs cannot objectively consider the case; hence, the accused will be deprived of the potential for self-defense. Concerning the situation at the plenum, Bukharin wrote:

Everyone had the materials (which were not verified by any evidence) except the accused; the accused was completely taken by surprise by the sudden and exceptionally monstrous accusations shown to him for the first time. In the face of the known, previously assigned, and constructed nature of the proceedings (the very nature of the formulation of the question, the unproven materials, the biases of the speaker, the press, the directed slogans such as Molotov's "accomplices and yes-men") all said: "I am sure," "there is no doubt," etc. They looked the accused in the eye and said, "But we do not believe, each of your words must be verified." While

on the other hand, the words of the accusers are taken as pure gold. . . .
In the general atmosphere of the present time no one dares to stand up for
the accused.

   And what happens then? In the later stages, after the obligatory party
verdict, etc., defense is almost impossible.

   In the breaks between the sessions of the Central Committee plenum,
Bukharin and Rykov arranged confrontations with E. F. Kulikov, L. S.
Sosnovsky, and Yu. L. Piatakov, whose depositions both Bukharin and
Rykov categorically denied. The plenum accepted the proposal of Stalin
"to consider the question of Rykov and Bukharin as unfinished, to continue with further examination and put off a decision on the case until
the next Central Committee plenum."

   However, no additional party examination of the accusations made
against Bukharin and Rykov was conducted. The case in essence was
transferred over to organs of the NKVD, which actively continued to
gather slanderous materials.

   At the end of 1936 and beginning of 1937, a number of people were
arrested, including K. B. Radek, V. N. Astrov, S. N. Padin, and B. N.
Nesterov. Radek gave depositions concerning the connections of the leaders of the former "right opposition" with the supporters of Trotsky and
Zinoviev, their terrorist activity, and the participation of Bukharin,
Rykov, and Tomsky in the murder of Kirov. Having become acquainted
with these depositions, on January 12, 1937, Bukharin sent a declaration
to the AUCP(B) Central Committee Politburo in which he categorically
refuted them as fabricated and slanderous. He also affirmed his refutation
on January 13, 1937, in the Politburo in a confrontation with Radek.

   V. N. Astrov played a provocative role in the fate of Bukharin. In one
confrontation he affirmed his deposition on the terrorism of the "right."
Later he declared that in the spring of 1932 "the center of the right
resolved to turn to the tactics of terror," that Bukharin had allegedly
talked about "the necessity to kill Stalin," and that the principal authors
of the so-called Ryutin platform were Bukharin, Rykov, Tomsky, and
Uglanov. He asserted that it was also personally known to him that
"Bukharin and Rykov continue to compose the center of the right, having
remained in their previous positions." Bukharin categorically denied
these charges.

Stalin took an active role in the interrogation of Bukharin in the confrontations. In particular, he accused Bukharin of forming an alliance with the SRs (Socialist Revolutionaries) during the period of the Brest-Litovsk Peace Treaty negotiations, to which Bukharin replied: "What sense does it make for me to lie about the Brest-Litovsk Peace Treaty period? At one point, the left SRs arrived and said, 'Let's set up a cabinet. We will arrest Lenin and form a cabinet.' I spoke of this later to Ilych (Lenin). 'Give me your word of honor that you will say nothing of this to anyone,' Ilych (Lenin) said to me. Then, when I fought with you against Trotsky, I brought this up as an example—what fractional struggle this could lead to! At that point this dropped like a bombshell."

After these confrontations, new and numerous arrests of former rightists and other opposition members followed, from which the "necessary" depositions on Bukharin and Rykov were obtained. The proceedings of the interrogations of these persons were sent to Bukharin in his apartment. For only one day, February 16, 1937, Bukharin received twenty such depositions. In his letters to Stalin and the Politburo, Bukharin denied the statements of all these individuals and protested against his persecution in the press, against the fact that *Pravda* was already proceeding from the "proven nature" of unprecedentedly grave charges against the "leaders of the right," and against the fact that in *Pravda* he had been "proclaimed an agent of the Gestapo."

At the beginning of 1937, when notified of a new analysis of the case in the Central Committee plenum, Bukharin sent a declaration to the Politburo concerning the fact that he would not appear at the plenum until the charges of espionage and wrecking were withdrawn, and in a sign of protest against the charges he declared a hunger strike. He also requested that his detailed explanation regarding the depositions obtained on him from those arrested, which he termed slanderous, be made public at the plenum.

For a day prior to the opening of the plenum, confrontations were held in the Politburo between Rykov and the previously arrested S. N. Radin, V. V. Shmidt, and B. P. Nesterov.

Radin testified that in 1932 Rykov allegedly provided the "right" with a directive on the use of terror and wrecking. Shmidt provided depositions concerning the fact that after 1929 the "center of the right continued to operate," that in 1932 a meeting of the "center" was allegedly held that considered the question of "the need for the violent elimination of the

AUCP(B) leadership—Stalin et al." Rykov completely denied similar types of depositions.

The Central Committee plenum opened on February 23, 1937, and for the second time considered the case of Bukharin and Rykov. Yezhov presented a report on this question that in essence repeated the accusations that had emerged at the previous plenum. He asserted that in 1929 they had betrayed the party, had not given up their "underground organization," had maintained it and continued the struggle with the party until very recently, had set the goal of seizing power by violent means, and had entered an alliance with Trotskyists, anti-Soviet parties, and Mensheviks.

Yezhov's report was based wholly on faked and falsified depositions obtained through prohibited methods of investigation. Almost all the individuals who had been arrested by organs of the NKVD and had given depositions in 1936–37 on Bukharin and Rykov have now been rehabilitated. There are some who by chance survived and who reported to a Central Committee commission that was working in the 1960s that during the interrogations, if they provided the "necessary" depositions, they were promised that they would not be killed and would be freed, while if they refused, they were threatened with violence. Those who resisted were subjected to physical and moral coercion. The information obtained in this manner was quickly provided to Stalin by Yezhov.

This is how the accusatory material on Bukharin and Rykov was fabricated. The participants in the plenum were deluded all the more in that all those arrested in the case of Bukharin and Rykov were presented by Yezhov as people who had willingly provided their depositions.

At the plenum, following Yezhov, A. I. Mikoyan delivered a major address, in fact a co-report, which contained pointed political accusations and appraisals.

The situation at the plenum was serious. Its participants had charged Bukharin and Rykov with very serious crimes and were not sparing in their insulting epithets and labels. Open pressure was put on the participants of the plenum by Stalin, who rudely snubbed Bukharin and Rykov, thereby strengthening the opinions of the participants concerning the authenticity of the NKVD evidence. Any attempt to object to the proceedings or defend Bukharin and Rykov was regarded as insincerity, duplicity, and slanderous of the NKVD organs. Here is a small fragment from an unofficial record of the Plenum:

BUKHARIN: Comrades, first I want to say several words concerning the speech that was delivered here by Comrade Mikoyan. Comrade Mikoyan, so to speak, has depicted my letters to members of the Politburo, the first and second [letters], as letters that contain methods for intimidating the Central Committee that are similar to those used by the Trotskyists.

First of all I should say that I know the Central Committee well enough to simply deny beforehand that the Central Committee plenum can be intimidated in such a way.

KHLOPLYANKIN: But why did you write that until the charges against you are dropped, you will not end your hunger strike?

BUKHARIN: Comrades, I beseech you not to interrupt, because it is very difficult, simply physically demanding, for me to speak: I will answer any question which you put to me, but do not interrupt me now. In the letters I portrayed my own personal psychological condition.

VOICE: Why did you write: not until the charges are dropped?

BUKHARIN: I did not say this in relation to the Central Committee. I said this not in relation to the Central Committee, because the Central Committee, as Central Committee, has not officially charged me in these matters. I was accused by various organs of the press, but the Central Committee has not charged me in these matters. I expressed my own condition, which is necessary simply from the point of view of human understanding. If, of course, I am not a human being, then there is nothing to understand. But I believe that I am a human being, and I believe that I have the right, at an extraordinarily difficult, vital, and serious moment for me, concerning my psychological condition to—

VOICE: But of course!

BUKHARIN: At an extraordinary, exceptionally difficult time—I wrote about it. And therefore here there is no element either of an intimidation or ultimatum. . . .

STALIN: And the hunger strike?

BUKHARIN: The hunger strike—at present I have not canceled it. I told you, I wrote you, because I seized upon it in despair, I wrote to a small circle of people because with such accusations hung on me it is impossible for me to go on living. I could not use a revolver because then they will say that I killed myself in order to harm the party; but if I die from illness, then what will you lose from this? (*laughter*)

VOICE: Blackmail!

VOROSHILOV: What baseness! A plague on you for saying such things! Foul. Think before you speak.

BUKHARIN: But understand that it is difficult for me to live.

STALIN: And it is easy for us?

VOROSHILOV: You only think: "I am not committing suicide, I am starving to death."

BUKHARIN: It is easy for you to talk about me. What do you have to lose? If indeed I am a wrecker, and a son of a bitch and so forth, who should be sorry for me? I certainly would not pretend for any reason. I am describing what I am thinking and what I am suffering. If this is related with any sort of even minute political damage I, undoubtedly, would accept all that you say. (*laughter*) What are you laughing at? There is absolutely nothing here to laugh at.

Mikoyan says that I want to discredit the organs of the NKVD as a whole. Absolutely not. I absolutely did not intend to do this. The passage about which Comrade Mikoyan speaks concerns certain questions that were asked by the investigators. What do I say about these? I say: Such questions are wholly impermissible and unnecessary, but in the present actual situation they lead to certain consequences.

In regard to the political situation, Comrade Mikoyan says that I wanted to discredit the Central Committee. But if the public is always reading in resolutions that are published in the newspapers and in the editorials of *Bolshevik* about what still must be proved as already proved, then it is completely natural that this becomes a determined, even directed, stream that seeps through everywhere. Is this really difficult to understand? This is not simply the work of random satirists.

PETERS: (*remark inaudible*)

BUKHARIN: I will tell everything. Don't shout, please.

MOLOTOV: I ask you not to respond. You are hindering the process.

BUKHARIN: Comrade Mikoyan has said that I have lied to the Central Committee on a whole series of matters, that with Kulikov I confused 1929 with 1932. That I was in error is true, but such personal errors can occur.

GAMARNIK: Let's take a break. . . .

Turning his attention to the most crude contradictions in the depositions brought against him, Bukharin, in particular, declared, "I did not know about a Trotskyist-Zinovievist block, or about a parallel center or about arrangements for the use of terror or about arrangements for wrecking, . . . let alone that I could have participated somehow in these matters. I protest against this in the most decisive manner. Here, despite the perhaps millions of many-sided statements that have been made, I cannot acknowledge this. This did not happen."

In their appearances at the plenum, Bukharin and Rykov rejected the accusations of duplicity brought against them as completely groundless and absurd. The accusations of duplicity concerned their formal recognition of their errors in 1929 and the continuation in recent years of a secret struggle against the party, the existence of an alleged illegal center of the right (from 1932 on), the platform of which was the alleged "Ryutin Platform," and the presence of a political connection with the supporters of Trotsky and Zinoviev. They also denied as completely absurd the charges that they were engaged in terrorist activity.

However, this was all disregarded. The participants of the February–March (1937) Central Committee plenum were under the influence of materials fabricated by the NKVD and under the pressure of Stalin.

Bibliographic Note

On Sources Old and New

Three major biographies of Stalin were written in the lifetime of the dictator. First was Boris Souvarine's *Staline. Aperçu historique du Bolshevisme*, Paris, 1935. An English edition appeared in 1939. The book was out of print for many years but was republished in France in the 1980s and also in the United States (New York, 1972). Bertram D. Wolfe's *Three Who Made a Revolution* first appeared in 1948. Isaac Deutscher's *Stalin, a Political Biography* was published in 1949. All three authors were former members of the Communist party; Souvarine was also active in the Communist International. Deutscher's biography is psychologically interesting; the author's sympathies are more with Trotsky (whose biography he subsequently wrote), but he tried so hard to do justice to Stalin and thought of so many extenuating circumstances that the picture that emerged in the end was too favorable to Stalin. To a certain extent, Deutscher tried to correct this in subsequent editions. Souvarine's biography is a powerful diatribe against Stalin, whom the author saw as a usurper who had betrayed the heritage of the Revolution. Ironically, seen in historical perspective, Souvarine was in some respects too gentle; thus he observed (in 1935) that while Stalin was a most brutal leader, he had managed to install himself as the supreme leader without shedding blood.

Among the earliest Stalin biographies are two wholly laudatory ones by S. Graham, *Stalin, an Impartial Study of the Life and Work of Joseph Stalin*, London, 1931, and Henri Barbusse, *Stalin, un monde nouveau vu à travers un homme*, Paris, 1935. Two other books were written by Soviet defectors: *Avec Stalin dans le Kremlin*, by B. Bajanov, who had been one of Stalin's secretaries in the 1920s; and *Staline, l'homme d'acier*, Paris, 1932, written by G. Besedowski, who had been an official of the GPU. Two other early biographies that are of some interest because the authors had firsthand knowledge of Russia are Essad Bey's (i.e., L. Noussimbaum) *Stalin*, Berlin, 1931, and Isaac Don Levine's *Stalin*, New York, 1931.

During the 1940s, the enormous interest in Stalin resulted in a flood of books. Some of the authors had no specialized knowledge of the subject; others had lived for years in Moscow (Eugene Lyons, *Stalin, the Czar of All Russians*, Philadelphia, 1940, and Louis Fischer, *The Life and Death of Stalin*, New York, 1953). J. T. Murphy (*Stalin 1879–1944*, London, 1945) had been a leading figure in the British Communist party. Yet none of these books added greatly to our knowledge of the subject. The same is true with regard to Yves Delbars's *Le vrai Staline*, Paris, 1950. Nikolaus Basseches, *Stalin, das Schicksal eines Erfolges*, Bern, 1950, had been a foreign correspondent in Moscow.

During the 1960s, Western academic studies on Stalin began to appear. The most ambitious and perhaps the best was Adam B. Ulam's *Stalin, the Man and His Era*, New York, 1973, a work of synthesis. Two books by American authors deal with Stalin's career up to the late 1920s: Edward Ellis Smith's *The Young Stalin* and R. C. Tucker's *Stalin as Revolutionary: A Study in History and Personality*, New York, 1973. Both authors had been diplomats in Moscow; Tucker subsequently became an academic with a special interest in psychohistory. Of the postwar popular biographies, the most reliable were Robert Payne's *The Rise and Fall of Stalin*, New York, 1965, and Alex de Jong's *Stalin*, London, 1987. Robert McNeal's *Stalin, Man and Ruler*, New York, 1988, is a brief account by an American professor who edited Stalin's works, vols. 14–16 (Stanford, 1967), after the Soviet edition (vols. 1–13) had stopped with the death of the dictator. R. Hingley's *Josef Stalin, Man and Legend*, London, 1974, is also a work of synthesis by a noted scholar, as is A. E. Adams's *Stalin and His Times*, New York, 1972. My own *Fate of the Revolution*, New York, 1967 (new, enlarged edition, New York, 1987), covers the historiography of the Revolution, Lenin, Stalin, and Stalinism.

Emil Ludwig's *Stalin*, New York, 1942, and H. Montgomery Hyde's *Stalin, the History of a Dictator*, New York, 1971, are the work of professional biographers rather than students of Soviet history.

Stalin's Russian biographies are few. The first was a brochure by A. Tovstukha, *Josif Stalin*, Moscow, 1927. Emelian Yaroslavsky's *O tovarishshe Stalin*, Moscow, 1939, appeared at the height of the cult. The same is true with regard to the *Kratkaia biografia*, Moscow, 1939, a small volume written by an authors' collective and containing virtually no information about Stalin as an individual. No biographical studies appeared in the Soviet Union between 1940 and 1987, but there were some works by Russian émigrés, especially A. Uralov (i.e., A. Avtorkhanov), *The Reign of Stalin*, London, 1953. Roy Medvedev's *Let History Judge*, New York, 1972 (new enlarged edition, New York, 1989), is the massive work of a Soviet dissident. It is of particular interest in view of the many interviews with surviving old Bolsheviks to whom Western authors had no access. The first glasnost biography was Dimitri Volkogonov's *Triumf i Tragedia*, first published in installments in the literary periodical *Oktiabr* in 1988 and 1989. According to an interview that appeared prior to publication, Volkogonov considered himself neither Stalinist nor anti-Stalinist. Subsequently, he became more outspoken in his criticism of Stalin. His book contains details not hitherto known, but the lacunae are even more striking; according to his own evidence, he had no access to many crucial files in the archives despite his high military rank (colonel-general) and his connections.

Furthermore, Volkogonov, a philosopher rather than a historian by training, frequently does not mention his sources, and it is difficult to establish what sections of his biography are based on documentary evidence and which were "re-created" by the author, direct speech and all. The second part of the biography (*Oktiabr* 7–9, 1989) covers, above all, the war years, and it appears that Volkogonov had many more hitherto unpublished military documents at his disposal than material from party and secret police sources a four-volume paperback edition subsequently appreared in Moscow. A samizdat work that first appeared in the West is Antonov-Ovseenko's biography of Stalin.

The books that deal with Stalinism are not many. The following, above all, should be mentioned: Robert C. Tucker (ed.), *Stalinism: Essays in Historical Interpretation*, New York, 1977, and G. R. Urban, *Stalinism: Its Impact on Russia and the World*, London, 1982. The former is based on papers submitted at a conference; the latter, on a series of interviews. There is a certain amount of overlapping as far as the contributors are concerned, but in the former volume, the "anticontinuity" believers have the upper hand, whereas in the Urban volume, most authors stress the impact of Leninism on Stalinism. Debates on Stalinism were published in *Russian Review* in 1986 and again in 1987, but they were to a certain extent overtaken by the glasnost revelations. Other works that should be mentioned include A. Avtorkhanov's *Tekhnologia vlasti*, Munich, 1935; R. Redlikh's *Stalinshshina kak dukhovni fenomenon*, Frankfurt, 1971; J. A. Armstrong's *The Politics of Totalitarianism*, New York, 1968; and R. Conquest's *The Great Terror*, New York, 1968. There is no need to mention in the present context works on totalitarianism in general, the working of the Soviet political system, and specialized works on specific periods of Soviet history, even though many have a direct bearing on our subject. No mention has been made so far of the Trotskyite literature on Stalin and Stalinism. Among these, L. Trotsky's *Stalin: An Appraisal of the Man and His Influence*, new ed., New York, 1967, and Jean-Jacques Marie's *Staline, 1879–1953*, Paris, 1967, should be singled out.

Several Soviet books about the Stalin period have been published under glasnost. Among them are:

Yu. N. Afanasiev (ed.), *Inogo ne dano*, Moscow, 1988.
L. Beladi and T. Kraus, *Stalin*, Moscow, 1989 (transl. from the Hungarian).
L. A. Gordon and E. V. Klopov, *Chto eto bylo?* Moscow, 1989
V. K. Gorev (ed.), *Stranitsy istorii KPPS*, Moscow, 1988.
V. Kannunikov (ed.), *Esli po sovesti*, Moscow, 1988.
K. Kobo (ed.), *Osmyslit kult Stalina*, Moscow, 1989.
Y. S. Kukushkin (ed.), *Rezhim lichnoi vlasti Stalina*, Moscow, 1989.
V. I. Kuptsov, *Stranitsy istorii KPSS*, Moscow, 1988.
V. S. Lelchuk (ed.), *Istoriki sporiat*, Moscow, 1988.
V. S. Moldavan (ed.), *Uroki gorkie . . .* , Moscow, 1988.
A. Proskurin (ed.), *Vozvrashennie imena*, 2 vols. Moscow, 1989.
Surovaia drama naroda; uchennie i publitsisti o prirode stalinisma, Moscow, 1989.
A. N. Svalov (ed.), *Istoriki otvechaiut na voprosy*, Moscow, 1989.
N. Vasetsky, *Likvidatsiia*, Moscow, 1989.
O. V. Volobuev and S. V. Kuleshov, *Ochishenie: Istoria i perestroika*, Moscow, 1989.

Essential for our purpose were the essays published in literary, artistic, historical and philosophical journals, as well as the occasional "roundtables." These articles appeared in the leading Moscow and Leningrad monthlies, such as *Novyi mir*, *Znamia*, *Oktiabr*, *Neva*, but also in popular scientific journals such as *Nauka i zhizn* and *Znanie sila* and even in the provincial literary magazines (for instance, *Ural*), where in previous years no one would have looked for them. The anti-anti-Stalinist opposition was fully represented in *Nash sovremennik* and *Molodaia gvardia* and less frequently in *Moskva* and *Literaturnaia Rossia*. The professional historical journals, such as *Voprosy istorii*, *Voprosy istorii KPSS*, and *Voenno-istoricheski zhurnal*, needed longer to get into the act, they began in 1988 to publish contributions of interest in virtually every single issue. *Voprosy filosofii* featured articles of value pertaining to the Stalin period, as did *Teatr*, and the journals put out by the moviemakers' union and even the circus performers. The most outspoken was *20th Century and Peace*, but one could not safely ignore any newspaper and journal published in the Soviet Union. The documents published in *Izvestiia Ts. K. KPPS* were most significant for the historian. Local journals and periodicals in the Baltic countries (*Daugava* and *Rodnik*), the Ukraine, Georgia, Voronezh, Sverdlovsk, and even far away

Kirgizia contained important accounts of recent Soviet history. Finally, the documentary films shown on Soviet television ought to be mentioned; many of them contained material that was of great benefit to the present writer with regard to the purges, the history of the gulag, and the fate of individual leaders.

The following list is no more than a small, though fairly representative, selection of the flood of interesting essays pertaining to the subject matter of the present book published in 1987–89:

S. Andreev, "Struktura vlasti i zadachi obshchestva," *Neva* 1, 1989.

L. Batkin, "Son Razuma," *Znanie sila* 3 and 4, 1989.

A. V. Bedov, "Chto obreteno v poiske?" *Voprosy istorii KPSS*, 5, 1989.

I. Bestuzhev-Lada "Byla li alternativa stalinismu?" *Politicheskoe obrazovanie* 3, 1989.

Y. Borisov, "Stalin, chelovek i simbol," in *Perepiska* . . .

Y. Borisov, "Stanovlenie komandno-biurokraticheskoi sisteme," *EKO* 1, 1989.

V. Bushin, "Kogda somnenie umesto," *Nash sovremennik* 4, 1989.

A. P. Butenko, "O sotsialno-klassogo prirode stalinskoi vlasti," *Voprosy filosofii* 3, 1989.

A. P. Butenko, "O myslakh na zakritikh zon," (series 12) *Vestnik M.G.U.* 3, 1989.

A. Chernichenko, "Knut i prianik," *Druzhba narodov* 5, 1989.

V. Danilov, "Kollektivisatsia kak eto bylo," in *Strannitsy istorii KPSS*

V. Danilov, "Fenomen pervikh piatiletok," *Gorizont* 5, 1988.

M. Gefter, "Stalin umer vchera," *Rabochi klass i sovremenny mir* 1, 1988.

M. Kapustin, "Kamo griadeshi?" *Oktiabr* 7, 1989.

Len Karpinsky, "Maska my tebia znaem," *Gorizont* 8, 1989.

I. Kliamkin, "Kakaia ulitsa vedet v khramu," *Novyi mir* 11, 1987.

I. Kliamkin, "Pochemu trudno govorit pravdu," *Novyi mir* 2, 1988.

I. Kliamkin, "Eshshe raz ob istokakh Stalinizma," *Politicheskoe obrazovanie* 9, 1989.

V. Kozhinov, "Pravda i istina," *Nash sovremennik* 4, 1988.

O. P. Latsis, "Problema tempov v sotsialisticheskom Stroitelstve," *Kommunist* 18, 1988.

O. P. Latsis, "Perelom," *Znamia* 6, 1988.

V. Lelchuk, "Industrialisatsia" in *Perepiska na istoricheskie temy*, Moscow 1989.

G. Lisichkin, "Mify i realnost," *Novyi mir* 11, 1988.

I. L. Mankovskaia and Y. P. Sharapov, "Kult lichnosti," *Voprosy istorii KPSS* 5, 1988.

A. Migranyan, "Dolgi put k evropeiskomu domu," *Novyi mir* 7, 1989.

V. P. Naumov et al., "Ob istoricheskom puti KPSS v svete novogo myshlenia," *Voprosy istorii KPSS* 10, 1988.

G. Popov, "Sistema i zubry," in *Uroki gorkie* . . .

"Priroda totalitarnoi vlasti," *Sotsiologicheskie issledovaniia* 5, 1989.

V. Selyunin, "Istoki," *Novyi mir* 5, 1988.

E. Sashenko, "Stalinshshina," *Obshestvennie nauki* 5, 1989.

Igor Shafarevich, "Russofobia," *Nash sovremennik* 6, 1989.

Y. A. Shetinov, "Rezhim lichnoi vlasti Stalina," *Vestnik M.G.U.* 3, 1989.

K. Simonov, "Glazami cheloveka moego pokoleniia," *Znamia* 3–5, 1988.

A. Tsipko, "Istoki Stalinisma," *Nauka i zhizn* 11 and 12, 1988, and 1 and 2, 1989.

N. A. Vasetsky, "L. D. Trotsky," *Novaia i noveishaia, Istoriia* 3, 1989.

Lastly, the impact of the Western Sovietological literature on the Soviet debate on Stalinism. Some Soviet specialists were familiar with Western writing in their field, but many were not. A few books had been circulated in samizdat, for instance, R. Conquest's *Great Terror* and Avtorkhanov. A few other titles had been translated for the benefit of members of the Politburo and key officials of the Central Committee. This changed under glasnost, where Western experts on Soviet affairs were invited to address Soviet audiences. No Western biographies of Lenin or Stalin or any general, comprehensive histories of the Soviet Union have been published to this writing; there was a clear preference for dissidents such as Roy Medvedev, Antonov-Ovseenko, and eventually even Solzhenitsyn. The last chapter of Deutscher's biography of Trotsky was also published in a Soviet journal (*Inostrannaia literatura*), as well as R. Slusser's book on Stalin in 1917 and excerpts from Alexander Orlov's *Secret History of Stalin's Crimes* (*Sovershenno sekretno*) and works of Viktor Serge and André Gide. Stephen Cohen's biography of Bukharin appeared in Moscow and was widely commented upon and quoted. The same is true with regard to Conquest's *Great Terror*, which appeared in the Leningrad journal *Neva*, which had previously featured Koestler's *Darkness at Noon*. *Voprosy istorii* published some articles by foreigners, but on topics other than Stalin and Stalinism. While in past decades Western fellow travelers had been singled out for praise in Moscow, they were widely criticized under glasnost; some even made them partly responsible for the all-pervasive Stalinist cult.

Stalin's private papers have not been discovered so far and no one can say for sure whether they still exist. This refers in particular to Stalin's "little book" (or books) with a black calico cover in which for years he made notes to refresh his memory. According to Epishev, who was at one time Beria's deputy and later became the boss of Volkogonov, Stalin's Soviet biographer, it is more than likely that Beria cleaned out Stalin's private safe immediately after the Soviet leader had suffered a stroke. But it is equally likely that the most important documents were destroyed during the lifetime of the dictator upon his instructions.

Those who knew most about Stalin's thoughts and actions (such as Poskrebyshev) almost certainly did not dare to keep a diary. It is virtually certain, on the other hand, that new documents will be unearthed once the archives hitherto kept closed in the Soviet Union will be made accessible. We have it on the authority of V. V. Tsaplin, head of the Soviet main state archives, that the files concerning "repression" have not yet been declassified and that reference to them in the press is not permitted. Mention has been made below of Tsaplin's own study on the number of victims caused during the purges and the terror.

Notes

Introduction

1. V. Grossman, *Everything Is Flowing*, London, 1988, p. 223. Written in the 1960s, this short philosophical novel was first published in the Soviet Union in 1989 (*Oktiabr* 6, 1989).
2. Students of the Third Reich discovered, much to their surprise, that a written order by Hitler concerning the "final solution" did not exist. The same may well have been true with regard to the major crimes of the Stalin era. The greater the crime, the less likely that documentary records would be found. A short verbal instruction—perhaps a simple nod—might have sufficed.

1. Josef Stalin, 1879–1953

1. According to the evidence of I. D. Perfilsev, another Turukhansk exile, reported by D. Volkogonov "Triumf i tragediia," *Oktiabr* 10, 1988.
2. Sebastian Haffner, *The Meaning of Hitler*, New York, 1975, p. 25.
3. Jan Kaplinsky, in *Raduga* 7, 1988.
4. *Iosif Visarionovich Stalin: Kratkaia biografiia*, Moscow, 1940, p. 74. The first full-length Stalin biography in the Soviet Union was published in 1989.
5. Henri Barbusse, *Stalin*, New York, 1935, pp. 282–83. This biography was apparently a work by several hands. It was reportedly written in large part by a German Communist, Alfred Kurella; Barbusse may have contributed to it, but not much. While Kurella's brother Heinrich was a victim of the purges, Alfred lived to become minister of culture in postwar Eastern Germany. He was a firm believer in Stalin and Stalinism, but so was his brother, who was executed. That he accepted (or volunteered) to act as anonymous hagiographer may have saved Alfred Kurella's life. *Habent sua fata libelli.* Even though the Barbusse biography was totally discredited, some neo-Stalinists thought that it constituted effective counterpropaganda against the "calumnies" of the anti-Stalinists. Excerpts from the Barbusse-Kurella book were therefore published in the *Voenno Istoricheskii Zhurnal* (12, 1989 and 1, 1990) even under glasnost.
6. J. T. Murphy, *Stalin: 1879–1944*, London, 1949, p. 242.
7. I. Deutscher, *Stalin*, London, 1949, pp. 466–67.
8. V. Kozhinov, "Pravda i istina," *Nash sovremennik* 4, 1988.

2. War Against the Peasants: The Bukharin Alternative

1. *Pravda*, February 7, 1988.
2. The most detailed Bukharin biography is Stephen F. Cohen, *Bukharin and the Bolshevik Revolution*, New York, 1973, a work that played a role in Bukharin's rehabilitation under Gorbachev; it appeared in Moscow in 1988. For a bibliography of Bukharin's works, see Sidney Heitman, *Nikolai Bukharin*, Stanford, 1969, and, more recently, *Sovetskaia bibliografia* 3, 1988.

   For a critical discussion of Bukharin's views, see Dora Shturman, *Mertvie khvataiut zhivykh*, Jerusalem, 1982.

   For a recent Soviet reappraisal of Bukharin, I. V. Emelianov, *O Bukharine: Revoliutsia, istoria, lichnost*, Moscow, 1989.
3. D. Volkogonov, "Triumf i tragediia," *Oktiabr* 11, 1988, p. 111.
4. A. M. Larina, "Nezabyvaemoe," *Znamia* 10–12, 1988.
5. It was originally published in *Sotsialisticheski vestnik* of Paris, December 22, 1936, January 17, 1937; later in English translation *The Letter of an Old Bolshevik*, London, 1938; also, in Nicolaevsky, *Power and the Soviet Elite*, New York, 1965; Lydia Dan's account in *Novyi zhurnal* 75, 1964.
6. "Letter," 1939, pp. 68–69.
7. *Znamia* 11, 1988, pp. 108–30.
8. Larina, *Znamia* 10, 1988, p. 165; Verigo and Kapustin in *Sovetskaia kultura*, October 6, 1988. Vrachev in *Uchitelskaia gazeta*, October 4, 1988; for an assessment of these comments, see Julia Wishnevsky, "Bukharin's Centenary," *Radio Liberty*, October 26, 1988.
9. Larina, pp. 134, 135.
10. *Sotsialisticheski vestnik*, April 25, 1931. Volkogonov adds: "Could it be that this prediction prompted Stalin (to act as he subsequently did)? Copies of this little journal were always filed in Stalin's cabinet" ("Triumf i tragedia, *Oktiabr* 11, 1988, p. 114). Anyone capable of believing that Stalin would be guided by the Menshevik weekly is capable of believing anything. The syndrome occurs more than once in Volkogonov's biography; thus he mentions the possibility that Stalin decided to engage in mass killings only after he had read in one of Trotsky's books that there were many anti-Stalinists in the Soviet Union. . . .
11. Quoted in W. Laqueur, *The Terrible Secret*, London, 1980, p. 207.
12. Larina, op. cit., p. 161.
13. Much new material about Bukharin has appeared under glasnost. The first major ideological reassessment was given by F. Burlatsky, *Literaturnaia gazeta*, June 22, 1987; the first detailed report about Bukharin's last days is in *Ogonyok* 48, 1987. These were followed by reappraisals in the party's leading journals, such as *Kommunist* (by G. Bordiugov and V. Kozlov) 13, 1988; *Voprosy istorii* (by L. K. Shkarenkov) 8, 1988; and *Voprosy istorii KPSS*, 1988, again by Bordiugov and Kozlov. V. D. Danilov in *Voprosy istorii* 3, 1988, also dealt with the "Bukharin Alternative," and there was new biographical material in the accounts of Volkogonov and Larina mentioned above.
14. James R. Millar in *Problems of Communism*, July 1976. There has been a discussion whether 1928 prices are the correct yardstick to apply; see Alec Nove, ibid. But whatever the correct approach, there seems to be general agreement that during the decisive period of the Five-Year Plan, agriculture made no major contribution to the

development of industry, if indeed there was any contribution at all. Taxes on vodka had, in all probability, a greater impact. On this see A. A. Barsov, *Balans stoimostnykh obmenov mezhdu gorodom i derevnei* (The Balance of Value Exchanges between City and Countryside), Moscow, 1969, and Michael Ellman "Did the Agriculture Surplus Provide the Resources for the Increase in Investment during the First Five Year Plan?" *Economic Journal*, December 1975.

15. The attacks against Y. Moshkov and V. P. Danilov in *Voprosy istorii KPSS* in 1966–68. Under glasnost, Danilov published an article sharply criticizing certain Western authors, who, he claimed, had exaggerated the number of victims of collectivization. But in the meantime Soviet authors have given even higher estimates.

16. This is the view of most articles in *Voprosy istorii* and *Voprosy istorii KPSS* mentioned above. In particular, there have been dissenting voices among the experts specializing in agricultural economies.

17. A. Tsipko, "Istoki Stalinisma," *Nauka i zhizn*, December 1988, p. 45.

18. A. Nove has written that there are circumstances in which people who have a particular set of beliefs do not regard a particular alternative as practical: "If there is a genuine alternative for me to eat either a cheese sandwich or a ham sandwich, this is not an alternative for a rabbi." *Problems of Communism*, op. cit. This is correct as far as it goes, but even from a theological point of view, if human lives are at stake, religious commandments might be disregarded in extreme situations, that is to say, if the issue of the ham sandwich were to become a question of life or death.

19. "Krugli stol: Sovetski Soyuz v dvatsatie gody," *Voprosy istorii* 9, 1988.

20. *Izvestiia*, December 22, 1934.

21. See, for instance, P. Vaganov, *Pravyi uklon v VKP(b) i evo razgrom*, Moscow, 1970.

22. See, for instance, the writings of V. Kozhinov in *Nash sovremennik* throughout 1987–89.

23. For open and veiled attacks see, for example, V. Kozhinov in *Nash sovremennik* 10, 1987, *Nash sovremennik* 1, 1989, and V. Bondarenko in *Moskva* 12, 1987.

24. For a review of activities connected with Bukharin during 1988, see Julia Wishnevksy, "Bukharin's Centenary," *Radio Liberty*, October 26, 1988, 483–88.

25. *Kniga*, Moscow, 1989.

26. Some authors writing under glasnost took the position that although the mood in the party contributed to Stalin's victory over Bukharin, this was by no means predestined (L. A. Gordon and E. V. Klopov, *Chto eto bylo?* Moscow, 1989, passim). But a reviewer rightly pointed out that the balance of power in the party leadership and the attitude of the militants remain to be investigated. G. Sobolev, *Kommunist* 9, 1989, p. 127.

3. Trotsky: "Demon of the Revolution"

1. He was one of the very few leaders of the extreme Left in Russia to have grown up in the countryside rather than the city. The first chapters of his autobiography are devoted to life in a little village in the Ukraine.

2. See, for instance, *Istoriia KPSS*, vol. 3, book 1, Moscow, 1967, p. 321; I. I. Mints, *Istoriia velikovo oktiabra*, Moscow, 1978, pp. 807–9 et seq. For a critical assessment of these writings, see Roy Medvedev, *Inostrannaia literatura* 3, 1988, pp. 167–74.

3. See Julia Wishnevksy, R. L. report 292/88.

4. P. Volobuyev, *Argumenty i fakty* 34/35, 1987.
5. *Literaturnaia Rossiia* 24, 1988. A similar demand was made by Otto Latsis, deputy editor of *Kommunist, Komsomolskaia pravda*, June 28, 1988.
6. P. Broué, "Voyage à Moscow," *Cahiers Leon Trotsky* 36 (1988), pp. 4–7.
7. *Moskovskie novosti* 13, 1989. Another great-grandchild became a militant member of the extreme right in Israel.
8. *Sovetskaia Rossiia*, September 27, 1987.
9. N. Vasetsky, "L. Trotsky, Mif i realnost," *Argumenty i fakty* 34, 1988; D. Volkogonov, "Triumf i tragediia," *Oktiabr* 12, 1988, pp. 90 et seq.; *Politicheskoe samoobrazovanie* 9, 1987, pp. 46–52.
10. *Agitator* 18, 1988, p. 38. In a later interview, Vasetsky presented a somewhat more positive account, stressing Trotsky's personal courage, conceding that he did play a central role in the civil war and mentioning that Lenin twice suggested that Trotsky should serve as his deputy. *Komsomolskaia pravda*, May 19, 1989.

    In yet more recent publications Vasetsky has again sharply turned against Trotsky, claiming that there was little to choose between the policies advocated by him and those of Stalin.

    According to K. Rash, in a long series of articles (*Voenno-Istoricheski Zhurnal*, throughout 1989), Trotsky was the greatest coward who had ever disgraced the Russian earth.
11. B. Kncipaz, *The Social and Political Thought of Leon Trotsky*, Oxford, 1978, p. 373.
12. V. Dolgov, *Komsomolskaia pravda*, October 22, 1988.
13. *Oktiabr* 12, 1988, p. 93.
14. "O Staline i Stalinisme," *Znamia* 1–4, 1989; quoted here from *Let History Judge*, New York, 1972, p. 140.
15. *Literaturnaia gazeta*, December 9, 1987. True, Volkogonov refers to Trotsky's call for a political revolution rather than murder, but he thinks that this amounted to a "coup" and that Trotsky's slogan "down with Stalin," the "outcome of his blind hate," was bound to have the same effect.
16. N. Vasetsky, "Likvidatsia," *Literaturnaia gazeta*, January 13, 1989.
17. I. Deutscher, *Stalin*, London, 1948, p. 377. Even sharp critics of Trotsky writing under glasnost did not use this argument. See, for instance, L. M. Minaev, "Borba za liderstvo," *Voprosy istorii KPSS* 12, 1989.
18. A point convincingly made by Sergo Mikoyan, "Asketism vozhda," *Ogonyok* 15, 1989.
19. Volkogonov, op. cit., p. 95.
20. D. Volkogonov, "Demon revoliutsii," *Pravda*, September 9, 1988.
21. "Demon revoliutsii" op. cit.
22. *Inostrannaia literatura* 3, 1989, p. 171.
23. "Mamin vopros," *Vek xx i mir* 3, 1989, p. 32.
24. N. Vasetsky, "Likvidatsia," *Literaturnaia gazeta*, January 4, 1989. However, a more positive approach toward Trotsky could be discerned in the writings of Vladimir Billik (*Sobesednik* 32, 1989) and also such mainstream writers as D. Volkogonov and V. Startsev (*Rodina* 7, 1989). *Voprosy istorii* (July 1989) began to publish in installments Trotsky's "Stalin School of Falsification." *Moscow News* featured an article by Albert Nenarokov, "A Good Name to Be Restored" (March 18, 1990). But these were still the exceptions. The approach in most Soviet periodicals vis-à-vis Trotsky was far more hostile than with regard to other Communist leaders, and for the

mouthpieces of the Right he remained the archvillain par excellence, much more odious than Stalin.

25. N. Vasetsky, "Likvidatsia," *Literaturnaia gazeta*, January 4, 1989.

26. Roy Medvedev wrote in 1989 that Krivitsky was killed by the NKVD, but he had apparently no access to Soviet archives and could not provide evidence. Ovidii Gorchakov, a writer and former intellience agent, praised Ignaz Reiss (who had denounced Stalin in an open letter to the Central Committee) as a true anti-Stalinist in a series of articles published under glasnost. "Nakanune ili tragediia Kassandri" ("On the eve, the tragedy of Cassandra"), *Nedelia* 42–44, 1988. His essay had originally been written in 1956. Krivitsky was also favorably mentioned by Gorchakov and others in connection with the publication in the Soviet Union of Koestler's *Darkness at Noon*.

27. The last chapter of Deutscher's Trotsky biography covering Trotsky's assassination was published in *Inostrannaia literatura* 3, 1989.

28. "Ubitsa Trotskovo, palach ili zhertva?" *Moskovskie novosti*, March 12, 1989. Efim Teper (*Neva* 3, 1989) writes that the official "legend" was, of course, nonsense, but no one knows what really motivated Mercader.

29. For instance, *Sovetskaia Rossiia*, September 27, 1987.

30. For instance, Yuri Trifonov's *Starik*, 1978.

31. One of the first to accuse Trotsky of the authorship of the collectivization and the terror in the countryside was the writer Vasili Belov; see his novel *Kanuny* (1972–89) and *Pravda*, April 15, 1988.

32. Vadim Kozhinov, *Moskva* 11, 1986.

33. A. Kurbatova, *Molodaia gvardia* 5, 1988.

34. *Nash sovremennik* 9, 1988, pp. 82–83. This is quite untrue; the same author claims that the poet Aleksander Gamin was shot in Vologda in 1925 (!) because he had written a poem critical of Trotsky.

35. Vasili Belov, "God velikovo pereloma," *Novyi mir* 5, 1988, p. 10.

36. *Ogonyok* 46, 1987; see Julia Wishnevsky, op. cit., p. 5.

37. *Moskva* 1, 1989.

38. His original name was Liova.

39. I. Deutscher, *The Prophet Outcast*, London, 1963, pp. 95–106. Pierre Broué, *Trotsky*, Paris, 1988, pp. 700 et seq.

40. Even a relatively objective account such as L. A. Radzikovsky's ("Boyazn demokratii," *Sotsiologicheskie issledovaniia* 3, 1989) exaggerates Trotsky's indirect impact on Stalin's thoughts and actions just as the juxtaposition of Lenin, the democrat, and Trotsky, the advocate of dictatorship, is historically inaccurate. As the result of many decades of censorship, Soviet writers are not familiar with the huge literature on Trotsky and Trotskyism, both for and against, published in the West.

4. The Great Terror: How It Came About

1. This refers to the Shakhty case in 1928, the Prom party (Industrial party) in 1930, the Menshevik trial in 1931, and the Metro-Vickers trial of 1933. There were also some other minor cases such as the historians' trial of 1931. Furthermore, beginning in 1930, groups of people were shot without trial. The use of stool pigeons was tried; one of them was Professor Ramzin, head of the "Industrial party."

2. Recent Soviet publications about the Kirov murder add little to what has been known. A. Kirilina in *Rodina* 1, 1989, and V. Lordkipanidze in *Argumenty i fakty* 6, 1989. A. Yakovlev, a member of the Politburo Investigation Committee, said in an interview that no documentary evidence has been discovered connecting Stalin with Kirov's murder.

3. U.S. intelligence was almost the only one that did not figure in the accusations, except in one or two marginal cases. It is also interesting to note that after 1936 there was hardly any mention of alleged Nazi espionage in public trials.

4. A good example is Alexander Orlov, a high-ranking NKVD officer; another is Victor Kravchenko, a foreign-trade official. Their revelations were bitterly attacked by some in the West as mere gossip picked up in the Moscow corridors of power, if not outright anti-Soviet fabrications. There were, of course, mistakes in their books, but this is less surprising than the amount of correct information they contained. Orlov remained a villain at first even under glasnost, whereas Krivitsky, another NKVD defector, fared much better, and Ignaz Reiss, the third of this group, became almost a hero (Ovidii Gorchakov, *Nedelya* 6, 1989).

Orlov's memoirs were first published in the West in 1953 but were dismissed by some U.S. academics as an unreliable source. In the Soviet Union in 1989, ironically, they became a bone of contention between several Soviet periodicals in a race to publish them first. *Ogonyok* did in November 1989.

5. R. Conquest, *The Great Terror*, London, 1968; R. Medvedev, *Let History Judge*, New York, 1971; A. Solzhenitsyn, *The Gulag Archipelago*, 3 vols., New York, 1973. Conquest's book was published in installments in *Neva*, 1989; excerpts from Solzhenitsyn appeared in *Novyi Mir*.

6. Marina Simonian, *Sotsialisticheskaia zakonnost* 1, 1988; Julia Wishnevsky, "Soviet Legality and the Falsification of History," Radio Liberty, August 20, 1987.

7. Feofanov, *Izvestiia*, June 14, 1988.

8. On the orders given between 1955 and 1960 to destroy the gulag archives, see the account by the member of one of the committees engaged in the destruction. Dmitri Yakovenko in *Zvezda vostoka* 1, 1989.

9. The circumstances of the escape are related in Solzhenitsyn *Arkhipel Gulag*, Paris, 1974, vol. 2, p. 57. There were more escapes in the 1920s and early 1930s of people who had been in the gulag; the most widely read at the time was the one written by Ivan Solonevich. Karl Albrecht, a deputy people's commissar, had been at Solovki as the head of a delegation and devoted a whole chapter in his book to his visit (Karl Albrecht, *Der verratene Sozialismus*, Leipzig, 1939, pp. 91–106). But these stories were seldom believed because the witnesses, like Albrecht, once outside Russia, became members of extreme right-wing or Fascist parties. In view of Goebbels's and Hitler's mendacious propaganda and in view of the horrors of the Nazi concentration camps, there was great skepticism with regard to information received from these quarters. However, when read fifty years after the event, there are not many discrepancies between the stories of Solonevich, Chernavin, Albrecht, and other witnesses of that period and the revelations made under glasnost.

10. Interview in *Argumenty i fakty* 50, 1988. See also Lev Korneshov, *Izvestiia*, December 21, 1988.

11. D. Yurasov, *Sovetskaia molodezh*, December 24, 1988.

12. L. Piyasheva in *Sotsialisticheskaia industriia*, January 14, 1988.

13. Ibid., September 27, 1987. See also Nikonov interview in *Literaturnaia gazeta* 32, 1987.

14. "Pokushenie na Sholokhova" in *Molodaia gvardia*" 5, 1989, pp. 174–93. If true, the account makes Sholokhov's immoral behavior toward persecuted Soviet writers after 1948 even more difficult to understand.

15. The appeal was first published in *Yunost* 12, 1988. The first revelations on the Ryutin affair were made by Arkadi Waksberg in *Literaturnaia gazeta*, June 29, 1988. Official documents concerning the Ryutin case appeared in *Izvestiia Ts. K. KPSS.* 6, 1989.

16. According to Volkogonov's biography, the other members of the Politburo were silent when Stalin made his demand. Stalin retreated when Kirov protested that Ryutin was not a hopeless case but a man who had gone astray. "Triumf i tragediia," *Oktiabr*, December 1988, p. 49.

17. It was not known whether this was because he betrayed his comrades or was a fellow Georgian, or for some other unfathomable reason.

18. V. A. Kumanev, V*oprosy istorii* 12, 1988, p. 19.

19. Volkogonov, *Oktiabr* 12, 1988, p. 51.

20. A local Leningrad historian has argued that although Yagoda, the head of the NKVD, may have been instrumental in Kirov's murder, Stalin might not have known. But this version is far from convincing. Alla Kirillina, *Moskovskaia pravda*, November 10, 1988.

21. Viktor Buzinov, "Mif o zelenoi lampe," *Leningradskaia panorama* 6, 1989.

22. Mrachkovsky and Ter-Vaganyan, two other defendants, had also been in prison throughout 1932 and 1934.

23. Bernard Pares, *Russia*, New York, 1943, p. 135.

24. Y. Feofanov, *Izvestiia*, June 14, 1988.

25. E. Kaplan, *Ogonyok* 5, 1989.

26. See, for example, N. Vasetsky in *Argumenty i fakty* 42 and 43, 1988; Dmitri Shelestov in *Nedelia* 29, 1988; E. Ambartsumov, *Moskovskie novosti* 25, 1988.

27. Interview with Vitali Glebov (Kamenev) in *Sotsialisticheskaia industria*, January 11, 1989.

28. *Ogonyok* 52, 1988.

29. Roy Medvedev wrote that 225,000 copies of the article were reissued in pamphlet form—an enormous figure at the time. *Let History Judge*, New York, 1972, p. 148. This sentence found its way into Volkogonov's biography, *Oktiabr* 11, 1988, p. 120.

30. Radek was murdered by a criminal who no doubt had been hired for the purpose. Sokolnikov died under circumstances that were not clear. *Moskovskie novosti*, June 19, 1988; *Ogonyok* 52, 1988.

31. *Sovetskaia Rossiia*, June 21, 1966.

32. A first attempt to come to terms with the new situation was the publication of a collection of 29 articles, *Vozvrashennie imena*, Moscow, 1989. A subsequent collection of essays was *Reabilitirovan posmertno*, Moscow, 1989.

33. A full-length article on Sokolnikov appeared in V*oprosy istorii* 12, 1988. But, significantly, it was not written by a professional historian but by Vladimir Genis, a leading Moscow designer, probably a relation or a friend of the family. A shorter version appeared in *Vechernaia Moskva*, October 4, 1988.

34. See, for instance, V. Kozhinov in *Nash sovremennik* 1, 1989, and in *Literaturnaia gazeta*, March 15, 1989.

35. The first was *Izbrannie proizvedeniia*, Moscow, 1989. A short biography by I. E. Gorelov was also published in 1989.
36. *Znamia* 10–12, 1988.
37. Only in 1989 did it become known that Bukharin had written from prison several dozen letters to Stalin that were preserved, but not made accessible, even to trusted Soviet writers such as Volkogonov. Moreover, an informer had been placed in Bukharin's cell, whose frequent reports about Bukharin's mood, etc., have also been preserved. One of Bukharin's letters, written before his murder, was read at a Central Committee meeting after 1956. It was very much in the same vein as the letter to Voroshilov. "Dearest (*rodnoi*) Koba, you know that I am not guilty. Why destroy me, why not send me for life to the White Sea? I shall work among the peoples of the north, to bring them the light of Marxist-Leninist truth. . . ." V. P. Naumov and D. Shelepin in "Problemy istorii i sovremennost," *Voprosy istorii KPSS* 2, 1989.
38. Among the articles devoted to their memory, to give but a short selection, were A. S. Senin, "Aleksei Ivanovich Rykov" in *Voprosy istorii* 9, 1988; the same journal also published an essay on Mikhail Tomsky, who had committed suicide before the trial. Also published were articles on Rykov, see Kolodezhni and Tepstov, *Nedelya* 18, 1988. A long interview on Rykov's last days with his daughter appeared in *Teatr*. On Professor Platner, V. Topoliansky in *Literaturnaia gazeta*, June 15, 1988. On Rakovsky—Dimitri Stanishev, in *Mezhdunarodnaia zhizn* 12, 1988. Television documentaries were devoted to the memory of Bukharin and Rykov in 1988–89.
39. One advocate of this line was the *Voenno istoricheski zhurnal* (the Military History Journal), which began to serialize in December 1989 Barbusse's biography of Stalin (1935), probably the most notorious document of the period of the "cult of the individual."

5. A Murky Affair: The Destruction of the Red Army Command

1. Krivitsky related that the Russians had an agent at the very center of an influential group in Paris, the Gutchkov circle—it was Gutchkov's daughter. The story of Vera Alexandrova Traill has been related in considerable detail in a recent book by a French academic. See Alain Brossat, *Agents de Moscou*, Paris, 1988.
2. Most prominently, Isaac Deutscher in his *Stalin*. Even in the new edition of 1960, despite all evidence to the contrary, Deutscher stuck to the old version. Only in 1966, with much reluctance, did he modify his account. He still believed, however, that there had been some sort of plot against Stalin. The other major biographer of Stalin, Boris Souvarine, never shared this belief: In an article in *Contrat Social* (July 1959), he disproved the allegations of a conspiracy once and for all.
3. In the National Archives in Washington, D.C., I found a curious Gestapo document entitled *Sonderbericht Tuchatschewski* that also throws doubt on the circumstances of his escape from a German prisoner-of-war camp (Ingolstadt) during World War I. But the author of this long anonymous report claims that he was helped in his escape by the Freemasons and the Bolsheviks then concentrated in Switzerland. . . . The report, submitted shortly before the trial, came from an outside consultant. On the cover is the revealing comment *Überholt* ("overtaken by events").
4. See P. Tastevin, *Rapport: Affaire de Miller. Confidentiel* (unpublished, from the Boris Nikolaevsky collection at the Hoover Institution).

5. Roman Gul, *Ya unes Rossiyu*, vol. 2, New York, 1984. Shortly after publication of the article, Alekseev managed to get himself arrested while trying to steal the blueprint for a submarine on which work had been discontinued. He told his French interrogators that he had reliable information from the Soviet general that Tukhachevsky was a German agent—which probably was the whole purpose of the exercise.

6. *Krasnaia zvezda*, July 26, 1988.

7. Leonid Mikhailov, in a series of three articles published in the weekly *Nedelya* in December 1989, 49–51. This sanitized publication provided evidence that at least some of the secret service archives had not been destroyed (as many had feared) but survived, even if access to them was carefully controlled.

8. Beneš's unwitting part in the intrigue is described by Ivan Pfaff in considerable detail on the basis of official Czech files in "Prag und der Fall Tuchatschevskij," *Vierteljahreshefte für Zeitgeschichte*, no. 1, 1987.

9. A debate has sprung up in the Soviet Union as to whether Stalin really believed the forgeries fabricated (or, at any rate, transmitted) by the Gestapo. Stalin's defenders have found mitigating circumstances: They suggest that he was hoodwinked by German intelligence (*Sovetskaia Rossiia* 18, September 1988). But another journal (*Sovetskaia kultura* 23, August 1988) has published an interview with General Nikolai Pavlenko, who rejected this version out of hand. According to another Soviet writer, F. Sergeev, the original information came from Skoblin ("a sworn enemy of the Soviet Union"), but the decision to use it was made by Hitler and Heydrich, so that there was no NKVD involvement (*Nedelya* 7, 1989). This rests on the assumption that Skoblin was an enemy of the Soviet Union; as we have seen, he was an agent of the NKVD.

10. Some Soviet media gave much publicity to an article published in the West German quarterly *Vierteljahreshefte für Zeitgeschichte*, by Ivan Pfaff, "Prag und der Fall Tuchatschevskij," 1, 1987. It was reprinted in full in *Voenno-istoricheski zhurnal* in several installments in 1988; a shorter version appeared in *Sovetskaia Rossiia*, September 18, 1988. But although Pfaff had done work in the Czech archives, his article did not deal at all with the reception of the forged material in Moscow or with its origins in Paris and London. It does in no way absolve Stalin from guilt. Upon opening the Tukchachevsky file in the Soviet foreign ministry, the director of the archives reported that no evidence had been found that the Heydrich-Beneš material had ever reached Stalin. Volkogonov, on the other hand, presents evidence that the first information of the alleged plot had emanated from ROVS, i.e., General Skoblin's organization. Ezhov had passed it on to Stalin, who sent it to some Politburo members (Volkogonov, *Oktiabr* 12, 1988, p. 137). According to files in Soviet archives made accessible in 1989, the Soviet ambassador in Paris also reported the Tukchachevsky plot, but the source seems to have again been Skoblin. N. Abramov, *Sobitie i vremya* 2, 1989.

11. That Stalin had a hand in the "Skoblin provocation" has been suspected in Moscow for a long time. Broad hints to this effect appear, for instance, in an essay on Tukhachevsky by Major General Isserson, written in the early 1960s but published only in 1988, in the literary journal *Druzhba narodov*. Isserson was arrested in 1939, but survived the camps. On his release in 1955, he was reinstated in the army but was demoted to the rank of colonel.

12. The *Short History of the Great War of the Fatherland*, 1965, gave even higher

figures, stating that virtually all divisional and brigade commanders disappeared. For a more recent assessment, see O. Suvenirov, "Vsearmeiskaia tragediia," *Voenno-istoricheski zhurnal* 3, 1989.

13. I. Korenblat, *Daugava* 5, 1989, p. 69.

14. Vladimir Borodin, *Voenny vestnik* 10, 1988.

15. A. Gorokhov in *Sobesednik* 18, 1988.

16. Volkogonov, *Oktiabr* 12, 1988, p. 147, adduces a sample.

17. On Nevsky, *Sovetskaia kultura*, May 14, 1988; on Bubnov, *Sovetskaia kultura*, March 8, 1988.

18. Interview with Irina Shliapnikova, *Moskovskie novosti* 50, 1987.

19. A. Van Goudoever, *The Limits of De-Stalinization*, London, 1986, p. 131.

20. On Antonov-Ovseenko, *Vechernaia Moskva*, January 9, 1988; *Nauka i zhizn* 8, 1988; *Moskovskaia pravda*, November 7, 1988; on Raskolnikov, V. Polikarpov in *Ogonyok* 26, 1987; *Nedelya* 33, 1988; and *Nedelya* 20, 1988.

21. Volkogonov, *Oktiabr*, December 1988, p. 137.

22. For a typical assessment of Yagoda under glasnost, see M. Liashko in *Turkmenskaia iskra*, August 20, 1988.

23. On Boky, Lev Razgon's fascinating memoirs "Nepridumannoe," *Yunost* 5, 1988.

24. A few old Chekists miraculously survived the various purges. One of them was Fyodor Fomin, who published his recollections in 1962. But Fomin had been in command of the NKVD border troops and, as such, not directly involved in domestic affairs.

25. Kamil Ikramov, "Delo moevo otsa," *Znamia* 5 and 6, 1989. Stalin's granddaughter (Svetlana's daughter) and Ikramov's granddaughter were classmates in Moscow in the 1970s.

26. For the Zelensky case, *Komsomolets uzbekistana*, April 15, 1988; for purges in Turkmenistan—*Turkmenskaia iskra*, November 10, 1988; in Kazakhstan—*Kazakhstanskaia pravda*, July 24, October 25, and November 26, 1988. On the murder of the Ukrainian Komsomol leadership—*Komsomolskoe znamia*, October 29, 1988.

27. *Krugozor*, December 1988, for a profile of Bagirov.

28. On Raibai—*Sovetskaia Latvia*, October 21, 1988. On Bykovnya, *Literaturnaia gazeta* 48, 1988, and Rupert Cornwell in *Independent*, March 10 and 25, 1989. The estimates of victims buried there vary between 6,329 and 240,000. In Kolpashev near Tomsk, thousands of graves were discovered in 1979. The local authorities tried to hush up the affair; it was claimed that these had been deserters from the Red Army. It took another ten years for the truth to emerge. Vladimir Zapetsky in *Biblioteka molodosti Sibiri* 5, 1989. There were countless other such reports. About a mass grave near Cheliabinsk in the Southern Ural, there were reports in *Sotsialisticheskaia industriia*, June 28, 1989.

29. The article was written by the Minsk archaeologist Zenon Pozniak and an engineer E. Shmygalev. It was published in *Literatura i mastatsva*, June 2, 1988. More details were revealed in an interview with Pozniak in *Molodezh Estonii*, May 20, 1989.

30. Dozens of reports and articles about Kuropaty were published in the Soviet press. Some of the more significant appeared in *Sobesednik* 46, 1988; *Daugava*, September 9, 1988; *Nedelya* 47, 1988; *Izvestiia*, September 12, 1988; *Sovetskaia molodezh*, September 22, 1988; *Daugava* 1, 1989; *Izvestiia*, November 27, 1988; and *Ogonyok* 39, 1988. For the most detailed account so far, *Neman* 4, 1990.

31. *Sovetskaia molodezh* (Riga), September 22, 1988. The official report of the Kuropaty investigation committee was published in *Sovetskaia Belorussia*, January 22, 1989.
32. The population declined from 12 million to 9.2 million in 1940: "Every fourth White Russian suffered from Stalinism." Pozniak in *Molodezh Estonii*, May 20, 1989.

6. Purges Everywhere

1. R. Conquest, *The Great Terror*, p. 322.
2. Interview with Beltov, *Vechernaia Moskva*, July 19, 1988; other interviews in *Zaria vostoka*, July 14, 1988 and *Vechernaia Moskva*, November 12, 1988.
3. A. Vaksberg, "Protsesy," *Literaturnaia gazeta*, May 4, 1988.
4. For the stories of Meyerhold's last days and how his private archive was hidden, see Konstantin Rudnitsky in *Ogonyok* 22, 1988 and *Neva* 11, 1988. About the murder of Mandelstam's wife, see *Ogonyok* 15, 1989.
5. Vaksberg, op. cit.
6. Y. Albats, *Moscow News* 46, 1987. Interview with Khvat in *Selskaia molodezh* 6, 1989.
7. E. Kolchinsky in *Voprosy estestvoznanii i tekhniki* 1, 1988, p. 124 and V. Filatov in *Znanie-sila* 10 and 11, 1987.
8. V. P. Filatov, *Voprosy filosofii* 8, 1988.
9. Yaroslav Golovanaov, *Literaturnaia gazeta*, November 9, 1988. For Korolev's story, *Znamia* 1 and 2, 1990.
10. Anna Livanova, *Ogonyok* 3, 1988.
11. See, for example, A. Latyshev, *Molodezh Estonii*, June 27, 1988.
12. G. Zhavoronkov, *Moscow News* 15, 1988; from a letter to Piatnitsky's son, dated December 23, 1987. See also Zhavoronkov on Piatnitsky in *Vozvrashennie imena*, Moscow, 1989, pp. 61–75.
13. F. I. Firsov and I. S. Yazhborovskaia, in *Voprosy istorii KPSS* 12, 1988, pp. 40–55.
14. H. Weber, *Die Wandlung des deutschen Kommunismus* Bd. 2, Frankfurt, 1969.
15. Günter Judick in *U.Z.*, May 4, 1988. For a critical comment, see H. Weber in *Deutschland Archiv* 4, 1988, pp. 580–83.
16. *Za rubezhom* 4, 1989. F. Firsov claims that "sometimes Dimitrov's letters brought results and sometimes not," but he provides no evidence. *Novoe vremya*, 18, 1989. The issue of the German Communists who had vanished in Moscow in the 1930s was prominently featured in East Germany after the censorship was abolished in October/November 1989.
17. A. Latyshev, *Sovetskaia kultura*, August 2, 1988.
18. A. Latyshev, *Molodezh Estonii*, June 23, 1988.
19. According to Kun's widow, Stalin disliked him because he had shown insufficient zeal in propagating the Stalin cult. B. I. Zhelitsky, Bela Kun, *Voprosy istorii* 1, 1989, pp. 80–81. See also "Novie dannie o gibeli Bela Kuna," *Voprosy istorii KPSS* 3, 1989.
20. Robert W. Thurston, "Fear and Belief in the USSR's Great Terror," *Slavic Review*, Summer 1986, pp. 230–31.
21. *Pravda*, July 4, 1989.
22. Yuri Feofanov, *Izvestiia*, April 19, 1988.

23. "Kto oni byli vragi naroda?" *Trud*, January 7, 1989.
24. Feofanov, loc. cit.
25. L. Babich, *Nauka i zhizn* 10, 1988.
26. *Ogonyok* 5, 1989.
27. M. Gurfinkl, *Moscow News* 28, 1988. On Kosarev and Bubnov, *Vozvrashennie imena*, Moscow, 1989, passim.
28. Arkadi Vaksberg, *Literaturnaia gazeta*, April 20, 1988.
29. The fullest acount of the "anticosmopolitan" campaign is Borshagorsky in *Teatr*, October 1988–March 1989. A detailed description of the anticosmopolitan campaign at Leningrad University by K. Azadovsky and B. Egorov appeared in *Zvezda* 6, 1989. The leading figures in this campaign, Professors Berdinkov and Bushmin, continued to prosper for many years after Stalin's death.
30. *Argumenty i fakty*, April 23, 1988; Viktor Demidov, *Knizhnoe obozrennie*, December 23, 1988.
31. Voznesensky, Kuznetsov, and Kapustin, perhaps owing to an oversight, had never been excluded from the party. For other accounts of the Leningrad affair, see S. Bardin, *Nedelya* 40, 1988; G. Romanov in *Sovetskaia Rossiia*, December 3, 1988; A. Afanasev, *Komsomolskaia pravda*, January 15, 1988; L. Sidorovsky in *Trud*, July 13, 1988, and, in greatest detail, L. Sidorovsky in *Avrora* 4, 1989, pp. 10–31 and *Izvestiia Ts.K KPSS* 2, 1989, p. 126.
32. K. Rudnitsky in *Teatr*; Rudnitsky had published a book on Mikhoels during the first thaw (1963) that was, however, far less detailed about the circumstances of his death. For a more recent account of the Mikhoels affair, M. Geiser in *Literaturnaia gazeta*, February 8, 1989.
33. A. Vaksberg, *Literaturnaia gazeta*, March 15, 1989. It also appeared that Grishaev, one of the main investigators in this as in other political trials of the late Stalin era, was still on the staff of a Moscow legal institute, had received various state honors, and said in an interview that he did not remember anything and that his conscience was clear.
34. David Gai, *Moskovskie novosti*, February 7, 1988.
35. Y. Rapoport, *Druzhba narodov* 6, 1988, p. 225.
36. On the fate of Professor Etinger and his family, see the account of his son, the historian Y. Etinger, in *Nauka i zhizn* 1, 1990, p. 126 et seq.
37. Y. Rapoport, op. cit., p. 236.
38. Natalia Rapoport, *Yunost* 4, 1988.
39. *New York Times*, May 13, 1988.
40. Hence, the arrest and murder in 1950 of Marshal Khudyakov, an Armenian who knew too much about Beria's role in Baku in 1917–18. *Kommunist*, Erevan, June 22, 1988.
41. A great many accounts were published under glasnost on the circumstances of his arrest. See, for instance. S. Bystrov in *Krasnaia zvezda*, March 18–20, 1988. For a general account of Beria's career and personal life, see A. Antonov-Ovseenko in *Zvezda* 9, 1988, pp. 141–64. See also "Berievshshina" in *Voenno istoricheski zhurnal* 5, 1989. The fullest account so far was published in *Dalnyi vostok* 1, 1990, the recollections of Major General Ivan Zub. Fifty volumes of evidence were collected in the preparation of the Beria trial; none has been published thus far.
42. Arkadi Vaksberg, *Literaturnaia gazeta*, January 27, 1988.
43. Volkogonov, *Oktiabr* 12, 1988, p. 121.

44. For a biographical sketch of Ulrich, see D. Tabachnik, *Radianska Ukraina*, February 3–5, 1989.
45. A. Lavin, *Chelovek i zakon* 11, 1988, pp. 89–99.
46. Vaksberg, op. cit.
47. Harold Laski, *Law and Justice in the Soviet Union*, London, 1935, p. 21.

7. Why They Confessed

1. Volkogonov, *Oktiabr*, December 1988, p. 132.
2. Among the first detailed estimates, David J. Dallin and Boris I. Nicolaevsky, "Forced Labor in Soviet Russia," New Haven, 1947, and the critique by Naum Jasny, "Labor and Output in Soviet Concentration Camps," *Journal of Political Economy*, October 1951. Jasny argued that a figure of 15–20 million forced laborers was grossly exaggerated. His critique was based mainly on a copy of the state plan for the national economy that had somehow found its way to the West.
3. B. Souvarine, *Stalin*, New York, 1939, pp. 640–41.
4. I. Deutscher, *Stalin*, London, 1949, p. 380.
5. The most detailed survey was S. Swianiewicz, *Forced Labor and Economic Development*, London, 1965. Also the exchanges between S. Rosefielde, S. G. Wheatcroft, and R. Conquest in *Soviet Studies*, January 1981, April 1981, July 1982, April 1983.
6. *Research Report 8533*. Department of State Bureau of Intelligence and Research, October 3, 1960.
7. *Argumenty i fakty* 5, 1989. This figure also appears in a new Soviet textbook by Yury Korablev, Y. Borisov, and others, *Istoria SSSR*, Moscow, 1989. See Thomas Sherlock and Vera Tolz, "Debates over numbers of Stalin's victims in the USSR and in the West," Report on the U.S.S.R., September 1989.
8. V. V. Tsaplin, "Statistika zhertv stalinisma v 30e gody," in *Voprosy istorii* 5, 1989, p. 181. It seems doubtful that 2 million Soviet citizens were permitted to leave the country during this period or succeeded to escape, even though the Asian borders of the country may have been more porous than generally believed.
9. N. Teptsov, "Veliki perelom," *Veteran* 50, 1988. Dimitri Yakovenko, "Osuzhden po 58 i" (sentenced according to paragraph 58), *Zvezda vostoka* 1, 1989, p. 85. According to an estimate by Y. Dyadkin in the nonofficial journal *Referendum* (29–30, 1989), some 3.2 million people died of other than natural causes in the Soviet Union between 1937 and 1940.
10. The estimates of some experts such as Wheatcroft and Danilov are perhaps too low, those of some Russian demographers such as Kurganov (66 million) almost certainly too high. W. Perevertsev in *Molodaia gvardia* 7, 1989; P. Palamarchuk, *Literaturnaia Rossiia* 27, 1989.

Quoting an official document dated February 1, 1954, Vladimir Nekrasov, a historian and major general, claims that from 1921 to 1954 some 3,777,000 persons were repressed, out of which 643,000 were sentenced to death. He also reports when the Second World War broke out, the camps had 2,300,000 inmates, but subsequently the numbers must have risen because he continues that during the war 3,400,000 died or were released from the camps and that by December 1, 1944, the camp population had fallen to 1,450,000 people. However, these figures certainly do not include the victims of collectivization and probably also several other major categories. *Komsomolskaia pravda*, September 1989.

11. Interview with Viktor Zemskov, *Argumenty i fakty* 45, 1989.

12. TASS, February 12, 1990. These figures were also published in *Argumenty i fakty* and became the subject of a public debate since they were much smaller than most earlier estimates. For the Zemskov-Nokhotovich article, see *Argumenty i fakty* 5, 1990. A considerably higher figure of executions between 1934 and 1954 (3.5 million) was given in an interview by Maj. Gen. Aleksandr Kurbainov, head of the new KGB public relations center in April 1990.

13. *Argumenty i fakty* 3, 1989.

14. V. Chaikova, *Neva* 10, 1988. Also his interview on the TV program *Vzglyad* and with *Sobesednik* and *Sovetskaia molodezh*, December 24, 1988. See also D. G. Yurasov in *Sovetskaia bibliografia* 5, 1988, pp. 61–67, and, in greatest detail in *Yunost* (Turkmenia) 1, 1990.

15. E. Genri quoted it apparently with some mistakes, in an open letter to Ilya Erenburg that found its way to the émigré press. See I. Makhovikov in *Vnutrennie protivorechia* 3, 1982, pp. 198–226.

16. See for instance, Volkogonov, *Oktiabr*, December 1988, pp. 149–50 and various essays in *Voenno-istoricheski zhurnal* from 1987 onwards.

17. *Neva* 7 and 8, 1988, in Andrei Kistyakovsky's excellent translation.

18. M. Zlobina, "Versiia Kestlera," *Novyi mir* 2, 1989.

19. Shatskin's letter complaining to Stalin from his prison cell is quoted in *Izvestiia Ts.K. KPSS* 6, 1989. On Shatskin, the founder of the Komsomol, the Communist youth organization, A. Galagan and A. Zinoviev, in *Vozvrashennie imena*, Moscow, 1985, vol. 2, pp. 305 et seq.

20. Thus Stalin is reported to have blamed Voroshilov for the murder of the Red Army commanders in later years. *Nedelya* 9, 1989.

21. For a discussion of this theory, Manfred Funke, *Starker oder schwacher Diktator?* Düsseldorf, 1989.

22. Volkogonov, *Oktiabr* 12, 1988, p. 162.

23. Deutscher, *Stalin*, London, 1949, pp. 375–80.

24. O. Volobuyev and S. Kuleshov, *Sovetskaia industria*, June 25, 1988.

25. N. M. Karamzin, *Predannia vekov*, Moscow, 1987, p. 572.

26. Reader's letter by Stepanov, *Dvatsati vek i mir* 10, 1988.

27. *Literaturnaia gazeta*, December 9, 1987.

28. Oleg Moroz, *Literaturnaia gazeta*, September 28, 1988.

29. N. Pavlenko, *Moskovskaia pravda*, September 4, 1988.

30. Above all, Robert Tucker, but also by Souvarine, Ulam, Medvedev, and others. For a critical survey see Daniel Rancour-Laferrière, *The Mind of Stalin: A Psychoanalytical Study*, Ann Arbor, 1988, chap. 2.

31. Lidia Shatunovskaia, *Zhizn v Kremle*, New York, 1982; A. Antonov-Ovseenko, *The Time of Stalin*, New York, 1983, p. 254.

32. A. Belkin, *Meditsinskaia gazeta*, November 11, 1988, and his interview in *Argumenty i fakty* 17, 1989. M. Buyanov (*Nedelya*, 25, 1989), comparing Stalin with Hitler, wrote that the former was lëss pathological or, rather, that his madness was more socially conditioned.

33. Report (1989) of a special Politburo commission on the so-called Moscow Center. *Izvestiia Ts.K. KPSS* 7, 1989, p. 84.

34. *Argumenty i fakty* 5, 1989.
35. I follow Y. Feofanov's account in *Nedelya* 41, 1988.
36. An investigation committee dealing with the Safonova case in 1989 reached different conclusions. True, the "party-needs-your-confession" argument was used against her, but in addition she was threatened with the arrest of her sister and her children and also the application of "physical measures." *Izvestiia Ts.K. KPSS* 8, 1989, pp. 86–88.
37. Colonel Alexander Litvintsev, *Sotsialisticheskaia industriia*, January 29, 1989.
38. Lev Razgon, "Nepridumannoe," *Yunost* 5, 1988, p. 19.
39. Report of the Commission of party control in *Isvestiia Ts.K. KPSS* 5, 1989, pp. 68–85.
40. On Ryutin, Ivan Anferter in A. Proskurov (ed.), *Vozvrazhennie imena*, Moscow, 1989, vol. 2, pp. 179 et seq.
41. Ibid., p. 84
42. Ibid., pp. 76, 84. Other members of Bukharin's circle also appeared in these confrontations (Kulikov, Radin, V. V. Schmidt). But it is more likely that they had been tortured, whereas Astrov's appearance was "particularly provocative" (ibid.).
43. It is possible that Stalin and the NKVD wanted to show that collaboration with the state security organs would be rewarded. Astrov served as a lieutenant in the war, was again arrested in 1949, and received a twenty-five-year sentence. Released from the camps after Stalin's death, he admitted to the Central Control Commission in 1957, 1961, and on other occasions that all his evidence had been mendacious. "Ispoved," *Literaturnaia gazeta*, March 29, 1989, and *Izvestiia Ts.K.*, loc. cit.
44. V. D. Polikarpov, *Literaturnaia gazeta*, March 29, 1989.
45. L. Anninsky, *Ogonyok* 36, 1988. Others who asked this question were the literary critic Latynina and General Gorbatov in his recollections published in the 1970s. Gorbatov had been arrested in 1937 but was released in 1940. Blyukher was not executed but beaten to death by his interrogators. *Argumenty i fakty*, January 13, 1990.
46. D. Zatonsky, *Nedelya* 28, 1988. Zatonsky's father was a leading Ukrainian Bolshevik.
47. L. Fink, *Nedelya* 46, 1988.
48. Interview with General Boris Viktorov, *Komsomolskaia pravda*, August 21, 1988.
49. Al. Borin in *Literaturnaia gazeta*, November 23, 1988. About her see also Larina's recollections published in *Znamia* 10 and 11, 1988.
50. V. Sirotkin, *Nedelya* 25, 1989. On Piatnitsky, G. Zhavoronkov in *Vozvrashennie imena*, Moscow, 1989, vol. 2, pp. 61 et seq.
51. Report of the Politburo Commission on the so-called parallel anti-Soviet Trotskyite Center, *Izvestiia Ts.K. KPSS* 9, 1989, p. 37.
52. General Putna and Primakov were arrested in August 1936; Putna confessed within eleven days, whereas Primakov made only unimportant and, from Stalin's point of view, unsatisfactory confessions until May 1937. Medvedev and Kork signed their confessions within two days, Eideman after three, Feldman after four days. Tukhachevsky resisted for seven days at most. Bloodstains were later discovered in his file. They were probably subjected to intensive "physical treatment" at once. Report of the Politburo special commission. *Izvestiia Ts.K. KPSS* 4, 1989.

8. Stalin at Home

1. A preglasnost source of some importance was Lydia Shatunovskaia, who had lived in the Kremlin in the 1930s; *Zhizn v Kremle*, New York, 1982. Another important source was, of course, Svetlana Stalin.

2. His account, "Ryadom s I. V. Stalinym," was published in *Sotsiologicheskie issledovaniia* 3, 1988. After Stalin's death, Rybin became "military commander" of the Bolshoi Theatre—that is to say, chief security officer. Some light was shed under glasnost on Rybin's boss, General Vlasik, who acted in many ways as the chief manager of Stalin's household. See A. N. Kolesnik, "Glavny telo-khranitel vozhda," *Voenno-istoricheski zhurnal* 12, 1989.

3. There are independent accounts of this meeting, for example, *Moskovskaia pravda*, October 16, 1988.

4. Rybin, op. cit., p. 91.

5. Volkogonov, *Oktiabr* 12, 1988, p. 66.

6. Rybin, op. cit., p. 92. In a subsequent article Rybin commented on Stalin's relations with his comrades-in-arms, which, according to the author, were rather distant. But this second Rybin article adds little to our knowledge. *Sotsiologicheskie issledovaniia* 5, 1989.

7. Rybin, op. cit., p. 93.

8. A. P. Miasnikov, "Konchina," *Literaturnaia gazeta*, March 1, 1989.

9. Lev Razgon, "Nepridumannoye," *Yunost* 2, 1989.

10. L. Shatunovskaia, op. cit., p. 184.

11. A detailed list appears in Volkogonov, op. cit., p. 164.

12. A. N. Kolesnik, "Voennoplenni starshi leitenant Jakob Dzhugashvili," *Voenno-istoricheski zhurnal* 12, 1988. Semen Apt, "Sudba," *Nedelya* 12, 1988.

13. Molotov had no son.

14. Kolesnik, p. 75.

15. Ibid., p. 77.

16. Published in the literary magazine *Prostor* 7–9, 1988; for comment, *Kazakhstanskaia pravda*, November 10, 1988.

17. A. Kolesnik, *Moskovskaia pravda*, October 23, 1988.

18. *Argumenty i fakty* 46, 1988. Vasili (in contrast to Jakob) had used the name Stalin until well after his father's death. A. N. Kolesnik, "Vzlet i padenie Vasilia Stalina," *Voenno-istoricheskii zhurnal* 2, 1989. Kolesnik makes Stalin responsible for the drunkenness of his son because of having offered him Georgian wine when he was still quite young.

19. *Vechernaia Moskva*, October 8, 1988.

20. Interview with Evgeni Stalin, "Preklonaius pered dedom" ("I bow before grandfather"), *Sovetskaia molodezh*, March 24, 1989.

21. A. Kolesnik, "Doch Stalina," *Argumenty i fakty* 1, 1989; A. Kolesnik, *Sovetskaia kultura*, April 20, 1989. Kolesnik, a former army lieutenant colonel, seems to have had a virtual monopoly so far inasmuch as access to the files of members of the Stalin family is concerned.

22. R. Domarus (ed.), *Hitler's Reden*, vol. 1, p. 613.

23. S. Mikoyan, "Asketism Vozhda," *Ogonyok* 15, 1989.

24. These quotations are from Otto Dietrich, *The Hitler I Knew*, London, 1955, pp. 20, 137, 147, 153, 196, and 214.

25. O. Moroz, N. Bekhtereva, M. Burno, and others. "Consilium," *Literaturnaia gazeta*, August 2, 1989.
26. O. Dietrich, op. cit., p. 136.

9. The Companions-in-Arms

1. He continued to sign even after they had taken his wife. Stalin promised him that he could have her back once the war was over and, for once, kept his word. By that time Kalinin was dying. Lev Razgon, *Ogonyok* 13, 1988.
2. Anastas Mikoyan, *The Memoirs of Anastas Mikoyan*, vol. 1, *The Path of Struggle*, Madison, Conn., 1988.
3. Y. Idashkin, *Literaturnaia Rossiia*, July 22, 1988.
4. Roy Medvedev, *All Stalin's Men*, New York, 1984. Antonov-Ovseenko's excerpts appeared in *Yunost*, *Zvezda*, *Teatr*, and other journals.
5. He had pneumonia that week, but this was not the reason for his tears. Vladimir Amlinsky, "Ten" (The Shadow), *Literaturnaia gazeta*, September 7, 1988.
6. Y. Idashkin, "Znakomi po portretam," *Literaturnaia Rossiia*, July 22, 1988.
7. Ibid. A Molotov autobiography, or sections of it, reportedly exists and may see the light of day at some future date.
8. Volkogonov, *Oktiabr*, December 1988, p. 81.
9. M. German, *Literaturnaia Rossiia*, January 27, 1989; *Nedelya* 9, 1989.
10. Brezhnev received as many; Sharaf Rashidov, head of the Central Asian mafia, got even more.
11. For instance, V. Kardashov, *Voroshilov*, Moscow, 1976; V. Akshinsky, *K. E. Voroshilov*, Moscow, 1979.
12. *Sovetskaia molodezh*, June 16, 1988. See also *Literaturnaia Rossiia*, June 8, 1988, for comment on this poster. A detailed portrait of Voroshilov by R. Medvedev appeared in *Yunost* 8, 1989.
13. Volkogonov, op. cit., p. 87. It has been estimated that 600 Soviet generals were killed in World War II, compared with 1,000 who perished in the purges of 1937–41.
14. Volkogonov, op. cit., p. 88. After Stalin's death, Voroshilov placed the blame for the executions on Stalin, Molotov, and Ezhov. See General Pavlenko, *Nedelya* 9, 1989.
15. L. Razgon, *Yunost*, January 1989.
16. Roy Medvedev in *Moskovskie novosti* 52, 1988, and *Nedelya* 51, 1988. See also *Voprosy istorii KPSS* 5, 1989; *Yunost* 5, 1989. On Kaganovich in the Ukraine, *Vitchizna* 4, 1989.
17. Vadim Kozhinov, "Pravda i istina" in *Nash sovremennik* 4, 1988, was one example of many such attacks.
18. R. Medvedev, *Veteran* 35/36, 1988; reprinted in *Pravda vostoka*, September 15–16, 1988, and in other regional newspapers.
19. S. Mikoyan, *Sovetskaia kultura*, August 13, 1988.
20. Khandyan, first secretary of the Armenian party, was shot on July 9, 1936. The official version lists the death as suicide.
21. These stories recur in semiofficial accounts and appear to be true.
22. Anton Antonov-Ovseenko, "Kariera palacha," *Zvezda* 9, 1988. Excerpts from the protocol of the Beria trial in 1953 (which was held in camera) were published

throughout 1989 in *Voenno-istoricheski zhurnal*. They show that his deputies, after their arrest, not surprisingly, turned against him.

23. S. Bystrov's report based on the recollection of Colonel (later General) Zub, one of the participants, is contained in *Krasnaia zvezda*, March 18–20, 1988. A fuller version appeared in *Dalnyi vostok* 1, 1990. See also A. Skorokhodov in *Literaturnaia gazeta*, July 27, 1988.
24. Volkogonov, op. cit., p. 89.
25. K. Simonov, "Glazami cheloveka moego pokolenia," *Znamia* 4, 1988.

10. The "Cult of Personality"

1. Boris Souvarine, *Stalin*, New York, 1939, p. 577.
2. Mikhail Heller, *Cogs in the Soviet Wheel*, London, 1988, p. 92.
3. Quoted in Heller, p. 68.
4. A. Lunacharsky, *Shtrikhi: Lenin: tovarish, chelovek*, Moscow, 1966, p. 178.
5. Nina Tumarkin, *Lenin Lives: The Lenin Cult in Soviet Russia*, Cambridge, Mass., 1983. The suggestion made by a Soviet author on television in April 1989 to close the mausoleum triggered off protest in the media.
6. I. V. Stalin. *Sochineniia*, Moscow, 1952, vol. 13, p. 19.
7. The *Nation*, August 13, 1930, quoted in Robert C. Tucker, "The Rise of Stalin's Personality Cult," *The American Historical Review*, April 1979. Fischer told Tucker that when the press officer of the foreign commissariat read out to Stalin a translation of the relevant passage, Stalin's comment was "svoloch" (the bastard).
8. *Pravda*, December 11, 1949. According to official statistics published in 1989, 706 million copies of Stalin's works were published until 1954; 279 million of Lenin's; and 65 million of Marx-Engels. *Kommunist* 7, 1989, p. 68.
9. *Izvestiia*, August 15, 1936; quoted in S. Labin, *Stalin's Russia*, London, 1949, p. 65.
10. *Pravda*, December 20, 1948.
11. Hans Schemm, quoted in Ian Kershaw, p. 59.
12. H. Barbusse, *Stalin*, New York, 1935, p. 281.
13. *Sopade, Deutschland Berichte*, vol. 2, pp. 278–79.
14. Quoted in Kershaw, p. 79.
15. Weissbecker in Kershaw, pp. 81, 122.
16. The most detailed survey of the Mussolini literature is August B. Hasler, *Das Duce-Bild in der faschistischen Literatur in Quellen und Forschungen aus italienischen Archiven und Bibliotheken*, Rome, 1980, pp. 420–505. See also Piero Melograni, "The Cult of the Duce," *Journal of Contemporary History*, 1976, pp. 221–37; Jens Petersen, "Mussolini, Wirklichkeit und Mythos eines Diktators," in K. H. Bohrer (ed.), *Mythos und Moderne*, Frankfurt, 1983; Emilio Gentile, in *Mondoperaio* 7/8, 1983; Gian Paolo Cesarani, *Ventrina del Ventennio*, Bari, 1981.
17. G. Gentile, *Genio Italico*, Napoli, 1935, p. 6. See also Renzo De Felice and Luigi Goglia, *Mussolini, Il Mito*, Bari, 1983, passim.
18. Hitler's success, too, was more lasting than commonly believed. A high percentage of Germans believed until well into the 1950s that but for the war, the murder of the Jews, etc., Hitler would have been a very great leader.
19. George Urban, *The Miracles of Chairman Mao*, Los Angeles, 1971, pp. 1–24.

20. New China News Agency, November 14 and December 6, 1967, quoted in Urban, pp. 138–39.
21. Henri Barbusse, *Stalin*, New York, 1935, text on flap.
22. Barbusse was ailing when he visited the Soviet Union; he died the year *Stalin* appeared.
23. David James Fischer, *Romain Rolland and the Politics of Intellectual Engagement*, Berkeley, 1980, p. 250.
24. Fischer, op. cit., p. 253.
25. *Moskovskie novosti*, March 27, 1988. See also Romain Rolland's Moscow journal published for the first time in V*oprosy literaturi*, March–April 1989.
26. André Gide, *Retour de L'URSS*, Paris, 1936, passim.
27. L. Feuchtwanger, *Moskau 1937. Ein Reisebericht für meine Freunde*, Amsterdam. He finished writing the book in May—the American edition appeared in print in August. For the background, see David Caute, *The Fellow Travellers*, London, 1988, pp. 129–30; E. Poretzky, *Our Own People*, London, 1969, p. 198; W. Jeske and Peter Zahn, *Lion Feuchtwanger*, Stuttgart, 1987, pp. 186–203.
28. *Moscow 1937* (U.S. edition), pp. 138–39.
29. Albert Plutnik, "Moskva 1937," *Moskovskie novosti*, October 30, 1988.
30. Plutnik, op. cit. See also "L. Feikhtvanger v Moskve" in *Sovetskie archivy* 4, 1989, pp. 55–62.
31. David C. Smith, *H. G. Wells*, New Haven, 1986, p. 311; David Caute, *The Fellow Travellers*, London, 1988, p. 92 et seq.; H. G. Wells in *New Statesman*, September 27, 1934, and subsequent issues.
32. *Pravda*, 15, November 1930.
33. Lilia Belaeva, *Literaturnaia gazeta*, November 23, 1988; Vadim Baranov, *Sovetskaia kultura*, April 1, 1989. Gorky's essays of 1917–18 that were critical of Bolshevik policies were republished for the first time in Soviet periodicals in 1988 (*Literaturnoye obozrenie*, etc.).
34. N. N. Maslov, "Kratki kurs istorii VKPb—Entsiklopedia kult lichnosti Stalina" ("The Short Course—an Encyclopedia of the Cult of the Individual"), V*oprosy istorii KPSS* 11, 1988.
35. G. Volkov, "Voznesenie," *Sovetskaia kultura*, June 7, 1988. On Stalin as literary editor, V. A. Kumanev, *Literaturnaia gazeta*, September 20, 1989.
36. *Trud*, August 31, 1988.
37. P. Boshshanov, "Rekord," *Komsomolskaia pravda*, October 15, 1988.
38. P. Boshshanov, "Rekordomania," *Komsomolskaia pravda*, January 22, 1989.
39. It is not clear whether Pavel was 12, 13, or 14 at the time. See Yuri Druzhinikov, *Voznesenie Pavlika Morozova*, London, 1989. Many of the facts of the case as related in the official media are dubious.
40. A. Uglanov, *Argumenty i fakty* 28, 1988.
41. A. Uglanov, loc. cit.
42. *Komsomolskaia pravda*, April 5, 1989, and *Chelovek i zakon* 1, 1989.
43. Yuri Zerkhaninov, *Yunost* 5, 1989.
44. Vladimir Karpov, *Znamia*, October 1989, pp. 50–51.
45. *Znamia* 2, 1990.
46. Quoted in Mania Chegodaeva, "A Double Life—A Double Art," *Moscow News* 9, 1989.
47. S. Korolev, *Sovetskaia kultura*, September 17, 1988.

48. Leonid Grekov, "Ne vse filosofy molchali" (Not All Philosophers Kept Silent), *Sovetskaia kultura*, January 26, 1989.
49. On June 20, July 4, and August 2, 1950, M. Gorbanevsky, "Konspekt po korifeyu," *Literaturnaia gazeta*, May 25, 1988.
50. M. Gorbanevsky, op. cit.
51. K. Simonov, "'Glazami cheloveka moevo pokoleniia" (Through the Eyes of a Man of My Generation), *Znamia* 4, 1988.
52. *Moscow News* 32, 1988.
53. *Stroitelnaia gazeta*, October 16, 1988; supplement *Arkhitektura* 19, 1988.
54. A. Belovanova and A. Razumova, eds., *Folklor Sovetskoi Karelii*, as quoted in Frank J. Miller, "The Image of Stalin in Soviet Folklore," *Russian Review* 39, 1980, p. 62.
55. Ibid., p. 67.
56. Y. Borev's *Memuary*; excerpts were published in *Knizhnoe obozrenie* and *Komsomolets Uzbekistana*, February 21, 1988; a longer version in *Daugava* 2, 1990.
57. George Bernard Shaw, *Man and Superman: Maxims for Revolutionists*.

11. Stalin as Warlord

1. Ernest Genri, *Moskovskaia pravda*, May 19, 1988. This is based on an open letter to Ilya Erenburg published in both samizdat and tamizdat more than twenty years earlier. For the full text, see *Druzhba Narodov* 3, 1988.
2. *Hitler's Table Talk*, *1941–44*, London, 1988, p. 361.
3. "If we talk about genocide and about the terror in Nazi Germany and the Soviet Union under Stalin, it is legitimate to compare them." N. N. Maslov, *Voprosy istorii KPSS* 2, 1989, p. 61.
4. Vitali Razdolsky, *Sovetskaia dramaturgia* 1, 1989, p. 205.
5. N. Popov, *Literaturnaia gazeta*, March 1, 1989.
6. For further documentation and references concerning this point, see W. Laqueur "The Strange Lives of General Skoblin," *Encounter*, March 1989 and March 1990.
7. M. S. Gorbachev, *Oktiabr i perestroika*, Moscow, 1987, pp. 23–25. This line was followed by many mainline Soviet historians, for instance, Vsevolod Ezhov, *Literaturnaia gazeta*, April 26, 1989, and General A. I. Mayorov, in *Voenno-istoricheskii zhurnal* 5, 1989, for a thorough apology for Stalin's policy in 1939. See also D. Yazov (the defense minister) in *Pravda*, May 2, 1989.
8. A. S. Yakushevsky, "Sovetski-Germanski dogovor o nenapadenii: Vzglyad cherez gody," *Voprosy istorii* 8, 1988.
9. Some Soviet authors claim, however, that German and Austrian Communists were deported to Nazi Germany because they opposed the pact. In fact, no one had asked them; they were taken from their prison cells and the labor camps where they had been kept since 1936–37.
10. M. Semiryaga, *Literaturnaia gazeta*, October 5, 1988, and the same author's article in *Ogonyok* 22, 1989.
11. Alexander Chubaryan, *Izvestiia*, July 1, 1989. See also the debate between Falin, Semiryaga, and others in "Krugli stol vtoraia mirovaia voina . . ." *Voprosy istorii* 6, 1989.
12. See, for example, *Komsomolskaia pravda* (Lithuanian edition), August 23, 1988,

and *Rahva Haal*, Tallinn, August 10, 1988, and eventually even *Voprosy istorii* 6, 1989.

13. For example, Y. Afanasiev in *Sovetskaia Estonia*, September 29, 1988; *Sovetskaia Litva*, April 21, 1989; *Atmoda*, June 12, 1989, and literally hundreds more articles.

14. Jonathan Steele, "Locked Basement Holds the Answer to Riddle of Stalin and Hitler's Deal," *Guardian* (London), June 15, 1989. Reluctant Soviet historians retreated from their denials only in the summer of 1989, when they argued that reference to their existence, albeit obliquely, had been made in *Izvestiia* in the fall of 1939 and in the first edition of the official history of the Great Fatherland War. (L. Bezymensky put the blame for the subsequent denials on the cold war.)

15. As quoted in V. M. Kulish, *Komsomolskaia pravda*, August 24, 1988.

16. Semiryaga, loc. cit.

17. For the state of preparedness of Soviet armed forces, see, for instance, Y. Perechnev, *Voenno-istoricheskii zhurnal* 4, 1988; M. Kiryan, *Voenno-istoricheskii zhurnal* 6, 1988; D. Volkogonov, *Pravda*, June 20, 1988, and the Kulish interview quoted above. See also the recollections of B. L. Vannikov, "Zapiski Narkomata," *Znamia* 1, 1988, and the memoirs of I. Konev, *Znamia* 11, 1987. See also Maj. Gen. V. L. Ivashov in *Voenno-istoricheskii zhurnal* 12, 1989. This journal published material of considerable importance during the years 1987–88, but subsequently the editorship went to neo-Stalinist hands, and the publication of critical articles was discontinued. See Samsonov, *Voprosy istorii* 11, 1989.

18. Perechnev, op. cit.

19. A. G. Khorkov, *Voenno-istoricheskii zhurnal* 4, 1988.

20. Perechnev, op. cit. A review of the discussions among the military historians in 1988–89 is given in H. H. Schröder, "Weisse Flecken in der Geschichte der Roten Armee," *Osteuropa* 5, 1989.

21. The dilemma was the subject of M. Shatrov's play "Brestski mir," which was staged in Moscow in 1987; Gorbachev no doubt saw it.

22. *Writings of Leon Trotsky, 1930–40*, New York 1969, p. 92.

23. The issue and the sources are discussed in some detail in *Das deutsche Reich und der zweite Weltkrieg*, Stuttgart, 1983, vol. 4, p. 72 et seq.

24. D. Volkogonov, "Triumf i tragediia," *Oktiabr*, 6, 1989, pp. 14–15.

25. V. Shlykov, "I tanki nashi bystry," *Mezhdunarodnaia zhizn* 9, 1988.

26. Colonel Krikunov published a reply: "Prostaia arifmetika V. V. Shlykova" in *Voenno-istoricheskii zhurnal* 4, 1989. Most Soviet military historians seem to be familiar only with Western works that were translated into Russian, such as Halder's *War Diary* and Mueller-Hildebrand's work on the German army. References to other non-Russian sources are few and far between.

27. V. Marinichev, "Na nebe ne naidesh," *Neva* 6, 1989. The numerical superiority of the Soviet air force is not denied by an establishment writer such as General Ivashov. See note 17 above.

28. V. Astafiev, *Moskovskie novosti*, May 8, 1988, and *Voprosy istorii* 6, 1988.

29. *Istoriia vtoroi mirovoi voiny, 1939–45*, vol. 2, p. 206.

30. Akhromeev, chief of staff, *Trud*, February 21, 1988; General Lizichev, head of political directorate of the Soviet army, *Kommunist vooruzhonnikh sil* 4, 1988; Colonel Filatov, *Krasnaia zvezda*, January 16, 1988; Major General Sidelnikov, *Krasnaia zvezda*, January 22, 1988.

31. K. Simonov, "Zametki o biografii G. K. Zhukova," *Voenno-istoricheskii zhurnal* 12,

1987, p. 54. See also V. Danilov, "Sovetskoe glavnoe kommandirovanie," *Novaia i noveishaia istoriia* 6, 1988.

32. M. M. Kiryan, *Voenno-istoricheskii zhurnal* 6, 1988; Kiryan had been one of the chief authors, or coauthors, of many of the preglasnost standard works.

33. A review of the changes in Soviet military historiography in H. H. Schröder, "Die Lehren von 1941," *Berichte des Bundesinstituts für ostwissenschaftliche und internationale Studien*, Cologne, 50, 1988.

34. Anfilov in *Krasnaia zvezda*, June 22, 1988; N. G. Kuznetsov, *Pravda*, July 29, 1988.

35. The interview was published in *Suomen Kuvalehti*, quoted here from *Svenska Dagbladet*, February 8, 1989.

36. N. Pavlenko in *Kommunist* 9, 1988, and in *Sovetskaia kultura*, August 23, 1988; V. Kulish in *Kommunist* 14, 1988.

37. A. Mertsalov, *Sovetskaia kultura*, March 25, 1989.

38. Boris Sokolov, "Velikaia otecheshestvennaia voina i tsena pobedy," *Literaturni Kirgizistan* 10, 1988. This is the shortened but politically more outspoken version of a more detailed paper published in V*oprosy istorii* 9, 1988. For a less radical reassessment of the question of Soviet losses, see V. V. Kozlov, "O liudskihk poterakh Sovetskovo Soyuza v velikoi otechestvennoi voine," *Istoria SSSR* 2, 1989. For Stalin and the number of Soviet victims at Stalingrad, G. B. Kliucharev, "Novy vzglyad na khod Stalingradskoi bytvi," V*oprosy istorii* 12, 1989.

39. Sokolov, *Literaturni Kirgizistan*, loc. cit., p. 102. See also A. Y. Krasha, "Opredeleniia liudskikh poter v velikoi otechestvennoi voine" (The Determination of Human Losses in the Great Fatherland War), *Sotsiologicheskie issledovaniia* 1, 1989. According to the same author, direct Soviet losses during the war were 26–27 million; indirect losses were 22–23 million, together equaling 48–50 million.

40. A. Seaton, *Stalin as Military Commander*, New York, 1976, p. 271; Kiryan, *Argumeny i fakty* 25, 1987.

41. Pavlenko, *Kommunist*, June 1988.

42. *Argumenty i fakty* 16, 1987; *Sotsialisticheskaia industria*, May 24, 1987; *Moskovskie novosti* 13, 1988; Samsonov's articles and many readers' letters were published as a book under the title *Znat i pomnit*, Moscow, 1988.

43. Stadniuk's novels tended to put the blame mainly on Stalin's underlings, especially "cosmopolitans" such as Mekhlis. *Sovetski patriot*, May 15, 1988; V. Morozov in *Sotsialisticheskaia industriia*, May 15, 1988; N. Saitsev, *Molodaia gvardia* 8, 1988.

44. A. M. Vasilevsky, *Delo vsei zhizni*, Moscow, 1988, p. 217.

45. A typical example for the old-school treatment was O. A. Rzheshevsky, *Pravda i lozh o vtoroi mirovoi voine* (Truth and Lies about the Second World War), Moscow, 1988; 255 pages of old-style polemics against Western reactionary warmongers who were trying to falsify the history of the Second World War.

46. They were all posthumously rehabilitated in 1957–58, but the text was published only in 1988; Lieutenant General Maltsev, "Kto vinovat?" *Voenno-istoricheskii zhurnal* 10, 1988, p. 28.

47. The text of the order was published for the first time in *Voenno-istoricheskii zhurnal* 9, 1988; see also the interview with academician Samsonov, *Izvestiia*, September 15, 1988.

48. Lev Kolodny, "Ispitanie," *Moskovskaia pravda*, October 15 and 16, 1987. The panic of October 16 was mentioned in standard Western works. See, for instance, John

Erickson, *The Road to Stalingrad*, London, 1975, pp. 106–7. For order 227: ibid., p. 507.

49. One of the sources is General Pavlenko, of whom mention has already been made. Another, D. Volkogonov (*Oktiabr* 7, 1989, p. 25). No reference to this episode has been found in the German archives, but there has been confirmation by Bulgarian sources.

50. V. Kulish, *Kommunist* 14, 1988, p. 90.

51. This refers, for instance, to the memoirs of Zhukov, Vasilevsky, Shtemenko, Konev, Rokossovsky, Grechko, and Meretskov, as well as civilians such as Vannikov, A. Yakovlev, and Konstantin Simonov's posthumously published interviews with Zhukov, Vasilevsky, and Admiral Kuznetsov. Some of these books came out in several editions, and there are marked differences in the text as the party line changed.

52. *Znanie-Sila* 11, 1988, pp. 79–80.

53. O. Suvenirov, "Vsearmeiskaia tragedia," *Voenno-istoricheskii zhurnal* 3, 1989. For an initiative by a group of senior officers to justify Stalin's action during the war, see *Literaturnaia gazeta*, March 7, 1990—in response to a new war movie, Lev Danilov's *Shtrafniki*.

54. Konev, op. cit.

55. Franz Halder, *Hitler as Feldherr*, Munich, 1949, pp. 20–21.

56. Zhukov, as quoted in *Kommunist* 14, 1988, p. 91.

12. Why Stalin? A National Debate

1. According to Stephen Cohen, the first writer to argue that Stalin's policies should be termed "Stalinism" was probably Walter Duranty, a *New York Times* correspondent in Moscow, who used the term in a series of dispatches in June 1931. See Robert C. Tucker, ed., *Stalinism*, New York, 1977, p. 5. Duranty was the greatest of Stalin's admirers among foreign correspondents. It is quite likely that the term was used concurrently (or even earlier) in the Russian émigré press. In Nazi Germany, "Stalinism" and "Stalinist" were used in a different sense, referring to German experts on the Soviet Union who (mistakenly, it was argued) welcomed the victory of Stalin's faction over its enemies as the triumph of the "national" over the "internationalist" element. See Hermann Greife, *Ist eine Entwicklung der Sowjetunion zum nationalen Staat möglich?* Berlin, 1939, p. 18.

2. For a discussion of these views, see G. P. Fedotov in *Novaya Rossia*, December 20, 1936. Reprinted in G. P. Fedotov, *Zashita Rossii*, Paris, 1988, p. 77.

3. Nikolai Berdiaev, *The Origins of Russian Communism*, Ann Arbor, 1972, p. 147.

4. S. Baron, "Between Marx and Lenin," in L. Labedz, ed., *Revisionism*, London, 1962, p. 50. This Plekhanov article was rediscovered under glasnost and quoted with approval for instance, by Vladimir Shubkin. "Trudnoe proshanie," *Novyi Mir*, no. 4 (1989): 168. The author did not mention the historical context, that the prophetic quotation was directed against Lenin's concept of the party.

5. M. Fainsod, *How Russia Is Ruled*, Cambridge, Mass., 1963, p. 59; Adam Ulam, *The New Face of Soviet Totalitarianism*, New York, 1965, pp. 48–49. The most detailed review of the "continuity" debate provided by one of its participants is

Stephen Cohen, "Bolshevism and Stalinism," in Robert C. Tucker, ed., *Stalinism*, New York, 1977, pp. 3–29.

6. Sheila Fitzpatrick, *Education and Social Mobility*, Cambridge, England: 1979, pp. 16–17.

7. See Peter Kenez in a discussion of Sheila Fitzpatrick's "New Perspectives of Stalinism," *Russian Review* (October 1986): 398–99.

8. *L'Express*, April 12, 1985.

9. Igor Kon, *Moskovskie novosti*, August 21, 1988.

10. The author was Lev Kvitko, who perished in the purge of the Jewish writers in the early 1950s.

11. Nikolai Mikhailov, "Sindrom otsa," *Ogonyok*, September 17, 1988.

12. L. N. Dzrnazian, "Kult i rabolepie" (Cult and Servile Worship), *Sotsiologicheskie issledovaniia* 5, 1988. The analysis shows familiarity with (and quotes) Western sources, such as the books of E. Fromm, W. Maslow, E. Harding, and others.

13. Aleksandr Tsipko, *Nauka i zhizn* 11 and 12, 1988, and 1 and 2, 1989. See also the same author's article in *Politicheskoe obrazovanie* 3, 1989.

14. *Nauka i zhizn* 2, 1989, p. 58.

15. Len Karpinsky, *Moskovskie novosti*, April 16, 1989.

16. Tsipko, *Nauka i zhizn* 11, 1986. A. Butenko claims that Tsipko's essay can be interpreted as an attempt to make Marx responsible for Stalin. *Vestnik MGU*, series 12, vol. 3, 1989, p. 51.

17. Igor Kliamkin's "Kakaya ulitsa vedet v khramu?" was published in *Novyi mir*, no. 11, 1987; "Pochemu trudno govorit pravdu," *Novyi mir*, no. 2, 1988. See also his article in *Politicheskoe obrazovanie* 10, 1988; his interview with Serge Yakovlev in *Literaturnoe obozrenie* 4, 1989; and his reply to critics in *Politicheskoe obrazovanie* 9, 1989.

18. Kliamkin had initially put much of the emphasis on support for Stalinism in the village. In light of criticism (by Latsis and others), he modified his view.

19. *Literaturnoe obozrenie* op. cit.

20. See, for instance, M. Kapustin in *Knizhnoe obozrenie* 38, 1988.

21. The difference between Old Believers and the official church concerned issues such as whether Hallelujah should be said twice or three times in prayer, whether believers should use two or three fingers while crossing themselves, and whether at a procession around the church, participants should first turn left or right.

22. V. Selyunin, "Istoki," *Novyi mir* 5, 1988.

23. If Kliamkin's arguments sound in some respects like Struve, Selyunin is clearly influenced by the views of another legal Marxist of the 1890s, the economic historian Tugan-Baranovsky, author of a classical history of Russian factories.

24. Olger Eglitis, *Atmoda*, April 17, 1989, to give but one example, drew attention to Lenin's call for mass terror and the establishment of concentration camps in which kulaks, clergymen, prostitutes, White Guards, and other questionable elements should be kept. There ought to be not a minute's delay executing these measures. And the observation, in passing: "Sombart is right, there are no ethics in Marxism."

25. Bordyugov and Kozlov in *Pravda*, September 30, 1988, and October 3, 1988. Their articles were edited by the director of the Marx-Engels Institute, the academician Georgi Smirnov. Their views were implicitly criticized by the Politburo ideological supremo, Vadim Medvedev, *Pravda*, October 5, 1988.

26. This refers, for instance, to *Voina*, by Ivan Stadnyuk, awarded the U.S.S.R. state

prize in 1983, or to Alexander Chakovsky's *Blokada* (1968–73), and also to his later novels.

27. *Voprosy istorii KPSS* 5, 1989, p. 91.

28. He was interviewed by V. Litov in 1980–81. The essay based on these interviews was published in *Molodaia gvardia* 4, 1989. Some sections appear dubious because they refer to issues and developments that occurred only years later under glasnost. But most of the essay has the ring of authenticity. There was a controversy among members of Benediktov's family as to whether the "interview" was genuine: some, writing in *Molodaia gvardia*, claimed it was; others, quoted in *Ogonyok*, maintained it was not.

29. There is an enormous German literature reflecting the widespread nostalgia for the good old days between Hitler's rise to power and the turn in the fortunes of war (1942–43). This refers to the recollections of people who served in the Third Reich in various capacities, military and civilian, but also to young people who were in no way prominent at the time. Typical examples for this mood can be found in virtually every issue of *Nation Europa* or the *National Zeitung*. The books expressing contrition, such as Baldur von Schirach, *Ich glaubte an Hitler*, Hamburg, 1967, or Albert Speer, *Erinnerungen*, Berlin, 1969, are the exceptions rather than the rule as far as former servants of Nazism are concerned.

30. M. I. Malakhov, *Molodaia gvardia* 4, 1988. In the 1940s, the author had been a party district secretary and, in later years, one of the leading figures in state planning. Another young bureaucrat, who began his career under Stalin, later wrote: "Fear pervaded literally everything, one's behavior, thought, and work. It was part of the atmosphere, and it hovered in the air." Aleksander Alekseev in *Ogonyok* 23, 1989, p. 30.

31. Igor Shafarevich, *Moskovskie novosti*, June 12, 1988. His tract on "Russophobia" has been published in *Vechi*, Paris, 1989, in *Vremia i my* (America) 104, 1989, and ultimately in a Soviet magazine, *Nash sovremennik* 6, 1989.

32. Vadim Kozhinov, "Pravda i istina," *Nash sovremennik* 4, 1988. Another landmark article of the right was Soloukhin's "Chitaia Lenina," *Rodina* 10, 1989, an open attack against Lenin and Leninism. There was an answer (by Bordiugov and Loginov) from an official party point of view in the same issue.

33. Kozhinov, p. 172.

34. Levan Khaindrava, "Nekotorie mysli . . . ," *Literaturnaia gruzia* 1(1989): 125.

35. Ibid., 148.

36. The most detailed such studies were Hermann Fehst, *Bolschewismus und Judentum*, Berlin, 1934, and Rudolf Kommoss, *Juden hinter Stalin*, Berlin, 1938. See Walter Laqueur's *Russia and Germany*, London, 1965, pp. 79–125 and 176–95.

37. R. Kommoss, op. cit., p. 210.

38. H. Fehst, op. cit., pp. 156–57.

39. A tract of this kind, widely circulated in samizdat, is based on a speech by Rudolf Hess at the Nazi Annual Party Congress in Nuremberg in 1936. A.B.B. in *Veche* 31, Munich, 1988, p. 55.

40. This was the thesis of H. Greife, *Ist eine Entwicklung der Sowjetunion zum nationalen Staat möglich?* Berlin, 1939.

41. The Russian extreme right has produced its own figures under glasnost. They claim, for instance, that in 1937, seventeen out of twenty-three ministers, seventeen out of twenty members of the Supreme Soviet, and fifty-three out of the fifty-nine leading

officials of the GPU were Jews. V. Sotnikov in *Molodaia gvardia* 1, 1990. These figures are even higher than the Nazi statistics.

42. There were exceptions, however, Varlam Shalamov, author of the *Kolyma Tales* and not a member of the Russian Right, once noted that the humanist Russian intelligentsia of the nineteenth century bore the responsibility for the bloodshed in the twentieth century. Such generalizations remind one of the attempts to make Nietzsche (or Hegel) responsible for Adolf Hitler. Perhaps more startlingly, the literary monthly *Kuban* 11, 1988, not only criticized the Revolution of 1905 but referred to October 1917 not as the "Great Socialist October Revolution" (the obligatory term) but as the "Bolshevik coup," as quoted in *Ogonyok* 22, 1989.

43. Otto Latsis, "Termidor schitat Briumerom," *Znamia* 5, 1989, p. 183.

44. G. Popov, "Programma kotoroi rukovodstvovalsia Stalin," *Nauka i zhizn* 7, 1989.

45. A. P. Butenko, "O sotsialnoe—klassovoi prirode stalinskoi vlasti," *Voprosy filosofii* 3, 1989, p. 65, and the same writer's article in *Nauka i zhizn* 10, 1989.

46. L. Bredneva, *Ural* 10, 1989, p. 139.

47. This refers, for instance, to a widely discussed article by S. Andreev, "Prichini i Sledstvii," *Ural* 1, 1988, and *Ural* 6, 1989. The *Lumpen* theory appears, for instance, in Aleksei Chernichenko, *Druzhba narodov* 5, 1989. See also "O Staline i stalinisme," *Istoriia SSSR* 4, 1989. Karyakin, too, has used the term *lumpenisatsia*.

48. Antonov-Ovseenko relates an extreme case. His older brother persuaded himself that their own father was both a Trotskyite and a Menshevik, that he was justly killed, and that he should not be rehabilitated. *Znamia kommunizma*, Odessa, April 26, 1989.

49. Other recent publications of relevance in this context include the roundtable discussion on the origins of totalitarianism in the Soviet Union in *Sotsiologicheskie issledovaniia* 5, 1989, and the collection of essays edited by U. P. Senokosov, *Surovaia drama naroda; uchennie i publitsisty o prirode stalinisma*, Moscow, 1989.

50. Few Soviet political scientists still argue (as they did in the early days of glasnost) that there was an obvious alternative to Stalinism in the 1920s. At most they maintain, as Butenko does, that while Stalinism was not inescapable, it was certainly not accidental; in fact, in the given conditions it was highly probable. As the result of the Stalinist experience, most Soviet writers see a much clearer dividing line between totalitarianism and authoritarianism than many Western historians and social scientists; for them totalitarianism is not a doubtful abstraction but a reality. See, for instance, *Sotsiologicheskie issledovaniia* 5, 1989. Even those who see in Stalinism a classic Thermidorian regime of an earlier historical period (Volobuev) admit that they do not have the answers to such crucial questions as: Why did it last so long? And why did it take the specific form of something akin to Eastern (medieval) despotism?

13. Memorial and Its Opponents

1. Stephen Cohen and Katrina Van den Heuvel, *Voices of Glasnost*, New York, 1989, p. 92.

2. *Literaturnaia gazeta*, January 20, 1989.

3. 2, Ulitsa Cherniachovskovo.

4. Essential documents about the early history of Memorial in *Vedomosti Memoriala*, January 28, 1989; also, *Osteuropa* 5, 1989, pp. 230–37.

5. *Ogonoyok* 29 and 46, 1988.
6. There were local initiatives in places such as Norilsk.
7. *Moscow Central Television*, March 3, 1989.
8. L. Ionin, *New Times* 22, 1989.
9. *Vedomosti Memoriala*, January 29, 1989.
10. *Moscow News* 29, 1989.
11. December 17, 1988. Among the signatories of the anti-Memorial appeal was General Grigori Samoilovich, a well-known Pamyat sympathizer.
12. *Atmoda* 20, 1989. Professor Igor Bestuzhev-Lada applied to the general procurator of the U.S.S.R. with the request to bring an action against the late Josef Stalin on the basis of Articles 102, 107, 177, 179, and others of the criminal code of the RSFSR as well as of Article 2 of the genocide convention of the United Nations. *Moskovskie novosti*, August 27, 1989.
13. V. G. Provotarov in *Sovetskaia kultura*, February 25, 1989.
14. G. Anishshenko in *Molodezh Estonii*, December 15, 1988, and April 13, 1989; see also *Russkaia mysl*, March 31, 1989.
15. M. S. Solomontsev, *Pravda*, August 19, 1988. The year after, a liberal member of the Politburo, A. Yakovlev, replaced Solomontsev as chairman. However, the overall constitution of the committee was still anything but radically anti-Stalinist. It included three members, or former members, of the KGB, as well as Vadim Medvedev, the chief party ideologist.
16. *Sovetskaia kultura*, February 25, 1989.
17. *Pravda*, op. cit.
18. *Izvestiia Ts.K. KPSS* 1, 1988, and 5, 1989. On the latter occasion, a report by the control commission was also published.
19. *Nedelya* 26, 1989.
20. *Trud*, May 1, 1989.
21. The debate raged all over the Soviet Union; a few examples should suffice: The interviews with V. P. Neroznak in *Krasnaia zvezda*, September 22, 1988, and in *Sobesednik* 35, 1988. See also Natalia Ivina in *Literaturnaia Gazeta*, September 28, 1988, and S. Korepanov in *Sotsialisticheskaia industriia*, August 27, 1988. Also *Nedelya* 37, 1988.
22. *Daugava* 4, 1989.
23. *Komsomolskaia pravda*, March 3, 1989.
24. *Semia* 36, 40, and 47, 1988.
25. Moscow Central Television, *Vzgliad*, May 12, 1989. The letter was originally sent to the newspaper *Vecherni Kiev*, but local censorship banned publication.
26. *Sovetskaia kultura*, May 19, 1988.
27. Extracts from the court proceedings were filmed and shown on Soviet television (*Ochishshenie*).
28. Interview with Shekhovtsov, *Komsomolskaia znamia*, Ukraine, April 9, 1989. On the Moscow trial, *Ogonyok* 41, 1988, *Sovetskaia kultura*, October 1, 1988; *Izvestiia*, September 23, 1988.
29. *Vechernaia Moskva*, January 5, 1989.
30. Ibid.
31. S. Tikhii, *Komsomolskoe znamia*, January 31, 1990.
32. *Nash sovremennik* 12, 1988.
33. Vladimir Korolenko, a liberal writer, had been in the forefront of the struggle for

human rights in tsarist Russia. After 1917, he tried to use his influence with Luna-charsky, the Bolshevik minister of education, in an attempt to save people, but without much success. His letters to Lunacharsky were published in *Novyi mir* 10, 1988, and were widely quoted.

34. "The House on the Embankment," 2 Serafimovich Street, was the subject of a novel by Yuri Trifonov; leading members of the Soviet establishment lived there. Many of them were arrested in 1937–39.

35. There always had been a streak of unreality in the thinking of the extreme Right in Russia, and this has not changed over time. "Russophobia" is a good example; in the late 1980s there was a great deal of it from Poland to the Baltic countries to the Caucasus and Central Asia. There was an explosion of anti-Russian resentment and, concurrently, a great deal of writing on "Russophobia." However, the writers in Moscow were not concerned with the real dangers, with their house on fire, but with the writings of some obscure Jewish-Communist poets in the 1920s or with the tracts of an émigré somewhere in the United States, who was not a Russophobe but had, tactlessly perhaps, arrogated himself the right to repeat what Cha'adaev, Lermontov, Herzen, Chernychevsky, and others had said about certain negative features of Russian history.

36. Typical examples were Valeri Khatiushin's articles in *Moskva* 10, 1988, and 4, 1989, as well as the essays by leading spokesmen of this group, such as Kozhinov, Lan-shikov, Bondarenko, et al.

37. *Molodaia gvardia* 5, 1989, p. 241.

38. According to a poll carried out by a Moscow newspaper, support for Stalin had declined from 16 percent to .8 percent within one year. But 30 percent still believed that although he had committed many crimes, he also had achievements to his credit. *Vechernaia Moskva*, August 27, 1988.

39. Interview with Y. Etinger in *Molodezh Estonii*, January 16, 1990. On the split in "Memorial," *Vechernaia Moskva*, February 1, 1990.

40. Some of the most interesting reading material emerged not from the capital but literary journals named *Ural*, *Pamir*, and *Literaturni Kirgizistan*.

14. Conclusion: Forty Years After

1. E. H. Carr, *Studies in Revolution*, London, 1950, pp. 226–27.

2. Y. L. Rapoport, *Na rubezhe dvukh epokh. Delo vrachei 1953 ogo goda*, Moscow, 1989.

3. V. Ravdin, *Novyi mir* 6, 1989.

4. L. Batkin, "Son razuma," *Znanie-sila* 3, 1989, p. 95.

5. For the "genocide" thesis see V. Manyak and L. Kovalenko in *Literaturna Ukraina*, July 13, 1989; V. Pakharenko, ibid., November 10, 1988; Y. Shebak in *Sobesednik* 49, 1988, and many other reports, including diaries, autobiographical studies, and interviews in Ukrainian journals during 1988–89. The same thesis had found many advocates in Western countries in earlier years. It had been studied by a U.S. congressional committee. The Western press had virtually ignored the famine at the time.

6. S. V. Kulchitsky in *Ukrainski istorichny zhurnal* 3, 1988, and the same author's articles in *Literaturna Ukraina* 2–5, 1988; V. Savelev in *Pravda Ukrainy*, July 8,

1989. Sergei Diachenko (*Ogonyok* 27, 1989) uses the term "holocaust" writing about the death of millions of Ukrainian peasants but does not consider it an action specifically directed against Ukrainians.

7. One of the few who did not like it was Romain Rolland, then on a prolonged visit to Moscow. *Voprosy literaturi* 3, 1989.

8. N. Shafer, "Paradoks Dunaevskovo," *Ogonyok* 30, 1988. Dunaevsky committed suicide in 1955.

9. The nearest that come to mind are some gushing entries concerning Hitler in Goebbels's diaries.

10. According to V. Khatiushin, an ideologist of the extreme Right, "very little depended on Stalin's will" who did little more than speed up the revolutions of the giant meat-mincing machine. . . . (*Moskovski literator*, March 31, 1989).

11. For a roundtable discussion of the impact of *Life and Fate*, *Literaturnoe obozrenie* 6, 1988, pp. 24–34. For the extreme Right in Russia, Grossman's novels became one of the most outspoken manifestations of "Russophobia"; they were invoked as an insult to Russian patriots.

12. O. Eglitis, "Leninu-119," *Atmoda* 15, 1989, and Maris Grinblats "Vernutsia ili idti dalshe? *Atmoda*, June 1989. A Latvian writer noted that he could not regard Lenin as "a wise helmsman" since he had attached morals to expediency and thus given the green light to future repressions. *Daugava* 7, 1989, p. 71.

13. See, for instance, *Rabochaia gazeta* on Viktor Erofeev's "Moya malenkaia Leniniana" (February 17, 1990).

14. *Sovetskaia Rossia*, June 9, 1989.

15. N. Molchanov, "Guilotina ili deklaratsia prav?" A reply to Andre Stil, *Literaturnaia gazeta*, July 12, 1989.

16. Ligachev speech at a Central Committee meeting, *Pravda*, July 12, 1989.

17. She continued to stick to her guns. Interview with David Remnick, *Washington Post*, July 28, 1989, and her letter in *Molodaia gvardia* 7, 1989, and 2, 1990.

18. Johannes Georgi, *Freideutscher Rundbrief* 3, 1948, quoted in Walter Laqueur, *Young Germany*, London, 1961, p. 202.

19. L. Gozman, "Psikhologia vlasti" in *Argumenty i fakty* 24, 1989. The author also mentions certain psychological peculiarities of the Russian (*Rossiski*) people that to a certain extent contributed to the emergence of a totalitarian system.

20. Sa'di, *Gulistan*, 8.8 (James Ross translation).

21. A. Migranyan, *Vek dvatsati i mir* 12, 1988; also his article in *Novyi mir* 7, 1989, and the dialogue with Igor Kliamkin in *Literaturnaia gazeta*, August 16, 1989.

22. L. Gozman and A. Etkind, "Ot kult vlasti k vlasti Liudei," *Neva* 7, 1989.

Index

About the Author

WALTER LAQUEUR is chairman of the international Research Council of the Center for Strategic and International Studies, Washington, D.C.; university professor at Georgetown University; and director of the Institute of Contemporary History (the Wiener Library) in London. He was the founder and first editor (1955–63) of *Survey*, a leading journal in the field of Soviet studies. His books, which have appeared in many editions and translations, include *The Long Road to Freedom: Russia and Glasnost*; *Russia and Germany*; and *The Fate of the Revolution: Interpretations of Soviet History from 1917 to the Present* (first published in 1967; updated and revised edition published in 1987).